Reading Renais

MW00829833

For three decades historicist scholars have reconnected Renaissance literature to its historical contexts, while formalist and rhetorical scholars have used improved historical resources to move closer to understanding how literary texts accomplish their cultural work. *Reading Renaissance Ethics* extends this study to question how Renaissance texts were read and put to use in their own time and how they continue to be used up to the present day.

Renaissance writers pursued the formative power of literature beyond explicit themes to include questions of genre, language and rhetoric with nuance and precision. *Reading Renaissance Ethics* questions the nature and mechanics of cultural agency and allows us to articulate with greater clarity just what is at stake when canon-formation, aesthetic evaluation and curricular reform are questioned and revised. Bringing together some of the best current practitioners of historical and formal criticism, *Reading Renaissance Ethics* assesses the ethical performance of renaissance texts as historical agents in their time and in ours.

Taking seriously the question of what to read requires us to consider exactly what it is that we do when we read and when we write about our reading. *Reading Renaissance Ethics* asks what sorts of events took place when Renaissance texts were first read and how this differs from the way we read – and teach – them now.

Contributors include: Sharon Achinstein, Harry Berger, Jr., Angus J. S. Fletcher, Victoria Kahn, Theodore B. Leinwand, David Lee Miller, David Norbrook, Anita Gilman Sherman, Richard Strier, Gordon Teskey, Vivienne Westbrook and Paul Yachnin.

Marshall Grossman teaches English at the University of Maryland, College Park. His publications include *"Authors to themselves": Milton and the Revelation of History*, and *The Story of All Things: Writing the Self in English Renaissance Narrative Poetry*, and numerous articles on Renaissance literature and literary historiography.

Reading Renaissance Ethics

Edited by
Marshall Grossman

Routledge
Taylor & Francis Group

NEW YORK AND LONDON

First published 2007
by Routledge
270 Madison Ave, New York, NY 10016

Simultaneously published in the UK
by Routledge
2 Park Square, Milton Park, Abingdon, Oxon OX14 4RN

Routledge is an imprint of the Taylor & Francis Group, an informa business

© 2007 Marshall Grossman, contributors for individual chapters

Typeset in 10/11½pt Baskerville by
Book Now Ltd, London
Printed and bound in Great Britain by
Antony Rowe Ltd, Chippenham, Wiltshire

British Library Cataloguing in Publication Data
A catalogue record for this book is available from the British Library

Library of Congress Cataloging in Publication Data
Reading Renaissance Ethics/[edited by] Marshall Grossman.
    p. cm.
1. Ethics in literature. 2. English literature–Early modern, 1500–1700–History
and criticism. 3. Literature and morals. 4. Ethics–England–History–16th century.
5. Ethics–England–History–17th century. 6. Literature and society–England–
History–16th century. 7. Literature and society–England–History–17th century.
I. Grossman, Marshall.

PR428.E85R43 2006
820.9'353–dc22   2006027742

ISBN 10: 0–415–40634–X (hbk)
ISBN 10: 0–415–40635–8 (pbk)
ISBN 10: 0–203–96264–8 (ebk)

ISBN 13: 978–0–415–40634–5 (hbk)
ISBN 13: 978–0–415–40635–2 (pbk)
ISBN 13: 978–0–203–96264–0 (ebk)

Contents

Figures

Contributors

Sharon Achinstein is currently Lecturer in English at Oxford University, and she has taught at the University of Maryland and Northwestern University. She is the author of *Milton and the Revolutionary Reader* (Princeton, 1994), winner of the Milton Society of America Hanford Prize, and *Literature and Dissent in Milton's England* (Cambridge, 2003). Her current work includes editing Milton's Divorce Tracts for *The Oxford Milton* and a book on Literature and Toleration.

Harry Berger, Jr., Professor Emeritus at the University of California, Santa Cruz, a critical West Coast octogenarian untrained in topics he writes about in order to know better, is the author most recently of *Situated Utterances: Texts, Bodies, and Cultural Representations* (2005) and *Manhood, Marriage, and Mischief: Rembrandt's "Night Watch" and other Dutch Group Portraits* (New York: Fordham University Press, 2006).

Angus J. S. Fletcher is Distinguished Professor Emeritus of English and Comparative Literature, CUNY Graduate School. Harvard published his *Time, Space and Motion in the Age of Shakespeare* (Spring 2007). His *New Theory for American Poetry: Democracy, the Environment and the Future of Imagination*, also from Harvard, won the 2005 Truman Capote Prize for Literary Criticism.

Marshall Grossman is Professor of English at the University of Maryland, College Park. His publications include *'Authors to themselves': Milton and the Revelation of History* (1987) and *The Story of All Things: Writing the Self in English Renaissance Narrative Poetry* (1998), an edited collection, *Aemilia Lanyer: Gender, Genre and the Canon* (1998), and numerous articles on Renaissance literature and literary historiography.

Victoria Kahn, Professor of English and Bernie H. Williams Professor of Comparative Literature, University of California, Berkeley, is the author of *Rhetoric, Prudence, and Skepticism in the Renaissance* (1985) and *Machiavellian Rhetoric from the Counter-Reformation to Milton* (1994). She is co-editor (with

Lorna Hutson) of *Rhetoric and Law in Early Modern England* (2001) and (with Albert Russell Ascoli) of *Machiavelli and the Discourse of Literature* (1993). Her previous work has addressed the relations between rhetorical form and social function in the renaissance.

Theodore B. Leinwand is Professor of English at the University of Maryland, College Park. He is the author of *The City Staged: Jacobean Comedy, 1603–1613* (1986) and *Theatre, Finance and Society in Early Modern England* (1999). He is currently writing a series of essays on Keats, Coleridge, Woolf, and Ted Hughes (among others) reading Shakespeare.

David Lee Miller, Professor of English and Comparative Literature at the University of South Carolina, is the author of *Dreams of the Burning Child: Sacrificial Sons and the Father's Witness* (2003) and is one of four general editors of the *Collected Works of Edmund Spenser*, in preparation for Oxford University Press.

David Norbrook is Merton Professor of English Literature at the University of Oxford. He is the author of *Poetry and Politics in the English Renaissance* (revised edition, 2002) and *Writing the English Republic: Poetry, Rhetoric and Politics 1627–1660* (1999) and has edited Lucy Hutchinson's *Order and Disorder* (2001).

Anita Gilman Sherman is an Assistant Professor of Literature at American University in Washington, D.C. She has published essays on Shakespeare, Donne, Montaigne, Thomas Heywood, and Garcilaso de la Vega. She is completing a book entitled *The Art of Doubt: Skepticism and Memory in Shakespeare and Donne*.

Richard Strier, Frank L. Sulzberger Professor, University of Chicago, is the author of *Love Known: Theology and Experience in George Herbert's Poetry* (1986) and *Resistant Structures: Particularity, Radicalism, and Renaissance Texts* (1995); he has co-edited a number of cross-disciplinary collections, and published essays on Shakespeare, Donne, Luther, Montaigne, and Milton, and on twentieth-century critical theory.

Gordon Teskey, Professor of English at Harvard, is author of *Allegory and Violence* and *Delirious Milton* (2006). He is editor of the Norton edition of *Paradise Lost* (1996).

Vivienne Westbrook is an Associate Professor of Renaissance Literature at National Taiwan University. She specializes in English Reformation Bibles and culture. She has published articles on a range of Reformation issues and culture from biblical translation through to Reformation historiography and contributed articles to the British Academy *John Foxe on-line* project, the *NEW DNB* and the *Yale Milton Encyclopedia*. Her first book, *Long Travail and Great Paynes: A Politics of Reformation Revision* (2001), was a study of neglected Reformation Bible translators. She is currently preparing two books for publication: *Richard Taverner, Reformation Humanist* and *Marginal Text and English Tudor Bibles*.

Paul Yachnin is Tomlinson Professor of Shakespeare Studies and Chair of the English Department at McGill University. He is also Co-Director of the Shakespeare and Performance Research Team and Director of the Making Publics project. His first book is *Stage-Wrights: Shakespeare, Jonson, Middleton, and the Making of Theatrical Value* (1997); his second, co-authored with Anthony Dawson, is *The Culture of Playgoing in Shakespeare's England: A Collaborative Debate* (2001). He is an editor of the forthcoming Oxford edition of *The Works of Thomas Middleton* and is editing Shakespeare's *Richard II*, also for Oxford. Work-in-progress includes a co-edited edition of *The Tempest* for Broadview Press and a book-length study, *Making Theatrical Publics: A Social History of Drama in Early Modern England*.

Acknowledgments

I would like to gratefully acknowledge the support and suggestions of the contributors to this volume as a group, with special thanks to Sharon Achinstein, David Norbrook and Theodore Leinwand who indulged my obsession during extended discussions of the project at the University of Maryland, and Dyanne Tsai, who assisted in the preparation of the manuscript. Also, at Maryland, Gary Hamilton and Irene Sanchez offered material help and moral support. Thanks are also due to Liz Thompson and Polly Dodson at Routledge, for their support of the project and their patience. I thank the Department of English and the Graduate Research Board of the University of Maryland for their generous help with the cost of the volume's many illustrations, which I gratefully acknowledge permission to reproduce as follows:

3.1 Jan Steen, *Cardplayers* (c.1660), private collection. Reproduced by permission of the owner.

3.2 Jan Miense Molenaer, *The Duet* [1] (c.1630–31). Gift of the Samuel H. Kress Foundation. Reproduced by permission of the Seattle Art Museum.

3.3 J.W. Delff, *Arquebusiers of the Fourth Squad* (1592), reproduced by permission of Delft, Stedelijk Museum Het Prinsenhof.

3.4 Dirk Jacobsz., *Civic Guard Group Portrait* (1529); 3.6. Werner van den Valckert, *Four Regents of the Amsterdam Leprosenhuis* (1624); 3.8 Jan Steen, *The Burgher of Delft* (1655). Reproduced by permission of the Rijksmuseum Amsterdam.

3.5 Frans Pietersz Grebber, *Banquet of the Officers and Subalterns of St George Civic Guard* (1619); 3.9. Frans Hals, *Regents of St. Elizabeth Hospital* (1641); 3.10. Frans Hals, *Regents of the Old Men's Alms House* (c.1664); 3.11. Frans Hals, *Regentesses of the Old Men's Alms House* (c.1664). Reproduced by permission of the Frans Hals Museum, Haarlem.

3.7 Cornelis van der Voort, *Regents of the Old Men's and Women's Home* (1618), reproduced by permission of the Amsterdams Historisch Museum.

6.1 "The Martyrdome and Burning of Mayster William Tyndall, in Flaunders by Filford Castle." Woodcut illustration from: Foxe, John, *Actes and Monuments*, 1580, p. 1229, sig. DDDiiii. Reproduced with the kind permission of the Dean and Chapter of York.

Part I

Introduction

1 Introduction

Reading Renaissance ethics

Marshall Grossman

After three decades in which historicist scholars have successfully reconnected Renaissance literature to its historical contexts, and formalist and rhetorical scholars have used improved historical resources to move closer to an understanding of how literary texts accomplish their cultural work, we think the time is right to question how Renaissance texts were read, how they were put to use in their own time, and how they may have been and continue to be used in subsequent times, up to and including our own. Following Kenneth Burke, we now ask: what sorts of "equipment for living" do Renaissance texts represent?[1]

The ethics of writing and reading were a pervasive concern in the Renaissance. Following Horace's dictum that poetry should delight and instruct, Renaissance writers understood their work as part of an ethical pedagogy, and reading in the Renaissance was understood to be an ethical performance. The right text might fashion a gentleman, build a citizen, or elevate the soul to the adoration of God.[2] But the wrong text might corrupt, enervate or confuse the reader.[3] Stringent censorship and an industrious polemical underground seeking to circumvent it assumed, implicitly and explicitly, the potency of renaissance texts as ethical agents.[4] Renaissance writers, appropriating classical forms for contemporary polemical purposes, were keenly aware of the ideological proclivities of given genres.

Our recent "culture wars" attest to the continued vitality of the old notion that what and how we read matters to who and what we are. Renaissance writers pursued the formative power of literature beyond explicit themes to include questions of genre, language and rhetoric with far greater nuance and precision than we have seen in our present debate. The "culture warriors" of the twenty-first century assume that our "values" are produced or conditioned by traditions that may or may not pass them down through generations, and across changing material and technological environments. Attention to the work of Renaissance writers not only raises the level of our own political discourse but also suggests a vocabulary and style of thought that allows us to move beyond the mere assumption that writing and reading matter and begin to articulate with greater clarity what is at stake when canon-formation, aesthetic evaluation and curricular reform are questioned and revised.

This question of what is at stake is distinct from the related questions of how canons, evaluations and curricula come to be shaped by material forces. We set about to question the nature and mechanics of cultural agency. To take seriously the question of what to read, we must first consider what we do when we read and when we write about our reading. We ask what sorts of events took place when Renaissance texts were read in various contexts and what sorts of events take place when we read them – and teach them – now? Our method for approaching these questions is inductive. The essays collected here implicitly work toward a phenomenology of reading, but not necessarily of reading in general. First, for the reasons stated above, we have chosen to read texts from a rather broadly defined English Renaissance, ranging from the early English bibles of the Tudor reign through the restoration poems of John Milton. Our attention extends also into the overlapping classical, neo-Latin and continental linguistic worlds of humanism and its descendents. Second, each of us has begun with questions arising out of the specific writing we discuss. Some of these questions are contextual, but in accordance with our interest in reading as an act, each of us has undertaken to read from the inside out rather than from the outside in. That is, we have attempted to let the texts we study speak first and last.

Understanding the sources and protocols of Renaissance textual ethics is a historical undertaking. Understanding the rhetoric of Renaissance texts requires sophisticated formal analysis. This analysis cannot take place without close reading. *Reading Renaissance Ethics* aims to restore the centrality of close reading to the task of assessing the ethical performance of Renaissance texts as historical agents in their own time and in ours. Doing so, we work against the naïve assumption that political speech is speech about politics, ethical speech, speech about ethics. Renaissance writers understood and engaged the formative power of literature beyond explicit themes to include considerations of genre, language and rhetoric more nuanced and precise than we have seen in our present cultural politics. This is another reason for addressing Renaissance texts in particular. Attention to them will, we hope, not only raise the level of our own discourse, but also suggest a vocabulary and style of thought that allows us to articulate with greater clarity what was felt to be at stake in Renaissance writing and what might be at stake in our reading of it.

This volume undertakes, then, specifically and self-consciously, to bring together two critical practices that have lately been at odds with or neglected by each other to acquire an improved apprehension of "the content of the form" exemplified in Renaissance discursive practices.[5] We aim to theorize and to set by example a protocol for future critical practice. To understand the scope and context of this proposed agenda, it is necessary to distinguish the historicist and formalist components of these essays from the "New Historicism" of the past 30 years and the "New Criticism" that preceded it.

As historicists, the New Historicists saw the need to dissociate their activity from a historicist tradition that, in their view, failed to recognize the nuanced content of literary form. Reading consistently from the ideological position of the powerful, the older historicists confused the material conditions in which a text is produced with the fictions represented within it – mistaking, for example, the "Elizabethan World Picture" for a picture of the Elizabethan world. New Historicists sought instead to reconnect the texts they studied not to an unmediated and reified version of the social world represented in them, but to a world as uniformly discursive and heteronymous as the texts themselves. They sought instead to formulate a uniform cultural field in which discursive practices could be seen in relation to material arrangements on the one hand, and literary historical contexts on the other. But it has become increasingly apparent in its second and third generations that New Historicism approaches two limits, one internal and necessary, the other external and contingent.

The internal limit, evident from the beginning, has been its inability to adequately theorize the notions of culture and text on which it depends.[6] The external limit is rooted in the history of New Historicism as a reaction against the pedagogical dominance of the New Critics. New Critical close reading brought not just a failure to historicize, but a positive resistance to it: the ideological fiction that what was most valuable in literature was autonomous and universal. To reach the art of literature one had to disencumber it of all that tied it to the time and place of its production. The New Historicists' primary mission of re-embedding the literary work in its culture reacted against the New Critics' "art-for-art's-sake" hermeticism, rather than against their interest in and facility with literary form.

But it has become apparent that diminished attention to close reading followed on from the attempt to treat discourse as a virtual total under the rubric "culture." The turn from text to context is implicated in the New Historicists' inability to derive and sustain protocols of reading that adequately recognize the literary historical and formal rhetorical contexts of Renaissance writing. In so far as New Historicism reacts less against the close reading of New Critics than against their isolation of the work of art from its material contexts, New Historicists worked to reconnect texts to a broader and more interactive social discourse. But the failure to recognize the heterogeneous and contradictory nature of even a synchronic discourse leaves New Historicist scholarship with an untheorized structuralist model that misses the resistance of the signifier – the unsystematic collaboration of historical intent and the intractable semantic effects asserted by linguistic, generic and literary historical forms that remain heteronymous to intention and contingent with respect to context.

It is the aim of this volume to explore and exemplify modes of reading that neither ignore nor privilege an extra-textual, material history putatively prior to the texts in question. The essays here presented insist rather that material history itself is already inhabited and colonized by literary form. By understanding history itself as a literary-rhetorical form and extending its close reading in all directions, this volume aspires to produce a criticism that is formally attentive, aesthetically sensitive and historically engaged.

The essays in this collection are further bound together by their foregrounding and attending to ethos as the – belatedly constructed – ground of the literary subject. The founding moment of this endeavor is Aristotle's insight, at the beginning of the *Poetics*, that *mythos* precedes *ethos* – that we derive the story of a character from his or her actions:

> Tragedy is an imitation not of persons but of action and life, of happiness and misery. Now happiness and misery take the form of action; the end at which the dramatist aims is a certain kind of activity, not a quality. We have certain qualities in accordance with character but it is in our actions that we are happy or the reverse. … Consequently the end of a tragedy is its action, i.e. its fable or plot; and the end is in all things paramount.[7]

What Aristotle says about tragedy is true of literature more generally. The activity of narration presents an action from which an ethos is deduced. The priority of action is easily confirmed by a simple thought experiment. Imagine a story constructed so as to create dissonance between character and action by attributing certain qualities to its characters but ascribing contradictory actions to them: "A ___ was a good son and an exemplary husband. He stole his mother's medications and frequently beat his wife." In such a case, readers invariably accept the action and dismiss the character description as unreliable or ironic. The narrator may be taken as a fool or a psychopath for *misrepresenting* the ethos, but only with a good deal of supporting narrative are the actions taken to be untrue. My example is outlandish, but an extant case in point would be *Othello*, in which Iago is consistently described as honest, dependable and trustworthy by the other characters, but easily identified as a villain by the things he does.

The nexus between character and action is choice. Ethos is not developed by what happens to a character but by what he or she chooses to do. Readers too make choices. One can choose to accept that Iago has been unfairly passed over for promotion, and share his suspicions that Othello and Cassio have had sex with his wife, and still be appalled at the revenge he chooses to exact. The reader's or spectator's own choices become more nuanced and perhaps more challenging when attention shifts from Iago to Othello. In the *Nicomachean Ethics* Aristotle conceives virtue in terms of habitual action. Here again ethos is deduced from mythos. A virtuous man is one who can be expected to choose actions conducing to the good. In these terms Othello appears to be a virtuous man until, put upon by Iago, he murders his wife. Do we then construe his evil act as an anomaly, a momentary lapse of otherwise customary virtue?

In his afterword to this volume, Theodore Leinwand (Chapter 14) recalls Horatio cautioning Hamlet not to "consider too curiously" the fate of the body after death.[8] If I may indulge the Hegelian move of referring to the Afterword in the introduction, this recollection helps me to think of Othello in Aristotelian terms. The *Nicomachean Ethics* posits the qualities of character as not desirable or repellent in and of themselves, assessing them rather as quantities along a scale that runs from deficit or deficiency to excess, with the mean conducing to virtue. If, as Horatio implies, Hamlet becomes ethically perplexed by thinking "too curiously" on the event, an Aristotelian might say that he has an excess of thoughtfulness, an overindulgence that interferes with his responsibility to make decisions and to act. Othello, in contrast, has a defect of curiosity that renders him criminally obtuse. Hamlet berates himself for being "unpregnant of [his] cause" (2.2.568). Aided by the midwifery of Iago, Othello is too easily delivered of "his monstrous birth" (2.1.403–04).[9]

Thinking one's way into Iago, however, presents a different sort of challenge. Hamlet and Othello continually make choices. Hamlet's indecision about how, when and whether to act on the ghost's charge is subsumed in the broadest possible choice of all: "to be or not to be." The second quarto text most explicitly brings this inability or unwillingness to decide to a decisive conclusion:

> Not a whit. We defy augury. There is special providence in the fall of a sparrow. If it be now, 'tis not to come; if it be not to come, it will be now; if it be not now, yet it will come. The readiness is all. Since no man, of aught he leaves, knows aught, what is't to leave betimes? Let be.
> (5.2.215–20)[10]

That final "let be," absent from the Folio text, supplies the ironically inverse answer to "the question" posed in 3.1. It makes clear that even indecision is a choice. Only after resigning the office of decision in favor of "providence" is Hamlet *ready* to attain his expressed desire, which has been from the beginning to: "melt, thaw and resolve ... into a dew." "Providence" offers him the resolution previously withheld by the "canon 'gainst self-slaughter" (1.2.129–32).

Othello too chooses to evade choice. When he exclaims of Desdemona, "Excellent wretch! perdition catch my soul / But I do love thee! and when I love thee not / Chaos is come again" (3.3.90–92), he sets out the alternative: Desdemona or perdition. Yet this choice is displaced by a choice he does not confront – that between Iago's and Desdemona's word. Iago is honest by epithet, and Othello never seriously questions his honesty. He demands of Desdemona that she "swear thou art honest," only that she may "swear it" and damn herself. Othello bets on Iago's word against Desdemona's. Minutes before these lines, Emilia articulates the soul-stakes of such a bet:

> I durst, my lord, to wager she is honest,
> Lay down my soul at stake: if you think other
> Remove your thought, it doth abuse your bosom.
> If any wretch have put this in your head
> Let heaven requite it with the serpent's curse,
> There's no man happy: the purest of their wives
> Is foul as slander.
>
> (4.212–19)

We see no such wagers on the part of Iago. Despite his occasional citation of grievances, about which he may or may not be serious, his evil is a given, a matter not of quantity – of excess or defect – but rather a quality of his nature. Interestingly, what evil-doing offers Iago is not self-respect or a misguided sense of retributive justice but joy. Hamlet and Othello are always engaged in the process of creating and/or discovering themselves. Iago, contrary to his "I am not that I am," is very much what he is – a set of actions bespeaking an incomprehensible ethos. His lack of narrative motivation makes him the mysterious and terrifying character that he is. The persistence of a character whose meanness is not subject to the dialectical interplay of action and reaction that governs a revenge play (like *Hamlet* – in which even Claudius is given a thwarted attempt at prayer and a genuine affection for his queen) is sealed off and impenetrable. The helplessness of Othello can be grounded in the story of his hard life and his racial isolation. But the meanness of Iago is the matter of his pleasure – his aesthetic joy – which the audience may resist sharing.

What, after all, does Iago want? When we voice inwardly the words of Hamlet or Othello we may experience vicariously some aspects of the choices they make. We may understand to some degree what it might feel like to face those choices and explore the ways in which we resemble and differ from these fictional people. Aristotle (and Freud after him) called this effect identification and argued that it facilitated the accumulation and the discharge of feelings in the spectators of tragedy on to the tragic protagonist. The impenetrability of Iago, the fact that we never really see him *choose* evil – never participate with him in selecting an action from among alternatives, moves us in a different direction. Evil, for Iago, as for his ancestor Richard III, is an aesthetic position, and as such it maintains an aesthetic distance from the audience. The power of Iago's evil strangely associates the repellency of his acts with an estranged appreciation of the power of his intellect. His "art" exceeds our thought, but I hope that few would think it sublime.

The conjunction in *Othello* of characters whose actions give the illusion of having come from a comprehensible dialectic of ethos and circumstances and a character like Iago, whose interiority is suggested, yet persistently opaque, tempts me to a, probably unseemly, leap from Shakespeare's time to our own and from the comfort of fiction to the brutal exigency of fact. The only excuses I can offer for this transfer of attention are existential – like most mental motions, it could not be thought until it was thought, and what occurs to one's mind, has, by necessity, already occurred – and that it is directional, by which I mean, it pulls the fictional world into relation with the "real" but resists a reciprocal aestheticizing of experience.

In the days after September 11, 2001, I experienced a visceral reaction against certain well-intentioned advice. I refer to admonitions to contextualize the event, to learn who the hijackers were and how their actions might make sense to them – to try to understand, in effect, where they were coming from. I could see how such efforts might be tactically useful, but my immediate, almost unthought, response was that I did not *want* to *understand* these men who flew planes full of people, into buildings full of people. Five years after the fact, I still don't![11]

It seems to me that to understand them would mean constructing a dialectical series of causes and effects, experiences and responses, to render intelligible the choice they made. This would move them from the category of Iago to that of Othello and thus (metaleptically) posit the story of their actions – their mythos – as the intelligible consequence of a comprehensible ethos – and, by doing so, to risk registering an aesthetic response.

In *The Critique of Judgement*, Kant, having distinguished between nature and art – "A beauty of nature is a *beautiful thing*; beauty of art is a *beautiful representation* of a thing" – makes the following assertion:

> Where fine art evidences its superiority is in the beautiful descriptions it gives of things that in nature would be ugly or displeasing. The Furies, diseases, devastations of war, and the like, can (as evils) be very beautifully described, nay even represented in pictures. One kind of ugliness alone is incapable of being represented conformably to nature without destroying all aesthetic delight, and consequently artistic beauty, namely, that which excites *disgust*. For, as in this strange sensation, which depends purely on the imagination, the object is represented as insisting, as it were, upon our enjoying it, while we still set our face against it, the artificial representation of the object is no longer distinguishable from the nature of the object itself in our sensation, and so it cannot possibly be regarded as beautiful.[12]

My determination not to understand the 9/11 hijackers is no doubt over-determined, but this passage from Kant helps me to explain (or rationalize) it as an intersection of the ethical and the aesthetic. If to understand the hijackers means to *represent* their action as the comprehensible continuation of a developing story, the mythos of an ethos, it seems to me that such an accommodation has one of two possible results. Either, as Kant says, the resulting tale's insistence that we enjoy it fails, and the representation simply evokes the disgust evoked by the action itself; or, more ominously, the conversion of fact to story succeeds in making us think we comprehend it and thus releases the joy it insists upon. It is this latter possibility that concerns me. I am uneasy when students take seriously the grievances with which Iago half-heartedly motivates his evil doing, because to do so risks making his reasoning plausible. It enables identification – seeing things from his point of view. Fortunately, I can point to things in the text of *Othello* that restore Iago's opacity. I am appalled at the thought of bringing the 9/11 hijackers into the purview of fiction because to do so requires an artifice that will inevitably (I fear) replace the blank fact of what they did with a fictional representation. Such a representation, by purporting to show us their point of view, sutures the ethical tear they enacted, authorizing even a covert joy – not in what they did, but in our illusionary belief that we understand it – even that we see a perverse beauty in it. To represent something is to make it iterable and thus to obscure the pathetic particularity of the evil doer – the sort of evil doer, that is, whom story cannot (ought not?) project into the universality of the commonplace. The presentation of this resistance of the particular to assimilation by the universe of precept is one source of the ethical efficacy of reading and writing, as is the danger of complicity with an aesthetics of villainy.

***

Reflecting this privilege of the particular, the essays in this volume join in regarding narration itself as a primary ethical action; each engages the ethics of reading through sustained practical criticism of specific texts. Part II, The Ethics of Renaissance Forms, presents four essays that begin with formal issues. David Lee Miller (Chapter 2) looks at Britomart's dream in the Temple of Isis in book 5 canto 7 of *The Faerie Queene*. Observing that the analogy of Britomart to Isis implicitly questions the divine sanction of male rule, Miller shows how Spenser's shift from Astraea to Isis and Osiris as patrons of Justice replaces "the myth of virgin withdrawal with one of militant sexuality" and probes "allegory as a poetic method," questioning not only the prince's divine warrant to rule, but also the "metaphysical basis of the symbolic mode that issues the warrant." Grounded in meticulous attention to the material weight and form of words in key passages, Miller's ethical turn highlights the commitments of a text that must choose between ideological comfort and its own procedures. Readers who follow that text discover that "to read 'right' rightly ... perhaps we need to read backward, undoing the reversal of language. Alertness to such double readings may be just what this legend (from *legendum*, that which is read) requires."

Harry Berger, Jr. turns our attention in Chapter 3 from the verbal *legendum* to the pictorial in his analysis of Dutch group portraits. Noting that in the *Poetics* "Aristotle uses *ēthos* to designate characters in drama and their moral quality as inferred or constructed by audiences" and "in the *Rhetoric* to designate the 'character' a speaker assumes – performs, or imitates – in order to persuade his audience of his moral authority," Berger recalls Keir Elam's observation that in "both cases Aristotle depicts moral character as effect rather than cause of dramatic or rhetorical speech – as the product of art rather than of nature. And in both cases, the production of a convincing 'character' is treated as the fictive effect of a performance and closely identified with acts of imitation." "The difference," Berger adds, "is that the dramatic *ēthos* is unproblematically fictional whereas the fictiveness of the rhetorical *ēthos* is morally problematical." Berger's strategic response is to place "the study of portrait poses within an epideictic framework that features the ethical concern, the competitiveness, the problem of fictive self-construction, and the performative anxiety common to speakers and sitters."

Berger's readings of group portraits of the regents and regentesses of seventeenth-century Dutch charitable institutions considers the purposes the paintings were expected to serve and the circumstances in which they were produced. Distinguishing two distinct kinds of composition: *portrait*, in which the subjects depicted appear to have gathered to sit for the painting, and *genre*, in which the painting purports to record a scene or event independent of it, Berger maps the genre and portrait elements of the paintings he discusses in terms of the ethics of paintings in which people pose as people who are not posing (genre) and paintings in which the subjects are posed as people who are posing, understanding the formal tensions in the paintings as also tensions in the structures of the Dutch Republic.

The essays by Marshall Grossman (Chapter 4) and Victoria Kahn (Chapter 5) see *Samson Agonistes* as a work that sets out to provoke a political response. *Samson Agonistes*, itself a reading of Judges 13–16, raises questions about the ethics of Milton's appropriation of biblical material for political ends, about the ethics of reading, and, most pointedly, about the ethics of Samson's decision to use the roof of the Philistine Temple as a weapon of mass destruction. While both Grossman and Kahn give precedence to the text itself, Grossman approaches these questions from a broadly psycho-analytic perspective, noting the structural similarities of psychoanalytic transference and ethical reading.

Kahn explores the form and contemporary purposes of *Samson Agonistes* in terms of Walter Benjamin's influential distinction between tragedy and *Trauerspiel*. In so doing, she adds another dimension to the ethics of reading by confronting the origins of that distinction in the writing of the notorious Nazi jurist Carl Schmitt. Kahn reads Benjamin reading (and writing to) Schmitt to draw a sharp distinction between Benjamin's *Trauerspiel* and Schmitt's.

For Grossman an ethical reading of Milton's text demands of modern readers that they examine Samson's undecidable decision – what Schmitt or Benjamin might call his "declaring the exception" – either rejecting it or making it their own. Readers thus incur the obligation to ask how their response to Samson might modify their own ethos. Kahn is concerned to show that Milton's closet drama is a call for continued political action and a formal resistance to the developing modes of restoration sentimentality. Both Kahn and Grossman are drawn to Milton's remarkable presentation of Aristotle's theory of tragedy in the epigraphs and the preface to *Samson Agonistes*, from which each draws a different conclusion.

Though each of the essays in this first Part is historically aware, historical contexts are addressed more prominently in Part III, Historicizing Renaissance Ethics. Vivienne Westbrook (Chapter 6) tracks the development of the English bible from the fourteenth to the middle of the sixteenth century, attending not only to the translations of the text but especially to the paratextual apparatus of marginal notes and commentary that accreted around them. Paratext brought the vitriolic debates of the time into the bible without "staining" the sacred text itself. Westbrook shows that while the translation of the bible was intended to free each individual reader from reliance on the teaching of others, "every attempt was made to control the readership through a broad range of paratextual strategies, and restrictive State interventions." Out of these crossed purposes – liberation and containment – came an ethics of translation and of bible reading that called for both personal and political reformation.

Paul Yachnin (Chapter 7) picks up the old story of Shakespeare's use of Montaigne's essay "On the Cannibals" in *The Tempest*. But his emphasis is not on the politics of colonialism in early Modern Europe, but rather on the ways in which Shakespeare and Montaigne aspire toward and achieve "an epistolary intimacy between writer and reader." Yachnin tracks "how the pressure of mortality registered in their texts ... seeks out reader-converts ... from among an anonymous, public readership – a group that, by virtue of its anonymity and far-flung membership, is capable of unlimited growth and deathless longevity." Yachnin shows how Montaigne's essay makes readers responsible for "taking in and making part of themselves the words of another." He sees in this transubstantiation of another's words "the generative closeness with the personality of the text that is so productive of the authorial presence characteristic of the high art of modernity" but which "also gives expression to the crisis in that ideal that emerged in the face of the trade in culture."

Like Kahn and Grossman, David Norbrook (Chapter 8) is interested in the "ethics of political violence," and, like Yachnin, he wants to understand the recipes seventeenth-century writers used to ensure the ingestion of their works. But where Yachnin looks at how Montaigne's *Essays* and Shakespeare's plays generate the "authorial presence" characteristic of modernity, Norbrook looks to the details of a single poem, whose form is peculiar to its time and place, a neo-Latin satire written to intervene in a specific political controversy. Asking how Marvell's "Scaevola Scoto-Brittannus" may have been digested by its politically embedded seventeenth-century readers, Norbrook looks to humanist pedagogy, recalling that Renaissance humanism was committed to, and greatly concerned with, the ethical agency of language and that its Latin pedagogy attended rigorously to linguistic details – "from basic vocabulary to the minutest details of quantitative prosody."

"Scaevola Scoto-Brittannus," little studied until now, is among the very last poems Marvell wrote. Norbrook treats it as perhaps the poet's crowning achievement. Implicit in Norbrook's reading of the efficacy of Marvell's poem in Restoration politics is an ethical/technical critique of the poem's neglect by modern critics. While recent historical critics may have slighted the intricacies of poetic form, the close-reading of more formally minded New Critics still favored the reflexive ironies of Marvell's lyrics, failing to appreciate the "rhetorical brilliance" of his satires. "The playfulness and formal self-consciousness inherent in the practice of emulating the register and prosody of poems written a millennium and a half previously offered a kind of excess with which the New Critics, always concerned in the end to vindicate the sacramental unity of form and content, were uneasy." Norbrook demonstrates his point by bringing the poem fully to life with a close reading that is aware of the formal practices of Renaissance imitation of classical sources and of the political situation in which the poem intervenes. Marvell's appropriation of a violent incident in the early history of the Roman republic and the accretions gathered to it by its many classical appropriations exemplifies the difficulty of locating a dividing line between violence and patience, suffering and agency. Norbrook's reading of it exemplifies the efficacy of combining formal and historical awareness in a criticism that works to historicize the former and formalize the latter.

We turn from the historicized attention to form in the essays by Westbrook, Yachnin and Norbrook, to four essays that – remaining both historical and formalist in method – address the issues of *Reading Renaissance Ethics* in more directly philosophical contexts.

Like Norbrook, Gordon Teskey (Chapter 9) is deeply responsive to the learning of the Renaissance. Pointing out that it was a time that "saw the revival of the most technical theories of the rules to be followed in making poems – theories, as Milton expressed it, of 'what the laws are of a true epic poem,'" he adds, however, that it "was also the period in which the question of enthusiasm in poetry, of divine inspiration, arose with peculiar force." The consequent status of the poem as something that hovers between the rule-governed artifact and a vessel of divine creation leads Teskey to consider the literary work as something created, which, in turn, raises the question of the character of its creator (a title which he notes first begins to be granted to poets in the Renaissance): "The question whether the laurel crown is a halo, glowing with celestial fire, is the quintessentially Renaissance question about the poet and about the artist in general: the question of what it means to bring into being what has never existed before."

Teskey's exemplary instance is Milton, whom he takes to be "the last major poet in the European literary tradition for whom the act of creation is centered in God and ... also the first major poet in the European literary tradition for whom the act of creation begins to find its center in the human." To occupy this doubly liminal position Milton turns from the hallucinatory simulacra of previous narratives (exemplified by *The Faerie Queene*) to what Teskey calls *delirious* narration. Where the poet of hallucination "delivers an experience" that is frankly fictive and subsequently discovers the displaced truth within it, the poet of delirium "undergoes an experience on our behalf." While the hallucinatory poet always stands elsewhere in relation to the poem he creates, the delirious poet is interior to his creation. In *Paradise Lost* the poet creates – by writing – not the *elsewhere* of allegory, but the same universe in which he must himself participate as a creature. If the poet is inspired, then this creation, in which he is contained, must be, at least in part, the work of something other that resides inside him. The space of allegory has migrated inward as a division of the self. But, Teskey asks, "If someone else is present, alongside the poet or within him, how can we speak of the character of the poet?"

Beginning with Bernard Williams's distinction between the moral and the ethical, Richard Strier (Chapter 10) argues that, like Williams, Shakespeare sensed the irrelevance of the moral to much of what we value, developing more and more fully and explicitly his sense of the limitation of the moral perspective as his career progressed. Strier traces this development from *Richard III* through the *Henry IV* plays to *King Lear* and *Antony and Cleopatra*. The distinction between the moral and the ethical is that between a prescriptive order and an internal mandate; the one asks conformity to a set of precepts, the other conformity to a sense of self. Strier grounds Shakespeare's preference for the latter in the exigencies of theatrical production, which, of its nature, favors the concrete particular over the abstract. Strier comes to articulate this persistent claim of the particular in a fundamentally Aristotelian way. He construes ethics as the pursuit of the good through a quantitative judgment of the mean and morality as the distinguishing of right from wrong according to a qualitative judgment of the absolute. It is this disparity that Shakespeare stages: "The problem with moralizing the represented experiences of Lear and Gloucester is not that it is difficult to do so. It could hardly, in fact, be easier. The problem is that it seems irrelevant to do so. Their sufferings are such as to make the whole question of 'desert' seem irrelevant – or, as in the case of Goneril and Regan's moral certainty, both niggling and cruel."

Anita Gilman Sherman (Chapter 11) also poses a question of philosophical compatibility. Turning to another strand of classical philosophy given new life in the Renaissance, she asks: "Is skeptical ethics an oxymoron?" Here the question of whether or not ethics and skepticism are compatible turns on what one means by *skepticism*: "If skepticism is defined as a principled refusal to pass judgment, then it may be wise to concede its incompatibility with ethics, the study of the grounds for choice. But if skepticism designates a program of inquiry based on a set of rhetorical techniques that will unsettle preconceived notions, then a skeptical ethics is not a contradiction in terms, but a plan for action." For a particular instance of skepticism as rhetorical inquiry, Sherman routes her question through John Donne's scabrous anti-Jesuit satire *Ignatius, his Conclave*, which, she argues, "both adopts and disowns a skeptical aesthetic – adopting rhetorical forms associated with skepticism while disowning the aestheticizing tendencies of its skeptical characters." While Donne's much studied Third Satire follows Aristotelian procedure, seeking a mean between competing religious postures, by the 1611 *Ignatius, his Conclave*, Donne, having had experience of legislative procedures – as an MP for Brackley and an ardent student of the Council of Trent – turned his attention to the more complex problem of group dynamics. Sherman shows how *Ignatius* thus becomes an occasion to ask "how a gathering of skeptical personalities goes about decision-making."

The final essay in Part IV is also the broadest in implication. Like Sherman, Angus Fletcher (Chapter 12) tracks how decisions are made by groups, with the corollary question of how decisions are made by individuals who are able to reflect on themselves as groups of conflicting desires and interests: "In politics [the] capacity to act is an equivalent of the individual's power to proceed as an ethical being, by making decisions and plans and then acting upon such initiatives. Now, while this analogy is broadly obvious on the political scale of government, it is not so obvious what altogether comprises the problem of 'committee' for an individual." Fletcher correlates "the power to proceed as an ethical being" with the turbulent politics of the seventeenth century and with the changes in thought associated with the new science. As Donne famously observed, the new science disrupted the moralized universe of circles and immanent motion, substituting a cosmos of straight lines, ellipses, inertia and external causes. Fletcher shows how a new ethics and a new politics followed. Like Sherman, Fletcher concludes that "baroque skepticism pitched philosophy (natural and moral) into a changed modern condition."

Reading Renaissance Ethics has been a collaborative project undertaken over a period of years by a group of scholars with diverse styles of thought and methods of inquiry but convergent interests; its last section, Part V, assesses the results of that project. The first of the two entries in this Part, Chapter 13, presents a straightforward experiment in a form of collaboration less mediated than that represented by the volume as a whole: an exchange between Sharon Achinstein and the editor on the politics of reading Renaissance ethics in Milton's *Areopagitica*. As the headnote explains, this exchange continues in print an on-going discussion (at times an argument) that began as a collegial response – suspicious of the politics of a volume on ethics.

Finally, Chapter 14, Theodore Leinwand's response to the project of *Reading Renaissance Ethics*, also negotiates the boundary between ethics and politics. Finding in our collaboration the marks of a common aesthetic response to contemporary political posturing, Leinwand formulates what he calls interpretive modesty as the mythos of an ethical response.

Notes

1 Kenneth Burke, *The Philosophy of Literary Form* (Berkeley, CA: University of California Press, 1973), pp. 293–304.
2 See respectively, Edmund Spenser, *The Fairie Queene*, "Letter to Ralegh," John Milton, "Of Education," and George Herbert, "Jordan I."
3 See for example, Ben Jonson, *The Alchemist*, "To the Reader."
4 Annabel Patterson, *Censorship and Interpretation: The Conditions of Writing and Reading in Early Modern England* (Madison, WI: University of Wisconsin Press, 1991) and *Reading Between the Lines* (Madison, WI: University of Wisconsin Press, 1993).
5 The phrase is taken from Hayden White, *The Content of the Form: Narrative Discourse and Historical Representation* (Baltimore, MD: Johns Hopkins University Press, 1987).
6 For a more detailed discussion of this failure, see James Holstun, "Ranting at the New Historicism," *English Literary Renaissance* 19 (1989): 189–225. See also Harry Berger, Jr., *Situated Utterances: Texts, Bodies, and Cultural Representations* (New York: Fordham University Press, 2005), pp. 19–98, Marshall Grossman, *The Story of All Things: Writing the Self in English Renaissance Narrative Poetry* (Durham, NC: Duke University Press, 1998), pp. 9–16, and Paul Stevens, "Pretending to be Real: Stephen Greenblatt and the Legacy of Popular Existentialism," *New Literary History* 33 (2002): 491–519.
7 *Poetics* 3.2 [1450a] cited from *Aristotle's Poetics, Demetrius on Style, Longinus on the Sublime*, trans. John Warrington (London: J.M. Dent & Sons, 1963), p.13.
8 William Shakespeare, *Hamlet*, ed. Harold Jenkins, The Arden Shakespeare (London: Methuen, 1982), 5.1.199. Theodore Leinwand, "Afterwords . . .," Chapter 14, this volume, pp. 107–12.
9 *Othello*, ed. E.A.J. Honigmann (Walton-on-Thames, Surrey: Thomas Nelson & Sons, 1997).
10 Victoria Kahn discusses Hamlet's inability to decide in terms of Carl Schmitt's and Walter Benjamin's different understandings of the baroque *Trauerspiel* in "Hamlet or Hecuba: Carl Schmitt's Decision," in *Representations* 83 (Summer 2003): 67–96, extending this discussion to *Samson Agonistes* in Chapter 5, this volume. See below, pp. 107–12.
11 On this point, of course, I drop the editorial "we" and speak only for myself, and not the other contributors to the volume.
12 Immanuel Kant, *The Critique of Judgement*, trans. James Creed Meredith (Oxford: Clarendon, 1952), § 48: pp.172; 173–74.

Part II

The ethics of Renaissance forms

2 Gender, justice and the gods in *The Faerie Queene*, Book 5

David Lee Miller

They must be called gods who are scarcely men ...
Erasmus

In Book 5, canto 7 of *The Faerie Queene*, Astraea as divine patron of Justice gives way to the Egyptian deities Isis and Osiris. Among the effects of this maneuver is to replace the myth of virgin withdrawal with one of militant sexuality. Isis doesn't just marry Osiris, she goes forth to gather his scattered remains and, when the phallus turns up missing, fashions a replacement for it.[1] She is an apt sponsor for Britomart, whose virile masquerade ends, in Book 5, with her determination to put the phallus back where it belongs. But the turn to sexuality in Book 5 does more than close down the gender-bending of the middle books. By carrying the analogy between Britomart and Isis to the point of deification it raises potentially awkward questions about the divine sanction of secular rule. Finally, it turns those questions back on allegory as a poetic method. In doing so, it not only questions the prince's divine warrant, it also unsettles the metaphysical basis of the symbolic mode that issues the warrant.[2]

To see why sexuality should be the common flashpoint for these concerns we might turn to Gordon Teskey's work on the history and theory of allegory.[3] Teskey argues that Plato's theory of ideas creates a logical impasse. Having separated matter from form absolutely, making form transcendent and immaterial while turning matter into the *prima materia* – a featureless, abstract substratum – Plato's metaphysic has no way to get the two back together again. The difficulty surfaces as a problem of predication: one may say with perfect redundancy that Justice is just, but to say that Agathon is just is to posit an immanence of the ideal within the material that the theory cannot strictly account for.

To explain the copresence of matter and form in existing objects – in other words, to make predication possible – Platonic idealism has recourse to the sexual imaginary, filling the gap in its logic with tropes of heterosexual union. In this way the primal aporia of metaphysics becomes instead its primal scene. Medieval allegory turns as well to the scriptive imaginary, stationing scribal figures called "genii" at the thresholds of the crystalline spheres. As ideal forms descend into the sublunary world, these genii write them into matter. The equivalence of writing with heterosexual union appears in this tradition when Bernardus Silvestris, for example, finishes off his *Cosmographia* by representing the testes as microcosmic scribes: the last pair of genii turn up inside the scrotum. The same equivalence appears in negative form when Alain of Lilles uses the language of grammar to mount a tirade against nonreproductive sexual practices: "The sex of active nature trembles shamefully at the way in which it declines into passive nature. Man is made woman, he blackens the honor of his sex; the craft of magic Venus makes him of double gender. He is both predicate and subject, he becomes likewise of two declensions, he pushes the laws of grammar too far."[4]

In Teskey's literary history, this primal scene of predication draws the slowly decaying pagan gods into its force field, capturing the residual glow of their numinous half-life. Like the primal scene of psychoanalysis, that of metaphysics is neither wholly real nor merely fantastic: instead it marks the point at which fantasy, having volunteered to fill a gap in the "real" of metaphysics, begins to generate real effects. The status of the pagan gods is similarly uncertain. Neither objects of faith nor empty figures of speech, they are personae in whom skepticism confronts an equivocal sense of the numinous as somehow spilling over the walls of doctrine, clinging to figures that may be human in origin but are so ancient, prepossessing, and mysterious that they inspire an awe verging on the religious. And so they are drawn into this warp space where fantasy and reality are knotted together.

Spenser situates *The Faerie Queene* at the edge of this primal scene to dwell in the uncertainty of its effects. From the time we leave Book 1 it is never clear to what extent the antique world is either Christian or pre-Christian. We can call this elusiveness syncretism and let it go, but if Teskey is right then the gods are more volatile than such labels imply. Two passages in Book 5, both linked to what we might call the Matter of Egypt, lend force to this equivocation by using it to insinuate the human origins of "divine right." The first is the proem, and the second is the opening of canto 7.

1. "So divine a read"

In the proem to Book 5 Justice, personified as a Goddess, is said to resemble

> . . . God in his imperiall might;
> Whose soveraine powre is herein most exprest,
> That both to good and bad he dealeth right,
> And all his workes with Justice hath bedight.
> That powre he also doth to Princes lend,
> And makes them like himselfe in glorious sight,

To sit in his owne seate, his cause to end,
And rule his people right, as he doth recommend.
                                        (st. 10.2–9)[5]

This affirmation uses God to consolidate "might" and "right": so long as a mimetic relation holds between God and the prince, justice will prevail on earth. But the proem has just informed us in some detail that the heavens are out of joint and the earth is spiraling down into a new stone age. This rehearsal of cosmic decay undermines the confidence of the closing turn to orthodoxy.

What if the prince who claims to borrow her power from God and to "sit in [God's] owne seate" were just as much a pretender as the Egalitarian Giant of canto 2? The language of weight and measure invoked in that episode comes from the Bible. The Giant might, for example, be admonished with a verse from Isaiah: "Who hath measured the waters in his fist? and counted heaven with the span, and comprehended the dust of the earth in a measure? and weighed the mountains in a weight, and the hills in a balance?" (40:12).[6] The same question might be put to the prince. Job 28 asks:

But where is wisdom found? and where is the place of understanding?
Man knoweth not the price thereof: for it is not found in the land of
    the living.
    …
God understandeth the way thereof, and he knoweth the place thereof.
For he beholdeth the endes of the world, and seeth all that is under
    heaven,
To make the weight of the windes and to weigh the waters by measure.
                                        (12–13, 23–26)

The proem to Book 5 may recall such passages when it burlesques the efforts of astrologers to mark off the heavens with a span. Ostensibly the poet is merely citing the disorder of the zodiac as further evidence for his thesis of universal decay. But as he turns to the sky something excessive begins, a cosmic Keystone Kops routine in which Capricorn forgets where he belongs and rams into Taurus, who then butts the Gemini, who topple onto Cancer and squash him. Cancer, presumably much the worse for wear, gets knocked into the grove of Leo, while all the other signs stray "out of their proper places farre away" (6.6).[7]

At some point the absurdity of this description may lead us not only to question the disposition of the heavens but also to impeach the practice that generates the description in the first place: "Star-read" (8.2). The underlying perception of decay – the discourse of historical pessimism – comes from a metaphor introduced in the opening lines of the proem: "So oft as I with state of present time, / The image of the antique world compare." But how much faith may be given to "those Aegyptian wisards old" who devise the star-read of stanza 8, or to any of the sources that describe a golden age? For that matter, how much faith may be given to sixteenth-century astronomy? Whatever the constellations might be doing, the experts were certainly stumbling over each other's explanations. If humans *have* decayed as far as the poet says, what would make us think they can accurately perceive heavenly affairs? Certainly not the Book of Job, and probably not the controversy touched off by Copernicus.

This questioning of star-read belongs to an insistent concern in the proem with reading, and in particular with reading the word "read." Human beings, the poet complains in stanza 2, are no longer "form'd of flesh and bone" (4), but instead

> Are now transformed into hardest stone:
> Such as behind their backs (so backward bred)
> Were throwne by *Pyrrha* and *Deucalione*:
> And if then those may any worse be red,
> They into that ere long will be degendered.
>
> (5–9)

The offspring of Pyrrha and Deucalion were "backward bred" because their progenitors threw stones over their shoulders, but men in the present age reverse even this backward breeding, metamorphosing from flesh back into stone and so literally un-breeding or "degendering" themselves. Or do they? Perhaps they have simply been degender-read, slandered by the golden-age fantasies that authorize this discourse of historical pessimism, underwriting its ability to discover in men the worst that "may ... be red." After all, we learn in stanza 4 that there has been a reversal in language as well: the terms "virtue" and "right" have changed places with their antonyms, "vice" and "wrong" (1–4). To read "right" rightly, then, perhaps we need to read backward, undoing the reversal of language. Alertness to such double readings may be just what this legend (from *legendum*, that which is read) requires.

Such alertness prepares us to retro-read the rhetoric of praise in the closing lines of the proem. There, as we saw earlier, God is figured as a monarch "in his imperiall might; / Whose soveraine powre is herein most exprest." To read this rhetoric backward is to see that an imperial God has been created in the prince's image. Given the displacement of the zodiac's residents, how can the earthly ruler know whether she is truly sitting "in the'Almighties place" (11.2)? Like all the "places" of ideology this one is rhetorically constructed, and the monarch's divine read, like the star-read of her wizards, may be a mis-read.

According to the proem, the shaky foundations of worldly justice depend on this analogy. If the "Souerayne Goddesse" (11.1) addressed there cannot secure God's "proper place" – if Virgo, or Elizabeth as Astraea, wanders *out*

of place like the other constellations – then Justice becomes an impossible
virtue and Spenser can only write the legend of its rhetoric. The reversal this
project would entail begins in the turn from the proem to canto 1, where we
learn that the golden age without force or fraud, described in stanza 9 of the
proem, was also a scene of so much vice that justice had to be established by
the "strong hand" (1.9) of heroic violence. Its Herculean patron Artegall
learned the "discipline of justice" (6.9) from Astraea herself – after she
kidnapped him. His education begins with fraud, the "gifts and speaches
mild" with which the goddess lures him to her cave (6.5–7). It continues with
force as the young knight practices "upon wyld beasts" because there are no
humans on whom to "make experience" (7.6–9). It reverts to fraud as Astraea
bestows upon Artegall the sword she has purloined from Jove (9.2–4),[8] and
turns back to force when the goddess absconds leaving Talus in her place
(12.1–2).

She abdicates to take up what the narrator, sweetly oblivious to contradiction, calls an "everlasting place" in the zodiac (11.5) – presumably the
same zodiac whose slapstick derangement was detailed in the proem. But
that tour of the zodiac stopped with Leo, the sign that precedes Virgo. The
text's reticence – which takes the form here of the narrator's complaisance,
or what I call the "Dan Edmund" effect – creates an ambiguous space
between the confusion of star-read and the apparent security of Elizabeth's
divine read.[9] When we get back to the stars in canto 1, we return to the place
where the proem left off. But now the zodiac has become decorous; it is "the
heavens bright-shining baudricke" on which Virgo appears "sixt in her
degree" (11.7–8). Is the text not asking us to think about the gap between Leo
and Virgo? Is it not questioning the decorum that ordains Astraea and her
justice?

The final stanza of the proem tells us that the analogy by which the
monarch resembles God lets her "aread" righteous doom to her people
(11.4). But a gap opens within "so divine a read" when the poet dares to
discourse of it (11.7). This gap is as large as the distance from Leo to Virgo, in
which the chaotic heavens are made decorous, and as small as the letter-
space that turns the verb of royal agency, "aread," into the noun of interpretation, "a read." It opens again as we approach Isis Church in canto 7.

2. Euhemerism

Canto 7 begins by reaffirming the divinity of true justice:

> Nought is on earth more sacred or divine,
> That Gods and men do equally adore,
> Then this same vertue, that doth right define:
> For th'hevens themselves, whence mortal men implore
> Right in their wrongs, are rul'd by righteous lore

> Of highest Jove, who doth true justice deale
> To his inferiour Gods, and evermore
> Therewith contains his heavenly Common-weale:
> The skill whereof to Princes hearts he doth reveale.

Here again Spenser invokes the paradigm of divine right in order to complicate it, insinuating doubt within a bland rhetoric that "presents" as affirmation. In doing so he works the gap that the proem has opened within
Elizabeth's power to "aread." The first line seems to assert the active presence
of divinity on earth, but it casts this affirmation as a negative, and in fact
asserts not that human justice is divine but that nothing else is more so. The
next line is no less equivocal: justice seems to join gods and men as the object
of their "equal" adoration, but the plural complicates this affirmation in turn.
Where the proem says "God" we now read "Gods." In this way Spenser
leaves the door open to a reading that would argue the human origins of the
figure – call him "Jove" – who reveals justice to the hearts of human princes.
   In the next stanza Dan Edmund strolls through this open door as if nothing
could be more innocent:

> Well therefore did the antique world invent,
> That Justice was a God of soveraine grace,
> And altars unto him, and temples lent,
> And heavenly honours in the highest place;
> Calling him great Osyris, of the race
> Of th'old Aegyptian Kings, that whylome were;
> With fayned colours shading a true case:
> For that Osyris, whilest he lived here,
> The justest man alive, and truest did appear.

> His wife was Isis, whom they likewise made
> A Goddesse of great power and soveranty,
> And in her person cunningly did shade
> That part of Justice, which is Equity,
> Whereof I have to treat here presently.

Spenser introduces the motif of euhemerism, a rationalizing or skeptical
discourse on the gods of the gentiles which sees their divinity as essentially an
epideictic trope.[10] He applies this trope directly to Osiris, not Jove, but of
course the texts that describe Osiris as an Egyptian king who "became" a god
make the same assertion about Zeus Ammon; indeed they make Osiris a son
of Zeus and Hera, and in the process they make Cronos, Rhea, Zeus, and
Athena into mortal Egyptian rulers who *achieved* immortality – that is, who
were deified. Spenser's narrator approves this act of deification, but in
affirming that the ancients invented well he also affirms that they invented,
"with fayned colours shading a true case."[11]

We recognize this language immediately from the standard defense of allegory, where truth is routinely "coloured with an historicall fiction, which the most part of men delight to read, rather for variety of matter, then for profite of the ensample."[12] The deification of mortals, then, is nothing but allegory. Such colors are warranted by the claim that they shade a true case. This is the force of "therefore," which assures us that the ancients invented well because in deifying judges they paid tribute to the divinity of justice. But they did so by creating the divine origin as an image of the human justice it inspired: Jove here rules not a pantheon but a "Common-weale" (1.8). Circularity comes back around to question the origins of the origin: does Jove really inspire the justice of the prince, or does she authorize the creation of Jove in her imperial image?

Dan Edmund goes on affirming truths in the same blandly inadvertent way. Britomart – without Talus – enters the temple and meets the priests, who among the other details of their attire

> wore rich Mitres shaped like the Moone,
> To shew that *Isis* doth the Moone portend;
> Like as *Osyris* signifies the Sunne.
> For that they both like race in equall justice runne.
>
> (4.6–9)

Evidently the priests of Isis don't know their Egyptian star-read, for as we learned in the proem the sun is far from consistent in running his "race":

> Ne is that same great glorious lampe of light,
> That doth enlumine all these lesser fyres,
> In better case, ne keepes his course more right,
> But is miscaried with the other Spheres.
> For since the terme of fourteene hundred yeres,
> That learned *Ptolomaee* his hight did take,
> He is declyned from that marke of theirs,
> Nigh thirtie minutes to the Southerne lake;
> That makes me feare in time he will us quite forsake.
>
> And if to those *Ægyptian* wisards old,
> Which in Star-read were wont have best insight,
> Faith may be given, it is by them told,
> That since the time they first tooke the Sunnes hight,
> Foure times his place he shifted hath in sight,
> And twice hath risen, where he now doth West,
> And wested twice, where he ought rise aright.
>
> (8–9.7)

Just as he did earlier in describing Astraea's retreat, the narrator in canto 7 "forgets" the difficulty human observers have in reading heaven. With Astraea the point is made by simple proximity, that of the first canto to the proem and that of Libra to Leo. With Osiris, it is made by the conspicuous reintroduction of the Matter of Egypt, which serves in both passages to disturb the discourse of divinity.

3. The justice of gender

Deification and divine sanction make up the central action of canto 7. Britomart first secures the warrant of the gods – or so the Hermeneutic Priest assures her – and then goes on to achieve the divinity she has dreamed of. The linked episodes of Isis Church and Radigund's defeat are framed by matching deifications of human rulers, that of Isis and Osiris at the canto's opening and that of Britomart at its close. Between these two moments, the poem intrudes its abiding concern with sexual politics.

Britomart's deification is anticipated in the "wondrous vision" that appears to her in the Church:

> Her seem'd, as she was doing sacrifize
> To *Isis*, deckt with Mitre on her hed,
> And linnen stole after those Priestes guize,
> All sodainely she saw transfigured
> Her linnen stole to robe of scarlet red,
> And Moone-like Mitre to a Crowne of gold,
> That even she her selfe much wondered
> At such a chaunge, and joyed to behold
> Her selfe, adorn'd with gems and jewels manifold.
>
> (st. 13)

Although Britomart and Isis remain separate persons in the dream, this transformation clearly identifies the dreamer at once with the Idol she has worshipped and with the iconography that made the queen of England an imperial idol.[13] It begins with an explicitly masculine identification, as we might expect. Britomart's struggle has from the start been largely internal, caused by her resistance to the fate read out by dynastic prophecy. From the moment she first approaches the Mirror of Venus in "her fathers closet" (3.22.2) only to find her self-image supplanted by the image of Arthegall, Britomart is caught between irreconcilable desires: she wants both to have and to be the masculine knight of her dreams. For most of her career in the poem she manages to finesse this contradiction, but when Radigund storms over the horizon to force the issue, anatomy turns to destiny and Britomart's story is over.

According to the narrator, Britomart's dream "did close implie / The course of all her fortune and posteritie" (5.7.12.9–10). It does so by looking at once backward and forward. It looks forward, as the Hermeneutic Priest explains, because it implies a prophecy of her marriage, rule, and motherhood; it looks backward because it recapitulates elements of her first experience with vision and prophecy in Book 3. The detail of her linen robe turning scarlet red, for example, implies a sexual transformation. The Priests mortify their flesh and are "tied ... to steadfast chastity" (9.7), which in context seems to mean they are celibate. The narrator tells us they neither eat meat nor drink wine, and this observation launches an etiological digression on wine as a return-of-the-repressed. When Jove slew the Titans, their resentful mother the earth stored up their shed blood, bringing it forth again in vines whose "liquor blouddy red" stirs the minds of men to renew the old rebellion (11.3–5). This is the immediate point of reference for the flush of color that "transfigured" Britomart's robe (13.4). The verb's allusion to Christ insists on the clash of associations as Britomart's transfiguration, instead of bathing her in an unearthly radiance, renews the stain of "proud rebellious flesh" (9.5).

The implications of this rubescence erupt in the following stanza:

> And in the midst of her felicity,
> An hideous tempest seemed from below,
> To rise through all the Temple sodainely,
> That from the Altar all about did blow
> The holy fire, and all the embers strow
> Uppon the ground, which kindled privily,
> Into outragious flames unwares did grow,
> That all the Temple put in jeopardy
> Of flaming, and her selfe in great perplexity.

The accumulating elements of vision, fire, blood, and rebellion not only anticipate the political wildfires that will challenge Britomart's right to the throne. They also recall the volcanic eruption in her own bowels that followed her vision of Arthegall in Book 3:

> For no no usuall fire, no usuall rage
> Yt is, O Nourse, which on my life doth feed,
> And sucks the blood, which from my hart doth bleed.
> ...
> Sithens it hath infixed faster hold
> Within my bleeding bowels, and so sore
> Nowranckleth in this same fraile fleshly mould,
> That all mine entrailes flow with poisnous gore,
> And th'ulcer groweth daily more and more;
> Ne can my ronning sore find remedee....
>   (3.2.37.3–5, 39.1–6)

In this way the dream figuratively locates the origins of political rebellion in Britomart's own "entrails." Commentators have noticed that what Britomart calls an "ulcer" sounds like the onset of menstruation, almost as if the image of Arthegall had triggered her sexual maturation.[14] But the logic of this conjunction is not really causal: what links the vision of Arthegall to the start of menses in Britomart is that each in its way genders her – and does so traumatically. The first thing the narrator tells us about the change in Britomart is that

> Thenceforth the fether in her lofty crest,
> Ruffed of love, gan lowly to availe,
> And her prowd portaunce, and her princely gest,
> With which she earst tryumphed, now did quaile. ...
>   (27.1–4)

The girl has lost her swagger. She regains it by putting on armor, a disguise that allows her to *be* Arthegall while questing to have him. At one point she carries the masquerade so far as to make "purpos ... / Of love, and other-whiles of lustfulnesse" (4.1.7.7–8) to poor Amoret, only just rescued from Busyrane and now subject to "abusion" (7.2) again as Britomart resumes the enchanter's suit.[15] Amoret's discomfiture is mercifully cut short by their arrival at the Castle of Compulsory Heterosexuality, where "hee / Which had no love nor lemman there in store, / Should either winne him one, or lye without the dore" (9.7–9). Britomart finesses the custom of the castle, first securing her right to Amoret through combat with the Ladyless Knight, but then in her female capacity demanding admittance for him as her consort:

> With that her glistring helmet she unlaced;
> Which doft, her golden lockes, that were up bound
> Still in a knot, unto her heeles downe traced,
> And like a silken veile in compasse round
> About her backe and all her bodie wound:
> Like as the shining skie in summers night,
> What time the dayes with scorching heat abound,
> Is creasted all with lines of firie light,
> That it prodigious seemes in common peoples sight.
>   (4.1.13)

The onlookers, we are told, "gan grow in secret dout / Of this and that" (14.2–3). They hover between the categories of knighthood and ladyhood, this and that, because of their comic inability to formulate the category "lady knight." Britomart can appear to this interpretive community only as a prodigy, like summer lightning. The "creasted" sky of the simile, recalling the drooping "crest" of Britomart's formerly downcast portance, aptly expresses the sexual contradiction she embodies, for it combines the implicitly gendered terms "creased" and "crested" into a kind of philological androgyne.

Britomart's dream in Isis Church prophesies the end of this prodigious career in a new Castle of Compulsory Heterosexuality. It looks forward not only to the eventual renewal of Ryence's dynasty in his grandson Conan, but also to the immediate rescue of Britomart's designated champion Arthegall. It does seem strange that Britomart has to rescue Arthegall now so he can save her future kingdom; she is obviously capable of saving kingdoms herself. But she cannot impregnate herself: this rather than warfare is Arthegall's true dynastic function. The dream rearranges temporal sequences, for according to its chronology, crocodile-Arthegall would first subdue political rebellion (devouring the flames of stanza 15) and only then submit grudgingly to Britomart (stanza 16). Of course Arthegall has long since submitted to Britomart, and she to him: "she yeelded her consent / To be his love, and take him for her Lord" back in canto 6 of Book 4 (41.7–8), after his first surrender in combat. But Arthegall's ability to follow through on the sexual contract has been compromised by his having got the submission part wrong. In thrall to Radigund he is emasculated, and cannot perform his dynastic duty; to fulfill it he must be remasculinized by the Isis before whom he originally humbled his crocodile pride.

Britomart, playing Isis and restoring the lost phallus to Arthegall, is by this circuitous route restoring it to herself. When she finds him dressed as a woman, "abasht with secrete shame, / She turned her head aside" (V. vii.38.3–4). Her shame here is a complex emotion. Insofar as Britomart has refused her castration as a woman, she has resisted the very desire that motivates her quest: she'd as soon do combat with Arthegall as grow enwombed of his game. But this desire, carried through to its logical conclusion, would make her Radigund. This is why Britomart must confront and defeat her double, not merely killing the Amazon queen but also beheading the corpse, insisting on its feminine castration. She confronts in the effeminized Arthegall yet another mirror of her disavowed desire. Breaking open Radigund's prison, Britomart encounters "that lothly uncouth sight, / Of men disguiz'd in womanishe attire" (37.6–7) without apparently recognizing that she, disguised as a knight, beholds in them her own reflection. Encountering Arthegall she can no longer avoid the thought: she can't look him in the eye because *this* mirror image would turn her inescapably into Radigund. In order for Britomart to disavow that reflection, Arthegall must resume the "dreadfull manly looke" he has put off. Until he does, she cannot enact womanhood in relation to him.

The Hermeneutic Priest began his exposition of her dream by looking through Britomart's disguise:

> How couldst thou weene, through that disguized hood,
> To hide thy state from being understood?
> Can from th'immortall Gods ought hidden bee?
>
> (21.4–6)

As the priest goes on to declare the knowledge of the gods, he makes it clear that the dream has arrived at a critical juncture:

> They doe thy linage, and thy Lordly brood;
> They doe thy sire, lamenting sore for thee;
> They doe thy love, forlorne in womens thraldome see.
>
> (21.7–9)

While Britomart's father laments a lost heir, the prospective father who will restore the lineage is himself lost to "womens thraldome." The function of the phallus, having failed in each, will be restored only when Britomart finds her way back to the sexual economy from which her disguise marks a protracted detour.

4. The gender of justice

As the exposition of Britomart's dream unfolds, a network of puns opens out of the names "Isis" and "Osiris."[16] James Nohnrberg has observed that the couples of the poem's central books seem destined for an onomastic fusion modeled on the name "Hermaphroditus" (Hermes + Aphrodite): thus we have "Scudamoret, Britomartegall, Osirisis, Paridellenore, Thamedway, and, in Book VI, Claribellamour," to which may be added "Florimarinell."[17] The compound "Osirisis" may indeed be shadowed in the line "For that same Crocodile *Osyris* is" (22.6). Once again the letter-space, the difference between "aread" and "a read," marks a crucial threshold, this time the one that keeps Isis – for now – from being folded into Osiris. This same threshold also identifies Isis with the copula that bridges the gap between genders, which corresponds in Teskey's reading to the gap between form and matter. In English her name, as a translinguistic visual pun, expresses an affirmation of pure being: "is is."[18] In doubling the verb "to be" this pun plays on the deep identity between predication and copulation, implicitly asserting that Isis, as the basis of all predication, is herself the *reason* "Osyris is." The text here is reading the primal scene *avant la* Teskey, dissolving masculine "justice" back into the feminine "just is."

If Isis affirms being, what does Osiris affirm? The answer was already implicit in stanza 21, where "thy love" and "thy sire" languish in a melancholy parallel construction, the one lamenting and the other forlorne. Stanza 23 confirms the link between them, reminding Britomart that her knight will restore "the just heritage / Of thy sires Crowne" (23.3–4). Restoring both her linage and her heritage, Britomart's Osiris will reestablish her continuity with the "sire" she has abandoned. His affirmation too may be heard in his name: "O sire is." His job is to recapture being for the phallus, turning "just is" into "justice."

Britomart's rescue of Arthegall spells out what this dream and its interpretation so cryptically prefigure: not the Briton maid's assumption in the fullness of time of her "sires Crowne," but her assumption a few stanzas later of gendered femininity. She enjoys a brief interval of sovereignty, "During which space she there as Princess rained" (42.3), but just as she has used her knightly prowess to restore Arthegall's manhood, she now uses her royal prerogative to restore all women "to mens subjection" (42.7) – and here the ambiguity of the phrase, which *could* refer to the condition from which Arthegall was just released, has no resonance. Britomart will give Nature no cause for complaint; she will not push the laws of grammar too far. The "true Justice" of her divine read (42.7) secures men and women on opposite ends of "subjection," disambiguating both the grammar and the politics of sexual subject-hood.

In return for this sellout to male supremacy, Britomart, like Isis before her, is "*made* / A Goddesse" (3.2–3, emphasis mine). But at what cost? Isis and Osiris were deified after death, "For that *Osyris*, whilest he lived here, / The justest man alive, and truest did appear" (2.8–9). While he lived *here*, he appeared as a man. Britomart pays a similar price, for although she doesn't die she does disappear, reenacting the fate of Amoret. The *femme coverte* has no legal personhood, and at moments like this Spenser dramatizes the woman's social death, the evanescence of what Elizabeth Fowler calls her "social person."[19] Britomart turns formerly subjected knights into magistrates, makes them swear fealty to Arthegall, and surrenders Arthegall to his quest. What remains for her is self-suppression, unhappiness, and a quick exit. Readers may fantasize a continuation for her story, but it would only be redundant, for she has already prefigured the fate Merlin prophesied for her, achieving rule only to yield up sovereignty, restoring the phallus only to have it "too rathe cut off" (3.3.28.8).

Far from endorsing this surrender, the poem dwells on its cost.[20] Stanza 39 compresses Britomart's ambivalence into a remarkable simile, likening her dismay at the spectacle of Arthegall-in-a-dress to Penelope's hesitation before acknowledging Odysseus:

> Not so great wonder and astonishment,
> Did the most chast *Penelope* possesse,
> To see her Lord, that was reported drent,
> And dead long since in dolorous distresse,
> Come home to her in piteous wretchednesse,
> After long travell of full twenty yeares,
> That she knew not his favours likelynesse,

> For many scarres and many hoary heares,
> But stood long staring on him, mongst uncertaine feares.

In the *Odyssey* Telemachus cannot understand his mother's resistance – he, Ulysses, and the nurse Euryclea all reproach her for it – and she herself seems at a loss to explain it: "My son, I am so lost in astonishment that I can find no words in which either to ask questions or to answer them. I cannot even look him straight in the face."[21] The simile is rooted in this moment of bewilderment: Britomart too is specifically unable to look Arthegall in the face. For Penelope, the demand for renewed submission after twenty years of deferring suitors is … abrupt. Her resistance to Ulysses prolongs ever so briefly her resistance to the suitors, famous as a sustained act of wifely loyalty but one that, under cover of fidelity, sustained *her* in a provisional autonomy. Out of loyalty to her husband's absence she now resists his return, delaying acknowledgment: in order to be certain, or in order to delay?

The sign Penelope accepts in the end is not the famous scar recognized by the nurse as Ulysses is bathing, but the secret of their shared bed. Wily as Ulysses himself, she asks the nurse to place this bed outside the chamber door. Ulysses knows that the centerpost of the bed is a deeply rooted olive stump, around which he built both the bed and the bedroom. For a bare moment, "during which space she there as Princess rained," Penelope has used her loyalty to this tree of dynastic genealogy in order to defer her inevitable return to the marriage bed it supports. But after this space of resistance opens, it closes again. Britomart's long sojourn has dilated Penelope's hesitation just as the simile here dilates Britomart's pause, but the ending was indeed forecast by Merlin:

> And eke enrooted deepe must be that Tree,
> Whose big embodied branches shall not lin,
> Till they to hevens hight forth stretched bee.
> For from thy womb a famous Progenee
> Shall spring. . . .
>
> (3.3.22.2–6)

This is the genealogical tree that anchors the conjugal bed of the wandering spouse. Spenser, mindful of what submission costs, transplants it figuratively into the womb of the dynastic bride. No wonder her bowels bleed; no wonder she hesitates before her destiny.

5. Just reading

The language of Book 5 insists that justice is a question of reading. It is not, however, a question of putting the spirit before the letter, for the letter itself is never one thing. I would like to offer a final illustration of this point by turning to the allegory of reading presented in stanza 55 of canto 2, at the end of the Egalitarian Giant episode. Don't bother looking for this stanza in your edition of *The Faerie Queene*. First published in 1839 in *The Plymouth and Davenport Weekly Journal*, it was written by John Keats in a volume of Spenser he was marking for Fanny Brawne when he died. According to Charles Brown it was "the last stanza of any kind that he wrote before his lamented death":

> In after-time, a sage of mickle lore
> Yclep'd Typographus, the Giant tooke,
> And did refit his limbs as heretofore,
> And made him read in many a learned book,
> And into many a lively legend look;
> Thereby in goodly themes so training him
> That all his brutishness he quite forsook,
> When, meeting Arthegall and Talus grim,
> The one he struck stone-blind, the other's eyes wox dim.[22]

Resurrected by the allegorical personification of textuality itself, the Giant is now reformed through education, rehabilitated by "goodly themes" rather than the "goodly thewes" in which Spenser's knights and ladies are characteristically trained (e.g. I.ix.3.9, I.x.4.4, and VI.iv.38.7). This sublimation of bodily power into pure literary force is clearly the work of Typographus, who inverts the *w* of "thewes" to read it as "themes." But even so tiny an alteration as this can be a revelation as powerful as Arthur's shield, able to blind Arthegall and dim even Talus's eyes.

In this fable, the egalitarian force of moveable typeface redeems the leader of the ignorant multitude. Forsaking his "brutishness," and with it no doubt his Britishness, or patriotic nationalism, he stops the agents of stone-age justice dead in their tracks. In the process they restore the balance of Spenserian justice. Talus, you will recall, rather ironically knocks the Giant *off balance* to destroy him, and of course the whole episode is taken up with the comedy of weighing and measuring abstractions. In this context, it wouldn't be surprising to find Spenser playing with poetic measures as he so often does; indeed, the episode begins, in stanza 29, with the narrator's droll observation that Talus and Arthegall "*measur'd* mickle weary way" in their journey, a phrase Keats seems to have picked up in his playful reference to "mickle lore."

Keats also seems to have measured their way: canto 2 begins with the episode of Munera and Pollente, which runs for a total of 27 stanzas (2–28). The episode of the Egalitarian Giant, beginning with the reference to "measur'd" in stanza 29, runs for 26. Keats, by adding what Brown describes as an "extra-concluding stanza" to the canto, brings its two episodes into balance as he stands the Giant back up on his feet. With this playful imitation of justice as calculation, he "justifies" a more radical reinvention of the allegory. This reinvention self-consciously textualizes justice as a way of reading learned books and lively legends. It is a way of reading, clearly, that Keats "invented" in the older sense – a way he came upon, or found – in *The Faerie Queene*. With his help, we too may reinvent (which is to say, rediscover) in Spenser an allegory in which justice emerges from the way we read. This is not the "practice of ritual interpretation" that Teskey associates with allegory; it is rather a way of reading solicited by what Harry Berger calls the text's *resistance* to allegory.[23]

Near the beginning of Book 5 Spenser tells us that Astraea taught Artegall "to weigh both right and wrong" and "to measure out" equity (1.7.1–2). In English law, equity is a name for the place where justice must be reinvented; it cannot be calibrated. Spenser says that Astraea taught Artegall to measure equity "out along / According to the line of conscience" (7.4). But he adds that this measurement takes place "When so it needs with rigor to dispence" (7.5) – that is, when justice must be dispensed with rigor; or, when rigor must be dispensed with. Two opposed and incommensurable answers to the question of justice coexist within the same line. Subject and predicate, male and female, justice and equity, change places undecidably. And the word in which their ambiguity is concentrated, the verb that means one or the other of two incompatible acts, is a characteristic pun on the poet's name.[24] This line of poetic conscience measures out equity as the aporia of the law, and it tells us that another name for this aporia is "Spenser." Unlike Britomart, unlike Arthegall, "he" can be at once predicate and subject, he becomes likewise of two declensions, he pushes the laws of grammar too far.

Notes

1 *Plutarch's De Iside et Osiride*, ed. and trans. J. Gwyn Griffiths (n.p.: University of Wales Press, 1970), p. 145; see also Katherine Eggert, "'*Changing all that forme of common weale*': Genre and the Repeal of Queenship in *The Faerie Queene*, Book 5" (*English Literary Renaissance* 26 [1996]: 259–90): "Unable to find Osiris' penis, Plutarch's Isis replaces it with a consecrated replica; and so too does Britomart reerect her husband's phallic power" (p. 276). Maureen Quilligan, *Incest and Agency in Elizabeth's England* (Philadelphia, PA: University of Pennsylvania Press, 2005), sees the marriage of Isis and Osiris as exemplary of the way female agency, in Britomart and in the culture at large, is shadowed by incest and intimations of monstrous sexuality (see esp. pp. 159–63).

2 The currently dominant reading of Book 5 sees it as critical of Elizabeth but not of sovereign power as such. See for example Richard Rambuss, *Spenser's Secret Career* (Cambridge: Cambridge University Press, 1993): "Not at all looking to subvert absolutist power, Spenser, on the contrary, appears to be championing a more vehement expression of it" (p. 112). My emphasis on a connection between the critique of sovereign power and the politics of gender is informed by a strong body of recent work, notably Eggert's impressive account of the relations between genre and gender in the second installment of *The Faerie Queene*, cited above;

Maureen Quilligan, "The Comedy of Female Authority in *The Faerie Queene*," *English Literary Renaissance* 17 (1987): 157–71; and Harry Berger, Jr., "Resisting Translation: Britomart in Book 3 of Spenser's *Faerie Queene*," in *Translating Desire in Medieval and Early Modern Literature*, ed. Heather Hayton and Craig A. Berry (Tempe, AZ: Medieval & Renaissance Texts & Studies Press, 2005).

3 Gordon Teskey, *Allegory and Violence* (Ithaca, NY: Cornell University Press, 1996). This and the two paragraphs that follow summarize material from pp. 14–22, 32–39, and 75–88.

4 *The Complaint of Nature*, trans. Douglas M. Moffat. *Yale Studies in English* 36 (1908): 3.

5 Citations throughout are to *Spenser: The Faerie Queene*, ed. A. C. Hamilton, text ed. by Hiroshi Yamashita and Toshiyuki Suzuki (New York: Longman, 2001). I have normalized i/j and u/v.

6 I quote the Geneva translation from a facsimile of the 1599 edition, *The Geneva Bible* (Pleasant Hope, MI: L. L. Brown, 1990), modernizing typography but not orthography.

7 Donald Cheney notes "overtones of slapstick in the random motions of Jupiter's menagerie," and comments that "the zodiacal signs are behaving in accordance with their nature as animals, though they may seem to have betrayed our higher estimate of them" (*Spenser's Image of Nature: Wild Man and Shepherd in "The Faerie Queene"* [New Haven, CT: Yale University Press, 1966], p. 153).

8 As Judith Anderson remarks, "it is odd that the sword of Justice should have been stolen by Astraea from Jove" ("'Nor Man it is': The Knight of Justice in Book V of Spenser's *Faerie Queene*," in *Essential Articles for the Study of Edmund Spenser*, ed. A. C. Hamilton [Hamden, CN: Archon, 1972], p. 453).

9 On Spenser's narrator as "Dan Edmund," see my essay "The Faerie Queene (1590)," in *The Palgrave Guide to Spenser Studies*, ed. Bart van Es (New York: Palgrave, 2006). For a subtle and extended exploration of the intertextual relations between Spenser and Chaucer, see especially Judith Anderson, "Narrative Reflections: Reenvisaging the Poet in *The Canterbury Tales* and *The Faerie Queene*," in *Refiguring Chaucer in the Renaissance*, ed. Theresa Krier (Gainesville, FL: University Press of Florida, 1998), pp. 87–105; "What Comes after Chaucer's *But*: Adversative Constructions in Spenser," in *Acts of Interpretation: The Text in its Contexts, 700–1600*, ed. Mary J. Carruthers and Elizabeth D. Kirk (Norman, OK: Pilgrim, 1982), pp. 105–18; "'A Gentle Knight was Pricking on the Plaine': The Chaucerian Connection," *English Literary Renaissance* 15 (1985): 166–74; "Arthur, Argante, and the Ideal Vision: An Exercise in Speculation and Parody," in *The Passing of Arthur: New Essays in Arthurian Tradition*, ed. Christopher Baswell and William Sharpe (New York: Garland, 1988), pp. 193–206; and "The 'Couert Vele': Chaucer, Spenser, and Venus," *English Literary Renaissance* 24 (1994), 639–59.

10 Bart van Es remarks on the "nicely balanced half-seriousness" of this passage, and notes that the "slippage from adored monarch to imagined god that underlies euhemerism is … played out" at the canto's end in Britomart's reform of Radegone. See *Spenser's Forms of History* (New York: Oxford University Press, 2002), p. 125.

11 Plutarch, alert to the subversive implications of euhemerism, rejects such interpretation of the gods as impious because it tends to atheism (p. 153). He proposes instead that Isis and Osiris began as "daemons" and were "translated through their virtue … into gods" (pp. 155, 159). Cf. Diodorus Siculus 1: 13: "And besides

these there are other gods, they say, who were terrestrial, having once been mortals, but who, by reason of their sagacity and the good services which they rendered to all men, attained immortality, some of them having even been kings in Egypt."

12 Spenser, Letter to Ralegh, ed. Hamilton, p. 715.

13 See Julia M. Walker, "Spenser's Elizabeth Portrait and the Fictions of Dynastic Epic," *Modern Philology* 90 (1992): 192–93 n. 34.

14 Hamilton's note to this stanza cites three critical comments on menstruation, to which may be added Walker, "Spenser's Elizabeth Portrait" (n. 13 above).

15 On the ambiguous sexual comedy of this scene, see Dorothy Stephens, *The Limits of Eroticism in Post-Petrarchan Narrative: Conditional Pleasure from Spenser to Marvell* (Cambridge: Cambridge University Press, 1998), pp. 30–41.

16 In "Words and Sex: The Language of Allegory in the *De planctu naturae*, the *Roman de la Rose*, and Book III of *The Faerie Queene*" (*Allegorica* 1 [1977]: 195–216), Maureen Quilligan demonstrates that the tradition of medieval allegory comes to Spenser already informed by a pervasive concern for the language and grammar of sexuality.

17 Nohrnberg, *The Analogy of* The Faerie Queene (Princeton, NJ: Princeton University Press, 1976), p. 607.

18 Reformation disputes over the words of the institution ("this is my body") brought extraordinary ideological pressures to bear on the verb "esse." For a lucid and informative account of what was at stake in the distinction between copulative and substantive modes of *is*, and a vivid sense of how the reformation debate over translation volatilized the metaphoricity of the verb of being, see Judith Anderson, *Translating Investments: Metaphor and the Dynamic of Cultural Change in Tudor-Stuart England* (New York: Fordman University Press, 2005), pp. 36–60. Teskey's argument about the role of the sexual imaginary in resolving the impasse of metaphysical idealism would imply (as I argued earlier) that the substantive mode of *is* actually depends on the copulative. Thanks to Sean Morris for calling my attention to the pun implied by "Osyris is."

19 On the concept of the "social person" in relation to that of the "legal person," see Fowler, *Literary Character: The Human Figure in Early English Writing* (Ithaca, NY: Cornell University Press, 2003), pp. 23–28. The disturbing implications of Britomart's disappearance from the poem have often been noted: Judith Anderson writes that Britomart "is used; she becomes unimportant in her own right. The demands of the fable require that she should *really become* Isis" ("'Nor Man it is,'" p. 461). Mihoko Suzuki, rejecting accounts of the episode that see Britomart emerging in positive contrast to Radigund, argues that poem "works to diminish and ultimately erase Britomart through her own destruction of Radigund" ("Scapegoating Radigund," in *Critical Essays on Edmund Spenser*, ed. Suzuki [New York: G.K. Hall, 1996], p. 190). Stephens, *The Limits of Eroticism*, keynotes an astute commentary on the Radigund episode with the observation that we cannot "extract the poem from its own cross-purposes" (p. 93).

20 Contrast Clare Carroll's very different reading of the "allegorical displacement of identities" in this episode ("The Construction of Gender and the Cultural and Political Other in *The Faerie Queene* and *A View of the Present State of Ireland*: The Critics, the Context, and the Case of Radigund," *Criticism* 32 [1990]: 181–86). For Carroll, "Spenser" names an ideological agent who pursues the same colonial program in the allegory of the poem that Irenius argues for in the prose treatise on Ireland attributed to Spenser. So, for example, "the language in which this

restoration [of male supremacy in Radegone] is achieved reveals the contradictions in Spenser's claims about the universality of the law in *The Faerie Queene*
and *A View*" (p. 184). Where a critic like Harry Berger, Jr. (see n. 20, below) reads
the text's resistance to allegory as part of its significance, Carroll identifies
"Spenser" with universalist "claims" and then sets the author *against* the work by
which the text reveals their contradictions. A similar insistence on constructing
the author against the text limits even Linda Gregerson's perceptive account of
the Britomart narrative in her impressive study *The Reformation of the Subject: Spenser,
Milton, and the English Protestant Epic* (Cambridge: Cambridge University Press,
1995), pp. 9–47.

21 Homer, *The Odyssey*, trans. Robert Fitzgerald (New York: Farrar, Strauss, 1961),
23.119–21.

22 *John Keats: Complete Poems*, ed. Jack Stillinger (Cambridge, MA: Harvard University
Press, 1978, 1982), p. 408; Brown is quoted in Stillinger's notes, pp. 484–85.

23 *Allegory and Violence*, p. 132: "allegories do not just reflect ideological structures;
they engage us in the practice of ritual interpretation by which those structures
are reproduced in bodies and reexpressed through the voice." Teskey does recognize more to the process of interpretation: "We become Christian imperialists
when we read the *Commedia* and Christian moralists when we read *The Faerie
Queene*. But it is only from submitting to this process that we learn from these
poems, or from moments inside them, how to do something else" (p. 133). Berger
affords more room in his account of Spenser for doing something else. In addition
to "Resisting Translation" (note 2 above), see "Sexual and Religious Politics in
Book 1 of Spenser's *Faerie Queene*," *English Literary Renaissance* 34 (2004): 201–42;
"Wring Out the Old: Squeezing the Text, 1951–2001," *Spenser Studies* 18 (2003):
81–121; "Archimago: Between Text and Countertext," *SEL* 43 (2003): 20–32;
"Displacing Autophobia in *Faerie Queene* I: Ethics, Gender, and Oppositional
Reading in the Spenserian Text," *English Literary Renaissance* 28 (1998): 163–82;
"Actaeon at the Hinder Gate: The Stag Party in Spenser's Gardens of Adonis,"
in *Desire in the Renaissance: Psychoanalysis and Literature*, ed. Valeria Funucci and
Regina Schwarz (Princeton, NJ: Princeton University Press, 1994), pp. 91–119;
"Narrative as Rhetoric in *The Faerie Queen*," *English Literary Renaissance* 21 (1991):
3–48. These essays are gathered in a volume forthcoming from Fordham
University Press under the title *Resisting Allegory: Interpretive Delirium in the 1590*
Faerie Queene. My considerable debt to these essays will be apparent to anyone
who reads them.

24 I have previously discussed other occurrences of this pun in several places: *The
Poem's Two Bodies*, "The Writing Thing," and "The Faerie Queene (1590)."

3 The ethics of posing

Visual epideixis in some seventeenth-century Dutch group portraits

Harry Berger, Jr.

I. On ethics and *ēthos*

The word "ethical" is normally used to mean something like "moral," "virtuous," "principled," etc. But "ethical" and "ethics" ultimately derive from the Greek word, "ēthos," which had a range of meanings that include custom, usage, character, disposition, bearing, manner. Aristotle uses *ēthos* in the *Poetics* to designate characters in drama and their moral quality as inferred or constructed by audiences. When a playwright (Aeschylus, Sophocles, Euripides) borrows a character from epic or other sources and remodels it, in Aristotelian parlance he "imitates" that character, as does the actor who plays the role. Aristotle uses the term *ēthos* again in the *Rhetoric* to designate the "character" a speaker assumes – performs, or imitates – in order to persuade his audience of his moral authority.

Keir Elam has brilliantly shown that in both cases Aristotle depicts moral character as effect rather than cause of dramatic or rhetorical speech – as the product of art rather than of nature. And in both cases, the production of a convincing "character" is treated as the fictive effect of a performance and closely identified with acts of imitation. The *Poetics* represents character as "a factor constructed or inferred by the audience, which attributes personal and moral integrity to the fictional individuals on the basis of their acts (*praxis*) and verbal expression (*lexis*). ... The character that appears to lie behind – but is instead the creation of – the ... [speech acts] of the stage speakers has much the same status as the product of the speech and acts of Aristotle's orator (who is, in this sense, a kind of actor-dramatist)."

In the *Rhetoric*, Elam writes,

> [Aristotle] proposes *ēthos* (the moral character of the speaker) as a strictly rhetorical rather than extra- or pre-discursive character. It is classified (1.ii.3) as one of the three "artificial proofs," i.e. "furnished by the speech" itself rather than by external ("inartificial") means. The orator's

ethical status (including the degree of moral commitment to what he says) is the single most influential factor in determining his rhetorical success. ... But this decisively weighty factor is itself a *product* of, rather than a determinant of, the oration.[1]

To fill out the Aristotelian account, the second artificial proof depends on the speaker's ability to affect his auditors and rouse them to emotion that leads them to assent to his arguments, "the third on the *logos* itself insofar as it proves or seems to prove" something.[2]

Elam's compressed account silently associates the ethical proof with one of the three kinds of rhetoric Aristotle describes in *Rhetoric* 1.3. He distinguishes them according to whether hearers act as members of the *ekklēsia* assembled to judge of things to come or as members assembled to judge of things past or "as the mere spectator[s] of the ability of the speaker." He calls these, respectively, the deliberative (*sumbouleutikon*), the forensic (*dikanikon*), and the epideictic (*epideiktikon*), and he sorts them out not only in terms of their functions but also in terms of temporality. Deliberative rhetoric is concerned with decisions affecting the future, the most important of which involve "ways and means, war and peace, the defence of the country, imports and exports, legislation" (1.4.8, pp. 40–41). Its "end is the expedient or harmful." Forensic rhetoric is concerned with the judgment of past actions. It deals chiefly with the five inartificial proofs discussed in 1.15: laws, witnesses, contracts, torture, and oaths (pp. 150–53). Its "end is the just or unjust." Epideictic rhetoric is concerned with praise and blame, its "end is the honorable and disgraceful," and its focus is on the present (the existing conditions of things that all who praise or blame have in view).[3] But as Aristotle will go on to show, the *now* of epideixis is not restricted to contemporaneous subject matter. It is also the reflexive *now* of the speaker's performance as an index to his *ēthos*. That too is among the conditions that those who praise and blame have in view.

Elam associates the ethical proof with epideictic rhetoric and appears to go beyond Aristotle in attaching special importance to that mode. Aristotle nowhere expressly ranks these three kinds, to each of which he devotes a chapter of the first book. I have been assured by classical scholars that he treats *epideixis* as the least important or "lowest" of the three modes of oratory. And indeed, a passing comment at 1.9.40 implies that, as common sense would seem to dictate, the topics considered in deliberative and forensic rhetoric make them weightier, more substantive and important, than *epideixis*, the subject of which consists of "actions that are not disputed; all that needs to be done is to attribute beauty and importance to them" (pp. 104–05). And this, he explains in a passage edged with oddly ironic or parodic tone, is most effectively accomplished by applying liberal doses of *auxēsis*, the trope of amplification that magnifies or exaggerates the virtue and vice, respectively, of the objects of praise and blame (1.9.38–40, pp. 102–05).

The whole of the chapter on *epideixis* (1.9) hums with a similar irony. It displays colors that were tightly furled in the opening remarks on artificial proofs, the third of which, as we saw above, depends "on the *logos* itself insofar as it proves *or seems to prove*" something. The italicized qualifier (*"deiknunai ē phainesthai deiknunai"*) glances at the disenchanted perspective of the author or speaker, who blandly advises would-be practitioners to "assume, for the purpose of praise or blame, that qualities which closely resemble the real qualities are identical with them; for instance, that the cautious man is cold and designing, the simpleton good-natured, and the emotionless gentle."[4]

Such assertions cast the shadow of a familiar suspicion – the suspicion of sophistry – over Aristotle's treatment of the artificial proof singled out by Elam, the one that depends on the speaker's *ēthos*. The shadow deepens in subsequent passages that emphasize the reflexive deployment of epideictic strategies:

> We will next speak of virtue and vice, the noble and the disgraceful, since they constitute the aim of one who praises and blames; for, when speaking of these, we shall incidentally bring to light the means of making us appear of such and such a character, which, as we have said, is a ... method of proof; for it is by the same means that we shall be able to inspire confidence in ourselves or others in regard to virtue.[5]

To paraphrase: as we speak of these qualities in themselves and attribute them to our subjects, we will do so in a manner that makes us appear to possess the virtues we praise. Our aim as orators is to inspire confidence – in ourselves as well as in others – "in regard to [*our*] virtue." In this passage, the authorial "we" loses its transparency and produces something like a self-portrait as the subject or object of its own praise.

"The orator persuades by moral character when his speech is delivered in such a manner as to render him worthy of confidence." This "confidence must be due" to the *ēthos* constructed in and by the speech itself rather than to "any preconceived idea of the speaker's character."[6] The redundancy is noteworthy. In order to inspire confidence in his arguments the orator should work to inspire confidence in the moral character (*ēthos*) of the fictional "character" (*ēthos*) he performs: it "is necessary not only that the speech itself be made demonstrative and convincing but also that the speaker should show himself to be of a certain character and should know how to put the judge into a certain frame of mind." Almost as if in passing, Aristotle slips in the most problematical qualification for rhetorical success: those in whom the orator should try to inspire confidence and trust "in regard to virtue" include himself.

By the beginning of the second book, two things have become clear. First, epideixis has an important reflexive function: no matter what kind of oratory is involved, an important element of any performance is the sustained if covert act of self-praise involved in the speaker's construction of his *ēthos*. Therefore, second, epideictic self-praise and self-promotion are basic constituents of deliberative and forensic rhetoric. The *technē* of *epideixis* is the hidden dimension (the orator attracting praise for his implicit praise of the audience) in all forms of oratory. The now of speaking is the radical tense that underlies, and determines the success of, the temporally removed and distinct foci of deliberative and forensic oratory. Epideixis is the radical proof from which the other two unfold:

> For it makes a great difference with regard to producing conviction – especially in demonstrative and, next to this, in forensic oratory – that the speaker should show himself to be possessed of certain qualities and that his hearers should think that he is disposed in a certain way toward them; and further, that they themselves should be disposed in a certain way towards him.[7]

Aristotle's Rhetoric *is a handbook for sophists*

This deeply skeptical account underlies Keir Elam's claim that the founding move in the Aristotelian system is

> the election of heart and soul not as internal cause for external expressive effect but as one effect (among others) of rhetorical *heuresis* or invention. ... Moral character becomes a question not so much of authenticity as of authority or power (imposition, persuasion), and ethics itself, of which rhetoric is a product, is synonymous with the science of power, or politics: "Thus it appears that Rhetoric is as it were an offshoot of Dialectic and of the science of Ethics, which may reasonably be called Politics."[8]

Elam finds Aristotle's statement about *ēthos* in the *Poetics* – that it denotes the character or dramatic person – entirely consistent with his statements about it in the *Rhetoric*. The difference is that the dramatic *ēthos* is unproblematically fictional whereas the fictiveness of the rhetorical *ēthos* is morally problematical. What is straightforward in poetry is devious in rhetoric. Dependent as it is on the will and whim of the audience, generated as it is in an arena of public competition, the rhetorical performance of *ēthos* is fraught with anxiety.

In the study that follows, I propose to transfer these formulations from poetry and rhetoric to portraiture, replacing the *ēthos* of character and orator with that of the portrait sitter. The aim of this strategy is to place the study of portrait poses within an epideictic framework that features the ethical concern, the competitiveness, the problem of fictive self-construction, and the performative anxiety common to speakers and sitters. To paraphrase

Aristotle, it makes a great difference with regard to producing conviction that the sitter should show herself to be possessed of certain qualities and that her viewers should think she is disposed in a certain way toward them, and further, that she acts as if they should be disposed in a certain way toward her.

II. Interpreting painted portraits in pre-photographic times: eight premises

Premise 1. *Acts* vs *identities: the portrait is the image not of a sitter but of the sitter's act of self-presentation*

Comment: Portraits are often defined, understood, and written about as pictures of somebody. Because I'm less interested in the persons portrayed than in their performances as sitters, I make a small but significant addition to this formula: for me, a portrait is a picture not simply of somebody, but of somebody posing; it's the painter's presentation of the sitter's act of self-presentation. In other words, to borrow a now trite distinction, I try to shift the interpretive focus from identities to acts, from the search for the historical identities of portrait sitters to the study of their acts of self-presentation as painters represent them. My emphasis is on the moment of epideixis and on the *ēthos* of the pose. *Portrait* designates any picture that contains the image of someone who appears to be posing for the image maker *and* for whatever viewers will inspect the image *after it has been completed*.

Premise 2. *Fictions* vs *facts: the portrait is the image not of an actual but of a fictional act of self-presentation*

Comment: The assertion that the portrait must be a copy of the prior act of posing it represents is easy to disconfirm. We know that sitters may not even have been present while the painters were at work. Painters sometimes used stand-ins and sometimes worked from memory or from textual descriptions or from other images of the sitter. So the evidence of empirical practice in the pre-photographic era makes it risky to assume that the act of self-portrayal any portrait delivers resembles or conforms to what the sitter actually did back then during the time he or she was posing for the painter. Even if a portrait presents itself as the copy of an original act of posing that occurred, let's say, on September 21, 1600, we can't take it as a reliable indicator of that event. We have to assume that the real studio event is irrecoverable and that what we look at is as fictitious as the starry sky on a clear night. A portrait doesn't simply offer its viewers the copy of a *now* that happened *then*. Rather, it delivers an imaginary *now* that we situate in an imaginary *then*. It delivers not an actual pose but the fiction of a pose.

Premise 3. Portrait genres differ structurally from narrative genres

Comment: I use the term *narrative* in a conventionally loose way to include pictures of mythological and historical events (both secular and religious) as well as examples of the chiefly Dutch genre confusingly called Genre.[9] The Genre genre may be considered a narrative form because it consists of scenes of everyday life in genteel, bourgeois, or rude settings (both private and public, indoors and out), scenes that are often skewed toward the status of cautionary tales.

To call a picture a Genre scene is to accept it as an image taken from life in the sense that it may be "realistically depicted" as if copied from life, but not in the sense that it was copied directly from the event it depicts. Rather, it's presented as a fictive event, the imaginary realization of a typical and thus often repeated slice of life. "Genre pieces are scenes that look to us as if they were taken from everyday life, depictions of situations as they *might* have been, but in fact they were *composed* in the artist's studio. They are never spontaneous records of a moment," never merely slices of life but fictive events: the Genre painter "generally depicted not real people but dramatis personae: types and characters."[10]

To call a picture a history is to accept it as the expressly imaginary representation of an actual past event. Even if it seems "realistically depicted" as if copied from life, the history never asks us to believe that it was copied directly from the historical event it depicts. On the contrary, "expressly imaginary" means that it's presented to viewers as an image with human figures whose features and gestures are not those of the original characters; they're not transcribed from life but borrowed from the painter's imagination, from his models, from other pictures, or from textual descriptions. Like Genre characters, historical characters differ from portrait sitters in that they are conventionally depicted as engrossed in their own lives and unaware of performing for the virtual observer.

To call a picture a portrait is to accept its fictive claim to be an image taken "from life" in a sense that differs from the claims to lifelikeness made by Genre and history: the portrait by definition is the record of the epideictic act of self-presentation we call posing, and to be a portrait sitter is by definition to acknowledge the observer. This holds even for sitters who gaze into observer space but studiedly avoid the observer point, an avoidance character-istic of the classic aristocratic or royal pose in which sitters give themselves to be seen but don't deign – conspicuously refuse – to return the attention they invite.[11]

Premise 4. Different genres deploy different oppositional "subject positions": patrons vs sitters in portraiture, models vs characters in history and Genre[12]

Comment: The patron is the person who commissioned and may have *posed for* the portrait while the sitter is the "person" who *poses in* it (the difference in verb tenses is significant). Sitters are the patrons' *representatives*, by which I mean that they get portrayed as if their performances are self-willed rather than externally imposed. Sitters appear to have chosen the poses they hold, and in that sense they are depicted as independent agents. But since their acts of posing are either invented by or mediated through the painter, sitters are at the same time the painter's representatives; creatures not of flesh but of facture, they carry out the painter's artistic designs on the viewer. If they appear to possess performative agency it is because the painter endows them with that power. Implicitly, therefore, sitters and the agency conferred on them are the products of negotiation between painters and their patrons.

Sitters are representations of figures who perform as themselves; models are representations of figures who perform, usually anonymously, as characters. When painted figures engage the observer in scenes we take to be narrative, we don't consider them to be sitters aware of being looked at while posing for their pictures. The sitter's situation differs from that of the characters in such narrative modes as history and Genre painting. For example, the effect of such figures as Nicolaes Maes's eavesdropper and Jan Steen's cardplayer (Figure 3.1) is identical with that of the interlocutor in an *istoria* as described by Alberti: when a painted figure makes contact with spectators of the painted event he or she transforms them into witnesses or participants standing in an imaginary extension of the istoria's space time.[13] Similarly, the object of the card player's gaze materializes as a participant, a fictional character whose complicity the painted character invites or fends off.

To distinguish between models and sitters enables us to highlight the originality of artists who, like Jan Steen, upset expectations by giving models the status of sitters. Steen's Genre and history scenes look staged. They feature models wearing out-of-date costumes. A "repertory of codified poses and rhetorical gestures" directs attention to models *as* models pretending to be characters.[14] This effect displaces the viewer's attention from the episode being depicted to the way it is being played, presented, performed by models posing as characters, as *ēthoi*, in a theatrically charged atmosphere.

Premise 5. The position of the virtual observer of a portrait differs from the position of the empirical viewer

Comment: The distinction between observer and viewer is comparable to the one we make in literature between the virtual and empirical reader. "Virtual reader" names a position (the famous Dear Reader) created and addressed

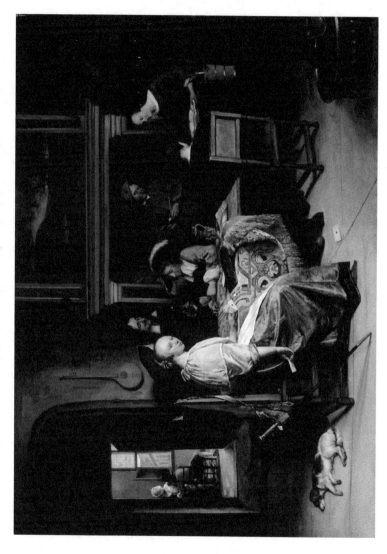

Figure 3.1 Jan Steen, *Cardplayers* (c.1660), private collection.

by a text before anyone reads it. The actual or empirical reader is anyone who subsequently occupies that position by reading the text. Similarly, the (virtual) observer is a permanent position created on this side of the picture surface by the form and content of the picture – by perspective, by paint facture, by light and shade, and, most important, by the direction of the painted figure's gaze. The viewer is anyone who happens along and looks at the picture and may (or may not) occupy the observer position. The observer is thus a blank or null position waiting to be filled by the parade of viewers who will occupy it. This position is itself variable, for in some cases painted figures appear to make direct eye contact with viewers while in others they aim their glances in the general vicinity of the observer without making direct eye contact. So we need to hypothesize both a virtual observer point and a more diffuse observer space within which that point is located. This distinction is especially important for group portraits, where different sitters may look out into different sectors of that space.[15]

Premise 6. Temporal relations between sitters and viewers in portraiture differ from those between characters and viewers in history and Genre

Comment: I noted earlier that when we identify a figure like Steen's cardplayer as a character in a Genre scene, her *now* becomes the viewer's *now*. By her glance and gesture, she brings the viewer into her game, into her room, into her world, as a participant, a supernumerary character. *We* are part of *her* story; she isn't part of *ours*. She is not perceived as a sitter posing for her portrait. Rather, the viewers of the Genre scene are invited to imagine themselves as her contemporaries standing in an imaginary extension of the space she occupies.

Such contemporaneity is not available to portrait sitters. The distinction between the (virtual) observer and the actual or empirical viewer advanced in Premise 5 makes it possible to take seriously the time difference between the act of posing or sitting and the subsequent act of viewing. The sitter's *now* never coincides with the viewer's *now*. If the portrait represents an act of sitting, it will not be available to viewers until it has been completed.[16] The term "observer" designates not an actual person or viewer but a position any viewer may occupy – a position constituted by the picture and waiting to be filled by the parade of viewers who will occupy it.[17] The latency and temporality implied by the phrase "waiting to be filled" is the most important part of this distinction. Under the hypothesis of the fiction of the pose, the portrait delivers an imaginary sitter's *now* that we, its viewers, situate in an imaginary *then* relative to us. It is therefore a *now* open or vulnerable to our constructive interventions, a *now* we view through a palimpsest of prior interpretations, the oldest of which are those expressed by the sitter's pose and the painter's imitation of it.[18]

This seems so obvious and trivial that it's easy to ignore. Nevertheless, the plot of portraiture depends on our taking temporal deferral seriously, and that means taking seriously the absence of the viewer to the sitter. To imagine that when sitters give themselves to be seen they pose for a viewer who hasn't yet materialized is to frame the sitter/observer relation in an atmosphere of drama, tension, and uncertainty. The portrait anticipates, with anxiety, many known and unknown viewers. It anticipates unforeseen interpretations. The emptiness of the observer position in the now of posing and the deferral of viewing until after the portrait has been finished place viewers in the position of authority as sources of power and danger. When we look at a portrait as the record of an act of posing, we see it as a trace, as a *now* that happened *then*, always in the sitter's present, always in the viewer's past. Thus in contrast to narrative genres, the primary message of any picture identified as a (commissioned) portrait is that the sitters are downstage performers who give themselves to seen by an observer they acknowledge but can't see, and by viewers who haven't yet materialized, viewers in the gallery of the future whose attention the sitters perpetually solicit and patiently await.

The gallery of the future: the phrase has a nice ring but as a metaphoric turn it is wildly misleading. It evokes an image in which generations of visitors parade by as portraits change residence and disseminate until they end up in our latterday collections, museums, and publications. If that were the future in question, it would be relatively easy to factor in the effects of deferral on the sitters portraits represent. Signs of performance anxiety could then be interpreted in terms of the premonition of the unknown: the premonition of public display in unimaginable alien spaces and of exposure to unimaginable alien gazes. Westermann mentions a related worry, the fact that the "attrition over temporal or spatial distance of sitter identity is ... inherent in portraiture."[19]

But of course what concerns portrait sitters and their contemporaries isn't the unknown long-term future but the uncertainties and pitfalls lurking in the too well known short-term future. The viewers they anticipate and hope to impress are not unborn hordes of anonymous museum visitors but the inhabitants of the sitters' spatial and temporal neighborhood: their peers, family, friends, associates, constituents, and descendants. Portraits are expressions of conservative desire: sitters give themselves to be seen as – to be transformed by painters into – talismanic household presences, guardian spirits who preserve and protect the ways of the past from the uncertainties of the future.

Portraits, then, are examples of visual epideixis, representations of *ēthos*. Since they are responses but not solutions to the uncertain future their sitters try to control, and since that uncertainty is built into the very structure of the portrait situation, portraits may themselves be causes as well as symptoms of social concern. To stipulate temporal deferral as a feature of the sitter/ observer relation is to generate a source of performance anxiety for sitters.

Their claim on the observer begins to appear less hegemonic than that of characters, more conditional, more fraught with uncertainty.

Premise 7. If an image gets re-classified from one genre to another, interpretation can respond by activating the principle of categoreal flexibility made possible through the institution of Premises 1 through 6

Comment: This is a fancy way of saying that if we've accepted the foregoing distinctions between portraiture and narrative genres, we can handle cases of reassignment by putting into play a conditional if/then procedure, a logic of "if x, then y." Generic attributions are contingent on our accepting previous classifications that are not set in stone. It is always possible that the connoisseur's exquisite discriminations, the historian's discoveries, the wonders of conservatorial science, or the whirligig of the market will lead what has been analyzed as a self-portrait to be transformed into a portrait, or a commissioned portrait into a head study, or a genre scene into a family portrait.

If we call an image a portrait we read it one way, if a narrative we read it another, because the structure of sitter/observer relations in portrait genres differs from that of character/observer relations in narrative genres. The element of deferral constitutes the dilemma peculiar to sitters in the scenario I imagine for them.

For example, Figure 3.2, by Jan Miense Molenaer, has been entitled *The Duet* and classified as a Genre scene, most recently by Dennis Weller.[20] It has also been identified as a [self]-portrait of the artist posing with his wife, the painter Judith Leyster.[21] If it is identified as a Genre scene, then the two characters are performing music and attentive to the effects of their performance on an audience present to them and located roughly in the observer's space. If it is identified as a portrait, then what they, as sitters, perform is not music but posing – posing as if playing, and holding that pose for the painter while they pleasantly, patiently, and quizzically court the approval of the still absent spectators who (they hope) will replace the painter when they are replaced by their image.

The principle of categoreal flexibility helps to lighten the load placed on visual interpretation by connoisseurial judgment, historical knowledge, and conservatorial science.

Premise 8. The group portrait is always a fiction, but for reasons other than those that determine the fictiveness of individual portraits

Comment: The picture of a posing group is not the result of a group posing. Painted group portraits have often been described as if they represented a prior event in which many individuals – sometimes very many – posed

Figure 3.2 Jan Miense Molenaer, *The Duet* [1] (*c*.1630–31), Seattle, Seattle Art
Museum. Gift of the Samuel H. Kress Foundation.

together at the same time in the same place while the artist reproduced the
scene. But that, as Groucho Marx would say, is a likely story. It's clear that
the end product must largely have been the result of sessions involving the
painter and individual sitters or their likenesses. Sitters can be presumed to
have posed separately for a picture that would pretend they posed together.
In some of those isolated acts of portrayal, they may have pretended to pose

as if interacting with others. Thus a better definition of a group portrait is that it's a picture in which sitters pretending to pose together actually posed separately. If we accept this definition, we won't be surprised to find the representation of collective posing so often transgressed by representations of individual posing – to find that sitters' attention to and interaction with each other is often overridden by their separate and competing claims on the observer's attention.

III. Interpreting group portraits: four structural features

1. Solidarity vs *competition*

There is a superficial resemblance between the tensions that affect visual relations among Dutch citizens as sitters in group portraits and those that affect their sociopolitical relations as members of institutional groups in the cities of the Dutch Republic. In *Fictions of the Pose* I tried to characterize this resemblance with the help of two terms borrowed from Simon Schama's *The Embarrassment of Riches:* the first is embarrassment; the second is disaggregation. Schama uses the phrase, "the embarrassment of riches," to designate both economic well-being and an uneasy sociocultural reaction to it, a reaction I associate with performance anxiety. As to disaggregation, Schama cites Paul Claudel's characterization of both Dutch still life and Rembrandt's *The Night Watch:* "an arrangement in process of disintegration" ("en train de se désagréger").[22] More generally, disaggregation is a threat built into the very constitution of the Dutch Republic, which rejected tyranny, eschewed monarchy, and settled for a decentralized coalition of provincial and urban governments. "Embarrassment" and "disaggregation" name symptoms of structural tensions in the Dutch Republic. Embarrassment is an index of strains in the republic's social, economic, and religious orders, disaggregation an index of strains in its political order.

Obviously, the *occasion* of group portraiture as an *institutional* practice is intended to promote and commemorate the kind of solidarity that defends against the threat of disaggregation. But the *form* of group portraiture as a *representational* practice is infiltrated by that threat, and reactivates it – as when, for example, the sitter's position in the portrait is determined not only by rank but also by competitive payment. In other words, the institutional desire for exemplary collaborative performance is activated in a practice that stimulates the conflicting desire for exemplary individual self-representation. Sheila Muller refers to speculations about "a practice by which families of retired regents took back the portraits they had paid for – in most cases by cutting up the whole and dividing the individual portraits among the various relatives."[23] Whether true or not, this is a perfect emblem or caricature of the competitive motive responsible for the push toward disaggregation.

Painters of group portraits tend to accentuate the conflict. By concentrating attention on the cusp of the delicate balance between these attitudes, they bring the performance anxiety of sitters into sharper focus. They seem to recognize that since competitive posing is the project common to all sitters, it is the feature that most unifies the group. Thus the rivalry that threatens to demystify the pretext of collective posing ultimately reinforces and justifies it. The sitters in group portraits are like the Provinces in the Dutch Republic.

2. Manual gestures

Devices that reinforce unity are often given a comedic form by their reliance on gestural conventions. Nothing could be more sociable, more gracious, than a hand resting on a neighbor's shoulder, or pointing toward a weapon, or a colleague, or a corpse, or inviting the observer to take in the scene.[24] J.W. Delff's *Arquebusiers of the Fourth Squad* (1592) carries the multiple acts of pointing introduced in Dirk Jacobsz.'s militia portrait of 1529 to hilarious excess (Figures 3.3 and 3.4). Such acts may be objective, reflexive, presentational, or collegial – directed at an object, at oneself, at another, or generally at the group. According to Alois Riegl, pointing "always had the function of drawing the viewer's attention in an eye-catching way to something that was contributing to the unity of the group portrait."[25] That may be its function but it is not necessarily its effect. An argument can be made that pointing contributes to disaggregation.

In the context of the competition that repetitively isolates each sitter, such presentational gestures archly signify the sociability and graciousness of the presenter's self-presentation. Very often, pointing fingers appear to point at nothing and thus suffer reflexive backlash: they point primarily to the sitter's act of pointing, and this reminds you that if the sitter was painted in isolation from the group, he may not have been pointing sociably at anyone or anything in particular; he may only have been pretending to participate in a scenario of mutual acknowledgment. *In short, pointing in group portraits is not necessarily reducible to the act of directing attention per se. It often seems to be the act of directing attention to the performance of directing attention.*

3. Scopic exchanges

Manual gestures are one marker of sociable interaction. Another is the attentive exchange of gazes – often reinforced by manual gestures – that supposedly links sitters in conversation or in some other act of mutual acknowledgment or activity. But what frequently happens is that the gazes don't quite connect with their putative objects. Scopic and conversational misfires occur in group portraits whenever sitters pretend to be socially engaged even as they or their painter seem unable or unwilling to conceal the fact that their primary attention is on themselves pretending to be socially engaged in a vacuum.

Figure 3.3 J.W. Delff, *Arquebusiers of the Fourth Squad* (1592), Delft, Stedelijk Museum Het Prinsenhof.

Figure 3.4 Dirk Jacobsz., *Civic Guard Group Portrait* (1529), Rijksmuseum Amsterdam.

4. Crowdedness

From the early sixteenth century on, militia portraits like those of Cornelis Anthonisz., Dirck Barendsz., Cornelis Cornelisz. van Haarlem, and Frans Pietersz. Grebber "grow into crowd scenes," and indeed crowdedness becomes a conspicuous *motif*, a motivating effect, as painters depict individual guardsmen gesturing "with or toward objects that refer to character traits, talents or skills intended to identify them among the crush of honored colleagues."[26] Sheila Muller's emphasis is on the way such portraits illustrate a change from religious to secular criteria of self-display. My emphasis is on "the crush" itself (Figure 3.5): on the consistent depiction of crowdedness as a visible influence on self-display and, more specifically, as the context that motivates, justifies, and enhances strenuous campaigns of competitive posing.[27]

Effects of crowdedness are often coupled with manual and scopic gestures of sociability that individualize sitters while purporting to bind them together.[28] The reliance on gestural conventions can be carried to ironic lengths that may suggest something either about the way conventions blind the patrons who commission pictures of themselves, or about the open-eyed wit of patrons who expect their portraits to compete with and differ from (and possibly send up) the portraits of others, or about the games painters play. But it would be a mistake if this discussion of group portraits left the impression that the genre as such is unavoidably comedic or farcical. Militia portraits obviously vary in this respect depending on the extent to which displays of manliness are the targets and not only the subjects of the painters' representational skill. In addition, there is another category of group portraits that occupies a more somber tonal range: the pictures of regents of charitable institutions. But even here, painterly irony can generate unexpected effects because the complex structure of that category features an odd collision of social requirements and aesthetic preferences.

IV. *Caritas* and charisma: the ethics of posing in regent group portraits

Officials of charitable institutions generally have an easier time of it in their portraits than do militiamen in theirs (Figure 3.6). There are fewer sitters, they have things to do with their hands, and the signs they make or objects they handle signify more than administrative activity. They signify the care, the *caritas*, the charitable works, of good Christian souls pursuing the Active Life.[29] In Alois Riegl's extensive analysis of regent group portraits the conflation of portrait effects with Genre effects plays a central role. He argues that Genre-like interactions among sitters increase the internal coherence of the portrait while displaying both the institutional functions and the general virtue of officials who perform important roles in a vital sector of Dutch public life. He also invested considerable stock in the idea that the portrayals

Figure 3.5 Frans Pietersz Grebber, *Banquet of the Officers and Subalterns of St George Civic Guard* (1619), Haarlem, Frans Hals Museum.

of these interactions often included addresses to participant viewers who were imagined to be recipients of the regents' largesse. Since the characteristics he picks out are partly determined by the institutional context, I preface my discussion of regent portraits with a profile of that context.

Charitable institutions in the Dutch Republic were designed to cope with two closely interrelated effects of a thriving economy on its chief beneficiaries: an embarrassment of riches and (to put it bluntly) an embarrassment of beggars. "Morally, the indigent and beggary constituted vexing problems as well as resources for prosperous Dutch citizens," who converted their two embarrassments into a system of charitable institutions sustained by both private investment and public monies.[30] The system was a response to more than *caritas* and guilt. It was also motivated by fear of the uprisings and riots that were a threat to burghers domiciled in the middle of towns whose prosperity "attracted tens of thousands of immigrants from all over northern Europe. ... The streets of the towns began filling up with beggars whose presence undermined the confidence of the charitable rich that things were under control."[31] Dutch urban society was "by modern standards a violent society" in which "men carried knives and used them particularly under the influence of drink."[32]

Caritas, guilt, embarrassment, fear: Muller acknowledges the complexity of motive, "the deeply felt ambivalence of rich toward poor which the Dutch of the seventeenth century sought to control through charity," but which limited the scope of their institutional responses to the problem.[33] The townships of Holland were not equipped to run the institutions of health and welfare as divisions of government, and had no desire to do so. Rather than assuming direct, city-wide responsibility for the welfare of the orphaned, the aged, the sick and the needy, they committed them to the care of boards of burgher regents, such as those that already ran other, non-church charities. The regents would supervise the institution's estates, invest its funds and use them for the good of their wards. The day-to-day running of the institutions was left up to paid administrators.[34]

The first residential home for orphans in Amsterdam was the *Burgerweeshuis* or Municipal Orphanage, founded in the early 1520s. It was not open to members of the urban underclass nor to the children of non-citizens. It accepted only the orphaned children of citizens of the middling classes, children whose parents had left property and assets. As Anne McCants observes in her excellent study of this institution, "the social position of the Burgerweeshuis children's deceased parents continued to influence the care of these children long after their parents had died." The orphanage offered "preemptive" rather than "ameliorative" poor relief, protecting "the social hierarchy not only from the usually hypothesized fear of social insurrection from below but also from the potentially destabilizing effects of downward social mobility."[35]

Popular chronicles attest to "a general policy of self-preservation" that

Figure 3.6 Werner van den Valckert, *Four Regents of the Amsterdam Leprosenhuis* (1624), Rijksmuseum Amsterdam.

began to prevail in response to the "unfavorable economic and political events" of the 1560s. Thus, even as charitable institutions were being granted public status and funding, most of them "closed their doors to all but *poorters* and demonstrated favor for those with the patrimony to subsidize their own upkeep."[36] "Poorters" designates not merely those within the city gates but specifically persons "with inherited citizenship from parents or grandparents who had also been *poorters*." The telling feature of the restriction, which discriminated against new immigrants unrelated to citizen families, was its ascriptive, or crypto-dynastic, character. Its objective was "to preserve the benefits of the institution for persons whose families had, by donation, contributed to its establishment and support in the past."[37]

In 1613 the Amsterdam burgomasters and town council belatedly founded the College of Almoners (*Aalmoezeniers*) to supplement the work of charitable institutions after a period during which expanding urbanization had increased the population of the indigent and compounded "the effects of poverty and unemployment."[38] The College was "the closest approximation in the city to a public welfare department."[39] It turned out not to be a forward-looking institution. It resisted modernization and followed outdated procedures that were basically conservative and religious. Muller cites evidence that at the time of its inception the College was expected to have only temporary interest in poor relief. Its main objectives were "to control a reserve immigrant labor force through poor relief ... and ... to enforce employment of an idle native work force and the most disruptive part of the immigrant group through coercion disguised as an idealistic attempt to rehabilitate the criminal element in society."[40]

By this time, a combination of strategies – restricted admission, prudent investment, the confiscation of Catholic property – and good fortune had made the other institutions wealthier and added prestige to the boards of the burgher charities. It was at this juncture that a new artistic tradition was born: the group portrait of charity regents. In 1617 and 1618, the first three such paintings came into being: the regents of the Amsterdam male house of detention, those of St. Peter's Hospital and of the home for the aged ... were all painted by Cornelis van der Voort (Figure 3.7). The sitters had themselves shown sitting and standing at their work table; around them were deeds, documents and account books referring to their administrative responsibilities.[41]

Muller argues that van der Voort's table format conspicuously alluded to and cancelled the image of lavish feasting associated with the portraits of civic guard at their banquets. The painter replaced foodstuffs with signifiers of the Active Life that referred not only to the sitters' "business acumen" but also to their virtue, and this convention, a variant of "older iconographic formulas," persisted into the middle of the seventeenth century.[42] In addition, according to Riegl, van der Voort introduced a participant observer, an "unseen party in the viewer's space," to whom the regents must be imagined as offering assistance.[43]

Figure 3.7 Cornelis van der Voort, *Regents of the Old Men's and Women's Home* (1618), Amsterdams Historisch Museum.

"The painted view of charity ... avoids the real faces of the poor in the seventeenth century."[44] Jan Steen's wonderful Genre/portrait of 1655, *The Burgher of Delft and his Daughter* (Figure 3.8), depicts a conspicuously idealized, or utopian, version of the wealthy burgher's relation to the rabble (the *grauw*, the drab and snarling mob). By "conspicuously idealized," I mean that signs of stress or trouble are not flatly excluded but depicted in muffled or displaced form. This is not a prelude to an ironic reading. We can assume with Perry Chapman that, rather than being "ironic criticism of the elite," *The Burgher of Delft* conveys "the burgher's moral imperative to act in the public realm," and that "to Steen's contemporaries this image would represent the natural

Figure 3.8 Jan Steen, *The Burgher of Delft* (1655), Rijksmuseum Amsterdam.

social order."[45] But perceived in the light of charity, the natural social order is a complex representation. Its hierarchic form is influenced by such motives as the fear of the rabble and of their potential violence. Charity is the entrepeneurship born of embarrassment. Impelled by *caritas*, condescension, and self-protective avoidance, it reflects a desire to find means of control more positive and less drastic than the impossible ideal expressed by Mr. Kurtz in Conrad's *Heart of Darkness*: "Exterminate the brutes."

Means of control include means of legitimation, and what lies behind "the burgher's moral imperative" is, appropriately, visible behind Steen's burgher: "most prominently, the tower of the Oude Kerk on the right and, above the burgher's shoulder, the Delflands Huis and the Prinsenhof," which, since 1597, had been "the headquarters of ... the municipal organization charged with overseeing charitable giving in Delft."[46] This iconography may be obvious to viewers familiar with the neighborhood, but it keeps a respectful distance. It contributes to the diffidence Westermann finds in the painting: "a narrative that is not spelled out entirely," an "evasive technique" that "draws viewers into a creative mode of looking."[47] To cite one example, the townscape is devoid of other people except for a single well-dressed man on the bridge. Viewed creatively, his lonely presence accentuates the bizarre sense of emptiness and, as in the sparsely populated townscapes of de Hooch, Berckheyde, and Vermeer, suggests what has been excluded.

The "evasive technique" also informs Steen's portrayal of the petitioners. Although the positions of both express deference, the woman's stance is more complex: she seems simultaneously to importune and to keep her distance, leaning forward and extending her hand but not her arm. The burgher strikes an even more complex pose of authoritative condescension and defended vulnerability. His stance is wide open toward the observer, and at the same time he seems to incline sympathetically toward the petitioner. But his foreshortened left shoulder with its cramped collar, the elbow on the railing, and the hand holding the paper, conspire to stiffen his demeanor and shield his openness from her.

The burgher's diffidence is reinforced by the way the young well-dressed woman turns her back and steps gravely away from the intrusive petitioners. She holds her left arm in a manner that echoes his, and lifts up her skirt as if to avoid contamination from the pavement – a needless gesture, given the spotless appearance of the tiles, and thus a repetition that both underlines and displaces his attenuated gesture of recoil. While the steeple confines the cumulus masses to the background, a few dark clouds breaking loose cast their shadows across the autumnal foliage and dapple the figures and trouble the young woman's face.

Steen's portrayal is idealist or utopian in part because the "humble yet respectable supplicants probably belong to the ranks of the *rechte armen* (right or deserving poor), as opposed to the vagrants, vagabonds, and the like, who were prohibited from begging."[48] His burgher's express attention to the poor is an informal and domestic version of what goes on in regent group portraits. If we tentatively accept Riegl's hypothesis about imaginary participant viewers as recipients of the depicted regents' charity, the burgher's relation to the beggars is a variant of the regents' relation to such viewers. Finally, the touch of self-protectiveness Steen gives the burgher seems associated with a regent's positive sense of – and concern for – prestige.

Unlike painters in van der Voort's tradition, however, Steen doesn't bestow on his sitter an aura that transcends prestige and derives from conspicuous allusion to the scriptural exemplar of charity. Van der Voort and his successors include scriptural allusions that play up the connection between the term *charity* and another term to which it is lexically if not etymologically very close: *charisma*. The portraits contribute to campaigns of self-representation aimed at transforming charitable activity to charismatic authority. The campaigns were not disinterested:

> In general, the members of the governing boards were appointed for life by co-optation, and came, needless to say, from the richest families. They saw their function more as a pious duty than a public trust. In the exercise of this duty, they were moreover in a position to safeguard the interests of their relatives in the clans which were the basic unit of the patriciate which ruled the towns. "Charity begins at home" is also a Dutch proverb, although couched in the somewhat obscure expression, "The shirt (that is one's own) is closer (to the body) than the robe (of public office)."[49]

Such pragmatism has made Anne McCants skeptical about the traditional explanation that members of "the regent patriciate" were impelled to serve as officials by such altruistic motives as "the strong hold of both Christian and civic duty." Her disenchanted alternative is that they were motivated primarily by prestige: charitable service provided the candidates with "a launching point to the highest echelons of Amsterdam politics and society" and at the same time gave those who selected them "a way of testing their suitability for later appointment to the city council."[50] But there were cultural reasons why the traditional and disenchanted alternatives were probably easy for regents to conflate.

Dutch Calvinism may have had only marginal success as a proselytizing ideology. But it played a central role in the moral life and culture of local communities as both a disciplinary force and a rhetorical framework. In the Burgerweeshuis, in other orphanages, and in all Dutch schools, education was suffused with religious concepts and practices, and overseen by predicants and rectors. Therefore, given the cultural environment McCants describes so well, it couldn't have required special knowledge or rhetoric to identify one's self-interest and career advancement (sincerely, un-hypocritically) with "the fulfillment of religious and social obligations to the less fortunate."[51]

Whether or not "charity wounds him who receives," it places the recipient under moral as well as political obligation.[52] It thus empowers and elevates not only the donor institution but also those who exercise its authority. This is transparently evident in "the regent portraits that hung in the orphanage" and "were commissioned and paid for privately by the regents themselves."[53] They celebrate terms of service dedicated to the Active Life and, as gifts to the regents' institutions, they remind viewers that the sitters they depict are also gifts to those institutions. The portraits obviously served as markers of prestige. But they were also instrumental in lending their sitters the aura of institutional charisma.[54]

I use the term "charisma" in its classic Weberian sense: charisma is personal magnetism that operates as a source of institutional authority. Its essential conditions are, first, that it be recognized as a gift from sources transcending human power, and second, that it be recognized as the embodiment of transcendent power in a human figure.[55] Those conditions make it a religious concept. Weber's account also makes room for institutional authority – a kind of derivative transcendence – that operates as a source of personal magnetism. Such functional reversibility is relevant to the roles and representations of regents not only in their supervision of charitable institutions but also in their group portraits. As noted above, van der Voort's sitters preferred portraits that showed them performing good deeds, which meant that their portraits were not restricted to lineup or table formats in which they simply posed as if posing. They posed as if in Genre scenes, pretending to interact with each other and with someone in observer space.

V. The ethics of posing in Frans Hals's regent group portraits

Hals attempted the first serious challenge to this format in his 1641 portrait of the Regents of St. Elizabeth Hospital (Figure 3.9). Riegl cites it as an illustration of the tendency in the early 1640s to treat "group portraits like genre scenes." At the same time he finds it unusual because it is entirely self-contained: no sitter looks out; no unseen participant viewer or beneficiary of *caritas* need be hypothesized.[56] These sitters may have elected to foreground their regential prestige. But the scenario they worked out with Hals departs from the models established by van der Voort and van den Valckert, who focused their scenes on acts of charitable donation and added symbols that gave them scriptural resonance. Hals's sitters seem instead to have opted for an image in which prestige was dissociated from charismatic authority – dissociated, that is, from the more powerful aura generated by a behavioral rhetoric expressly imitative of good works in the scriptural tradition.

The dissociation is effected by having the portrait feint toward and then studiedly ignore a Genre interaction, a business transaction:

The gallery of his early group portraits of officers gathered around a banquet table has been replaced appropriately by a new dignity and sobriety. An unspecified business matter, not a spectacular performance of eating and drinking, is the order of the day. An inkpot has replaced the *roemer*, and a ledger, instead of a dish of oysters, is found on the table. A few coins lying before the regent seated on the right may identify him as the treasurer of the group.[57]

Like Riegl, Slive finds the portrait unusual in its treatment of internal coherence: "Some of the regents [Regents 2 and 3, numbering from the left] glance at the man in the front plane, but the latter appears quite unaware of their attention."[58] Regent 1's gaze is less focused and its direction less certain because it is affected by a contorted or dyspeptic posture, which regent 5 seems to be placidly contemplating. But the conspicuous disconnect between Regent 4 and the two who eye him sets the tone for the whole portrait and makes us wonder how seriously to take the evident indications of Genre action. The sheer theatricality of posing as if not posing stands out in a manner that both questions and freezes any pretense of Genre. At first sight, the viewer seems invited to enjoy the sitters' vivacity, their congeniality, and their communicative openness. But the invitation is rudely canceled at the door.

In the fantasy Riegl concocts, Regents 1 and 3 listen excitedly as 2 speaks to 4 who looks to his "left with a thoughtful expression" and "passively" resists 2's argument while 5, "obviously the treasurer," sits "calmly awaiting the results of the others' deliberation."[59] Degrees of tension are registered by the variety of knuckles on tightly or loosely clenched hands, including those of the more detached figure of Regent 5. The repetitive triangular tilting of hats, collars, hands, glances, and half-lit faces adds intensity to the rightward surge of Regents 1 through 3, but Regent 3 reflects by his uprightness the jolt of the opposing force of Regent 4, who seems to hold them off even as Regent 5 appears ready to push back his chair. Regent 5 may seem, as Riegl says, to be "calmly awaiting" something, but there's no reason why that should be a Genre outcome ("the results of the others' deliberation") rather than a portrait outcome, that is, the results of the painter's "deliberation."

The difference between the anxiety of prestige and the aura of charismatic authority is sharply focused by the question of the profile. Riegl finds the profile view of Regent 4 "inappropriate for a portrait" and necessitated only by the demands of the Genre scene Hals invents: "to provide a strong contrast to the other three men who are pressing him for a reply."[60] Slive, who mentions the "Dutch bias against the profile view," concurs: patrons and artists "must have felt there was something archaic about stressing the topographic contours of half a face. ... Moreover, it sharply limits the range of a sitter's glance, a serious restriction to portraitists who want their subjects

Figure 3.9 Frans Hals, *Regents of St. Elizabeth Hospital* (1641), Haarlem, Frans Hals Museum.

to appear to make direct contact with the beholder."[61] Obviously, this was not what Hals wanted here. He wanted the beholder to make direct and sustained contact with Regent 4 so as to derive pleasure from Regent 4's delight in refusing to return the compliment. For this reason, profile notwithstanding, his expression surely has as much portrait value as Genre value. If he is the observed of all the observers on the left, he ignores them, just as Regent 5 ignores Regent 4 and observes Regent 4's observers. The gestures of Regents 1, 2, and 3 are rendered all the more operatic, more dyspeptic, because so blithely ignored by Regent 4 and so coolly measured by Regent 5.

Pierre Descargues' comment comes closer than Riegl's to what we see: although two of the sitters seem to be addressing him, Regent 4 "looks away with smiling indifference, as if thinking of something else."[62] What could that something else be, if not the pleasure with which he presents his profile to the painter and basks in the radiance of his self-regard? Self-fascination is what the painter chooses to accentuate, and if we center our attention on Regent 4's face and hand – the hand brightly but lightly poised at the edge of the table – another look at the three regents on the left shows them shrinking back as if the power of the *fascinum* lurks in the luminous hand.

The variable rhythm of spacing adds resonance to that strange undertone. Regents 4 and 5 comfortably occupy their half of the painting; in contrast, Regents 1, 2, and 3 are crowded together in their half. Crowdedness here, as always, sharpens the accent on competitive posing and shifts the balance from the Genre state (posing as if not posing) to the portrait state (posing as if posing). On the one hand, the Genre situation features sitters who pretend to engage in the good works that signify not merely their institutional authority but also the charisma they derive from doing the Lord's work. On the other hand, competitive posing is flatly oriented toward prestige. Here, a shift of emphasis from the first to the second is decisively marked by the focus on Regent 4, a shift that belies the pretense of Genre and confronts the group with the threat of disaggregation.

The threat arises partly because, although the signifiers of charitable work are on display, the sitters ignore them as well as the observer. Some twenty years later Hals returned to the subject in the portraits of the Regents and Regentesses of The Old Men's Alms House. This time there is less to hold the sitters together and the threat of disaggregation increases: in one, the isolated pyramidally self-enclosed figures of four regentesses accompanied by a matron or housemother; in the other, acts of self-presentation restlessly dispersed by a busy play of hands and a scatter of glances under five space-consuming hats tilted at different angles as if pressed to make room for each other and for the housefather crammed against a wall beside a window. Slive is surely justified in criticizing the portraits for "lack of compositional coherence."[63]

Two interrelated characteristics set these portraits off from portraits that

Figure 3.10 Frans Hals, *Regents of the Old Men's Alms House* (*c.*1664), Haarlem, Frans Hals Museum.

Figure 3.11 Frans Hals, *Regentesses of the Old Men's Alms House* (c.1664), Haarlem, Frans Hals Museum.

feature the Genre-type interactions analyzed by Riegl. First, they disavow any pretense of collective sociality. Each sitter poses for and by herself / himself and against the others. Competitive isolation is conveyed by the separated pyramidal forms of the regentesses and by the overlap and clash of disconnected poses among the regents. Second, they conspicuously refuse the Genre option. Riegl nevertheless insists that the conditions of Genre once again apply: the officials in both portraits "are deliberating with an applicant who is assumed to be standing in the position of the viewing subject."[64] This is more imaginable in the case of the regentesses (in part because three of them pick out the same observer point) than in the slightly mad circus of regent poses. But as we'll see, even the regentesses don't pose as if working. They pose as if posing. The two servants archly displaying messages highlight this alternative by the irrelevance of their offers of messengerial service. Their diffident postures are justified: they present reminders of the Genre scenario the other sitters abjure.

In all three of his regent portraits Hals seems to have included the symbols of charitable activity only so that they could be disavowed (see below) and the viewer's attention more strictly redirected toward the drama of posographical negotiations. But the spirited portrayal of 1641 has been easier to like and praise than the relatively constipated poses populating the later group pendants. At one time the unflattering details and supposed grimness of the pendants were rumored to have been the product of artistic malice, payback by a painter who had been badly treated by the represented officials.[65] But P.J. Vinken and Eddy de Jongh successfully debunked that rumor while accounting for the negative qualities on historical and generic grounds. They locate the misreading in an anachronistic attempt to compensate for the relative impassivity of the portrait as a genre, and to explain Hals's apparently unflattering portrayal, by injecting into his two group pendants novelistic scenarios that are more appropriate for nineteenth-century art.[66]

Here and elsewhere de Jongh emphasizes the taciturnity or reticence (*zwijgzaamheid*), the "limited communicativeness" (*beperkte mededeelzaamheid*), of "old portraits" in general and of Hals's two regent pieces in particular.[67] His work has cleared the path for critics who acknowledge this effect but try to come to grips with it in ways that build toward a less reductive evaluation of Hals's achievement in these late portraits. Christopher Wright finds that although Hals made "no real attempt at a conversation piece," he managed to produce "a series of ... exceptionally powerful [single] portraits in two pictures."[68] Similarly, Pierre Descargues comments on "the aloofness and solitude imparted to each figure" and Sheila Muller sees in the regents' portrait only "a collection of rhetorical posturings that do not follow from any depicted stimulus (e.g., from each other, from objects, from a child or other visitor), except perhaps the occasion of posing for a portrait."[69]

In Muller's excellent account, Hals gives that occasion a suspiciously polemical turn by having his sitters pose in formats that allude to other institutional group portraits, but do so in the rhetorical mode of disavowal that I call conspicuous exclusion.[70] For example, Wright is content to describe the regentesses as "gloomy old women, responsible for the administration and dispensation of public charity."[71] But Muller points out that this particular group of officials is not exactly putting its responsibilities on parade. She alludes to institutional group portraits by Hals's contemporaries (Van der Valckert, Bol, Verspronck, de Bray) in which "busy women" sit at tables filled with conventional items that identify their official duties.[72] Some pretend to discharge those duties. Others strike poses that emblazon their domestic virtue, their industriousness, and their commitment to the Active Life of public service. In contrast, Hals's regentesses, posed around a "noticeably uncluttered" table, seem "strangely unoccupied" and unapologetically "inactive."[73]

This inactivity is most dramatically enacted by the regentess on the right, whom I'll refer to as Regentess 4, numbering from left to right. The book that signifies her administrative role is closed and securely tied, and, as Muller observes, she "makes no move to open or close it." Instead, she eyes the observer and keeps "her right hand pocketed in her apron," a gesture dandified by the modest if defiant Renaissance elbow it produces.[74] But her other hand, however conventional it is as a gesture, is remarkable.[75]

In the posographic contest, the perpetual risk for sitters is that the artist yield to the epideictic impulse and compete with them by decentering attention from the displays of their virtue to the play of his virtuosity. Regentess 4 anticipates this danger. She keeps his brush at bay by exposing her long slender skeletal left hand to its caresses. Hals has duly set the hand apart from the busily clenched and gnarled and stubby extremities of her colleagues. The same hues brushed smoothly over the book have been crumbled into the daubs and slashes and flakes of her painted flesh. It barely sustains its form against the pecking of the birdlike brush that eats away its contour. Seen in those terms the hand is grotesque as an object but it remains eloquent as a gesture. And he has made it beautiful in its confident inactivity.

The inactivity of her colleagues is equally strenuous. Regentess 1 may rest "one hand on a crucifix as though claiming her preference ... for the Contemplative Life," but with her parted lips and the expressively obscure gesture of her other hand she is the most active of the four in her demands on the observer.[76] It has been suggested that her manual gesture is traditional and conspicuously alludes to a prior portrayal of service and the Active Life: "Verspronck had already used it in 1641 to identify the treasurer."[77] If so, the allusion may be urged on the viewer only so that it can be cancelled, conspicuously excluded by the absence of the symbols of treasure.[78] The gesture now serves the anecdotal rhetoricity of a portrait sitter who displays her respect for Christ's good works but who invites auditory attention and visual curiosity more as a sitter than as a treasurer.

Confronted by such pious showmanship, Regentess 2 stolidly opposes the closed fist to the open hand as she looks toward but not necessarily at her neighbor. One of the effects of the conventional exotropic or wall-eyed glance in portraiture is to suggest abstracted attentiveness. If Hals depicts Regentess 1 pretending to speak and Regentess 2 pretending to listen, he may have wanted to show the latter fixed in unseeing audition. But it is easy to translate that behavior into the aesthetic correlative it resembles: the patience of the long-term Rembrandt sitter whose body continues holding the pose from which his or her attention has begun to lapse. The touch of rigidity and tightness in the pose, with left arm more fully extended and left fist more tightly clenched, registers the threat from the other side. She inclines slightly toward Regentess 1 to make room for the upright Regentess 3, against whose territorial enchroachment her arm and fist provide a barrier.

Regentess 3 is Muller's scapegoat, or, rather, her candidate for Hals's scapegoat. She chastises her for yielding to worldly desire: accoutered with both fan *and* gloves (an embarrassment of symbols), her "concern . . . extends only to her own fashionable dress and fancy collar."[79] It's true that she excels in wimpled cuffs and that her collar with its two butterfly-shaped ties is a more elaborate production than the casually tied circlet within which Regentess 4's head is pilloried. But to judge the sitter in isolation is to shear away the context of the competitive group dynamics that gives her figure its meaning within the ethics or politics of posing. What her outfit and demeanor may suggest about her moral condition is a matter of conjecture. What they tell us about her role in the dynamics of the group pose will no doubt be more trivial in psychological terms, but they lend themselves to a form of impressionistic description that is, if not fully disconfirmable, at least open to debate over the meanings to be educed from a limited array of visual effects.

Within these limits, we can say that although Regentess 3 appears, relatively speaking, dressed to kill, she also appears less complacent than Muller implies because she is hemmed in by the dogged posture of Regentess 2 and by Regentess 4's aggressive elbow. Everything about her becomes more tentative, less resolute and definite. Compare, once again, the relatively smooth, stiff, and starchy collar worn by Regentess 4 with the gauzy off-white undulations that seem to dissolve Regentess 3's sloping shoulders. Even the blurred pentimenti transfer uncertainty from painter to sitter. Compare also the decisiveness of Regentess 4's hand and elbow with the wavy contours, the puffy shape, of her neighbor's hands as they awkwardly manage a display of fan and gloves.[80] The two sets of properties are dynamically interconnected: an overall awkwardness is introduced into Regentess 3's pose by the way she turns her body and pulls in her left elbow to accommodate the intrusion into her space not only of 4's elbow but also of the matron's message-bearing hand. Hers is a collegial performance. It deserves respect, even sympathy, rather than censure.

Muller's moral judgment on Regentess 3 supports her argument that

Hals's sitters reject the Active Life in rejecting the Genre performances featured by other group portraits. The only vestigial gesture toward institutional activity is assigned to the matron, and once again, Muller illuminates its parodic force: this is "a device observed in many portraits where it is intended to give the impression that a meeting of the group is under way."[81] Here, it serves as a trope of conspicuous exclusion, a reminder of the sort of business meeting the Regentesses usually have but aren't having now. The sitters are gathered together for another purpose. The role assigned the matron – the awkward tilt of whose body signifies arrested forward motion – is to intrude on a portrait session. Both formally and symbolically, her folded message competes with Regentess 3's folded fan.

The qualities that distinguish Regentess 3 and make her vulnerable to Muller's indictment also distinguish Regent 3 in the other portrait. There are compositional similarities between the two portraits. Regentesses 1 and 2 correlate positionally and gesturally with their male counterparts. Generally, however, the two groups perform under very different conditions. Descargues comments on "the cruelty of Hals's delineation of these charitable old ladies" yet finds them more "stern" and "serene" than the men and "more harmonious" as a group.[82] On the one hand, if they seem calmer it is partly because they have more room to pose in. They are five instead of six and economically organized in four separate pyramidal forms with very little overlap – a compositional economy capped by tightly coiffed heads.[83] On the other hand, the men with their aggressively wide-brimmed hats and flowing hair are larger, closer to the picture surface, and crammed into a smaller space. They are forced to overlap in a manner that increases the need for competitive posing. So, for example, unlike his counterpart, the Regents' housemaster is pushed back into the shadows. Patiently, genially, deferentially, he doffs his hat and accepts his place.[84] But – with the same patience and deference – he continues to exhibit his message, as if hoping for the painter to move him onstage and into the wonted messengerial pose of aggressive delivery.

Descargues concedes that "this portrait of six solitudes is indeed the work of an old man who no longer cares about what it is that brings his sitters together."[85] Presumably he means that Hals ignores the desire of the sitters to be portrayed interacting as a collective group with a particular institutional identity. His "no longer" may imply a contrast to the practice or attitude of the younger Hals. But it may also suggest the old painter's careless response to the *durée* of this commission: the task of planning, scheduling, and executing by the painter presumably in accord with the wishes of his posing subjects. The comment recalls the correspondence concerning the Amsterdam militia group portrait completed by Codde.[86] And Descargues's lurking question is, how could they possibly have wished for *this*?

David Smith arrives at a comparably perplexed judgment by way of a different itinerary. Taking issue with Vinken and de Jongh's minimalist conception of portraiture, he distinguishes between two modes of portrayal, "rhetoric and prose – between figures who present and, in effect, perform themselves before an audience and figures caught in the midst of an ongoing narrative."[87] His readings of a variety of portraits (of individuals, couples, and families) demonstrate in impressive detail how these modes exist in tension and dialogue with each other. But when he comes to Hals's portraits of the Regents and Regentesses, his verdict is unclear.

At one point Smith seems to claim that the criticism of Vinken and de Jongh was preempted by Hals's portrayal: "Hals has intentionally obscured their rhetoric." Usually in the portraits of officers of charitable institutions, sitters "engage in active, explicit gestures that allude to their good works," but in these portraits the sitters' hands "are pointedly inexpressive. Only the regent with the cocked hat makes a rhetorical gesture, and its effect is almost entirely cancelled by the man in the center of the composition."[88] A few sentences later, Smith's own rhetoric shifts responsibility from painter to sitters: "their rhetoric is half-hearted"; although they "could have acted out their parts in a narrational mode," they adopted "a rhetorical stance" and failed "to commit themselves to it."[89] Is this an observation about what the painter did to the sitters or about what the sitters failed to do on their own? Is it a criticism of what Smith *sees* (the sitters in the *now* of posing) or of what he *infers* (the patrons posing *then* for the painter)?

Confronted by these questions, my preference is to rewrite all the above statements, some of them critical, as strictly descriptive insights into an unorthodox scenario. It is unorthodox for the reasons persuasively laid out by Muller: the portraits are institutional performances that conspicuously exclude the usual signifiers of administrative responsibility and commitment to the Active Life. The scenario is also unorthodox because the sitters display varying levels of responsibility and commitment to their acts of posing. Several pose as if they *have been* posing – as if they have been patiently sustaining, and in some cases are now relaxing, the effort to hold the pose. In Smith's terms, they appear to have become half-hearted about their commitment to the rhetoric not only of institutional responsibility but also of collective posing. This, at least, is the narrative on which they collaborate. And it is a narrative that makes them more than functionaries with ordinary faces in repose. It makes them individuals striving – within a restrictive conventional framework – to differentiate themselves at two levels: first, from sitters in other institutional group portraits, and second, from each other as they try to compete for the viewer's attention by variations in dress, posture, gesture, or expression.

The conflict between the claims of institutional representation and those of personal self-display is suggested by the fact that although the table contains more evidence of their responsibilities as governors than does that of the regentesses, the additional evidence (a tray of writing materials) is partly concealed and flamboyantly ignored by Regent 3. There is nothing half-hearted about his performative rhetoric. Muller sees in his excessive and awkward double gesture (arm akimbo and hand over heart) "no more than a fashionable pose struck for the moment with the portrait occasion in mind."[90] But "no more than" is too dismissive since the remainder of the sentence expresses portraiture's normative motive or rationale. Regent 3 has his own portrait occasion more fully in mind than the occasion, say, of his colleague, Regent 4. Since the latter appears to be presenting Regent 3, it seems a shame that his manual gesture "is almost entirely cancelled by" Regent 3's showboating.[91] But maybe it isn't.

Regent 4 is famous as the supposedly drunk or neurologically challenged regent.[92] Riegl gives him little respect: he infers from "[t]he dissipated expression of the unkempt speaker … with his crooked hat and disheveled hair" that these sitters are "aging bon vivants."[93] In their survey and convincing refutation of such views, Vinken and de Jongh conclude that his strange appearance could better be explained by medical than by moral or physiognomic diagnosis. They also try to domesticate his performance by noting that his is not the only dangerously cocked hat in art history: Hals gives a similarly rakish tilt to the same kind of hat with very different effect in two single portraits produced during the 1660s.[94]

We can acknowledge the persuasiveness of their defence against the malignity argument without letting it diminish the strangeness of Regent 4's role in the collective performance Hals depicts. Whatever the cause of his physical abnormalities (paralysis of the *nervus facialis*, lagophthalmos, ectropion, etc.), they conspire with a crazy hat to draw the viewer's gaze past Regent 3 and toward his shadowy form. Even his presentational gesture is so conspicuously diffident that it calls attention to itself. To present another is to compete with another. The longer we fix on the claims these two Regents make on the observer, the more intense their conflict seems.

In this conflict, the angle of Regent 4's hat is decisive. He might otherwise appear to be patiently posing, as if the task of self-presentation has been prolonged until he has begun to withdraw into himself while holding on to the pose. But the obvious need to sustain a balancing act over time transforms the message his gaze sends from introspective withdrawal to proprioceptive effort. The effort is underlined by details that stiffen the pose: the set of his chin in its collar, the way the occasionally thick mask-like contour lines around face and forehead contribute to an effect of rigid self-immobilization, and the highlights on the knuckles of his left hand, which indicate that the hand exerts pressure on the table. Ironically, the only sign of relaxation, of forgetfulness or distraction, is the curling of the fingers with which he presents Regent 3.

Regent 4's act of presentation is one of three such manual gestures – Regents 1 and 5 perform the others – and all three could be construed as presenting Regent 3, which may be the dominant motif of the portrait, especially if Regent 3 is also construed as presenting Regent 3. The gestures of Regents 1, 4, and 5, but surely not that of Regent 3, qualify as members of

Smith's category, "half-hearted."[95] The adjectives "tired" and "flaccid" also come to mind. In all three cases, the presentational gestures exhibit incipient or advanced relaxation – signs of extended posing. They remind us that "a fashionable pose struck for the moment" may take many moments to produce. And they increase our admiration for the sustained enthusiasm, the patience, the focused energy, with which Regent 3 tirelessly gives of himself to his painter and posterity.

Regent 3's most spirited competitor is Regent 2 – spirited in the sense that, like his counterpart among the regentesses, he doggedly faces left, though why he does so is not clear. Either he offers the painter a three-quarter view of his noble countenance by looking posefully past Regent 1 into observer space. Or he plays the auditor whose attention to Regent 1 confirms the latter's half-hearted attempt at a conversational demeanor.[96]

In contrast to Regents 3 and 2, the red-legged Regent 5 has begun to show signs of the wear and tear of posing. Hals helps the process along with his brushwork. On the left, he makes the regent's waterfall of a shirt terminate in one of two gloved hands destroyed by the same paint that builds them up. On the right, slapdash fingers of paint applied in a scrupulously careless manner double as the dangling gloved hand of a straw man. The vibrant hatchwork for which Regent 5's upheld sleeve provides an excuse shatters solid form and transforms linen into origami-like fantasies. Within that burst of energy, the sitter's gesture is not fully legible. It hovers between sprezzatura and fatigue. And as all this "happens" before the viewer's eyes, Regent 5 casually but fixedly sustains the most awkward of the five poses: a travesty of midmotion frozen into the stillness of the field over which the painter's brush restlessly starts and stops and flickers and darts.

"Slapdash" brushwork: the metaphor conjures up the painter's haste to catch and fix a momentary pose. It conjures up the fiction of a sitter who may be restless or in need of a rest or about to interrupt the pose. When the art historian speaks of "rapid brushwork on the cuffs and collars" he picks out a conspicuous effect, the representation and souvenir of the painter at work; in particular, the representation of the rapidity and haste that signify painterly bravura.[97] But Hals's painting also features a kind of granular chiaroscuro that animates small areas like the surfaces of hands and at the same time models and solidifies them. These passages of "careful" therefore "slow" painting are juxtaposed to the areas of "careless" and "rapid" painting. Together, they enhance the effect of temporality – the effect of the *durée* as well as the work of posing and painting.

To focus on these effects is to bring the *now* of painting and sitting, the situation of painter and sitters, into the picture. It is to make oneself aware that something has been happening since first the sitters gathered together to plan and sit for their portrait. Hals's sitters are not only setting up for the observer in their future. They are also waiting now for the painter to finish. They *appear to be* patiently posing, as if the task of self-presentation has been prolonged until some have begun either to hold on to the pose, or to sign off and let the painter do as he likes. Their communicative gestures are stalled or frozen (as the paint flickers about) in the time warp produced by our decision to focus on the act of *sustaining* the pose.

Nevertheless, something has happened. The pretext of corporate occasion has lost its hold. The fabric of collectivity has eroded. For Pierre Descargues, only "six [or eleven] solitudes" remain, but Christopher Wright elegiacally confabulates a context for them in their life beyond painting: "we sense the quivering hands, the bleary eyes blinking, the mutterings about questions of finance, and the indomitable gazes of men and women who have had seventy years of having their own way."[98] Here it will help to recall Vinken and de Jongh's caveat: we might "sense" these quiverings, blinkings, and mutterings but we don't see them. The portraits are not synecdoches – stills extracted from the film of life – nor are they stoppages in the passage of time. Portraits represent special events of one kind only – the event of posing. But this event may take either or both of two forms: *posing as if posing* and *posing as if not posing*.

These two alternatives frame Muller's important contribution to the debate about Hals's portraits. She would prefer less of the former and more of the latter, and she bases this preference on moral grounds. In citing Riegl's "pioneering work," she states her intention to go beyond him by documenting the impact of the Christian humanist concept of the Active Life on a series of group portraits made for charitable institutions.[99] The strength and novelty of her position derive from the attempt to correlate moral critique with formal analysis, as when she imagines that Hals must have intended to underscore the subversion of the Active Life "by depicting sitters who are inactive – almost torpid," and who have thus let him down by giving him too "little with which to work." She goes on to speculate metapictorially about his reason for inserting an Italianate landscape painting into the women's portrait: it is to suggest that an adornment like this portrait, "commissioned by the regentesses to decorate their institutional boardroom, has little to do with the true meaning of *caritas*."[100]

This may add a new twist to the sorts of negative judgment Vinken and de Jongh had criticized (as Muller herself notes), but it falls within their range and in so doing it veers away from the more profound question that lurks in her argument, the question about the portraits' ambivalence of motive. Do they – does Hals – emphasize the perverseness of the sitters' refusal to show themselves productively occupied? Are they being wicked to insist on posing as if posing? Or do they present posing, self-commemoration, as a productive activity that needs no apology? Muller opts for the former and casually dismisses the latter in the description of the regents I cite above: "a collection of rhetorical posturings" with no apparent motivation other than "the occasion of posing for a portrait."[101]

Given her emphasis on what can only be called the flakiness of the sitters portrayed by Hals, she has to work hard to explain why the patrons might have approved of the painting. She decides that they must have enjoyed seeing themselves in his "immediate and vivid images of real characters appearing to comport themselves naturally before the viewer."[102] Yet her concluding opinion contains an odd throwaway: Hals is less "engaged in sending up his sitters" than in "revealing what they perceive the Active Life to be."[103] But she had previously argued that Hals reveals their perception of the Active Life to be frivolous and to have "little to do with the true meaning of *caritas*." How could he not be sending them up? The answer isn't complicated, but it presupposes a return to the first principles of the fictions of the pose.

"A collection of rhetorical posturings." We saw while examining Aristotle in Part I of this essay that since his text acknowledges all forms of rhetoric as forms of "posturing," its more subversive message is that *epideixis* is king: the orator's performance of *ēthos*, his "presentation of self," is central to deliberative and forensic no less than to epideictic success. The same holds true for the portrait sitter. The product of this complex articulation is a performance of *ēthos*, the basic form of which is posing as if posing. This form takes precedence over any Genre dramatization of institutional function or membership.

Yet although posing as if posing is the signature stance of portraiture, during the first half of the seventeenth century it was often partly masked or varied by the tendency of painters of group portraits to experiment with Genre situations that featured sitters who pose as if not posing. Sitters in regents' portraits from the time of van der Voort and van den Valckert on have been interpreted as pretending to engage with participant viewers in the discharge of their charitable responsibilities.[104] This scenario supplies the pretext of a corporate activity more altruistic and important than that of the portrait activity through which it is being represented.

Muller convincingly shows that Hals's sitters refuse this scenario. The contents of the Regentesses' table are reduced to the cross under the hand of Regentess 1 and the closed account book under the cuff of Regentess 4. Does the fact that the account book signifying charitable activity is closed comment on the cross signifying Christian activity? Have both been "demoted," rendered conspicuously vestigial by the transfer of the locus of charismatic authority from symbols of Active Life to sitters actively posing? In the case of the regents, the single attempt to index institutional activity, Regent 1's manual gesture toward the closed book, deserves David Smith's epithet, "half-hearted," in part because the gesture could just as well be aimed, or half-aimed, at Regent 3. Finally, the gestures with which the matron and housemaster offer messages appear incongruous because the motivating Genre context is missing – and because the other sitters ignore them so completely.

If, then, Hals is not "sending up his sitters," if it seems unlikely that they have commissioned him to portray them sending up the Active Life of *caritas*, and yet if scrutiny of the portraits doesn't justify the opinion that they reveal what the sitters "perceive the Active Life to be," what possibilities remain? My preference, predictably, is not to dispense with the idea of a sendup but to redirect it toward a more reflexive scenario: Hals and his sitters have decided to send up the pretense of Genre and along with it the pretentious display of participation in the Active Life that earlier regents' portraits featured. They conspicuously reject that option, conspicuously refuse to pose as if not posing.

Hals's sitters have chosen instead to acknowledge their investment in what they are actually and self-interestedly doing at the moment. They pose as if posing. Their prestige doesn't have to be demonstrated by displays of good works. They have required the painter neither to demonstrate their *caritas* nor to visualize their claim to charismatic authority. They prefer to concentrate on doing what figures of authority eventually and inevitably do, sit for their portrait and for posterity.

Yet eventually and inevitably, the painter has the last say, and his statement is at once strangely perverse and deeply respectful. Hals betrays his sitters' tired attempts at institutional and social gestures. He assigns them different levels of attentiveness. Some, like Regent 3 and Regentesses 3 and 4, are still making the effort to hold the pose. But all have the look of sitters who have been posing for a long time. Most have begun to drift into themselves. The gestures of Regentesses 1 and 2, and of Regents 1, 2, 4, and 5, are studiedly vague or indeterminable. It is as if the pretext of corporate occasion has lost its hold and posing has lost its edge.

Partly, then, what makes the pendants so poignant, so powerful, is their stark refusal to transcend the swerve toward disaggregation. Hals's groups are on the verge of falling apart. Nevertheless, the sitters persevere. They will not let the painter or themselves down. Even when small explosions of restless white facture indict the contentious or pretentious performances of Regents 3 and 5, Hals accords them the respect the painter owes to the long-term sitter: one bravely holds on to the pose (and to himself); the other tries to maintain contact amid signs of imminent relaxation. Charismatic authority can come in darker, more distant, and haunting shades than those that surround the energetic agents of *caritas* in earlier regents' portraits.

I conclude this essay with a methodological caveat. The drama and the psychology of posing may not loom very large in the economy of human life. Posographical interpretations of sitters are at once more limited and more expressly hypothetical in their claims than those we associate with general psychology. They are more likely to be comic than tragic in mode and tone. They may not shed much light on the physiognomic or psychological or emotional makeup of the person portrayed – on his or her soul, character, or personality. Vinken and de Jongh's emphasis on the pragmatic limits to the disclosure of inwardness encourages a healthy skepticism about these sources of revelation. The methodological limits placed on interpretation by the "rules" of the fiction of the pose support that skepticism, but at the same time they mark out a field within which it becomes possible to say something specific about the sitters' demeanor, their expressions, their gestures, and their attention or inattention to each other and to the observer. Whether we can say more depends on the possibility of expanding the interpretive field so that our accounts of the act of posing include reference to the institutional and social scenarios it performs – or betrays.

Notes

1 Keir Elam, *Shakespeare's Universe of Discourse: Language-Games in the Comedies* (Cambridge: Cambridge University Press, 1984), p. 217.

2 Aristotle, *The "Art" of Rhetoric*, 1.2.2–6, trans. John Henry Freese (1926; rpt. London: William Heinemann Ltd, 1947), pp. 14–17. Page references include those of the original text and its translation.

3 Ibid., 1.3.2–6, pp. 32–35.

4 1.9.28, pp. 96–97.

5 1.9.1, pp. 90–91.

6 1.2.4, pp. 16–17.

7 2.1.1–3, pp. 168–69.

8 Elam, *Shakespeare's Universe of Discourse*, pp. 217–18; Elam cites *Rhetoric* 1.2.4, but the quoted words appear in 1.2.7, pp. 18–19.

9 The term "Genre" is capitalized here and hereafter when it is used to designate the particular "genre" described and defined below rather than "genre" as a general category. For a recent account of the origin of the term, see Wayne Franits, *Dutch Seventeenth-Century Genre Painting* (New Haven, CT: Yale University Press, 2004), pp. 1–2.

10 Eddy de Jongh, *Questions of Meaning: Theme and Motif in Dutch Seventeenth-Century Painting*, trans. Michael Hoyle (Leiden: Primavera Pers, 2000), p. 85.

11 The distinction between portraiture and history is complicated – and may be interrogated – by the ambiguities of historiation, but the distinction itself remains normative.

12 *Definitions*: Let the term *sitter* designate the painted figure, the likeness, and the term *patron* the nominal original and referent of the likeness. Let the term *model* designate the originals but not the referents of painted figures in history and Genre scenes. Let the term *character* designate their referents – the singular figures of history and the typical figures of Genre.

13 The figure Alberti characterizes as an interlocutor acts as if he were in the presence of imaginary spectators of the depicted event: he "beckons them with his hand to look, or … challenges them not to come near, as if he wished their business to be secret, or … invites you to laugh or weep": Leon Battista Alberti, *On Painting and On Sculpture*, ed. and trans. Cecil Grayson (London: Phaidon Press, 1972), p. 83.

14 H. Perry Chapman, in *Jan Steen: Painter and Storyteller*, ed. Chapman, Wouter Th. Kloek, and Arthur Wheelock, Jr. (New Haven, CT: Yale University Press, 1996), p. 205. In addition to the excellent studies in this volume, especially those by Chapman and Mariët Westermann, see Westermann, *The Amusements of Jan Steen: Comic Painting in the Seventeenth Century* (Zwolle: Waanders, 1997); Westermann, "Jan Steen, Frans Hals, and the Edges of Portraiture," *Nederlands Kunsthistorisch*

Jaarboek 46 (1995): 298–331 – revised as chapter 6 of *The Amusements of Jan Steen*; H. Perry Chapman, "Jan Steen as Family Man: Self-Portrayal as an Experiential Mode of Painting," *Nederlands Kunsthistorisch Jaarboek* 46 (1995): 372–76; Chapman, "Persona and Myth in Houbraken's Life of Jan Steen," *The Art Bulletin* 75 (1993): 135–50.

15 Along the same lines, Richard Wollheim distinguishes between the spectator *in* the picture and the spectator *of* the picture. The first, the "internal spectator," is "located in the virtual space … the painting represents," while the second, the "external spectator," is "located in the actual space … the painting itself occupies." Richard Wollheim, *Painting as an Art* (Princeton, NJ: Princeton University Press, 1987), p. 102. See, more generally, pp. 101–85 *passim*. I reserve the term "observer" for the internal spectator and the term "viewer" for the external spectator.

16 The sitter's immediate viewers will be the painter and casual onlookers in home or studio as well as the virtual observer constructed by that sitter's gaze.

17 Initially I thought of the observer position as blank or null, but this is a misleading way to characterize an address and relation that are intrinsically rhetorical.

18 The order implied by "the sitter's pose and the painter's imitation of it" is itself a mystification, since the portrait pretends to imitate or copy what in fact it creates. The true order is: the patron's pose and instructions > the painter's representation > the sitter's pose.

19 Westermann, *The Amusements of Jan Steen*, p. 271. Westermann notes that "the responses of sitters to the genre-bending portraits of Steen and Hals are unknown," but speculates that they may have "appealed to viewers in the know about the pictorial genres practiced in the Dutch Republic" (ibid.).

20 *Jan Miense Molenaer: Painter of the Dutch Golden Age*, ed. Weller (Raleigh, NC: North Carolina Museum of Art, 2002), p. 85.

21 By W.R. Valentiner and Colin Eisler. Cited by Weller, ibid., 86, note 7.

22 See Simon Schama, *The Embarrassment of Riches: An Interpretation of Dutch Culture in the Golden Age* (New York: Alfred A. Knopf, 1987), pp. 10–11 *et passim*; Paul Claudel, *The Eye Listens*, trans. Elsie Pell (New York: Philosophical Library, 1950), p. 48; Claudel, *L'oeil écoute* (1935), *Oeuvres Complètes*, vol. 17 (Paris: Gallimard, 1960), p. 46.

23 Sheila D. Muller, *Charity in the Dutch Republic: Pictures of Rich and Poor for Charitable Institutions* (Ann Arbor, MI: UMI Research Press, 1985), p. 233n.40.

24 See Margaret Iversen, *Alois Riegl: Art History and Theory* (Cambridge: MIT Press, 1993), p. 106.

25 Alois Riegl, *The Group Portraiture of Holland*, trans. Evelyn M. Kain and David Britt (Los Angeles, CA: Getty Research Institute, 1999), p. 159.

26 Ibid., 11.

27 For example, in Thomas de Keyser's 1633 portrait of 21 shooters in the Amsterdam Historical Museum, figures overlap and squeeze against each other in such a way as to indicate that there was not enough room to accommodate all of them comfortably. The hiatus created right of center by the pike man in front of the doorway only accentuates the problem; his expansive, oversized figure demands so much space that the tight little duo huddling in front of him seems crushed together.

28 See, for example, Dirk Jacobsz., *Civic Guard Group Portrait of 1529* (see Figure 3.4), and Dirck Barendsz., *Banquet of Eighteen Guardsmen of Squad L, 1566*, both in the Rijksmuseum, Amsterdam.

29 On this see Muller, *Charity in the Dutch Republic*, chapter 1 *et passim*.
30 Westermann, *The Amusements of Jan Steen*, p. 264.
31 Gary Schwartz, *The Dutch World of Painting*, catalogue for the exhibition organized by the Netherlands Office for Fine Arts and the Vancouver Art Gallery, April 6–June 29, 1986 (Maarssen: Gary Schwartz, 1986), p. 66. Schwartz relies heavily on, and expresses his indebtedness to, Sheila Muller's *Charity in the Dutch Republic*.
32 J.L. Price, *Dutch Society, 1588–1713* (New York: Longman, 2000), p. 152.
33 Muller, *Charity in the Dutch Republic*, pp. 3–4.
34 Schwartz, *The Dutch World of Painting*, p. 65.
35 Anne E.C. McCants, *Civic Charity in a Golden Age: Orphan Care in Early Modern Amsterdam* (Urbana, IL: University of Illinois Press, 1997), pp. 76, 28. One of the many strong points of this study is its account of the complementary relations between the form and development of the charitable institution and the development of the nuclear or "newly privatized family" on which the orphanage was modeled and which it was designed to support. See pp. 30–37, 148, and 201.
36 Muller, *Charity in the Dutch Republic*, p. 8.
37 Ibid., 229n.14, 8.
38 Ibid., 51.
39 Schwartz, *The Dutch World of Painting*, p. 70.
40 Muller, *Charity in the Dutch Republic*, pp. 51, 82.
41 Schwartz, *The Dutch World of Painting*, p. 67.
42 Muller, *Charity in the Dutch Republic*, pp. 13–16, *et passim*.
43 Riegl, *Group Portraiture*, p. 223.
44 Muller, *Charity in the Dutch Republic*, p. 3.
45 Chapman, *Jan Steen: Painter and Storyteller*, p. 21.
46 Ibid., p. 119.
47 Westermann, *The Amusements of Jan Steen*, p. 264.
48 Chapman, *Jan Steen: Painter and Storyteller*, p. 121.
49 Schwartz, *The Dutch World of Painting*, p. 65.
50 McCants, *Civic Charity in a Golden Age*, pp. 106–07.
51 Ibid., p. 106. For a much richer speculation about the motives of regents, see Muller's remarkable close reading of Werner van den Valckert's 1624 portraits of the regents and regentesses of the Amsterdam Leprozenhuis in *Charity in the Dutch Republic*, pp. 14–20. The "image of virtue" portrayed in these works

> was meant to be seen as an exemplar of charity and not as a factual description of administrative acivity within the Leprozenhuis. ... To the sitters ... this image of virtue was perhaps a way of justifying for themselves the advantages they enjoyed over their fellow men: their regency was a position of privilege but it was only from that position that they were offered the opportunity to practice charity in a manner approaching the biblical ideal. (19)

52 Marcel Mauss, *The Gift: Forms and Functions of Exchange in Archaic Societies*, trans. Ian Cunnison (New York: Norton, 1967), p. 63.
53 Ibid., 199.
54 On this, see Jonathan I. Israel, *The Dutch Republic: Its Rise, Greatness, and Fall, 1477–1806* (Oxford: Clarendon Press, 1995), p. 356.
55 To diagram this relation, the human figure stands at the center; above is the Power, the source of the figure's gift and favor; around the figure is the audience that recognizes this power and confers the status of charismatic embodiment.

Charismatic stability depends, first, on the relative strength or weakness of collective belief in the authorizing Power; and second, on the extent to which both the central figure and the audience can repress or ignore the disabling suspicion that charisma lies in the eye of the observer (or simply that charisma lies).

56 Ibid., p. 346.
57 From the catalogue entry by Seymour Slive in *Frans Hals*, ed. S. Slive (Munich: Prestel, 1989), p. 284.
58 Ibid.
59 Ibid., pp. 340–42.
60 Ibid., p. 342.
61 Slive (ed.), *Frans Hals*, p. 288.
62 Pierre Descargues, *Frans Hals*, trans. James Emmons (Geneva: Skira, 1968), p. 99.
63 Seymour Slive, *Dutch Painting 1600–1800* (New Haven, CT: Yale University Press, 1995), p. 54.
64 Riegl, *Group Portraiture*, p. 348.
65 On the deterioration of the portraits, see Karin Groen and Ella Hendriks, "Frans Hals: A Technical Examination," in Slive (ed.), *Frans Hals*, pp. 120–21.
66 P.J. Vinken and E. de Jongh, "De boosardigheid van Hals's regenten en regentessen," *Oud Holland* 80 (1963): 1–24.
67 See E. de Jongh, "Oude portretten, hun zwijgzaamheid en mededeelzaamheid," Koninklijke Nederlandse Akademie van Weterschappen. Verslag van de Verenigde Vergadering van de beide Afdelingen der Akademie op maandag 8 April 1991: 15–44; and *Portretten van echt en trouw: Huwelijk en gezin in de Nederlandse kunst van de zeveniende eeuw* (Zwolle: Waanders, 1986), p. 33.
68 Christopher Wright, *Frans Hals* (Oxford: Phaidon Press, 1977), p. 6.
69 Descargues, *Frans Hals*, p. 127. Sheila D. Muller, *Charity in the Dutch Republic: Pictures of Rich and Poor for Charitable Institutions* (Ann Arbor, MI: UMI Research Press, 1985), p. 46.
70 Conspicuous exclusion expressed as a statement might be, "we want you to think of other institutional group portraits when you look at us so that you'll see we aren't doing and *wouldn't* do the sorts of things they're doing – for whatever particular reasons (emulation, parody, or critique that might reflect aesthetic social, political, or moral motives)." See, for example, my two essays on conspicuous exclusion in Vermeer, reprinted in *Second World and Green World: Studies in Renaissance Fiction-Making*, ed. and intro. John P. Lynch (Berkeley, CA: University of California Press, 1988), pp. 441–509.
71 Wright, *Frans Hals*, p. 13.
72 Muller, *Charity in the Dutch Republic*, p. 44. These are the types of portraits that Riegl converts to hybrids dominated by Genre-type interactions involving participant observers.
73 Ibid., pp. 44–45.
74 Ibid., p. 45.
75 See the catalogue entry in Slive (ed.), *Frans Hals*, p. 362.
76 Ibid.
77 Descargues, *Frans Hals*, p. 127.
78 Muller's reading of the placement differs from that of Descargues: she claims that the treasurer's position is occupied by Regentess 2, who "has her hands spread far apart to show that there are no coins on the bare table" (*Charity in the Dutch Republic*, p. 45).

79 Ibid. The different styles and positions of their collars reinforce their different gestures. For example, the longer collar and tabs of Regentess 2 accentuate her reliance on the table for support. A similar collar on the matron subtly accentuates the deferential forward tilt of her upper body. Regentess 1's shorter and more protuberant collar seems to facilitate as well as to emphasize the rhetorical placement of her arms. In the triangulated drama of Regentess 3's self-display, the eye attracted to the distanced gauziness of her collar is led downward and forward from the smaller to the larger of the butterfly-shaped ties to the climactic stage business with fan and gloves. Finally, the single tie that adorns Regentess 4's collar (noticeably more reserved than her neighbor's display) is closely enough related in form to the tie that fastens her book to reiterate its insistence on the priority of posing and portraiture to business and Genre.

80 Such qualities prompted Grimm to reassign the portrait from Hals to his "Workshop" (*Frans Hals*, pp. 158, 242–43).

81 Ibid., p. 45.

82 Descargues, *Frans Hals*, p. 127. But notice that he calls them "old ladies," whereas no such epithet is applied to the regents. Are regentesses supposedly older and more motherly than their more vigorous manly counterparts?

83 The dominant authority of the regentess with the book beside her is reinforced by the inclusion of the matron in her pyramid.

84 His "friendly and guileless expression" endears him to Riegl, who judges him to be the most congenial figure in the painting (*Group Portraiture*, p. 350).

85 Descargues, *Frans Hals*, p. 123, my translation: "un vieillard qui ne croit plus à ce qui rassemble ses modèles" (*Hals: Étude biographique et critique* [Geneva: Skira, 1968], p. 123).

86 For details, see Slive (ed.), *Frans Hals*, pp. 390–91.

87 David R. Smith, "Rhetoric and Prose in Dutch Portraiture," *Dutch Crossing* 41 (1990): 72.

88 Ibid., pp. 85–86.

89 Ibid., p. 86.

90 Muller, *Charity in the Dutch Republic*, pp. 46–47.

91 Smith, "Rhetoric and Prose," pp. 85–86. The presentation is noted by Muller, *Charity in the Dutch Republic*, p. 47.

92 In *Frans Hals: Life Work Restoration* (Amsterdam: Uniepers, 1989) Norbert Middelkoop and Anne van Gravenstein speculate that "the dullness of his look" signifies a disease of the eye (p. 34). They may be referring to the evidence of paresis discussed by Vinken and de Jongh in "De boosardigheid van Hals's regenten en regentessen," 4.

93 Riegl, *Group Portraiture*, p. 350.

94 See Vinken and de Jongh in "De boosardigheid van Hals's regenten en regentessen," 4. For a skeptical opinion about Regent 4's condition and a comment on other portraits by Hals that feature cocked hats, see Slive (ed.), *Frans Hals*, p. 367. See also Harry Berger, Jr., *Fictions of the Pose: Rembrandt Against the Italian Renaissance* (Stanford, CA: Stanford University Press, 2000), pp. 299–301.

95 Regent 1 looks "in the approximate direction of the speaker, while not looking directly at him. A corresponding movement of his right index finger supports this interpretation of his orientation" (Riegl, *Group Portraiture*, pp. 348–50).

96 In Wybrand Hendricks's watercolor copy, the roles are reversed: Regent 2 appears to be addressing Regent 1, whose manual gesture is thereby rendered irrational.

97 Wright, *Frans Hals*, p. 6.

98 Ibid.

99 Muller, *Charity in the Dutch Republic*, pp. 6 and 228n.4.

100 Ibid., pp. 45–46. On attempts to identify the landscape, see Slive (ed.), *Frans Hals*, p. 362.

101 Ibid., p. 46.

102 Ibid., p. 48. This contradicts her emphasis on the way the contorted pose of Regent 3 influences the viewer's "feeling for the portrait as a whole" (p. 47).

103 Ibid., p. 48.

104 Genre actions with possible participant observers appear earlier in militia portraits. See Riegl, *Group Portraiture, passim*.

4 Textual ethics

Reading transference in
Samson Agonistes

Marshall Grossman

The transference is unthinkable unless one starts out from the subject who is
supposed to know. … He is supposed to know that from which no one can
escape, as soon as he formulates it – quite simply, signification.[1]

This mystery is, in the final analysis, the mystery of the *transference* itself: to
produce new meaning, it is necessary to *presuppose* its existence in the other.[2]

1.

By textual ethics I mean the perseverant and transformative performance of
texts in and on those who produce and consume them, and the relative
openness of readers and writers to transformation. Textual ethics, then,
examines the way texts act and how their efficacy may be embraced or
resisted by readers. I am, therefore, concerned with two distinct but related
ethical moments with respect to textual agency. On the side of reading: the
well worn thought that reading might be a transforming experience,
constituted as and resulting in an ethical choice. On the side of writing: the
willingness of an author to submit himself or herself to the logic of his or her
text and to follow its tropes and schemes to places unanticipated by authorial
intention. Taken together these processes make up two sides of the same
ethical coin. The features that lend to a text whatever transforming power it
may have emerge in the course of the writer's more or less intrepid
collaboration with his or her medium, genre and material and the reader's
willingness to engage in a similar collaboration with the resulting text. For
both reader and writer openness to the ethical moment of the text means
understanding the rhetorical and linguistic material from which the text is
fashioned as a third term, distinct from reader and writer, yet irreducibly
implicated in the potential agency of the text. This agency inheres in the
text's ability to discover a plurality of universes by configuring and reconfiguring the possible relationships among its signifying elements.[3] Varied
configurations result from choices made among possible ways a text may be

construed, and they result in further choices when they project the reader or writer into various delineated situations. Aristotle understood this when he made *ēthos* subordinate to *mythos*. The plot offers the protagonist choices. These choices disclose the customs or habits that determine his character. As we read, the unfolding of the plot appears to be determined by the character's choices; the character-effect is thus metaleptic. From the point of view of the writing, character is caused by plot, which is then represented as an effect of character. My agenda in this essay is to propose a version of psychoanalytic transference as a way to detail how readers and writers encounter ethical choices and how the choices they make not only disclose but also determine character. In the latter part of the essay, I hope to demonstrate the efficacy of the model by bringing it to bear on a curious detail of the presentation of *Samson Agonistes* in Milton's 1671 volume.

One way to think about textual agency is to consider the writer as the first reader, transformed by the text as he or she encounters himself or herself as its author. Although the existence of the author prior to the text may seem a given, a moment's reflection confirms that, in the process of writing, the writer is transformed into the author of the text he or she has written. The case of Milton is an example. The author of *Eikonoklastes* and *Defensio Pro Populo Anglicano* emerges unequivocally as a regicide – much less ambiguously so than the author who began those works. Of course it is possible that Milton held these views before he wrote his polemics, but the fact remains that the act of writing entails placing whatever views he held within a determined textual universe, and publishing the texts bound Milton to them. In fact, the publication of these texts would turn out to be a decisive public moment for John Milton. Earning him some anxious time in hiding and a brief incarceration at the Restoration, they committed him irreversibly to the republican cause.[5] This public commitment may or may not also have been a decisive private moment; but, for the sake of illustration, it is not difficult to imagine the author of these texts, one English, the other Latin, following not only his arguments, but the internal logic of his tropes and schemes and transforming into the confirmed regicide in the course of the writing. In so far as he set out to persuade others that regicide was right, Milton engaged also to persuade himself. Even an argument cynically advanced, if constructed to persuade, must be judged by its writer on its persuasiveness to himself.

In writing his name on *Eikonoklastes* and the *Defensio*, which were undertaken not on his own initiative, but on behalf of the government that employed him, Milton identified publicly and, quite likely, privately, with the writer who supported the execution of the King. He thus put in play, as lived experience, the commonplace metonymy whereby we call a book by its author's name in expressions like: "Would you hand me *The Norton Shakespeare* please?" or "Remember to bring the *Milton* to class tomorrow." Milton's royalist and Presbyterian opponents looked forward to the day when he would be "brought to book" for writing the regicide tracts; the metonymy attained ominous ontological force on 29 August 1660, when, with Milton in hiding, his books were publicly burned by the hangman at the Old Bailey.[6]

This was not the first time Milton was brought to book for his published writing. Five years before the regicide, on 13 August 1644, his divorce tracts were attacked in a sermon before Parliament by Herbert Palmer, a prominent member of the Westminster Assembly. A petition sent to the Commons on 24 August by the Stationers' Company was referred to the Committee on Printing on 26 August, with instructions to "inquire out the Author, Printers and Publishers of the Pamphlet … concerning Divorce." When Milton responded by attacking the statute intended to suppress unlicensed pamphlets like *The Doctrine and Discipline of Divorce*, the commonplace metonymy of cause for effect that allows us to name the work by its author extended its ontological reach through a famous trope: the metaphoric identification of writing and sexual procreation in *Areopagitica:* "For Books are not absolutely dead things, but doe contain a potencie of life in them to be as active as that soule was whose progeny they are; nay they do preserve as in a violl the purest efficacie and extraction of that living intellect that bred them" (*Areopagitica, CP* 2, 492).

Milton goes on, again famously, to say that to destroy a good book is to kill "the Image of God, as it were, in the eye" (ibid.). The seminal book, then, represents not the material image of a man but the creative word of which men are made. It is the man *in potentia*, and as such it is form awaiting matter, an unrealized thought that enters print as an individual enters life – determined by parentage and historical situation, but undetermined with respect to the lifetime of choices that lie ahead. The metaphor of the unprinted book as the fetal state of authorial progeny underlines the notion that the processes of writing and publishing are interactive, neither the author nor the book is completed until the book-child emerges into the light, is read and elicits response. The unprinted book as the "image of God in the eye" can be no less than consciousness of self as the consequence of reasoned choice. Its author's posterity waits upon the vicissitudes of his offspring sent into the world. In very practical terms, then, the book becomes the cause of its author. This exchange of cause for effect is evident in the considerable branch of modern criticism that continues to advance competing claims for Milton's affinity – as a religious radical or a liberal champion of civil society, a revolutionary actor in the class struggle or a bourgeois cog in history's march toward the corporate state, who, if he were alive today, would be a militant feminist or a raging opponent of female emancipation. These critical inventions and reinventions of Milton exist only because there is no Milton to whom we have access, save the one caused by what he wrote and what is written about him. Each of our critically constructed Miltons exists in one or more of a determinate but undetermined multiplicity of universes capable of being negotiated between text and reader.[8] This is emphatically not to say, in the popular argot of "the culture wars," that "anything goes," or that Milton is whatever an individual or a social interest wants him to be.[9] Quite the opposite: ethical reading mandates two constraints on the reader: 1) The range of possible universes generated by a text is determined by the text; that is, by what may be logically, rhetorically and grammatically construed, as much as possible without resort to a preconception of context or intention, though ideas of context and intention may be brought to bear as a second order of evidence. This is the province of close reading. Any claim made about a text should be supported by specifiable philological, rhetorical, grammatical or logical determinations. 2) An ethical reader accepts that once a range of possible universes has been construed, choices among them are his or her responsibility. Such choices represent preferences and ought to be justified or defended on ethical rather than ontological grounds. In other words, our contest is not over who Milton was, but over who he ought to have been. When we encounter two or more defensible readings of a given textual construction, we may either defer interpretation by recognizing what is strictly undecidable, or we may prefer the alternative we think conduces to a better world, while acknowledging that this choice is extrapolated from an undecidable text. A reading may be more or less answerable to the text but not to the presumed intention of a historically situated author.

Following a Platonic commonplace, Milton's metaphor in *Areopagitica* assigns an author the responsibility of a parent. If we are to take seriously the metaphoric identification of a child and a book, it follows that although our children may be our "image in the eye," before they are born, nevertheless we understand that they will gradually come to speak for themselves; we, as parents, do not own what they mean.[10] The sustainable critical claim is not "Milton agrees (or perniciously disagrees) with me," but "Milton's text can be literally construed as inviting sets of thoughts or lines of argument that I consider valuable in one way or deleterious in another."

By way of a more concentrated example, from a less overtly political author, we might consider the following crux in Othello's account of how he won the love of Desdemona:

> My story being done
> She gave me for my pains a world of sighs,
> She swore in faith 'twas strange, 'twas passing strange,
> 'Twas pitiful, 'twas wondrous pitiful;
> She wished she had not heard it, *yet she wished*
> That heaven had made her such a man.[11]

Jacobean syntax allows us to read *her* in this passage as either an indirect or a direct object of *made*. Either Desdemona wished that heaven had "made [for] her such a man [as Othello]," or that heaven had "made her [into or as] such a man." I suspect a philological argument could be made – citing the prevalence in the time of the dative without preposition in similar constructions – for the simpler, first reading. Desdemona finds an appropriately modest way to tell Othello that she desires him by displacing the desire from the individual to the class: "a man like him." The context supports this reading too, since Othello, who here recounts Desdemona's words, clearly understands her to want a man like him. But the price of this determination is to foreclose a possible universe in which Desdemona's desire for Othello includes a desire to acquire a masculine and exotic being whose radically contingent adventures are the antithesis of the enclosed life of a Venetian gentlewoman acting in accordance with her father's expectations. I do not know whether this spectral secondary reading falls within Shakespeare's intention or to what degree it would have been available to his audience. Similarly twinking syntax at the intersection of gender, desire and agency certainly occurs elsewhere in Shakespeare.[12] But the undecidable reading is neither willful, random nor without justification on the reader's part. It falls reasonably within the grammar of the text. We can say too that such a double reading is productive in terms of how we might read the play. One can generate sustained readings that take account of the interplay of desire to have and desire to be in the exchange of affections between Othello and Desdemona. Such a consideration extends also to Iago's emulous style of resentment and the overlap of gender and race in the play's construction of differences – General and ensign, wife and courtesan, Venetian and Moor, husband and father – so that one could argue that the ambiguity is integral to the design. Such an argument is only necessary, however, if we wish to attribute the ambiguity to Shakespeare; that is, if we want the text to cause one Shakespeare rather than another. Otherwise, we can say that the ambiguity, regardless of its status as authorial intention or conscious design element, or its availability to any particular audience – in Shakespeare's time or in ours – is clearly a feature of the text. The very fact that it generates discussion validates its efficacy. The strictest philologist could not say it is not there unless the construction was haunted by the possibility that it is. Rather than saying that Shakespeare remains the same and the text, subjected to the *distortions* of time, politics, linguistic change and cultural displacement, needs to be restored to its original determination, I believe we do better to say that the text remains the same. It is the author whom we construct as its posterior effect that constantly changes. The ethical efficacy of the literary text inheres in this collaboration of anterior and posterior causes through which the reader may potentially recognize himself or herself as among the text's over determined, yet legitimate, causes.

2.

Psychoanalytic transference suggests a paradigm of how this metaleptic exchange of cause and effect extends its functions in the experience of the reader. Because reading submits the present of speaking to the expectations of a represented speaker, it installs a peculiar temporality in the reader, who comes to locate him or herself by voicing the *I* of the text at the constantly moving intersections of anticipation and retrospection and self and other. The signifier, as Lacan remarks, "always anticipates meaning by unfolding its dimension before it."[13] Psychoanalytic transference may be understood as an analogous instance of affective-linguistic mediation. Lacan identified the structure of the unconscious as that of a language. Reading allows varied mediations of the text's language and that of the reader. Using psychoanalytic transference as a model for the reading and writing process, I am going to suggest that *the ethical moment of a text*, as opposed to *the determinative moment of choice* depicted in the text, lies not in choosing a reading – or conscious interpretation of the text – but rather in deferring that choice. The ethics of reading and writing dwell in the unfolding of possibilities that are never fully under control. Thus reading, like analysis, is interminable.

Transference in Freud's work takes three distinct forms.[14] Early on, Freud argues that the emotions attendant on a repressed trauma, although they are never consciously experienced, remain mobile in the unconscious. Because these archaic emotions remain unthought, without a narrative context to accommodate them to a "cause," they persist in the unconscious as what Freud called "unbound affect." They are felt in conscious life only when on occasion they are transferred to something in consciousness that lends itself to representing – though not disclosing – the repressed material. Freud first notices this transference of affect in dreams, when targets of opportunity in what he calls, elegantly, "the remains of the day" may be seized on to represent something in the latent – that is unconscious – dream thoughts.[15] While the traumatic cause of these emotions remains unconscious, the emotions themselves may gain access to consciousness by a transference that ascribes them – at least in part – to some conscious cause. The unbound affect is then bound to a conscious narrative that is not its cause but is, in fact, posterior to the affect itself. This mobility of emotion is facilitated when disparate chains of signifiers are imbricated, enabling associated feelings to jump from an unconscious chain of signifiers to a conscious one, the links of which are similarly configured. Rhetoric has long supplied the nomenclature for such enabling semantic transfers in its lexicon of tropes describing the paths by which one thing may come to be called by the name of another.[16]

When analyzing Dora's first dream, in the earliest of his case histories, Freud imagined the structural intersections joining one signifying chain to another as railroad switches across which affect jumps:

> Now, in a line of associations ambiguous words (or, as we may call them, "switch-words") act like points at a junction. If the points are switched across from the position in which they appear to lie in the dream, then we find ourselves upon another set of rails; and along this second track run the thoughts which we are in search of and which still lie concealed behind the dream.
>
> (Freud, *Fragment of an Analysis of a Case of Hysteria*, *SE* 7.65, n.3)

Lacan recognizes the rhetorical structure that underwrites the transfer of emotion from one track to another and rewrites the transfer of affect in terms that recall the rhetorical itinerary we encountered in Milton's *Areopagitica*. He identifies the mechanism underlying "the line of associations" as metonymy and that of the "points of junction" or "switch words" as metaphor (*Ecrits*, pp.156–59). The operative distinction here is between associations based on contiguity – one thing adjacent to another – and those based on resemblance – one thing like another.[17] Metonymies extend the tracks along which the semantic train rolls; metaphors establish the switches that allow it to cross from one track to another.[18]

Thus an early Freudian reading of *Hamlet* sees emotions arising from Hamlet's archaic oedipal associations become manifest in conscious life, when they are able to cross at the word *father*, from King Hamlet to Claudius.[19] However, it is not necessary to posit Hamlet's unwritten childhood to see the transference of emotion across a switch word dramatized in exchanges like this:

> Gertrude: Hamlet, thou hast thy father much offended.
> Hamlet: Mother, thou hast my father much offended.[20]

Hamlet resists the assimilation of Claudius to King Hamlet by redirecting the object of *offended* in Gertrude's sentence from Claudius to King Hamlet in his own. In doing so, he rejects, as he had in his first soliloquy, the implication that the word *father* can be deployed metaphorically to evoke a resemblance between the two brothers. Later in the scene, he reiterates this resistance by comparing pictures of King Hamlet and Claudius: "look here upon this picture, and on this, / The counterfeit presentment of two brothers" (3.4.53–54). That Polonius lies dead on the floor while Hamlet conducts the comparison further illustrates the potential violence of unthought emotions misdirected by metaphoric naming: "How now? A rat! Dead for a ducat, dead" (3.4.22). My point here is not to support an Oedipal reading of *Hamlet* but to indicate how Hamlet's resistance to a certain linguistic identification invokes the consequences of what is unsaid. By tracking the possible (and resisted) nominal assimilations of King Hamlet, Claudius and Polonius, we become aware of a textual unconscious without speculating about Hamlet's unconscious or its historical contents.[21]

Metaphor depends on a perception of impertinent predication. When the poet says, "My love is a rose," metaphor occurs only if the literal predication is rejected as impertinent. A neurotic, prevented by repression from recognizing the impertinence – for whom "a rose is a rose" – might present symptoms of *floraphilia*, which analysis could hope to resolve by eliciting from the unconscious the repressed tenor of the metaphor. But, as will become clear in what follows, the tenor thus elicited need not be a *literal* fact of memory; a serviceable fantasy, itself a secondary metaphor, will do as well.

In this respect, the truth of desire inheres not in the desired object but in the formal (and temporal) structure that situates it with respect to the subject. Hamlet treats the appellation of *father* to Claudius as impertinent, because Claudius is not literally (or biologically) his father; but he also rejects the metaphoric assimilation of Claudius to King Hamlet within the parallel classes of kings of Denmark and husbands of Gertrude, which it implies. Claudius is neither his father nor can he be understood to resemble his father. The issue is not whether Hamlet is arrested by a repressed childhood memory of his father – any more than it would be the discovery of a traumatic rose in the history of our hypothetical floraphiliac. Rather it is the formal structures of trauma and transfer by which King Hamlet and King Claudius, the historical and the metaphorical rose, are assimilated one to the other. These structures inhere not in a putative memory of the past but in the present encoding of the text. We use our awareness of a text haunted by a set of implied but unspoken alternative locutions to make sense of what we read against a background of what we may have read. Thus, without imputing textual features to a putative cause distinct from the text, we can see that the transference of emotion across words in a text correlates two or more contemporaneous and specifiable representations.

Unlike readers, the psychoanalyst aims to elicit the unthought associations that comprise an unconscious by working back through the distorted form in which they have reached consciousness. Bringing the repressed past into the discursive present is the putatively therapeutic work of "the talking cure." However, I have tried to demonstrate with the previous example that becoming aware of the configurations on which stray emotions map does not require constructing a narrative memory of some originary trauma. What psychoanalysts call "repetition automaton," for example, may also be understood as the circulation of emotion between two linked chains, in which the rhetorical scheme of an earlier chain unconsciously configures succeeding engagements according to a pattern similar to its own. Freud called these pre-emptive configurations, "complexes." I have been at pains to show that the recovery of the repressed memory that formed the complex is a separate issue from the recognition of its rhetorical structure. Once the complex is established the structure is constant, the content variable – until it becomes available to conscious thought.

Transfer of affect is a general mechanism of the mobility of emotion, a way to explain, for example, why neurotics invest certain seemingly trivial objects, events, or performances, with apparently disproportionate import-ance. The talking cure, itself, relies on a form of transference specific to it. This specifically analytic transference occurs, during the course of analysis, when the analysand comes to identify the analyst with a significant figure in the repressed drama from which his or her putatively archaic emotions derive. This identification is not a matter of mistaking the analyst for the repressed figure but of placing the analyst structurally in the position once held by the analysand so as to *project* onto the analyst emotions originally evoked by the figure he or she has come to represent. Freud at first thought this phenomenon, which he experienced as illusory love or hate directed toward him by his patients, represented the most difficult to overcome of the resistances.[22] Later, however, he came to see the transference as an essential element of the analytic process. Identification of the analyst with a key figure from the past enabled the analysand not simply to recall what had been repressed but to "work through" or experience the free-floating emotions attached to it. "Remembering" and "working through" in this way bind these emotions and allow them to be discharged into conscious memory, thus freeing the neurotic, for example, from repetition compulsion in which the emotion is bound by endlessly repeating the configuration of the unremembered scene in various opaque representations.[23] So I come by this circuitous route to something that shares the general shape of Aristotle's melioristic view of tragedy, in which by identifying with the tragic hero, the spectator is able to purge himself of pity and fear, to achieve as Milton puts it in *Samson Agonistes,* "calm of mind, all passion spent."[24]

3.

To further explore this coalition of Aristotle and Freud I propose to investigate what sort of transference might be in play when, in the front matter of *Samson Agonistes,* we read Milton reading Aristotle. Milton's tragedy "never intended for the stage" first appeared in a peculiarly constructed volume printed by John Starkey, in 1671. The title page of this volume reads *Paradise Regained. A Poem. In IV Books. To which is added Samson Agonistes.* Following the text of *Paradise Regained,* a second title page introduces "*Samson Agonistes. A Dramatic Poem* / The Author John Milton." Two epigraphs appear on this page. The first epigraph is an abbreviated excerpt from the definition of tragedy in the *Poetics* V (1449b) given in Greek: "*tragôidia mimêsis praxeôs spoudaias, &c.*" The second epigraph repeats and slightly expands the first, but this time in Latin: "*Tragœdia est imitatio actionis seriæ, &c. Per misericordiam & metum perficiens talium affectuum lustrationem.*"

To complicate the picture further, on the page following, Milton's *Preface,* "Of that Sort of Dramatic Poem which is Called Tragedy," begins by paraphrasing a still larger portion of the same passage, yet again; this time in English:

> Tragedy, as it was anciently composed, hath been ever held the gravest, moralist, and most profitable of all other poems: therefore said by Aristotle to be of power by raising pity and fear, or terror, to purge the mind of those and such like passions, that is to temper and reduce them to just measure with a kind of delight, stirred up by reading or seeing those passions well-imitated.
>
> (Leonard, p. 463)

Why would Milton repeat the same information in three different languages? To answer this question would be to engage on some level the nature of Milton's desire. This question of desire not only is, but *ought* to remain, unanswerable. However, by tracking what happens to the theory of catharsis as Aristotle's words journey through time, language and space in the front matter of *Samson Agonistes*, we can learn something of the structure of desire in relation to the *ethos* both of Milton's Samson and of the author we might choose to deduce from the poem.

By way of example, I am going to engage two small details of Milton's repeated, and repeatedly translated, epigraphs: the translations of Aristotle's *katharsis*, as *lustratio* in Milton's Latin version and then as *purging* in his English paraphrase, and the puzzling substitution of *passions* for *actions*, in the Preface, where Aristotle's "*mimêsis praxeôs spoudaias*," which Milton rendered into Latin as "*imitatio actionis seriæ*," becomes "*passions well-imitated*." *Katharsis*, in the *Poetics*, appears to refer specifically to the purging or cleansing of emotions from the spectators at a tragedy, and thus directly answers Plato's objections to the theater in, among other places, the *Republic*.[25] The word appears in the Greek corpus in sacrificial contexts, but with purely medical references as well.[26] The English *purge* in Milton's paraphrase answers well to the original it translates, and the following sentence emphasizes the physiological aspect of the word: "Nor is nature wanting in her own effects to make good [Aristotle's] assertion: for so in physic things of melancholic hue and quality are used against melancholy, sour against sour, salt to remove salt humours" (Leonard, p. 453). *Lustratio*, in the intervening Latin version, however, appears to have had a somewhat more restricted use. Lewis and Short define it as "a purification by sacrifice, a lustration," and the adjectival form, lustral(e), appears in the phrase *aqua lustrale* (Liv. 1, 28) in which Milton's contemporaries likely would have heard something like "holy water." Now, I am not saying that Milton was unprecedented or overly strategic in choosing *lustratio* to translate *katharsis*. Given its Roman associations, it is also not hard to imagine why he might avoid *purgatio* in the Latin epigraph, while choosing its English cognate for the Preface. But whatever the motive, the Latin epigraph on the title page of *Samson Agonistes* tropes the classical text in the direction of Milton's Christian narrative. This little bit of work is erased in the English paraphrase, which, it should be noted, opens a Preface that explicitly engages the vexed incongruity of writing a Christian tragedy. To state it grandly, then, the three versions of Aristotle recapitulate an ecclesiastical history also marked by the passage of scripture from Greek to Latin to English and the appearance and disappearance of purgatory.

This final point brings me briefly to the supplementary and anachronological position of the tragedy in *Paradise Regained. A Poem. In IV Books. To which is added Samson Agonistes*, because *Samson Agonistes* is precisely not a Christian tragedy, but a Hebrew one. Like Aristotle's pagan *Poetics* it cannot (for Milton) be properly understood in its native languages until it has been illuminated by a Roman light in Jerusalem from which it is subsequently purified. *Samson Agonistes* retells the story from Judges of a Nazarite, consecrated at birth to the service of God, who, in the end, strikes down the supporting columns of the Temple of Dagon, and in the process meets his own cruciform death. In Milton's characteristically typological reading, the story makes sense in its time but yields its full meaning only when illuminated by the subsequent events anticipated in it. We have then a parallel set of two actions purported to have transpired at different times in the same geographical region constituting a structural repetition through four linguistic and dispensational mediations. The Hebrew story of Samson in ancient Gaza is to be understood as a repetition before the fact of the Greek Gospel accounts of the acts of Jesus in Roman-occupied Jerusalem, which were mediated to Europe, first in the Latin of the Vulgate and then in the vernacular bibles of the reformation. The temporal complication requires an effort of understanding. By placing the chronologically later story first, Milton's volume provides to the reader the antitype that Samson could not have known. The reader is placed in the position of the analysand who recovers and restructures an archaic trauma through the mediation of a later representation. The knowledge of Christ forever bars the reader from the experience of Samson, which can therefore be recovered only in the register of fantasy.

In the second of the details I want to look at, we may see the deferred action of typology verbally enacted as a collapse in the distinction between the cause and effect of representation. Milton translates Aristotle's "*tragôidia mimêsis praxeôs spoudaias*" first as "*imitatio actionis seriæ*" and then as "passions well-imitated." The Latin translation of *praxeôs* as *actionis* is unexceptional. However, the substitution of *passions* for *actions* in the Preface again tropes Aristotle in a specific direction. On a purely verbal level "passions well-imitated" brings forward Milton's plan to represent Samson's catastrophe as a prefiguration of Christ's passion. But more interesting is the way the translation accommodates the typological gap between the two events as a shift from active to passive – from *praxeôs* to *pathos*. The catastrophic action imitated in *Samson Agonistes* is clearly an act. Samson pushes out the pillars that support the roof. But Samson's "heroic" and sacrificial action is represented as a premature imitation (both representation and anticipation) of "deeds above heroic" that will have been made comprehensible by Christ's inaction and suffering on the cross.[27] Milton's pathos-*para-praxeôs* suspends the heroism of deed in and behind – before and after – the moment of its putative sublimation into the "better fortitude" of Christ's *passion*.

Milton's 1671 volume is a Christian book, but the Hebrew decorum of *Samson Agonistes* is treated seriously, Samson's knowledge of God is mediated by the law and his two attempts to transcend the law through direct intuition have been his disastrous (and violent) marriages to gentile women (a situation Milton discusses in *Tetrachordon* and *Colasterion*). Samson is separated from the Christian reader by the reader's anti-typal knowledge and the putative presence of the in-dwelling spirit. The reader, turning the page from Jesus's return "private to his mother's house" at the end of *Paradise Regained* to discover the poly-epigraphed title page of *Samson Agonistes*, meets a public man who understands his Nazerite mission, precisely in terms of the letter, as to throw off the coercive power of the Philistines – an understanding which, from the reader's point of view, Jesus will have rejected, just a few pages earlier. I think, Milton's Samson is both heroic and a failure. He fails to transcend the letter because Jesus has not yet come to enlighten it, but he is heroic because he wagers eternity on inward motions he cannot verify. But to be heroic is not necessarily to be a hero. He succeeds because, in meta-historical terms, the origins of his internal promptings do not matter. By acting out the type he has established the retrospective frame in which *Paradise Regained* is read. Samson therefore serves God, even by failing him. The poignant picture of the blinded and captive insurgent at the poem's opening makes Samson available as a figure of the recently failed English revolution and of the blind poet "fallen on evil days." Samson tried to seize state power, got a lot of people killed and failed – even in death – to dislodge the Philistines. When restructured through the deferred action of *Paradise Regained*, however, the story changes. Samson becomes, as Manoa had predicted, a signifier – but not locally, through a monument to rally the Hebrew youth to armed resistance. Rather he shows how risky it is to serve God; but also and more importantly, his typological narrative demonstrates that even if the good old cause is not validated by victory, even if it turns out that it was indeed too good to be fought for, it has not been extinguished. The public men of the interregnum are gone, but the revolution continues its work "in private houses."[28]

The ethical question I wish to raise is not whether Milton is justified in translating Aristotle as he does – whether his translation is correct or not – but rather the agency or efficacy of the translation in reconfiguring the language of Milton and his reader and the choices made by author and reader in accepting or resisting the agency of the text. To examine this triangular relation of author, text and reader I want to extend the model of transference one more step to include what came to be called the counter transference: the reciprocating effect of analysis on the analyst, his or her projection of emotions onto the analysand. An analyst, like a reader, must recognize that his or her unconscious is submitted to modification by its engagement with that of another. Lacan understands the reciprocal trans-actions of transference in relation to fantasies of knowing. He argues that in the transference, the analysand, wishing to engage the desire of the analyst, may produce associations of which (he or she thinks) the analyst will approve. The analysand seeks, that is, to persuade the analyst that the analysis is going somewhere, or, in literary terms, that it is heading toward narrative closure. If the desire of the analyst is for the truth and the analysand wishes, therefore, to produce the truth to satisfy this desire, he or she first constructs the analyst as the one who knows the truth and so can distinguish progress from resistance, analytic work from evasion. Transference occurs when the analyst is presumed to know; yet what the analyst is presumed to know is the unconscious desire of the analysand. Similarly, in counter transference, an analyst, whose desire is, indeed, the patient's truth, might presume that the patient knows the truth and produces or withholds it so as to express pleasure or displeasure with the analyst. It is the task of the analyst to refuse both positions. The analyst understands that although the truth – that is, the true path of his or her desire – is in the analysand, it is not known to the analysand or by the analyst, nor will it be known except by the mediation of its signifier. The temptation of the counter transference is interpretation. To interpret is to presume to know, and a premature interpretation forecloses the unconscious from which the structure of the truth may become manifest. For Lacan, the mutual projection of desires that comprises the transference is a kind of love: "[W]hat is there, behind the love known as transference, is the affirmation of the link between the desire of the analyst and the desire of the patient. ... It is the patient's desire, yes, but in its meeting with analyst's desire."[29]

John Rajchman spells out the ethical import of this love, in terms that curiously recapitulate the sublimating journey from Greek to Latin to English that we have traced in the front matter of *Samson Agonistes*:

> In Lacan's eyes, analysis would be the form of love which never supposes that it knows what is good for someone else. ... In this way, it would be distinguished from *philia* and *caritas*. For *philia* is a love that brings men together in the knowledge of the good that is the same in each of us, and *caritas* supposes a knowledge of salvation or grace. ... Psychoanalysis is a form of love that is not based in those ideal parts of ourselves that would allow us to master our fate or to obtain salvation. On the contrary, it would open up even our first love, our love of ourselves, to a traumatic and fateful cause.[30]

This cause is inherent to the traumatic stitching of our desire to our selves. At once historical, radically contingent and non-signifying, it is the result of our coming to represent ourselves to ourselves by interposing a symbolic representation between us and the unmediated self-presence we never had, but whose absence we retrospectively construct. I propose a similar engagement with literature.

What will it mean to love the text in this way? Perhaps the hint of an answer may be found in Milton's misprision of *praxeôs* as *passions*. We have already considered what might be termed the ideology of this translation. By substituting *passion* for *action*, however, Milton also collapses the cause and effect of the passions to be discharged through catharsis. For Aristotle, the tragic mythos imitates actions so as to arouse and then purge passions. But in

Milton's English version it is passions themselves that are imitated. What is performed by this strangely collapsing exchange? Is this Milton's counter-transference onto the Aristotelian text to which he has been listening? It is not an interpretation or a correction, but rather a repetition of the *Poetics*, supplemented by a slight slippage that overlays it with Milton's desire of that other Greek, Latin, English text – the Gospels – which he returns to Aristotle in this inverted form. And yet, the passion of another can only be manifest in his or her actions. Milton's elision of action in favor of the higher fortitude of suffering is an oddly non-signifying object of imitation, a silence calling forth some private working-through as opposed to a heroically repetitive acting out.[31] I submit that the ethical moment of a text, as opposed to the deter-minative moment of choice depicted in the text, lies not in choosing a reading but in deferring that choice, not in generating a mythos to fill the silence, but in holding its space sublimely open. The ethical position with respect to the text is neither remembering nor repeating, but working-through the silence of that which does not appear.

Deferring the interpretation implies, not a refusal to interpret, but an admission that interpretation is an action, a decision that determines not the text but me in relation to my desire for and of the text. I do not think that Milton thought the text open in this way, but Milton operated with an epistemology based on absolute truth that is not available to me and which I choose not to allow to my contemporaries. I admire in Milton that his texts generally allow me to distinguish between what he may have wanted – in the case of *Samson Agonistes* and *Paradise Regained*, action against the restored monarchy, an underground movement for spiritual freedom along Quaker lines – and his implicit diagnoses of the ethical risks involved.[32] I think it likely that Milton's desires lie in relating his historical moment as he understood it to the two moments represented in the 1671 volume – geographically the front matter of *Samson Agonistes* lies between Jesus's moment, after the failure of zealous action on the national level, and Samson's moment of trying to foment such action; for Milton, the epistemology of Samson is radically open until it is anti-typically completed in the other testament, and, perhaps, so is that of the English revolution, which, like Jesus at the end of *Paradise Regained*, must, in the restoration, return to its mother's private house – to work in the earth like Marx's old mole. Was the good old cause too good to be fought for? Not if it can survive in the wilderness and prepare its militant return. But whether or not the questions raised are resolved in Milton's mind does not change the fact that his text includes a profound understanding of the possibility that Samson may be wrong, that action may both risk everything *and* be necessary. The parallel moment for interpretation (with milder stakes for now) is to recognize that the text is open to different readings. Deferral, then, does not mean not interpreting, but rather taking responsibility for one's interpretation without soliciting Milton's authority to arbitrate it.

This view of the ethics of interpretation entails recognizing one's own

desire in its meeting with Milton's desire as mediated by the text. Such recognition brings the reader's ethos into focus. If I choose one Milton among a
number of possibilities, it is not because I am committed to an unchanging
truth, vested in an author prior to the text that bears his name, but because I
believe that one reading in someway leads to a better world than another. If,
for example, I find joy in the patriarchal elements of *Paradise Lost,* I ought to
ask myself what attracts me to them. I find Milton's text an ethical one,
because it records both patriarchy and resistance to patriarchy.[33] Neither
Samson Agonistes nor I can say definitively whether Samson is a hero or a fool.
Milton never tells us whether the inward motions that initiate the catastrophe
are from God or from Samson. But what I think and how I feel about a man
who acts as Milton's Samson does can help discover the transferential *ēthos*
that passes between us. Reading *Samson Agonistes* thus provides an opportunity
to think through my desires in terms of the alternatives it presents. The
efficacy of textual ethics in relation to my reading depends on my taking the
opportunity to think through my desire as it is revealed in the encounter with
the text. As long as the text is construed in its details, my interpretive preferences are my responsibility. If I am wrong in my understanding of a word, an
allusion, a grammatical construction, I ought to be corrected. But there will
still be choices to make that are both faithful to the text and open to
preferences that enlighten my understanding of myself. I am interrogated by
the text, and I may be called upon to change.

Now, I am aware that in the foregoing I have at times spoken of "Milton's
counter transference" and "Milton's elision of action," despite my having
earlier proscribed such notions of a "Milton" prior to his texts. Who, then, is
this "Milton" to whom I refer authorial choices against my own directions?
He is the "Milton supposed to know," for whom I must take responsibility.
His appearance, here, at the end (though not the completion) of analysis
marks a continuing transference. Surely there is, even in the front matter of
Samson Agonistes, "a potencie of life … as active as that soule was whose
progeny they are." But to think that one can reason back from the child to
the father is a disservice to the child – and to the reader who, in the meeting
of his own desires and the desires disposed in the text, becomes, at least for a
moment, the child of that child – as Milton must have, when his verses were
read to him and he discovered whom he wrote.

Notes

A first and much shorter draft of this chapter was presented to a seminar on translation
and ethics at the 2002 meeting of the American Comparative Literature Association
in San Juan. In expanding and reworking it, I have benefited greatly from the advice
and suggestions of friends and colleagues. In particular, the contributions of Theodore
B. Leinwand, Victoria Kahn, Vivienne Westbrook and Gordon Teskey require
grateful acknowledgment.

1 Jacques Lacan, *The Four-Fundamental Concepts of Psycho-Analysis*, ed. Jacques-Alain Miller, trans. Alan Sheridan (New York: Norton, 1978), p. 253.

2 Slavoj Žižek, *The Sublime Object of Ideology* (London: Verso, 1989), p. 185. [Žižek's emphasis.]

3 This case for the configuring agency of texts is made in detail in my *The Story of All Things: Writing the Self in English Renaissance Narrative Poetry* (Durham, NC: Duke University Press, 1998).

4 See Jonathan Culler, "Fabula and Sjuzhet in the Analysis of Narrative: Some American Considerations," *Poetics Today* 1 (1980): 27–37. A story unfolds as one thing after another, and moves toward a denouement that discloses the sequence as one thing because of another. "Introduction to the Structural Analysis of Narrative," *Image, Music, Text*, trans. Stephen Heath (Boston, MA: Hill and Wang, 1977), pp. 79–124.

5 A month-by-month summary of events befalling Milton at the Restoration may be found in Gordon Campbell, *A Milton Chronology* (London: Macmillan, 1997), pp. 190–94. For narrative accounts, see William Riley Parker, *Milton: A Biography*, 2 vols (Oxford: Clarendon, 1968), 1, pp. 567–87, and Barbara K. Lewalski, *The Life of Milton: A Critical Biography* (Oxford: Blackwell, 2000), pp. 398–404. Milton remained in hiding from early May, 1660 until the King's Assent to the Act of Oblivion on August 29th. On June 16th an order for his arrest was issued and his books were removed from the Bodleian. On August 29th Milton's books were publicly burned by the hangman at the Old Bailey. In October, he was arrested and briefly incarcerated.

6 Milton was the object of continual invective by Royalist writers, who attributed his blindness to divine retribution for his anti-monarchial tracts. John Heydon, for example, achieves a notable historical specificity by reporting that Milton was struck blind by God as he wrote the second word of *Eikonoklastes* (*The Idea of Law Charactered* [June, 1660], cited in Campbell, *A Milton Chronology*, p. 191).

7 Ernest Sirluck, "Introduction," in *Complete Prose Works of John Milton*, ed. Don M. Wolfe *et al.* (New Haven: Yale University Press, 1953–82), 2, p. 142. This edition of Milton's prose is hereafter cited as *CP*.

8 On the contested inventions and reinventions of Milton, see John Rumrich, *Milton Unbound: Controversy and Reinterpretation* (Cambridge: Cambridge University Press, 1996).

9 For a clear and lucid refutation of the "anything goes" position, see Jacques Lacan, *The Four-Fundamental Concepts of Psycho-Analysis*, pp. 251–52.

10 Plato, *The Phaedrus*, 274c–275e. Plato's Socrates rejects writing for the very reason that Milton praises publication: the written text, speaking without the supplemental presence of the writer, can provoke ideas unthought of at its composition. On Plato's distrust of writing, see Jacques Derrida, "Plato's Pharmacy," in *Dissemination*, trans. Barbara Johnson (Chicago, IL: University of Chicago Press, 1981), pp. 61–171. The uncanny resemblance of Milton's seminal metaphor to elements of Derrida's deployment of "dissemination" against the paternal metaphors of the *Phaedrus* suggests the possibility of a latently ironic reading of Plato, awaiting its theory at least since 1644. More generous than Derrida's theory, Milton's rhetorical practice validates as it refutes – allowing Plato's metaphors to express themselves in *Areopagitica*'s contradictory conclusions.

11 William Shakespeare, *Othello*, ed. E.A.J. Honigmann, The Arden Edition, 3rd series (Mayfield on Thames: Thomson, 1998), 1.3.158–64. [Emphasis mine.]

12 Notably in sonnet 20.9–12: "And *for* a woman wert thou first created, / Till nature as she wrought thee fell a-doting, / And by addition thee of me defeated, / By

adding one thing to my purpose nothing." *Shakespeare's Sonnets,* ed. Katherine Duncan-Jones, The Arden Shakespeare (London: Thomas Nelson, 1997) [my emphasis]. At the level of dramatic discourse, one sees this strategically ambiguous syntax also in the structure of the plot of *Twelfth Night,* in which the audience's attention is riveted to the figure of Viola, enacted by a boy, pretending to be a girl, pretending to be a man. See also, *Macbeth* 1.3.139–41: "My thought, whose murther is yet fantastical, / Shakes so my single state of man, / That function is smother'd in surmise," where "murther" appears to be the partitive genitive of "thought" ("my thought of murder is only a fantasy"), but "thought" can also be construed as the object of "murther" ("the murder of my thought is still a fantasy"). The undecidable reading is nicely recapitulated by the line that closes the passage: "And nothing is, but what it not" (1.3.142). *Macbeth,* ed. Kenneth Muir, The Arden Edition (1951, Methuen, rpt. Mayfield on Thames: Thomson, 1997).

13 "The agency of the letter in the unconscious or reason since Freud," *Ecrits: A Selection,* trans. Alan Sheridan (New York: Norton, 1977), p. 153.

14 For a succinct and useful account of the development of the theories of transference, see the entry for *Transference* in J. Laplanche and J.-B. Pontalis, *The Language of Psychoanalysis,* trans. Donald Nicholson-Smith (New York: Norton, 1973).

15 *The Interpretation of Dreams* in *The Standard Edition of the Edition of the Complete Psychological Works of Sigmund Freud,* trans. James and Alix Strachey, 24 vols (London: Hogarth, 1953–73), 5, p. 562. This edition is hereafter cited as *SE.*

16 For an illuminating and thorough examination of the way tropes can redescribe experience, see Paul Ricoeur, *The Rule of Metaphor: Multi-Disciplinary Studies in the Creation of Meaning in Language,* trans. Robert Czerny, with Kathleen McLaughlin and John Costello (Toronto: University of Toronto Press, 1977).

17 Lacan thus follows the distinction between metonymy as figure of contiguity and metaphor as figure of resemblance made by Roman Jakobson in Roman Jakobson and Morris Halle, *Fundamentals of Language* (The Hague: Mouton, rev., 1975), pp. 72–76.

18 For a more nuanced and detailed discussion of this rhetorical interaction, see *The Story of All Things,* pp. 34–55.

19 Ernest Jones, *Hamlet and Oedipus* (London: Gollancz, 1949).

20 William Shakespeare, *Hamlet,* ed. Harold Jenkins, The Arden Edition (London: Methuen, 1982), 3.4.8–9.

21 Lacan distinguishes between the contingent associations that may occur in the course of speaking and those which are established in the structure of language in the unconscious:

> [Freud] understood and formulated admirably the distinction to be made between the operation of language as a function – namely, the moment when it is articulated and, in effect, plays an essential role in the preconscious – and the structure of language, as a result of which those elements put in play in the unconscious are organized. In between, those coordinations are set up, those *Bahnungen* [facilitations], that concatenation, which dominate its whole economy.
>
> (*The Seminar of Jacques Lacan, Book VII: The Ethics of Psychoanalysis 1959–1960* ed. Jacques-Alain Miller, trans. Dennis Porter (New York: Norton, 1992), p. 45)

Such facilitated pathways are similarly established in the literary text. For example, Hamlet's iterated references to post-mortem decay of the body not only establish a connection, specific to him, between death and disgust; they also pave paths of association connecting the various contexts in which they occur. These pathways are, properly speaking, features of the text. On a more thoroughly structural level, *Hamlet*, the play, is marked by an intricate network of doubled chiasmi that almost silently direct traffic through its associative interchanges. This argument is further developed in my "*Hamlet* and the Genders of Grief," in *Grief and Gender, 700–1700*, ed. Lynne Dickson Bruckner and Jennifer C. Vaught (New York: Palgrave, 2003), pp. 176–93.

22   "The Dynamics of Transference," in *SE* 12, pp. 97–108.

23   "Remembering, Repeating and Working-Through," in *SE* 12, pp. 145–56. On transference and repetition, see also, *Beyond the Pleasure Principle*, in *SE* 18, pp. 18–23. The process of binding emotion through unconscious repetition underlies the classic readings by Freud and Jones of *Hamlet* as a reenactment of unresolved oedipal passions. In *The Interpretation of Dreams*, Freud remarks that:

> Hamlet is capable of doing anything – except take vengeance on the man who did away with his father and took that father's place with his mother, the man who shows him the repressed wishes of his own childhood realized. Thus the loathing which should drive him on to revenge is replaced by self-reproaches, by scruples of conscience, which remind him that he himself is literally no better than the sinner whom he is to punish.
>
> (*SE* 4, p. 265)

See also, *Introductory Lectures on Psychoanalysis*, XXI:

> But let us now turn from the direct observation of children to the analytic examination of adults who have become neurotic. What help does analysis give towards a further knowledge of the Oedipus Complex? ... Analysis ... shows that each of these neurotics has himself been an Oedipus or, what comes to the same thing, has, as a reaction to the complex, become a Hamlet.
>
> (*SE* 16, p. 335)

24   Aristotle, *Poetics*, 1449b; Milton, *Samson Agonistes*, line 1759, cited from *John Milton: The Complete Poems*, ed. John Leonard (New York: Penguin Books, 1998); subsequent references to Milton's poetry are to this edition, hereafter cited as Leonard; see also, Jacques Lacan, "The Tragic Dimension of Psychoanalytic Experience," in *The Seminar of Jacques Lacan, Book VII: The Ethics of Psychoanalysis 1959–1960*, pp. 289–325. This and the preceding two paragraphs repeat material presented in a different context in Marshall Grossman, "The Onomastic Destiny of Stanley Fish," *Milton in the Age of Fish: Essays on Authorship, Text, and Terrorism*, ed. Michael Lieb and Albert C. Labriola (Pittsburgh, PA: Duquesne University Press, 2006), pp. 45–46.

25   D.W. Lucas cites *Republic*, pp. 605C–606B, where:

> Plato's strictures on the moral weakness caused by indulgence in epic and tragedy suggest that the audience luxuriated in the community sorrow, "surrendering itself" to lamentation and taking part in the mourning along with actors and chorus. ... As an answer to Plato's strictures the theory of *katharsis* is a triumphant success; so far are we from pandering to our emotional frailty when we visit the theatre that we actually strengthen our emotional resistance ready for the trials of real life.
>
> (Aristotle, *Poetics*, with intro., commentary and appendixes by D.W. Lucas [Oxford: Clarendon, 1968], Appendix II, "Pity, Fear and Katharsis," pp. 273, 283)

26 See entries for Kathario and Katharsis, in Henry George Liddell and Robert Scott, *A Greek-English Lexicon,* rev. and augmented by Sir Henry Stuart Jones with the assistance of Roderick McKenzie (Oxford: Clarendon, 1940, rpt. 1951). Liddell and Scott cite the passage from the *Poetics* to exemplify the medical use of the term: "*clearing off of morbid humours,* etc., *evacuation,* whether natural or by the use of medicines." Aristotle's sentence specifies the humors to be cleared off or evacuated by the mythos of the tragedy: *eleos* (pity) and *phobos* (fear). See also, Lucas, "Pity, Fear and Katharsis":

> The verb *kathairo* means to "cleanse" or "remove impurities." The impurities may consist of visible dirt or of invisible sacral contaminations ... With the growth of medical science in the fifth century the word came naturally to be applied to the removal or evacuation of morbid substances from the human system. Finally *kathairo* was used in a sense partly religious, partly medical, for the psycho-therapeutic treatment of emotional disorders by ritual and music. (p. 276)

27 Stanley Fish, "Inaction and Silence: The Reader in *Paradise Regained,*" in Joseph A. Wittreich, Jr., ed., *Calm of Mind: Tercentenary Essays on Paradise Regained and Samson Agonistes* (Cleveland, OH: Case Western Reserve University Press, 1971), pp. 25–47.

28 See Gary Hamilton, "*Paradise Regained* and Private Houses," in P.G. Stanwood, ed., *Of Poetry and Politics: New Essays on Milton and His World* (Binghamton, NY: Medieval & Renaissance Texts & Studies, 1995).

29 Lacan, *Four Fundamental Concepts of Psycho-Analysis,* p. 254.

30 John Rajchman, *Truth and Eros: Foucault, Lacan, and the Question of Ethics* (New York: Routledge, 1991), p. 43.

31 The resemblance of this non-signifying object to what Lacan calls the "not all" of feminine *jouissance* (Seminar 20) suggests a direction for further exploration of the literary text as both subjected to and eluding the phallic function. See my "The Rhetoric of Feminine Priority in *Paradise Lost,*" *ELR* 33 (2003): 394–413.

32 On *Samson Agonistes,* see Victoria Kahn, Chapter 5, this volume. I am indebted for whatever clarity is achieved in this and the following paragraph to the probing and sympathetic questions put by Victoria Kahn in response to an earlier version of this essay.

33 I discuss the resistance of Milton's text to its own patriarchal assumptions in *The Story of All Things,* chapter 7.

5 Aesthetics as critique

Tragedy and *Trauerspiel* in *Samson Agonistes*

Victoria Kahn

> Compassion is disreputable.
> Adorno and Horkheimer

> Forgive us if we seem heartless.
> Brecht

It is one of the ironies of literary history that Milton's place in the history of aesthetics has been largely determined by eighteenth-century readers who praised the stylistic sublimity of *Paradise Lost*. As Nicholas von Maltzahn has recently argued, this "aestheticizing" reading of Milton's forceful style to the exclusion of all else resulted in the depoliticization and secularization of his work. Milton, that is, was one of our first victims of aesthetic ideology: against his own stringent emphasis on ethical deliberation, his high style was interpreted as an instance of the "pathetic sublime" and appropriated for the theatrical and sentimental politics of the Restoration. In the context of civil war and Restoration politics, however, it is surely more appropriate to see Milton as one of our earliest critics of aesthetic ideology, that is, of the purely affective response to the work of art that places art in the service of the political status quo.[1] This is particularly the case with *Samson Agonistes*, the poem in which Milton is most explicitly engaged with theatrical culture of the Restoration. Central to this poem is an attack on effeminizing pity, compassion, and sympathetic identification that foreshadows modern critiques of aesthetic ideology in the work of Benjamin and Brecht. Reading Milton alongside these modern theorists may help to produce a different history of aesthetics, one in which stylistic and political alienation is central, while compassion is disreputable.

Milton's critique of sympathy and pity has a long history, one that is frequently entwined with a suspicion of theatricality.[2] In *The Tenure of Kings and Magistrates*, Milton ridiculed the "dissembl'd and seditious pity" the Presbyterians felt for Charles I, thus linking the inappropriate affective response to the charge of feigning and hypocrisy (*CP* 3: 193). This attack on pity became all the more urgent after the royalists appropriated the image of the suffering Christ to represent the martyrdom of the king. In *Eikon Basilike*, "Charles" and Gauden used Christ's passion not only as an emblem of divine pity for mankind, but also as an image designed to elicit the properly "pitiful" response from the spectators or readers. The "king's book" thus anticipated the royalists' affective response to Charles's downfall by proleptically casting that tragedy as a romance. In this romance, the emotion of pity was not purged or tempered (as it would be in Aristotelian tragedy) but rather romantically heightened. In response, Milton compared Charles to "the Person of Richard III," whom Shakespeare represents as "a deep dissembler, not of his affections only, but of Religion," and he went on to attack Charles's appropriation of Sidney's *Arcadia* as a "heathen fiction" propping up Charles's feigned religiosity (*CP* 3: 362). Instead of pity or sympathy for the fallen Charles, Milton urged the unsentimental application of justice (*CP* 3: 584–96).

Samson Agonistes is Milton's critique of aesthetic ideology, updated for the 1660s. Milton's attack is two-pronged. First, *Samson Agonistes* continues Milton's critique of the sentimentalism of royalist culture, including the sentimental drama (both literal and figurative) of the Restoration.[3] Against the crown's "spectacles of state," which revived the cult of royal martyrdom and politicized public expressions of joy as consent to the new regime, Milton in the 1660s aimed "to assert the philistinism of those in power," and to claim a "monopoly over learning and culture [for the] excluded."[4] He aimed in short "to conduct a fundamental exercise in delegitimation."[5] Second, the object of Milton's critique was not only royalist supporters of the Restoration but also his own fellow republicans, who were guilty of backsliding in the late 1640s and 1650s and who were guilty of passivity in the 1660s. As Florence Sandler has argued, after the Restoration, "the burden of carrying the pathos of the witness of Christ passed from the royalists back again to the sectaries."[6] The question was how this pathos should be construed. In *Samson Agonistes* Milton argued against both royalists and republicans that the aesthetic responses of pity and fear were disreputable. Against a politically vitiated notion of aesthetic response, Milton in *Samson Agonistes* attempted to preserve what Adorno and Benjamin called "aesthetics as critique," and thus a genuine conception of politics.

Restoration sentiment

As Steven Zwicker has argued, spectacles of state were not the only kind of theater Milton had in mind in writing *Samson Agonistes*. Equally important was the Restoration creation of heroic drama by Dryden, William Davenant, Robert Howard, and others – a drama characterized by, in Zwicker's words, "its swooning excesses, its rhetoric and rhymes, and not least its exaltation of a Court whose acts and ethos were celebrated in the guise of exotic emperors and queens," even as it also criticized the court's "corruption, its moral squalor, its manners, arms, and arts."[7] Milton was familiar, as well, with the manifesto of the new genre, Dryden's essay *Of Dramatick Poesy*, which defined poesy as the "imitation of humour and passions," and tragedy as "nature wrought up to an higher pitch."[8] According to Dryden, the end of tragedy was "to beget admiration, compassion, or concernment." In his later "Heads of an Answer to Rymer," and "Grounds of Criticism in Tragedy" (1679), Dryden made the sentimental and non-Aristotelian basis of tragedy even clearer: English poets have added to the beauties of Greek tragedy by focusing on "new passions; as namely, that of love." One goal of the tragic poet is now to stir up the passion of pity through the representation of suffering lovers.[9]

In his emphasis on the passions, Dryden participated in a general seventeenth-century shift in accounts of tragic pleasure. Up to the middle of the seventeenth century, there were two main accounts of tragic pleasure. The first subordinated delight to instruction and understood catharsis as purging or moderating those passions that hindered ethical action. The second explained tragic pleasure in terms of the delight the audience takes in the artist's manipulation of artistic form. In the middle of the seventeenth century, these theories began to be qualified or supplanted by accounts of tragic pleasure influenced by Descartes's physiology and Hobbes's psychology. Followers of Descartes such as Rapin and Dennis explained the effects of tragedy in terms of the natural delight individuals take in the "sheer physical stimulation of the animal spirits." Hobbes adopted a similar materialist perspective when, alluding to Lucretius's *De rerum natura*, he explained aesthetic pleasure in terms of the physical distance that ensures the spectator's personal safety.[10]

Together, Descartes's physiology and Hobbes's psychology contributed to an increasingly sentimental understanding of tragedy. Influenced in part by Descartes, critics now argued that the representation of intense emotional moments was more important than the plot taken as a whole in producing the desired tragic effect. Influenced in part by Hobbes's argument regarding the primacy of self-interest, critics proposed a variety of counterarguments about the pleasures of tragedy which emphasized the audience's natural sympathy with those who suffer. In both cases, the new account of tragic pleasure involved a "division of labor," according to which it was now the poet's job to "cause" pity and fear, and the spectators' to temper and purge these passions by means of contemplation.[11] In Rapin's influential commentary on Aristotle's *Poetics* we still find the homeopathic theory of catharsis, a theory of countervailing passion, which views catharsis as rectifying the passions by the passions themselves.[12] But, in Dryden and others, a truncated version appears: poetry is now described as simply "begetting" admiration or "causing" pity and fear, rather than also purging these emotions.[13] In this new account of tragic pleasure, the spectators' tears, we might say, are the goal of tragic representation and sympathy is seen as shoring up rather than undermining the status quo. The obvious telos of this argument would be someone like Edmund Burke, for whom

> public affections, combined with manners, are required sometimes as supplements, sometimes as correctives, always as aids to the law. The precept given by a wise man, as well as a great critic, for the construction of poems, is equally true as to states. *Non satis est pulchra esse poemata, dulcia sunto.* There ought to be a system of manners in every nation which a well-formed mind would be disposed to relish. To make us love our country, our country ought to be lovely.[14]

Milton would have agreed with Burke that the construction of poems can tell us something about the construction of states. But, against Burke, in *Samson Agonistes*, Milton challenged the royalist equation of aesthetic pleasure with sympathy and with support for the status quo.

Modern critiques

Along with Restoration debates, modern discussions of the relationship between aesthetics and politics can also shed light on *Samson Agonistes*: these discussions frequently use the early modern period as a touchstone and some of the most important analyses focus on the genre of tragedy. In a study of Shakespeare's *Hamlet*, the German jurist Carl Schmitt argued that the notion of the aesthetic emerged historically in conjunction with a new, liberal notion of politics. Liberalism, which was ushered in by the Hobbesian sovereign state, institutionalized the principle of formal neutrality in politics – that is, an official indifference to substantive goals. Liberalism, in this view, involves a purely instrumental conception of politics as the technical means for harmonizing conflicting interests, without pronouncing on the relative value of those interests. According to Schmitt, the artistic equivalent of such formal neutrality is the notion of aesthetics, which emphasizes the pleasure we take in aesthetic form at the expense of any substantive content. In Schmitt's account, the historical emergence of the Hobbesian state and of aesthetics affected the genre of tragedy. Drawing on Hegel, Schmitt argued that the Hobbesian state initiated a regime of "objective reason beyond theology whose *ratio* put an end to the heroic age, the age of heroic law and heroic tragedy."[15] Against the anti-heroic Hobbesian state, Schmitt counterposed the tragedies of Shakespeare, in particular *Hamlet*, which dramatized for Schmitt a genuine crisis of decision – not only Hamlet's crisis about whether or not to kill Claudius, but also the crisis of decision which the Reformation posed for early modern Europe. Hobbes in this interpretation was linked to the rise of liberalism and aesthetics, while Shakespeare stood for a moment before the aesthetic – when something like genuine politics was still possible.

After Hobbes, the political and the aesthetic were equally vitiated separate spheres; whereas with Shakespeare, art was political through and through.[16]

Schmitt, of course, was not the only twentieth-century figure who articulated the relationship between aesthetics and politics in this way. In *Dialectic of Enlightenment*, Adorno and Horkheimer presented Kantian aesthetics as the historical and dialectical counterpart of liberal, Enlightenment instrumental reason. Marcuse linked a certain notion of aesthetics to liberalism in "The Affirmative Character of Culture." And Hannah Arendt articulated a similar complaint in *The Human Condition*, where a liberal, instrumental conception of political action went hand in hand with an aesthetic concept of the artifact.[17]

On the other hand, unlike Schmitt, these writers also tried to save aesthetics from liberalism. Adorno tried to develop a theory of aesthetic form as the vehicle of ideological critique; Marcuse argued for the political potential of "aesthetic form as such" in *The Aesthetic Dimension*; and Arendt read Kant's *Critique of Judgment* as adumbrating a notion of political critique as well as aesthetic judgment. In other words, at the same time that these writers recognized the complicity of a certain notion of aesthetics with the dominant ideology, they also wanted to recover a notion of aesthetic form as enabling radical political critique of and resistance to the status quo.[18]

In this context, it is above all Walter Benjamin, in his *Origin of German Tragic Drama*, who elaborates a notion of dramatic form that helps us understand *Samson Agonistes*'s critique of the emerging notion of aesthetics. This is not only because Benjamin's work is actually about seventeenth-century European drama and so responsive to early modern history and genre in a way that most of these other twentieth-century writers are not. It is also because Benjamin conceived of the *Trauerspiel* book as a political critique of the aestheticizing tendencies of his own day. In particular, the allegorical dimension of the *Trauerspiel* is in Benjamin's analysis both a symptom of the real fragmentation of contemporary life under the regime of aesthetics and a critical method of reading and interpreting. As such, it can serve as a model for Milton's double-edged reflection on aesthetics in *Samson Agonistes*. As we will see, Milton turns the aestheticizing tendencies of the Restoration against themselves and in the process elevates *Samson Agonistes* from a *Trauerspiel* to a tragedy.

Like Benjamin's essay on Goethe's *Elective Affinities*, which was written at about the same time, the *Trauerspiel* book marked Benjamin's break with the radical youth movement and its charismatic leader Gustav Wyneken, whose rhetoric of submission to genius and the world spirit drew uncomfortably close to the conservative political rhetoric of the period. In both works, Benjamin implicitly criticized the vitalism and aestheticizing glorification of myth associated with the Stefan George circle. (The Goethe essay in particular took aim at Friedrich Gundolf's 1916 book on Goethe, written under the influence of George.) At the heart of this critique was an attack on the romantic notion of the symbol, which Benjamin defined as "the indivisible unity of form and content." In advancing this critique of the romantic symbol, Benjamin drew on Alois Riegl's analysis of late Roman art in a period of political and cultural decay. Benjamin, following Riegl, wanted to establish "the contemporary relevance of the baroque after the breakdown of German classical culture" in the aftermath of World War I. The *Trauerspiel* book, in short, was not only Benjamin's attempt to recuperate a marginalized literature of the late Renaissance and a polemical intervention in contemporary methodological debates. It was also Benjamin's diagnosis of postwar Germany, with its rampant inflation, political incoherence, and cultural decay. In contrast to the sentimental and mystifying cult of the symbol, the *Trauerspiel*'s landscape of ruins provided a more accurate analogue for this decay; in its fragmentation of all pretensions to totality, it also provided a more potent weapon against the aestheticizing myths of George and his acolytes.[19]

The English translation of Benjamin's book is entitled *The Origins of German Tragic Drama* but this translation of *Trauerspiel* as tragedy obscures Benjamin's main argument. According to Benjamin, whereas Greek tragedy turns on the fateful decision of an individual character, the seventeenth-century baroque play of mourning depicts a world in which such absolute or quasi-divine powers of sovereign decision-making can no longer be taken for granted. Here Benjamin was drawing on Carl Schmitt's earlier work of political theory, *Political Theology*, which defined the sovereign as the individual who "decides the exception" – who makes decisions in cases of national emergency – when positive law has been suspended. Benjamin argued that *Trauerspiel* represents a dislocation of sovereignty and thus a dislocation of a world in which decisions can take place.[20] "The theory of sovereignty which takes as its example the special case in which dictatorial powers are unfolded, positively demands the completion of the image of the sovereign, as tyrant." And yet, the tyrant, "who is responsible for making the decision to proclaim the state of emergency, reveals, at the first opportunity, that he is almost incapable of making a decision."[21] Benjamin linked this dislocation to the Reformation, to a new focus on the individual believer, and to the priority of faith over works, which deprived human action of any immanent meaning or worth and thus provoked melancholy in the hero.[22] The world of the *Trauerspiel* is a world in which history is no longer the medium of eschatology or even of significant action. Instead, action has been replaced by acting. This gives rise to the meta-theatrical reflexivity of *Trauerspiel* – as in the well-worn trope of the world as a stage.

Unlike Schmitt, who viewed *Hamlet* as an exemplary tragedy, Benjamin reads *Hamlet* as exemplifying the conventions of *Trauerspiel*. In Hamlet, we find the self-conscious theatricality characteristic of *Trauerspiel* (p. 82), as well as the link between mourning and ostentation (p. 140). Hamlet's play within a play is characteristic of "the playful miniaturization of reality and the introduction of a reflective infinity of thought into the finite space of a profane fate" (p. 83). In contrast to the tragic hero who decides and acts, Hamlet in his indecisiveness and melancholy "betrays the world for the sake of knowledge" (p. 157). Hamlet also illustrates the preoccupation with "the misery of mankind in its creaturely estate" (p. 146). His famous soliloquy, "What a piece of work is man," contains "both the philosophy of [Lutheran] Wittenberg and a protest against it" (p. 138).[23] Finally, the accidental manner of Hamlet's death is also typical of *Trauerspiel*: "The death of Hamlet, which has no more in common with tragic death than the Prince himself has with Ajax, is in its drastic externality characteristic of the *Trauerspiel*. ... Whereas tragedy ends with a decision – however uncertain this may be – there resides in the essence of the *Trauerspiel*, and especially the death scene, an appeal of the kind which martyrs utter" (p. 136).

According to Benjamin, one consequence of the subordination of action to acting is a greater prominence of affect or of the passions in the *Trauerspiel*. In contrast to Aristotle's *Poetics*, which defines tragedy as the imitation of an action, in the *Trauerspiel*, "Fear and pity are not seen as participation in the integral whole of the action, but as participation in the fate of the most outstanding characters. Fear is aroused by the death of the villain, pity by that of the pious hero."[24] In addition, the hero is himself defined in terms of the passions: instead of acting, the hero emotes, mourning the loss of transcendence, belief, unproblematic agency – or even, in the case of Hamlet, the possibility of tragedy itself.[25] Hence the prominence of martyr dramas in the genre of the *Trauerspiel*, that is, dramas concerned not with the deeds of the hero, but his suffering. In Benjamin's account, the martyr is the flipside of the tyrant, or rather "the tyrant and the martyr are but the two faces of the monarch": "for the 'very bad' there was the drama of the tyrant, and there was fear; for the 'very good' there was the martyr-drama and pity."[26]

Benjamin goes on to argue that the force of the passions in *Trauerspiel* is manifest as a strange kind of externality. Observing that in the *Trauerspiel* "the tempo of ... emotional life is accelerated to such an extent that calm actions, considered decisions, occur more and more infrequently,"[27] Benjamin concludes that "passion is distinguished from [a] psychological motive [for] action," and becomes more like a stage-property. That is, passion is not so much an attribute of an individual as something that happens to him. For example, the martyr-drama, according to Benjamin, was frequently concerned "not so much with [the martyr's] spiritual torment as with the agony of the physical adversity which befalls him."[28] As Benjamin remarked of the characters of the Silesian dramatist, Caspar von Lohenstein:

> What is conspicuous about [these characters] is ... the sheer arbitrariness of a constantly shifting emotional storm in which the figures ... sway about like torn and flapping banners. And they also bear a certain resemblance to the figures of El Greco in the smallness of their heads, if

we understand this in a metaphorical sense. For their actions are not determined by thought, but by changing physical impulses.[29]

As a result, the *Trauerspiel* or drama of fate appears at once contingent and staged: "chance [breaks] ... down ... action into fragmented elements or things."[30] The plot is disarticulated into discrete events, much like the medieval chronicle history but without the medieval faith in redemption (p. 77). History is reduced to nature, specifically nature deprived of grace or what Benjamin calls the "bare state of creation" (p. 81).

This observation brings us to the last defining characteristic of the *Trauerspiel*: its fragmentary and allegorical mode – as manifest, for example, in the prominence of emblems and iconography. Benjamin identified allegory with a certain foregrounding of the materiality of signs, that is, with contingent relation between material signs and their significance. In seventeenth-century baroque drama, a heightened emphasis on materiality goes hand in hand with a heightened awareness of convention, of literature as an art of invention or construction, and a corresponding awareness of the reader's own activity of interpretation.[31] This unmooring of sign and significance, this materiality or externality of signs produces the baroque effect of "ostentation" and provokes a kind of sublime frenzy of interpretation on the part of the reader.

The allegorical dimension of *Trauerspiel* then precipitates a turn in Benjamin's argument. On the one hand, allegory refers to the reified or petrified landscape of baroque drama – the reduction of history to nature, time to space, and action to acedia. On the other hand, allegory provokes action in the reader, who disassembles and reassembles the text in a new constellation of ideas. "Criticism," Benjamin writes aphoristically, "means the mortification of works" (p. 182). Allegory thus comes to name a new critical method, which undermines the illusory totality of aesthetic ideology. To the extent that aesthetics is predicated on the organic unity of signified and signifier in the symbol, it performs the ideological operation par excellence of mystifying culture as nature. In contrast, allegory is the linguistic mode that calls attention to the arbitrariness or conventionality of signification. Allegory is then synonymous with the critique of ideology, with the unmasking of nature or natural signs as culturally constructed.[32] "In the field of allegorical intuition," Benjamin writes, "the image is a fragment, a rune. ... The false appearance of totality is extinguished."[33] In its emphasis on the fragmentary, allegory amounts to "a deep-rooted intuition of the problematic character of art."[34] But it is this extinction of totality – this critique of a certain notion of art – that allows for the transcendence of a mystified notion of aesthetics. Here, it is clear that Benjamin is no longer thinking of the characters in *Trauerspiele* simply as figures of melancholy or acedia. Instead, he seems to imagine them as containing "the prolegomena of interpretation" (p. 228) which in turn holds out the promise (however endlessly deferred) of redemption.[35]

While the allegorical method was a constant in Benjamin's later work, he would not always hold to this semi-mystical view of the *Trauerspiel*. In a later essay on Brecht's "epic theater," Benjamin placed greater emphasis on the political legacy of the *Trauerspiel*'s non-Aristotelian emphasis on fragmentation, its foregrounding of acting, and its critique of aesthetic ideology. Benjamin argued that Brecht's Marxist epic theater is the modern equivalent of the *Trauerspiele* of Gryphius, Shakespeare, and Calderon.[36] Whereas Aristotelian catharsis depends on empathy or identification (Einfühlung), which precludes a critical approach to social and political problems, the goal of epic theater is to reconcile the emotions with the critical spirit.[37] Where Aristotelian theater is simply "the occasion of feelings," epic theater also obliges the spectator "to decide."[38] The hero of epic theater is not a tragic hero in the strict Aristotelian sense because he doesn't provoke identification. Rather, through the technique of the alienation effect, the characters prompt the spectator to think about the proper conditions for action. Instead of creating the illusion of false harmony or idealization, epic theater uncovers the inconsistencies and contradictions of actual life.[39] In revealing these inconsistencies and thus the possibilities for change, epic theater provokes "astonishment" rather than empathy, and "leave[s] its spectators productively disposed."[40] In this reading of the epic theater as political critique, Benjamin also revises – or makes explicit – the political agenda behind his reading of German baroque drama in 1928.

Trauerspiel and tragedy in *Samson Agonistes*

If we now return to Milton we can see that many of the features that Benjamin identifies in the marginalized genre of baroque play of mourning appear in *Samson Agonistes*. And, as in Benjamin's *Trauerspiel* book, these features appear both as a symptom of decline and a critical mode of reflection. To the extent that Samson succumbs to mourning and ostentation, he remains a Hamlet-like figure out of *Trauerspiel*. To the extent that *Samson Agonistes* dramatizes a critical mode of reflection, however, it rises to the level of genuine – that is, Greek – tragedy. Whereas Benjamin turned to early modern drama to intervene in contemporary political and methodological debates, Milton turned ultimately to Greek drama to comment on the Restoration aestheticizing of politics.

At first glance, *Samson Agonistes* appears to be a *Trauerspiel*, a play of mourning about the impossibility of action under the Restoration. Like the sovereign of baroque drama who is faced with a state of emergency, Samson is faced with what Benjamin calls "a state of emergency in the soul, the rule of the emotions."[41] Samson needs to decide the exception – needs to decide whether he himself is an exception as prophesied – and yet seems unable to do so. Prophecies, signs, or promises seem in excess of their significance. At the very least, it's not clear how signs and their significance are related, how signs become meaningful. The main character seems unable to "shake off [his] immanence"; that is, even as he seeks some kind of transcendence, some otherworldly meaning, he remains preoccupied with "the hopelessness of the earthly condition."[42] In his posture and complaints, he seems the very personification of Renaissance melancholy: "Myself mine own Sepulcre, / A moving grave." Like the martyr-drama, *Samson Agonistes* focuses on the suffering of the hero, at the same time that it renders this suffering in unusually physical terms: Samson's thoughts are "a deadly swarm / Of hornets" (ll. 19–20); he is "eyeless in Gaza at the mill with slaves" (l. 41); his griefs pain him "as a ling'ring disease," as "wounds" that "rankle, and fester, and gangrene, / To black mortification" (ll. 618–21). In addition, his passions seem strangely material, and thus, by the logic of *Trauerspiel*, they also come to seem theatrical, artificial, or conventional. Then there is the question of forward movement in the plot of *Samson Agonistes*. From Samuel Johnson onwards, critics have worried about the play's middle. They have debated whether the serial encounters really add up to the growth of Samson's mind, especially when Samson seems – like Lohenstein's characters in Benjamin's description – to be caught up in a constantly shifting emotional storm, and to bear a certain resemblance to the figures of El Greco in the smallness of his head ("O impotence of mind, in body strong!" [l. 52]).[43] Most famously, Samson's own motive for going to the Philistine temple is occluded for us in a phrase – rousing motions – that equates emotion with physical motion.[44] Above all, *Samson Agonistes* is like the *Trauerspiel* in linking the prominence of the passions to the play's metatheatrical dimension.[45] In his ostentatious performance of suffering, Samson asks us to consider the meaning of pathos; while his final violent act of pulling down the temple / theater prompts us to reflect on the metatheatrical dimension of his actions. In all these ways, *Samson Agonistes* draws near to the baroque *Trauerspiel*, with its subgenres of martyr play and revenge tragedy.

Despite these similarities or rather because of them, I think it is more accurate to say that Samson *thinks* he's a character in a *Trauerspiel* and it is by "seeing" this play acted out before him that Samson is roused to his final catastrophic action. Milton doesn't simply foreground the passions as a symptom of the state of emergency in Samson's soul and as a cause of Samson's inaction. Rather, in a fundamental way the plot is *about* the aesthetic responses of pity and fear. Although in the Preface to *Samson Agonistes*, Milton famously revises Aristotle's definition of tragedy ("the imitation of an action") in the direction of the Restoration concern with the passions, he also sub-scribes to an ethically inflected homeopathic theory of catharsis. According to this theory, tragedy elicits the passions in order to purge or temper them to a just measure. This concern with tempering the passions is in direct opposition to Dryden's interest in eliciting sentiment and sympathy. In this light, critics who observe that we don't feel pity for Samson or fear for the Philistines at the end of the tragedy are right on target.[46] Like his contemporary

Rapin, Milton believed that tragedy "rectifies the passions by the passions themselves," that it cures pride and hardness of heart; "but because man is naturally timorous, and compassionate, he may fall into another extreme, to be either too fearful, or too full of pity; *the too much fear may shake the constancy of mind, and the too great compassion may enfeeble equity.*"[47] The goal of *Samson Agonistes* is to turn such passions into action, to make passion the spur to action, through the mediation of dramatic representation or aesthetic form.[48]

Samson Agonistes is, in short, Milton's version of epic theater. This means that Milton's understanding of Aristotle, both in the Preface and in the poem as a whole, has much less to do with empathy or Einfühlung and much more with exposing the conditions of political action by alienating the reader from the aesthetic ideology of the Restoration.[49] Milton achieves this "alienation effect" by precisely those aspects of the play that have seemed most trouble-some to readers: the lack of a middle and the paratactic relation of scenes to each other, the suppression of motivation, and the strangely external or what Brecht might call "gestic" quality of Samson's actions. As we will see, Samson is ultimately not simply or even primarily the patient sufferer of *Trauerspiel* but rather an exemplary tragic figure who raises "acting" to the level of action. All these elements of *Samson Agonistes* serve to call attention to the artifice of the play and, ideally, to provoke the audience's "astonishment . . . at the conditions under which they function" – where "they" refers not only or primarily to the characters but to Milton's readers. Samson is purged of or alienated from pity and fear by seeing his own passions mirrored back to him by other characters. Similarly, instead of feeling pity and fear, the reader is ideally astonished by and alienated from the real-life theater of Restoration state. In achieving this understanding, Samson and the audience alike con-vert what might have been only a *Trauerspiel* into a genuine tragedy on the order of Sophocles, Euripides, or Gregory of Nazianzen's *Christus patiens*.[50]

Let me give a few examples. If there were ever a soliloquy that illustrated what Benjamin described as a "constantly shifting emotional storm in which the figures . . . sway about like torn and flapping banners," it's the opening soliloquy of *Samson Agonistes*, filled as it is with Samson's self-pity, lamentation, and despair.[51] The ensuing encounters with Manoa, Dalila, and Harapha enable Samson to reject these and other passions by seeing them represented. Manoa represents the response of pity: "O miserable change!" he proclaims upon seeing Samson (l. 340). In response, Samson rejects Manoa's pity. He insists on not being ransomed, on not being "to visitants a gaze, / Or pitied object" (ll. 567–68). But, not finding a real outlet for action, Samson succumbs again to a Hamlet-like despair: "My hopes all flat, nature within me seems / In all her functions weary of herself" (ll. 595–96). And he glosses his condition in theatrical terms, seeing himself as "reserv'd alive to be *repeated* / The subject of [Philistine] cruelty, or scorn" (ll. 645–46).[52]

Dalila arrives, announcing not only her "tears" (l. 735), but also her repentance. She urges her fear: "I saw thee mutable / Of fancy, fear'd lest one day thou wouldst leave me" (ll. 793–94). Above all, she solicits Samson's pity: "And Love hath oft, well meaning, wrought much woe, / Yet always pity or pardon hath obtain'd" (ll. 813–14). Like Manoa, she promises the consolation associated with domestic tragedy: "Life yet hath many solaces, enjoy'd / Where other senses want not their delights / At home in leisure and domestic ease" (ll. 915–17). The effect of this theatrical performance of the passion – which is perceived as such by Samson – is to intensify his "uncompassionate anger" (l. 818), his resistance to the theatrical temptation of pity.[53]

Unlike Manoa and Dalila, Harapha doesn't pretend to offer consolation. Instead, he represents a theatrical or parodic version of Samson's own uncompassionate anger. Parodic because it is clearly motivated by vainglory, which Samson conjectures is related to Harapha's fear for his own self-preservation. At the same time, he mirrors back to Samson his own earlier despair, telling him: "Presume not on thy God, whate'er he be, / Thee he regards not, owns not, hath cut off" (ll. 1156–57). In response, Samson accuses Harapha of "feigned shifts" (l. 1116), and of mere aesthetic contemplation: "Cam'st thou for his, vain boaster, to survey me[?]" (l. 1127).

These three encounters, in other words, function as plays-within-the-play, meta-theatrical moments in which Samson is alienated from his passions by seeing them represented. Manoa's and Dalila's representations of pity counteract Samson's self-pity; Harapha's fear, in the words of one Renaissance commentator on Aristotle's *Poetics*, "teaches [Samson] to have no fear of that of the body, and makes [him] perceive within [himself] the force of justice."[54]

But it is above all the encounter with the Philistine messenger that dramatizes the transformation of the passions of *Trauerspiel* into tragic action. Initially, Samson refuses the Philistine command to "play" at work, to "sport with blind activity" (l. 1328):

> Although thir drudge, to be thir fool or jester,
> And in my midst of sorrow and heart-grief
> To show them feats, and play before thir god,
> The worst of all indignities, yet on me
> Join'd with extreme contempt? I will not come.
> (ll. 1338–42)

Like the hero of the *Trauerspiel*, Samson links his sorrow and heart-grief to the impossibility of genuine action, to the theatrical hollowing-out of agency. Shortly after this, however, he feels rousing motions and agrees to go along with the messenger. Whether rousing motions refers to emotion or divine impulse – in either case, the word "motions" suggests both the materiality and the strange externality of motive characteristic of *Trauerspiel*. But what is unlike *Trauerspiel* is the fact that the word "motion" *renders emotion or passion in the form of action*. In this respect, the word "motion" is a semantic mini-drama of the way representation can convert passion to action.[55]

Equally important, rousing motions appear to involve neither pity nor fear. Samson has rejected self-pity and pity for others in his encounters with Manoa and Dalila. He has rejected fear for his self-preservation and despair in his encounter with Harapha. At the same time, what he seems to have learned through all three is the power of theatrical representation to turn passion into action. Thus, immediately after experiencing the rousing motions, Samson acts the part of the fearful and obedient captive; he feigns fear for his life, or at least he equivocates in a way that allows for this interpretation: "Masters' commands come with a power resistless / To such as owe them absolute subjection; / And for a life who will not change his purpose?" (ll. 1403–05). In the Messenger's account, Samson's actions are rendered in even more theatrical terms: "he still perform'd / All with incredible, stupendious force" (ll. 1626–27); he stood at the pillars "as one who pray'd" (l. 1637). But a crucial part of Samson's newfound understanding of the power of theatrical representation to turn passion into action is a critique of aesthetic contemplation. Thus Samson himself mocks the aesthetic pleasure derived from his own play-acting when he addresses the Philistine audience:

> Hitherto, Lords, what your commands impos'd
> I have perform'd, as reason was, obeying,
> Not without wonder or delight beheld.
> Now of my own accord such other trial
> I mean to show you of my strength, yet greater;
> As with amaze shall strike all who behold.
>
> (ll. 1640–45)

In other words, the aesthetic responses of wonder, delight, and amazement are fatal when not properly understood – when they are understood as the occasion for mere contemplation. In contrast, and unlike the hero of *Trauerspiel*, Samson has elevated *Spiel* or play or representation to the enabling condition of tragic action. For it is under the cover of play-acting that Samson transforms his servitude into an act of political resistance.[56]

Here it is helpful once again to return to Benjamin, who illustrates the contrast between *Trauerspiel* and tragedy by the polemics about the regicide of Charles I. According to Benjamin, seventeenth-century *Trauerspiele* share with medieval religious drama the view that "world history [is] a tragedy, not in its form but in its content," that is, not essentially but merely contingently (p. 78). In support of this claim, Benjamin cites Claude Salmasius's description of the tragic outcome of the English Civil War.

> Ce qui restoit de la Tragedie iusque à la conclusion a esté le personnage des Independans, mais on a veu les Presbyteriens iusques au quatriesme

acte et au delà, occuper auec pompe tout le theatre. Le seul cinquiesme et dernier acte est demeure pour le partage des Independans; qui ont paru en cette scene, après avoir sifflé et chassé m'auroient pas fermé la scene par une si tragique et sanglante catastrophe.

(The Independents were the tragic element which remained right up to the conclusion, although the Presbyterians were seen to occupy the whole theater in pomp until the fourth act and beyond. The fifth and final act alone was left for the Independents, who appeared after howling down and chasing off the previous actors. It is possible that the latter would not have brought the drama to a close with such a tragic and bloody catastrophe.) (p. 78)

According to Benjamin, in viewing tragedy as the contingent result of circumstances Salmasius betrays his misunderstanding of the real meaning of Greek tragedy. A similar misunderstanding of tragedy is evident in Salmasius's attempt to "find the origin of kingship in the state of creation," that is, to derive kingship from Adam's original dominion over the world (p. 85). For Benjamin, Salmasius's patriarchialism is simply the political and legal equivalent of *Trauerspiel*'s reduction of history to nature. Only on the basis of such naturalism could regicide be condemned as parricide (ibid.).

At the same time, Benjamin also reads Salmasius as a critic of the hyper-theatricality of baroque kingship. In the *Trauerspiel*, according to Benjamin, "kings and princes appear with their crowns of gilt paper, very melancholy and mournful, and they assure the sympathetic public that nothing is more difficult than to rule" (p. 123). Benjamin then comments:

> Political philosophy, which must have held such points of view as sacrilegious, provides the counter-test. Salmasius writes: 'Ce sont eux qui traittent les testes des Roys comme des ballons, qui se ioüent des Couronnes comme les enfans font d'vn cercle, qui considerent les Sceptres des Princes comme des marottes, et qui n'ont pas plus de veneration pour les liurées de la souueraine Magistrature, que pour des quintaines.
>
> (It is they who treat the heads of kings like balls, who play with crowns as children play with hoops, who regard the scepters of princes as jesters' staffs, and who have no more respect for the insignia of sovereign magistracy than for quintains.) (p. 124)

That is, Salmasius recognized, even as he condemned, the puppet-like representation and treatment of the king by the regicides. In this way, he unwittingly supports Benjamin's claim that, in the world of the *Trauerspiel*, kings are mere puppets and true action has been replaced by acting.

Milton also saw Salmasius as undermining his own defense of Charles I. In the opening pages of the *Defence of the English People* against Salmasius's *Defensio regia,* Milton mocks Salmasius's syntax in the phrase concerning "the murder among the English in the person of the king" (*CP* 4: 1, 309). He points out that the Latin word *persona* means mask and conjures up the division between actor and role that Salmasius is at pains to deny.

> What, I ask you, is "committing murder in the person of the king," what is "in the person of the king"? When was Latin ever spoken like that?
>
> Unless perhaps you are telling us about some pretender like the false-Philip who assumed the guise of king and carried out some murder or other among the English: In this you may have spoken more truly than you thought, for a tyrant, like a king upon the stage, is but the ghost or mask of a king, and not a true king. (p. 310)

With his bad Latin, Salmasius has revealed that Charles I is a tyrant who is merely pretending to be a king. He has, in short, exposed the self-conscious theatricality of Charles's rule in much the same way as Milton did in his attack on Charles's feigned religiosity in *Eikonoklastes.* There Milton also made it clear that Charles's theatrical self-presentation – as in his "portraiture before his book drawn out to the full measure of a masking scene" – aimed to prescribe both the reader's interpretation and his affective response. In the "person" of Charles, real action was replaced by acting, which in turn prompted a merely sentimental response from the English people.

Against the hypertheatricality and sentimentality of the royalist *Trauerspiel,* with its reduction of history to nature and action to acting, Milton counterposes Greek tragedy: contrary to Salmasius's claims, Aeschylus, Sophocles, and Euripides all testify to the right of the people to resist tyranny (p. 440). This suggests that there is another way of reading the meaning of *persona,* which runs counter to Salmasius's insistence on the identity of the king's person and his power (p. 488). As Milton comments later in the *Defence*: "If you are unaware that a single man may play several roles, each of which may be perceived or thought of as distinct from the individual himself, you must be without either common sense or Latinity" (pp. 488, 489). Self-conscious theatricality may be a feature of baroque sovereignty, but it may also be adapted to republican political goals. Milton gives the example of the Israelites who made acting a vehicle of political resistance after they had been conquered by Eglon, king of Moab: "while they openly rewarded him as their king they slew him by secret plots as an enemy" (p. 401). And he goes on to compare Ehud, the slayer of Eglon, to Samson who, "whether prompted by God or by his own valor ... thought it not impious but pious to kill those masters who were tyrants over his country" (p. 402). Through a tissue of citations, Samson comes to represent the correct understanding of ancient Greek tragedy. The same is true, I have argued, of *Samson Agonistes,* which turns the conventions of royalist *Trauerspiel* against themselves in order to free the reader from a sentimental understanding of tragedy.

In this light, it's clear that both Manoa's and the Chorus' response to Samson's actions are inadequate. Manoa understands that Samson has escaped from the confines of a *Trauerspiel*. He also understands that lamentation and mourning are activities properly reserved to the Philistines. But his plan to build a monument for Samson, with his "Acts enroll'd / In copious Legend, or sweet Lyric song," misreads the genre Samson has brought to conclusion. Manoa's vision of valiant youth being inspired to "matchless valor" construes Samson's actions simply as a humanist example to be imitated rather than an exceptional drama of conscience, while the references to "virgins ... bewailing / His lot unfortunate in nuptial choice" returns us again to the sentimental world of *Trauerspiel*, or perhaps even melodrama.

The Chorus also understands that mourning is reserved to Gaza. But, judging by Samson's earlier rejection of the consolations offered by Manoa and Dalila, the Chorus errs in its emphasis on peace and consolation, as well as in its declaration of "calm of mind, all passion spent." This interpretation of catharsis implies that pity and fear have purged (or, depending on how you read spent: tempered) by witnessing the final action of Samson. But the excesses of pity and fear have been tempered long before this, both in Samson and in the reader. Moreover, "calm of mind, all passion spent" does not invite the audience to move from passion to action. To the contrary, in its antinomian complacency ("All is best, though we oft doubt, / What th' unsearchable dispose" [ll. 1745–46]), the Chorus displaces action from Samson to God: "Oft he seems to hide his face, / But unexpectedly returns / And to his faithful Champion hath in place / Bore witness gloriously" (ll. 1749–52). It is God who acts here, bearing witness to Samson, rather than vice versa.

In both cases, we can see how a certain theological complacency goes hand in hand with aesthetic contemplation and the eclipse of agency. I have been arguing, in contrast, that both the explicit subject and intended effect of *Samson Agonistes* is not calm of mind but rather (to return to the language of the prefatory note) the "stirring up" of Samson and the reader by means of imitation. The reader sees the passions of pity and fear well imitated by Manoa, Dalila, and the Chorus, and sees them rejected by Samson. For Samson, aesthetic ideology, including the aesthetic passions of pity and fear, is undone by the metatheatrical dimension of representation. But – as in Benjamin's analysis of the *Trauerspiel* – this critique of aesthetic ideology is not only a theme but an effect of *Samson Agonistes*. Confronted with the deliberate opacity of Samson's rousing motions (which turns passion into action on the level of semantics), the reader is provoked to a sublime activity of interpretation which is itself rousing. In Benjamin's vocabulary, the aesthetic appearance of totality is extinguished by a strange and fragmentary ostentation that provokes a surplus of interpretation; in Milton's vocabulary, sight is displaced by reading. In either case, the lesson is not one of consolation or aesthetic contemplation but of "fiery virtue rous'd."

Against the pathos of Restoration tragedy, which Dryden associated with the sublime, Milton creates a different kind of tragic sublimity. This sublimity is not an effect of what Dryden called "concernment" or sympathetic identification with the hero, nor is it an effect of what Hobbes described as the feeling of physical security confronted at a distance with the suffering of another. It is instead what we might call the hermeneutical sublime, in which representation or even quotation allows for the reinterpretation of past experience, including the experience of the passions.[57] In this light, the Restoration and Restoration drama taken together appear as a sentimental *Trauerspiel*, which the tragedy of *Samson Agonistes* both represents and critiques. In doing so, *Samson Agonistes* places the conventions of Greek tragedy in the service of the "good old cause."

I want to conclude with a final thought about aesthetics as critique. As we saw at the outset of this essay, early Renaissance commentators on Aristotle can be divided into those who moralized catharsis as a vehicle of the ethical and political dimension of tragedy and those who emphasized the pleasure we derive from artistry of imitation (Minturno on the one hand and Castelvetro on the other). In the middle of the seventeenth century, pleasure and instruction joined forces in a new way. Critics now emphasized the pleasure the reader or spectator derived from indulging the passions, while insisting these passions should illustrate moral truths or follow from what Dryden called "poetical justice."[58] Milton, I have been suggesting, refuses the alternatives of the early Renaissance theories of tragedy, and the conflation of the later theories of tragic pleasure. In doing so, he anticipates modern theories of aesthetics as critique which make the alienation effect of representation itself the condition of ethical and political action. For this reason, *Samson Agonistes* may allegorize what Benjamin saw as the historical shift from a world governed by a transcendent God to one mired in immanence. By suppressing motivation, by exacerbating the issue of the criterion of Samson's judgment, Milton demonstrates the internalization of judgment that is a feature of the Reformation conscience. This internalization of judgment represents a kind of historical way station between theology and aesthetics, which we have come to know as the process of secularization. Yet this internalization of judgment also makes available a new kind of ethical autonomy and political agency that is linked to the historical emergence of the autonomous aesthetic artifact. Benjamin writes that "for the theater of profane society ... the power of salvation and redemption only ever lies in a paradoxical reflection of play and appearance."[59] *Samson Agonistes* is a *Trauerspiel* in which reflection on *spiel* or the play of representation becomes the enabling condition of both tragic action and political critique.

Notes

1   See Nicholas von Maltzahn "The War in Heaven and the Miltonic Sublime," in
    A Nation Transformed: England after the Restoration, ed. Alan Houston and Steve
    Pincus (Cambridge: Cambridge University Press, 2001), pp. 154–79. Maltzahn
    sees this aestheticization of Milton as a response to his mid-seventeenth century
    poetics (p. 159). Maltzahn contrasts Milton's rational sublime with

> the more affective thrust of the pathetic sublime [which] we may associate
> especially with the heroic drama of the Restoration, and its increasingly
> nationalist aesthetics, and secondarily with Dryden's influence on the aesthetics
> of Dennis, Gildon, Blackmore, and others in the 1690s. For Dryden's Whig
> acolytes after the Revolution, the sublime seemed especially useful as a means
> of gaining consensus in national issues, a coercion without coercion, which we
> might style propaganda or more broadly ideology. (pp. 161–62)

An earlier version of this paper was presented at the International Milton
Symposium in Beaufort, SC, in June 2003.

2   As early as *The Reason of Church Government* (1642), Milton stressed precisely the
    opposite qualities: the "pious and just honouring of our selves" as the proper
    motive for heroic action in both romance and epic (*Complete Prose Works of John
    Milton,* ed. Don M. Wolfe *et al.* (New Haven, CT: Yale University Press, 1953–
    82), 1, pp. 841–42. This edition of Milton's prose will be abbreviated *CP* here-
    after). In his comments on the *Iliad,* as Colin Burrow has argued, "Milton avoids
    the sentimental revision of Homer, and sidesteps the galloping rush of 'piety'
    towards 'pity' by yoking it with justice." See Colin Burrow, *Epic Romance* (Oxford:
    Clarendon, 1993), p. 246.

3   On the Restoration context of *Samson Agonistes,* see Christopher Hill, *Milton and the
    English Revolution* (Harmondsworth: Penguin, 1977), pp. 428–50; Nicholas Jose,
    "*Samson Agonistes*: The Play Turned Upside Down," *Essays in Criticism* 30 (1980):
    124–50; Laura Lunger Knoppers, *Historicizing Milton: Spectacle, Power, and Poetry in
    the Restoration* (Athens, GA: University of Georgia Press, 1994); Steven N. Zwicker,
    "Milton, Dryden, and the Politics of Literary Controversy," in *Culture and Society in
    the Stuart Restoration,* ed. Gerald MacLean (Cambridge: Cambridge University
    Press, 1995), pp. 137–50; and in the same volume, Blair Worden, "Milton, *Samson
    Agonistes,* and the Restoration," pp. 111–36; Sharon Achinstein, "*Samson Agonistes*
    and the Drama of Dissent," *Milton Studies* 33 (1996): 133–58; and Achinstein,
    "Milton's Spectre in the Restoration: Marvell, Dryden, and Literary Enthusiasm,"
    Huntington Library Quarterly 59 (1997): 1–29.

4   On royalist spectacles of state, see Knoppers, *Historicizing Milton,* chapter 1. On
    the revival of the cult of Charles I as martyr, see p. 28. On joy, see chapter 3. Such
    an emphasis on spectacle and on the audience's emotional response was
    ideological in the sense of being politically motivated; it did not constitute an
    aesthetic ideology in the modern sense of a mystified belief in the organic
    wholeness of the work of art. Contemporaries themselves were skeptical of public
    expressions of joy: as Edward Hyde, Earl of Clarendon, commented in his
    autobiography, "The joy was universal; and whosoever was not pleased at heart,
    took the more care to appear as if he was" (p. 67). As Knoppers herself argues,
    "Restoration spectacle was marked by self-consciousness, anxiety, and ambiva-
    lence," but this did not prevent the court from staging theatrical displays designed
    to elicit the subjects' passions, however feigned. See also Harold Weber,
    "Representations of the King: Charles II and his Escape from Worcester," *Studies*

in Philology 85 (1988): 489–509, on how the court of Charles II "projected an idealized courtly mythology" and "question[ed] the terms of its own idealizations" (p. 491).

5 Derek Hirst, "The Politics of Literature in the English Republic," *The Seventeenth Century* 5 (1990): 147–58, here 149. Hirst is describing the royalists in the 1650s, but my contention is that Milton adopted this strategy during the Restoration.

6 Florence Sandler, "Icon and Iconoclast," in *Achievements of the Left Hand*, ed. Michael Lieb and John T. Shawcross (Amherst, MA: University of Massachusetts Press, 1974), p. 182.

7 Steven N. Zwicker, "Milton, Dryden, and the Politics of Literary Controversy," p. 151. Zwicker traces Milton's interest in something like heroic drama, with its conflicts of love and honor, in his earlier sketches for dramas, and reads *Paradise Regained* as a response to Dryden's dramatic success. Milton alludes to the Howard–Dryden debate on rhyme in the prefatory note to *Paradise Lost*.

8 Dryden, *Of Dramatic Poesy: and Other Critical Essays*, ed. George Watson, 2 vols (New York: Dutton, 1962), 1:56, and 87: in tragedy "the plot, the character, the wit, the passions, the descriptions, are all exalted above the level of common converse." See p. 76:

> And though the fury of a civil war, and power for twenty years together abandoned to a barbarous race of man, enemies of all good learning, had buried the Muses under the ruins of monarchy; yet, with the restoration of our happiness, we see revived poesy lifting up its head, and already shaking off the rubbish which lay so heavy on it. We have seen since his Majesty's return many dramatic poems which yield not to those of any foreign nation.

Should we hear an ironic echo of Milton's allusion to Samson in *Areopagitica*: "Methinks I see in my mind a noble and puissant nation rousing herself like a strong man after sleep, and shaking her invincible locks" (Milton's *Complete Poems and Major Prose*, ed. Merritt Y. Hughes (Indianapolis: Odyssey, 1957), p. 745)?

9 Dryden, "Heads of an Answer to Rymer," in Watson, ed., *Of Dramatic Poesy*, 1:212, and 218. See "The Grounds of Criticism in Tragedy," 1:245, 247.

10 This paragraph summarizes the lucid argument of Earl R. Wasserman, "The Pleasures of Tragedy," *ELH* 14 (1927): 283–307; the quote appears on p. 288. See also Baxter Hathaway, "John Dryden and the Function of Tragedy," *PMLA* 58 (1943): 665–73; and Eric Rothstein, "English Tragic Theory in the Late Seventeenth Century," *ELH* 29 (1962): 306–23. On Hobbes, see also Baxter Hathaway, "The Lucretian 'Return upon Ourselves,'" *PMLA* 62 (1947): 672–80.

11 Rothstein, "English Tragic Theory," pp. 311, 315.

12 See ibid., p. 311.

13 Hathaway, "John Dryden," p. 669.

14 Edmund Burke, *Reflections on the Revolution in France*, ed. Conor Cruise O'Brien (Harmondsworth: Penguin, 1973), p. 172. The Latin quotation is from Horace's *Ars poetica*, 99: "It is not enough for poems to be fine; they must charm."

15 See Carl Schmitt, *Hamlet oder Hekuba: Der Einbruch der Zeit in das Spiel* (Düsseldorf: Diederichs, 1956). I quote from the translation by David Pan of Schmitt's Appendix to the book, "On the Barbaric Character of Shakespearean Drama: A Response to Walter Benjamin on *The Origin of German Tragic Drama*," in *Telos* 72 (1986): 149, citing in a footnote Hegel, *Rechtsphilosophie*, pars. 93 and 218. I have discussed Schmitt's reading of *Hamlet* in greater depth in "Hamlet or Hecuba: Carl Schmitt's Decision," in *Representations* 83 (Summer 2003): 67–96.

16 It's an interesting fact of intellectual history that, while Benjamin drew on

Schmitt's *Political Theology* in his *Trauerspiel* book, Schmitt in turn used the *Trauerspiel* book in his analysis of *Hamlet*. But he also took issue with Benjamin's reading. In his chapter on "The Source of the Tragic," Schmitt begins his discussion of *Hamlet* as *Trauerspiel* by calling attention to the word *Spiel* or play. He asserts that the essence of theater is play, and that "in play lies the fundamental negation of the serious situation, the state of emergency" (p. 139). Here, again, we can see that the distinction between *Trauerspiel* and tragedy maps onto the traditional distinction between aesthetics and politics. Schmitt concedes that Shakespeare's plays are *Trauerspiele* in the self-reflexive, theatrical sense which Benjamin and others found characteristic of baroque drama. He writes, "Men of action in this epoch saw themselves on a rostrum before spectators, understood themselves and their activities in terms of the theatricality of their roles" (pp. 139–40). Yet, in contrast to Benjamin, Schmitt argues that there is something in *Hamlet* that transcends *Trauerspiel*, that Shakespeare "succeeded in elevating *Trauerspiel* to tragedy" (p. 142). In Schmitt's view, *Hamlet* and Tudor England are characterized by a sublime "religious fanaticism and feudal anarchy," by "medieval barbarity," in contrast to that "remarkable troika of modern progress," "politics, police and *politesse*" (p. 149). *Hamlet* and the character Hamlet, in Schmitt's reading, thus stand for the authentic world of politics, whereas Hecuba stands for artifice and aesthetics.

17 See Adorno and Horkheimer, *Dialectic of Enlightenment*, trans. John Cumming (1944; New York, 1969): "To the Enlightenment, that which does not reduce to numbers, and ultimately to the one, becomes illusion; modern positivism writes it off as literature" (p. 7). See also Herbert Marcuse, "The Affirmative Character of Culture," in *Negations*, trans. Jeremy J. Shapiro (Harmondsworth: Penguin, 1968), pp. 88–133; and the intriguing remarks by Arendt in *Origins of Totalitarianism* (1951; New York: Harcourt Brace Jovanovitch, 1973) on Hobbes' anticipation of the novel and the death of drama (p. 141 n37).

18 In her *Lectures on Kant's Political Philosophy*, trans. Ronald Beiner (Chicago, IL: University of Chicago Press, 1982), Arendt builds on Kant's analysis of aesthetic judgment to elaborate her own account of democratic politics. She thus antici-pates a variety of postmodern political theories that links aesthetic judgment to the possibility of democratic politics. See, for example, Jean-François Lyotard, *The Differend: Phases in Dispute*, trans. Georges van den Abbeele (Minneapolis, MN: University of Minnesota Press, 1968); and Anthony J. Cascardi, *Consequences of Enlightenment* (Cambridge: Cambridge University Press, 1999), esp. chapter 5. On the critical potential of "aesthetic form as such," see Herbert Marcuse, *The Aesthetic Dimension* (Boston, MA: Beacon Press, 1978), p. ix.

19 This paragraph draws on John McCole, *Walter Benjamin and the Antinomies of Tradition* (Ithaca, NY: Cornell University Press, 1993). The quotation comes from p. 128. Benjamin's definition of the symbol appears in *The Origin of German Tragic Drama*, trans. John Osborne (London: NLB, 1977), p. 160. Although he recog-nized that Goethe championed the symbol against allegory (see p. 161), Benjamin read Goethe's *Elective Affinities* as advancing an immanent critique of the symbol or what McCole calls "a scathing critique of the bourgeois form ... of life ... as a world permeated by mythic compulsions" (p. 123).

20 See Carl Schmitt, *Political Theology*, trans. George Schwab (Cambridge, MA: MIT Press, 1985), 5; Benjamin, *Origin*, pp. 70–71. On the differences between Schmitt's concept of the sovereign and Benjamin's views of the baroque sovereign, see the excellent article by Samuel Weber, "Taking Exception to Decision: Walter Benjamin and Carl Schmitt," *Diacritics* 22 (1992): 5–18.

21 Benjamin, *Origin*, pp. 69, 71.
22 On melancholy, see ibid., pp. 139 ff.
23 See also ibid., pp. 138–39: "In that excessive reaction which ultimately denied good works as such ... there was an element of German paganism and the grim belief in the subjection of man to fate. Human actions were deprived of all value. Something new arose: an empty world."
24 Ibid., p. 61.
25 On this last point, see Samuel Weber, "Genealogy of Modernity: History, Myth and Allegory in Benjamin's *Origin of the German Mourning Play*," *MLN* 106 (1991): 465–500, esp. 493–94.
26 Benjamin, *Origin*, pp. 72, and 69. According to Benjamin, this emphasis on the characters' passions meant that Aristotle's *Poetics* was, accordingly, either neglected by writers of *Trauerspiel* or interpreted through the lens of a Christian stoicism, e.g. Lipsius: "The *Trauerspiel* should fortify the virtue of its audience," and encourage stoic apatheia, "understood as an active impulse to alleviate the physical and mental suffering of others, and not as a pathological collapse at the sight of a terrifying fate, not as *pusillanimitas* but as *misericordia*" (p. 61). Here Benjamin begins to suggest that *Trauerspiel* may offer an immanent critique of the passions it stages. It is significant for *Samson Agonistes* that the violent oscillation between tyrant and martyr in turn produces the plotter typical of revenge tragedy. The question is whether Charles II or Samson is the plotter.
27 Benjamin, *Origin*, p. 99. On the importance of passions in the *Trauerspiel*, see also p. 132.
28 Ibid., p. 72. The allegorical mode informs Benjamin's own description of baroque character, which becomes as an allegory of allegory.
29 Ibid., p. 71.
30 Ibid., p. 133.
31 Ibid., pp. 178–79.
32 Moreover, as the mode that calls attention to the materiality of signs, allegory foregrounds both the linguistic relations of production and the agency of the interpreter.
33 Benjamin, *Origin*, p. 176. According to Benjamin, the arbitrariness of allegory gives rise to an antinomy:

> Any person, any object, any relationship can mean absolutely anything else. With this possibility a destructive, but just verdict is passed on the profane world: it is characterized as a world in which the detail is of no great importance. But it will be unmistakably apparent, especially to anyone who is familiar with allegorical textual exegesis, that all of the things which are used to signify derive, from the very fact of their pointing to something else, a power which makes them appear no longer commensurable with profane things, which raises them onto a higher plane, and which can, indeed, sanctify them. Considered in allegorical terms, then, the profane world is both *elevated and devalued*. (p. 175)

34 Ibid., p. 176. Hence "the conflict [in allegory] between theological and artistic intentions" (p. 177).
35 Adorno famously drew on this analysis, while secularizing the meaning of redemption, in his essays on literature, where he argued that allegory allowed the reader to see the [totalizing] ideological effect not only of aesthetics but also of politics. Kafka's allegories, his "artistic alienation," were the "means by which objective estrangement [became] visible." See Theodor W. Adorno, "Notes on

Kafka," in *Prisms*, trans. Samuel and Shierry Weber (1967; Cambridge, MA: MIT Press, 1982), p. 269.

36 Benjamin, "What is Epic Theater?," in *Illuminations*, ed. Hannah Arendt, trans. Harry Zohn (New York: Schocken, 1978), p. 149.

37 See Bertolt Brecht, "Über eine nichtaristotelische Dramatik", in *Schriften zum Theater*, 7 vols (Frankfurt am Main, 1963–64), 3.25.

38 "The Modern Theater is the Epic Theater" (*Notes to the Opera Aufstieg und Fall der Stadt Mahogany*, in *Brecht on Theater*, ed. and trans. John Willet (New York: Hill and Wang, 1964), p. 36.

39 Bertolt Brecht, "A Short Organum for the Theater," in *Brecht on Theater*, ed. and trans. John Willett (New York: Hill and Wang, 1964), p. 277.

40 Ibid., p. 205; Benjamin, "What is Epic Theater?," p. 150. (It may be for this reason that Brecht chose to rewrite Marlowe's *Edward II* and to set some of his other plays in early modern Europe.)

41 Benjamin, *Origin*, p. 74.

42 Ibid., pp. 67, 81.

43 See Eric Rothstein, *Restoration Tragedy* (Madison, WI: University of Wisconsin Press, 1967), pp. 15–16, on the serial form of Restoration drama. Here and following, all quotations from *Samson Agonistes* are taken from the edition of Milton's *Complete Poems and Major Prose*, ed. Merritt Y. Hughes (Indianapolis: Odyssey, 1957). The following reading of *Samson Agonistes* incorporates several paragraphs from my *Wayward Contracts: The Crisis of Political Obligation in England, 1640–1674* (Princeton, NJ: Princeton University Press, 2004).

44 See Benjamin, *Origin*, p. 139.

45 Like baroque drama in Benjamin's characterization, *Samson Agonistes* is meta-theatrical, from the prefatory note, to the Chorus' interpretation of Samson's condition in terms of medieval theories of tragedy ("O mirror of our fickle state" [l.164 and ff.]), to the Messenger's narration of Samson's final performance, his pulling down the theater of the Philistines. On the metatheatricality of *Samson Agonistes*, see Mary Ann Radzinowicz, "The Distinctive Tragedy of *Samson Agonistes*," *Milton Studies* 17 (1983), 267–70. Radzinowicz describes the Messenger's narration as a play-within-a-play. See also David Loewenstein, *Milton and the Drama of History* (Cambridge: Cambridge University Press, 1990).

46 Cf. C.M. Bowra's complaint that "Samson's fault is stressed so strongly that we hardly pity him, and if we feel any fear, it is less for him than for the Philistines"; Bowra is cited in Hughes's ed. of Milton's *Complete Poetry and Major Prose*, p. 546. See also A.S.P. Woodhouse, "Tragic Effect in *Samson Agonistes*," in *Milton: Modern Essays in Criticism*, ed. Arthur E. Barker (New York: Oxford, 1965), pp. 447–66, esp. p. 463, on how the end mitigates sense of tragedy since we don't feel sorry for the death of the Philistines. For a recent defense of our lack of pity for the Philistines, see Feisal G. Mohamed, "Confronting Religious Violence: Milton's *Samson Agonistes*," *PMLA* 102 (2005): 327–40. In *Shifting Contexts*, Wittreich cites numerous seventeenth-century comments to the effect that Samson elicits wonder but not pity because he is a flawed hero whose vengeful actions are not to be imitated. I come to a different conclusion about the meaning of our not pitying Samson.

47 Rothstein, "English Tragic Theory," p. 313.

48 Elsewhere in this volume Marshall Grossman argues that Milton's "translation" of action as passion places *Samson Agonistes* in a typological relation to the Passion and also signals an ethical moment of withholding interpretation which is prior to any determinate choice or action that might be represented in the text. I think it's

also possible to argue the opposite: that *Samson Agonistes represents* the withholding of interpretation in its deliberate obfuscation of the meaning of Samson's rousing motions but that, behind this, the text insists on the necessity of a decision.

49 Broadly speaking, this pedagogical goal is consistent with the vast majority of Renaissance commentators on Aristotle's *Poetics* whom Milton read. However they understood catharsis, they saw the ultimate goal of poetry as the didactic one of educating the reader's judgment. Where Milton differed from his Italian predecessors was in advocating a radical critique of the status quo. In this he was preceded by Euripides and, in a different way, by Gregory of Nazianzen, whom Milton believed to be the author of the twelfth-century tragedy *Christus patiens*. See below.

50 Milton's understanding of these tragic models is, of course, itself subject to debate. In *Shifting Contexts: Reinterpreting* Samson Agonistes (Pittsburgh: Duquesne University Press, 2002), Joseph Wittreich has argued that Euripides and Gregory, together, support a reading of Samson as a flawed Hebraic hero under the law, one who is not intended to be exemplary for Christian readers. Renaissance commentators on the Greek tragedians, including Euripides, however, support the exemplary reading of Samson. See, among others, Margaret J. Arnold, "*Graeci Christiani*: Milton's Samson and the Renaissance Editors of Greek Tragedy," in *Milton Studies* 18 (1983): 235–54. That Milton found a model for his own tragedy in *Christus patiens*, a pastiche of quotations from Euripides, makes the case for Samson's exemplarity even more forcefully. For the Christ who appears in this text is not simply the martyr figure associated with the *Trauerspiel*. Instead of emphasizing Christ's crucifixion, the text dramatizes Christ's role as "victor" and liberator. Wittreich has presented his case most recently. John Rogers argues that Milton finds *Christus patiens* exemplary for its proto-Sociaian understanding of redemption as atonement, rather than repayment or sacrifice, and that this Sociaian understanding of redemption is dramatized by Samson's refusal to be ransomed in *Samson Agonistes*. See his "Delivering Redemption in *Samson Agonistes*," in *Altering Eyes: New Perspectives on* "Samson Agonistes," ed. Mark R. Kelley and Joseph Wittreich (Newark, NJ: University of Delaware Press, 2002), pp. 72–97.

51 Samson also illustrates the iconography of melancholy. See among others Mary Ann Radzinowicz, *Towards* "Samson Agonistes" (Princeton, NJ: Princeton University Press, 1978).

52 Cf. Benjamin, *Origin*, p. 137: "The *Trauerspiele* of the seventeenth century treat [their subjects] … in such a way as to permit, indeed necessitate, repetition."

53 In a comment on an earlier draft of this essay, Marshall Grossman noted that Samson's rejection of Dalila also involves an evasion of her argument – that she, like him, acted on behalf of her country. I address the symmetry of Samson's and Dalila's actions in a related essay: "Milton's Disappointed Nationalism," in *Milton and Nationalism*, edited by Paul Stevens and David Loewenstein (Toronto: University of Toronto Press, 2005).

54 Battista Guarini, in Allan H. Gilbert, *Literary Criticism: From Plato to Dryden* (Detroit, MI: Wayne State University Press, 1962), p. 518. See Brecht, "Short Organon":

> Observation is a major part of acting. The actor observes his fellowmen with all his nerves and muscles in an act of imitation which is at the same time a process of the mind. For pure imitation would only bring out what had been observed; and this is not enough, because the original says what it has to say with too subdued a voice. To achieve a character rather than a caricature, the

actor looks at people as though they were playing him their actions, in other words, as though they were advising him to give their actions careful consideration. (p. 54)

55 See Erich Auerbach's discussion of the dual meaning of passio as action and passion, motus animi, in *Literary Language and its Public in Late Latin Antiquity and in the Middle Ages*, trans. Ralph Mannheim (Princeton, NJ: Princeton University Press, 1993), p. 70; cited in Kevis Goodman, "'Wasted Labor'? Milton's Eve, the Poet's Work, and the Challenge of Sympathy," *ELH* 64 (1997): 439.
56 Here one could say that the combination of rousing motions and play-acting corresponds to the strange coincidence of materiality and artifice that Benjamin found characteristic of *Trauerspiel*.
57 For Dryden's association of tragic pathos with Longinian sublimity, see "Grounds," pp. 254–55. On the republican sublime in Milton, see Annabel Patterson, *Reading Between the Lines* (Madison, WI: University of Wisconsin Press, 1993), pp. 256–72; and David Norbrook, *Writing the English Republic* (Cambridge: Cambridge University Press, 2000). On quotation in relation to the Longinian sublime, in particular Longinus's quotation of "Let there be light" as an example of sublimity, see Neil Hertz's reading of Longinus in *The End of the Line* (New York: Columbia University Press, 1985). Patterson stresses the political implications of "the Longinian claim that a writer can ameliorate his servitude, take back mastery, by *quoting* the texts of older defiances" (p. 267). But Patterson also points out the ideological ambiguity of the sublime offers the reader a choice of interpretations, which itself is the readerly equivalent of Arminianism or hermeneutical free will (p. 272). As I noted above, Nicholas von Maltzahn links the aestheticizing of the Milton sublime with the process of secularization in "The War in Heaven and the Miltonic Sublime." See note 1.
58 Dryden, "Grounds," p. 245, on poetical justice, or the punishing of vice and rewarding of virtue.
59 Benjamin, *Origin*, pp. 81–82.

Part III

Historicizing Renaissance ethics

6 The ethics of Renaissance bible translation

Vivienne Westbrook

Introduction

The history of the English Bible from the fourteenth century to the mid-sixteenth century is a history of translation in conflict; of rebellion against Church and State, of continual revision in pursuit of a stable text, of didactic paratextual intervention to bring the unlearned readers to an understanding of the Bible: and its erasure by the authorities that had licensed the Bible for that purpose; of persecution, condemnation, and conflagration of Bible translators within what purported to be a Christian Commonwealth. The ethical struggles out of which English Bibles emerged are reflected in the pages of the Bibles themselves, through the decisions and revisions that vied for the claim to truth, but most especially in the paratext to the Bibles, in the prefaces, annotations, and framing devices that overtly engaged with rival readings of what was most necessary to know for the good of the Commonwealth.

Bible historians make clear distinctions between the textual histories of Anglo-Saxon, Medieval, and Renaissance Bibles. The so-called Wyclif versions were recognizably English, but they were translated from Jerome's fourth-century Latin Vulgate Bible and copied by hand. Over one thousand words were introduced into the English Language through these Bibles, but because they were manuscript books their circulation and influence was limited.[1] Tyndale translated from the Hebrew and Greek texts, and with the advantage of the printing press his New Testaments and Pentateuchs circulated more easily. All subsequent Protestant Bibles printed throughout the sixteenth century contained, in varying degrees, revisions of Tyndale's work. But Renaissance Bible translators recognized themselves within a translation tradition that reached back to Anglo-Saxon times and the translation efforts of Bede, Alcuin, and King Alfred. The tradition that gave translators precedent and authority for translating the biblical text enabled Archbishop Matthew Parker to establish a heritage for the newly formed Church of England.[2]

Beginnings

In his preface to Gregory's *Pastoral Care*, Alfred implied that perhaps worse than the fact that the Vikings had destroyed so many libraries, an act that he understood in terms of Divine retribution for neglecting the educative agenda of Bede and Alcuin, was the fact that no one had even read those books:

> [T]he Churches throughout the whole of England stood filled with treasures and books, and there was also a great multitude of God's servants, but they had very little knowledge of the books, for they could not understand anything of them, because they were not written in their own language.[3]

In spite of the fact that the translation of good books was deemed to be good for the nation, there was a reluctance on the part of scholars to translate into their own language. Perceiving the miserable state of ignorance into which England had fallen, Alfred placed translation at the center of his agenda for social reform and defended his decision by arguing that the Hebrew Law had been translated by the Greeks and then the Romans before being translated in part by all other Christian nations (Sweet, p. 6). Although biblical texts were translated, even by Alfred himself, it was not until the fourteenth century that a Bible was translated into recognizable English.

Two Middle English versions of the Bible were inspired by John Wyclif's teaching. A prominent Oxford Theologian, Wyclif advocated a transfer of Obedience from the Church and its precepts, to an individual's Obedience to God's Laws as they were written in the Bible. Important to the promotion of this idea was the provision of a Bible in English. The first version was produced between 1380–84, a word-for-word translation of the Vulgate, and the second, *ca.* 1396, which was rendered into a more natural English style by John Purvey. At this early stage of English Bible production two ideas about how the Bible should be translated into English emerged; one that attempted to transfer the text from one language to another by following the word order exactly and another that attempted to transfer the meaning of the text across languages.

The second Wyclif Bible contained a prologue which offered both a defense of translation and an account of the translation ethics adhered to. In the prologue Purvey pointed out that:

> Bede translated the Bible, and expounded much in Saxon, that was English, the common language of this land, in his time; and not only Bede, but also King Alfred, that founded Oxford, translated in his last days the beginning of the Psalter into Saxon, and would more, if he had lived longer.

By returning to Bede and Alfred, Purvey demonstrated that there was authority and precedent for vernacular Bible translation.

His first step towards translating the Bible was to gather up many old Bibles, commentaries, and glosses. He consulted with Divines and Grammarians about the more difficult words, and translated the text as meaningfully as possible. The finished text was then corrected by many good and knowledgeable men. Whilst he invited correction from any learned person who might perceive that his translation was at fault, he cautioned him to first check his source: "for no doubt he shall find full many Bibles in Latin full false, if he look many, namely new; and the common Latin Bibles have more need to be corrected," he argued, than consulted. Where there was a textual discrepancy he gave the Hebrew and some contexts for establishing meaning in the margin. Purvey argued that the words were not inherently meaningful and must be made to serve meaning. When the same word in the source text was ambiguous he chose the word that was best suited to the context. He followed Augustine's example of Psalm 13.3 in which the Greek could equally be translated as "sharp" or "swift": "the feet of him be swift to shed blood." Purvey pointed out that "he that translated sharp feet, erred, and a book that hath sharp feet, is false, and must be amended." Finally, upon strong precedent, he elided the procedure for translating with the procedure for living; only a man divested of worldly distractions and open to the influence of the Holy Spirit would be capable of producing a true translation.

In his 1563 *Actes and Monuments* John Foxe compared Wyclif to Simon, son of Onias, in Ecclesiasticus 50: 1–21: "Even as the morning star ... so doth he shine and glitter in the temple and church of God." This was not how the Church regarded him. Wyclif was called to answer for his heretical doctrines at Lambeth, where he complained, among other things, that within the Church "the verities of the scriptures are reputed as Cockel [weed]." Foxe reports that the Bishops, unable to answer Wyclif, let him go.[4] Wyclif was eventually condemned in 1380 and forced into retirement at Lutterworth, where he died in 1384. Many of his followers were "most cruelly judged to the fire" (Foxe, 1563, L.iii.r.). Milton was later to argue that God had chosen Wyclif to begin reformation as a sign of grace and honor to the English people, and that he was the lamp by which all of Europe lit its taper, "whilst to his Country-men but a short blaze soon dampened and stifled."[5]

In 1408 Archbishop Arundel's convocation decreed that no further translation of the Bible into English should be made or read without prior permission. More than a century later, inspired by the progress that European scholars such as Erasmus and Luther had made in the translation of the Bible, scholars in England began to turn again to the possibility of translating the Bible into English.

In 1526 William Tyndale produced his first complete translation of the New Testament in English; he did so in exile and in defiance of Church authority.[6] That Tyndale was a pioneer of English biblical translation can

Figure 6.1 "The Martyrdome and Burning of Mayster William Tyndall, in
Flaunders by Filford Castle." Woodcut illustration from: Foxe, John,
Actes and Monuments, 1580, p. 1229, sig. DDDiiii.

hardly be disputed, but he was also considered a dangerous rebel infected
with Lutheran plague, and a threat to the realm. In 1536 he was strangled
and burned as a heretic in Vilvoord, and less than two years later Henry VIII
licensed his work in the Matthew Bible. To his account of William Tyndale's
life and martyrdom John Foxe added a woodcut that encapsulated his final
conflict with earthly authority in a final prayer, "Lord Open the King of
England's Eyes," by which the Elizabethan reader would understand that
God had heard the voice of the martyr and had granted his petition (Foxe,
1563, BBii.r.).

Renaissance English Bibles

Tyndale never completed his translation of the Bible. Miles Coverdale
produced the first printed English Bible in 1535, translated largely from the
Vulgate, the text of the Roman Catholic Church. John Rogers produced the
pseudonymous "Thomas Matthew" Bible in 1537 that contained William
Tyndale's translations, from Hebrew and Greek, of the Pentateuch, Joshua-

II Chronicles, and the New Testament, supplemented by Miles Coverdale's translations of the poetic and prophetic books. The Matthew Bible contained 2,200 marginal notes to help the reader to understand the text correctly. Whilst the marginal space in Medieval books was ever a site of supplementation and contestation,[7] the notes in the margins of the Matthew Bible ranged from simple word alternatives to those used in the text, to detailed diatribes of over 500 words that even transgressed the boundary of the margin and spilled into the space of the text. The Matthew Bible note to Job 1.6 cut not only into the text, but into the middle of the word "Satan":

> **Sa** Came and stood before the lord. ... The devil then is counted to have come into the sight of God not that the most wicked come indeed into the sight of the good God but because his cruel and most wicked thoughts came into the sight of God. And thus even nowadays also cometh the devil with them into the sight of God in that he daily accuses, finds fault, vexes, persecutes and troubles the Godly.**tan**.

At the most literal level the point was made that the godly were surrounded by "Satan." The notes made the Bible the focus of controversy. As John Foxe later defended his own book against attacks by Roman Catholics, he recalled in his preface to Elizabeth that the bishops:

> renewed . . . again an old wonted practice of theirs; doing in like sort herein, as they did sometimes with the Holy Bible in the days of your renowned father of famous memory, King Henry the Eighth who, when they neither by manifest reason could gainsay the matter contained in the book, nor yet abide the coming out thereof, then sought they, by a subtle devised train, to deprave the translation, notes, and prologues thereof.
>
> (Foxe, 1570)

Because of the trouble that the Matthew Bible annotations had caused, books with marginal annotations were subsequently subjected to censorship.

Richard Taverner, who had already produced several translations of Humanistic works for Cromwell, produced a revision of the Matthew Bible, retaining approximately two-thirds of the annotations. The margins of the Matthew Bible had hosted an impressive range of authorities that included historians, theologians, and Hebraists, but Taverner's procedure was to keep the note whilst removing the authority, with the notable exception of those notes in which Erasmus was cited. An example of Taverner's erasure strategy occurs in Matthew 2.1, by way of explaining the identity of the wise men at Herod's court who are on a mission to seek Christ. Rogers had included a marginal note which read: "a*These were neither kings nor princes, but as Strabo says (which was in their time) sage men among the Persians as Moses was among the Hebrews, he says also that they were the priests of the Persians." Rogers had included a double authority by naming his source and then endorsing it with the detail that he was a contemporary witness. Taverner cut the authority and gave: "f These were sage men among the Persians as Moses was among the Hebrews also they were the priests of the Persians." This was not merely a space-saving exercise; Taverner's margins could certainly have accommodated the full note here, as elsewhere. Such systematic erasure signaled a willingness to use, but a refusal to recognize a potentially distracting authority.

Although the Matthew Bible translation was preferred by Archbishop Thomas Cranmer and Thomas Cromwell, it was Miles Coverdale, rather than John Rogers, who was entrusted with its revision for Church use. Both Taverner's and Coverdale's revisions of the Matthew Bible were produced in 1539. In the absence of any marginal notes to his revision Miles Coverdale offered a short explanation that there was insufficient time for the annotations to be approved by the censors before the printing of the Bible, but that they would be printed in a separate subsequent volume – it never materialized. Further revisions of the Matthew Bible and Taverner's Bible were published by John Day between 1549 and 1551, edited by Edmund Becke. Becke's 1549 Matthew Bible revision included edited versions of the annotations in the Matthew Bible, his own annotations, plus the anti-papal annotations from Tyndale's previously printed works, such as the provocative note at Exodus 32: "the Pope's bull slays more than Aaron's calf," that John Rogers had left out of the Matthew Bible in 1537. Becke supplemented the New Testament with annotations from a 1548 New Testament revision that used John Bale's newly printed *The Image of Bothe Churches* to explicate the Book of Revelation.

In 1553 the fifteen-year-old Protestant King Edward VI died unexpectedly. Although the Protestant Lady Jane Grey was named as his successor, it was Mary, his Roman Catholic half-sister, who succeeded. With her coronation Protestant Bible printing ceased and around 800 scholars and theologians fled to Europe to escape persecution. From Geneva, a company of these scholars, led by William Whittingham, produced a Bible that was a revision of the Matthew Bible but with a new section of the prophetic books translated from Hebrew, making it the first printed English Bible translated entirely from the original languages. In 1558 Queen Mary died and many of the exiled Protestants returned home to see the Protestant Queen Elizabeth crowned. The exodus caused some delay in the finishing of the Bible, but it was eventually printed in 1560. It was furnished with maps, and thousands of annotations that were keyed into the text and packed into the marginal space. This Bible was subsequently revised and printed in numerous editions throughout the sixteenth century, finally in Edinburgh by Thomas Stafford in 1640.

The English Bishops took exception to the Geneva Bible's annotations and petitioned Queen Elizabeth for a new revision in order to remove perceived errors in the Great Bible and divert readers away from the dangerous Geneva Bible. Archbishop Matthew Parker led a committee of translators in producing what was subsequently known as the Bishops' Bible. It was printed in 1568 and was set up in the Churches to replace worn-out Great Bibles, but because it was a lectern Bible it was expensive and cumbersome. It failed to draw readers from the sociofugal or private enjoyment of their Geneva Bibles into the sociopetal collective space of interpretative constraint.

In the same year, Cardinal William Allen established a seminary at Douai. In 1578 the seminary was transferred to Rheims, where Gregory Martin, one of a number of Oxford scholars who had fled Queen Elizabeth's Protestant England, began work on translating the Bible into English for Roman Catholics. There were insufficient funds to print the whole Bible, so the New Testament was printed first in 1582, which Martin followed up with *Manifold corruptions of the Holy Scriptures by the heretike*; before he died later that year.[8] The Old Testament was eventually printed in two volumes in 1609/10. In their preface to the New Testament Allen and Martin maintained that the biblical text was not, and never had been, the whole of religion. Their version was intended merely to provide the Roman Catholics who had been reading the Geneva Bibles with a version of their own.

Although the stated role of the paratextual apparatus in the Protestant English Bibles produced throughout the sixteenth century was that of edification, the fact that readers were being edified in-line with Protestant perspectives made the annotations a constant target of the more conservative English Bishops, and, of course, Roman Catholics abroad. Allen and Martin's Roman Catholic version was copiously furnished with paratextual aids that included essays dispersed throughout the Bible, prefatory and end notes, marginal notes to the text, and even marginal notes to end notes to the text that were less taken up with explication than they were with defending the Church, its ceremonies, and its saints. The texts were read through the lens of Patristic authority; to attempt to interpret the Bible upon their own authority was deemed to be supremely arrogant, even heretical, two faults with which they charged Protestant interpreters. Evelyn Tribble has suggested that the inclusion of a plethora of paratext in Allen and Martin's version was a deliberate strategy to stop the reader: "Rather than deceiving the reader that the Scriptures are familiar, they choose to force the reader to stay at the difficult passages – to stop reading."[9] But what the paratext actually did was to force the reader onto a path of reading that was authorized by the Church, thereby undermining not the reading process so much as the individual's control over meaning.

For Protestants, "The Revelation" both accommodated the whole of human history and promised its end, but it was the most difficult text of the Bible because of its figurative language. For Roman Catholics "The Apocalypse" was mysterious. In the Rheims New Testament the first end-note to Apocalypse 1.1 explained that according to Eusebius, Denis of

Corinth had found the book "exceedingly mystical and marvellous" and that Augustine had agreed that "many things are obscurely spoken." The annotators cautioned the reader to be humble and advised that in this book they would "only or chiefly note unto the studious, such places as may be used by Catholics, or abused by Heretics, in the controversies of this time." The battle between the true and the false Churches, between Christ and the Anti-Christ told in the Apocalyptic text, was pursued in the paratextual arena of the Geneva and Rheims translations. At Apocalypse 10.18 the Rheims note pointed to: "The Calvinists heresy concerning the Saints confuted by S. Jerome long ago," and at Apocalypse 13.11: "Another false prophet inferior to Antichrist, shall work wonders also, but all referred to the honour of his master Antichrist. So doth Calvin & other Arch-heretics pervert the world to the honour of Antichrist, and so do their scholars also for the honour of them." The end note to 13.18 demonstrated why the Pope could not be the Antichrist, to refute a point that the Geneva Bible had expounded at some length. It began,

> If the Pope had been Antichrist, and had been revealed now a good many years since, as these fellows say he is to them, then the number of this name would agree to him, and the prophecy being now fulfilled, it would evidently appear that he bares the name and number here noted.

The marginal note to the end-note alerted the reader "The Pope can not be Anti-Christ." The defense was continued in the end note to 17.9, in an exposition of the seven hills:

> The Angel him self here expounds these 7 hills to be all one with the 7 heads and 7 kings: & yet the Heretics blinded exceedingly with malice against the Church of Rome, are so mad to take them for the seven hills literally, upon which in old time Rome did stand: that so they might make the unlearned believe that Rome is the seat of Antichrist.

In the margin to the end-note, a note read: "The Protestants' madness in expounding the 7 hills, of Rome: the Angel himself expounding it otherwise." Throughout the Rheims Apocalypse, then, refutation was integral to the expository strategy in which "Protestants," "Calvinists," and "Heretics" synonymously signified the adversaries of the true Church.

The aggressive annotations in the Rheims New Testament turned it into a weapon with which English Roman Catholics could now beat back the Protestant attacks on their Church that had dominated the margins of English Bibles for 80 years. Aggressive responses to paratext had by now become part of the history of English Bible printing. With the printing of the Rheims New Testament in 1582 it was now the turn of English Protestants to respond aggressively to Roman Catholic paratext.

What is surprising about the paratextual controversies is that no one questioned the ethics of carrying on a verbal war with contemporary Christians within the Holy Bible itself. There were plenty of opportunities to engage in vitriolic debate in the wider press and in public debating arenas, which were of course seized, without staining the Bibles with it. In 1583 Thomas Cartwright was given an advance of one hundred pounds by Sir Francis Walsingham to write a refutation of the Rheims New Testament. He was encouraged in the work by a large group of divines and scholars, among whom were the prominent Cambridge divines, William Whitaker and William Fulke. Cartwright took a long time over the work, so Fulke produced his own powerful confutation of both Martin's *Manifold corruptions* (1582) in his *A defense of the sincere and true translations* (1583) and the Rheims New Testament (1582) in his *A Confutation of all such arguments, glosses, and annotations* ... (1589). Meanwhile, William Whitaker engaged with William Rainolds, a student at Rheims, in *An Answere to a certeine booke ... entituled, A Refutation of Sundrie Reprehensions, Cavils, &c.* (1585), concerning the accuracy of the Hebrew text, a defense of the English Bible, and the Rheims annotations, which he argued demonstrated "blasphemous audacity in controlling the word of God" (O2.r.). Cartwright died before he could complete the commissioned work but it was posthumously printed in 1618; "the small defects by mice, through 30 years neglect" (A2.v.) and other gaps in the work were supplied with sections of Fulke's work.

The printed disputations over the Rheims annotations were, of course, the work of highly educated theologians, but the paratextual disputes within the bibles encouraged disputation among laymen and women within the commonwealth. The Jacobean Swetnam controversy provides an ample demonstration of misogynistic misapplications of biblical text and Protestant women's manipulation of Geneva Bible annotations.[10] Allen and Martin reminded the reader in their preface that the Council of Trent's prescription was that the Bible should not be read by everyone. It was deemed insufficient to exhort the reader to read the Bible in the right way, as the Protestant prefaces had done. They argued:

> [T]he holy Scriptures, though truly and Catholically translated into vulgar tongues, yet may not be indifferently read of all men, nor of any other than such as have express licence thereunto of their lawful Ordinaries, with good testimony from their Curates or Confessors, that they be humble, discrete and devout persons, and like to take much good, and no harm thereby.

To ensure that the true character of the Bible was understood the character of the reader had first to be assessed by a representative of the Church.

An ethics of Bible reading

In the prefaces to secular translations authors demonstrated an anxiety about malicious readers, and frequently pleaded with the intended patron for protection. In the prefaces to the English Bibles there was even more concern about how the Word might be misunderstood and its authority misapplied. Since the object of reading the Bible was to fashion one's life and conversation accordingly, it was necessary to alert the readers that the Bible contained narratives of evil as well as good, and that it was necessary to be able to distinguish between what was poisonous and what was efficacious. Inspired by Erasmus, Myles Coverdale provided steps for the reader in his 1535 Bible preface:

> Again, it shall greatly help you to understand scripture, if you mark not only what is spoken or written, but of whom, and unto whom, with what words, at what time, where, to what intent, with what circumstance, considering what goes before, and what follows after. For there are some things which are done and written, to the intent that we should do likewise: as when Abraham believes God, is obedient to his word, and defends Lot his kinsman from violent wrong. There are some things also which are written, to the intent that we should eschew such like. As when David lies with Uriah's wife, and causes him to be slain. Therefore (I say) when you read scripture, be wise and circumspect: and when you come to such strange manners of speaking and dark sentences, to such parables and similitudes, to such dreams or visions as are hid from your understanding, commit them to God or to the gift of his holy spirit in them that are better learned than you.

In his 1540 preface to the Great Bible that was set up in the Churches, Archbishop Thomas Cranmer asserted that "In the scriptures be the fat pastures of the soul, therein is no venomous meat, no unwholesome thing, they are the very dainty and pure feeding." Nevertheless there were "venomous" readers in urgent need of guidance, and it was to these that Cranmer's preface was chiefly addressed. Before reading the Bible it was necessary first to prepare one's mind to read it in the right way: "every man that comes to the reading of this holy book ought to bring with him first and foremost this fear of almighty god, and then next a firm and stable purpose to reform his own self according thereunto." Truly understanding the Bible meant applying its precepts to one's daily life; one would then become a teacher by example within the community "with his living and good example, which is sure the most lively, and most effective form and manner of teaching."

Citing Christostom, Cranmer outlined the importance of developing a reading habit and resisting the ready excuses for not reading. The more distracted and busy with worldly affairs one was, the more one needed the defence of the biblical texts: "You are in the midst of the sea of worldly wickedness, and therefore you need the more of ghostly succour and comfort." Cranmer maintained that far from being difficult to understand, the biblical texts were open to those who had the patience to read and learn. Unlike secular texts written by the learned for the learned to demonstrate their art, the Bible had been written by Apostles and Prophets with the intention of making God's message accessible to every kind of reader. The key to understanding was patience. When one came across a difficult text one was merely to "read it again and again" and God would "open to you that which was locked from you." This message was echoed in the preface to the 1568 Bishops' Bible:

> Christ himself will open the sense of the scriptures, not to the proud, or to the wise of the world, but to the lowly and contrite in heart: for he has the key of David, who opens and no man shuts, who shuts and no man opens. Math.xi. Esai.lxi. i.Cor.xii. Apoc.iii. Sapi.i. Iob.xiiii. Sapi.i.

The claims for the transformative power of text for the individual and society continued throughout the prefaces to Renaissance Bibles. When Edmund Becke produced his revision in 1549 it contained extensive marginal and end annotation that was meant to ensure right reading; the problem was how to persuade men to read the Bible at all. He advised Edward VI that the key to a happy reign over an obedient Commonwealth was to encourage men to read the Bible as they had:

> Chronicles and Canterbury tales, then should they also abandon and banish from their private houses and families all blasphemies, swearing, carding, dicing (the very adversaries and mortal enemies, to all virtue, study, godly reading of scripture and learned talk) and put away all pride, prodigality, riot, licentious and dissolute living, and all other enormities and vice, whereby God is offended and provoked to pour forth his indignation and anger upon us. Oh what a flourishing commonwealth should your grace enjoy and have? What loving and obedient subjects would they be?

Even as translators and revisers were engaged in semantic battles in the public arena and in the prefaces and margins across the editions of the English Bibles, the rhetoric of the efficacy and ease of reading the Bible was asserted. This assertion amounted to an open defiance of the Roman Catholic Church's argument that the biblical texts were too difficult and mysterious for an unlearned reader. Protestants argued that this opinion was maintained only to keep people in ignorance of the fact that Roman Catholic Religious practice had no biblical precedent, and therefore no authority.

In his Geneva Bible preface Whittingham departed from the rhetoric of simplicity, and rather sympathized with the reader in finding the text difficult. The way forward was not to patronize readers by pretending they were easy, but to help them to understand the obvious difficulties in the text. Whittingham noted: "what errors, sects and heresies grow daily for lack of the true knowledge thereof, and how many are discouraged (as they pretend) because they can not attain to the true and simple meaning of the same." Unfortunately, the paratextual helps that Whittingham's translators provided to meet this need were precisely what made this Bible unacceptable to English Church authority. In spite of its numerous editions and widespread popularity no Geneva Bible was ever authorized in England. In the Geneva Bible preface, "To our Beloved in the Lord the Brethren of England, Scotland, Ireland, &c.," Whittingham asserted that the translation was faithful both to the word and to the meaning: "For God is our witness that we have by all means endeavoured to set forth purity of the word and right sense of the holy Ghost for the edifying of the brethren in faith and charity." The procedure was to transliterate Hebrew names in their original forms, even in the Greek New Testament, and, where in the translation the meaning could not be rendered without straying too far from the Hebrew and Greek source texts, English words were inserted in italics so that the reader could discern between the biblical text and the dynamic departures authored by the translators to achieve narrative flow.

To facilitate referencing and memorization the text was divided into verses, for the first time in a complete English printed Bible. Authoritative endorsements of translated texts were signposted with * and what were considered to be the most important elements to glean from the text were signposted with paragraph markers. Arguments to books and chapters and running heads were added to each page, again to direct the reader in understanding "the chief point of the page." For instance, at Genesis 3.1–10 the marginal annotations made the serpent Satan's first victim, configured Adam's fall as the result of his own ambition and his blaming of Eve as wicked, whilst the running head read "The woman seduced." That Lanyer, Leigh, or Speght understood Eve both as the perfection of creation and as a victim rather than an imperfect, crooked rib that had caused mankind's suffering is the natural consequence of Geneva Bible reading. Maps and copious marginal explanations were added as a further aid to understanding and memorization.

Although the paratextual apparatus was intended to supplement the text with meaning, it amounted to a sophisticated system of prescribed reading that was necessarily doctrinally biased, even as it was asserted that the text was "pure." Invoking Matthew 7.6, Whittingham presented the Geneva Bible as the figurative pearl to be gratefully accepted by God's chosen church, a treasure that only the swine would refuse. "Therefore, as brethren that are partakers of the same hope and salvation with us, we beseech, you, that this rich pearl and inestimable treasure may not be offered in vain, but as sent from God to the people of God, for the increase of his kingdom, the comfort of his Church, and discharge of our conscience, whom it hath pleased him to raise up for this purpose." In the aftermath of the Marian persecutions, Whittingham exhorted Elizabeth to be as Zerubbabel in rebuilding the temple, and as Josias, in stamping out idolaters.

The Geneva translation was superior in every way to its predecessors, but Elizabeth's Archbishop Matthew Parker insisted on using the Great Bible, the official Bible of the Church, as the foundation for the Bishops' Bible. Any alteration in their text, Parker argued, was in the interest of improved accuracy, not private opinion or agenda:

> [Y]ou may be well assured nothing to be done in this translation either of malice or wilful meaning in altering the text, either by putting more or less to the same, as of purpose to bring in any private judgement by falsification of the words, as some certain men have been over bold so to do, little regarding the majesty of God's scripture.

Parker asserted that the Bishops' Bible was ethically superior to all other translations, and offered an example of what he considered to be unethical translation at Romans 6.13. He noted:

> one certain writer to prove his satisfaction, was bold to turn the word of Santificationem into the word of Satisfactionem ... That is, as we have given our members to uncleanness, from iniquity to iniquity: even so from henceforth let us give our members to serve righteousness into satisfaction: where the true word, is into sanctification.

A slip in biblical translation was inexcusable because of the consequences for faith, and salvation, but Protestant and Catholic translators accused each other of deliberately mistranslating to bend the Bible to their doctrine and win souls. In 1582 Allen and Martin made mistranslation a reason for the Roman Catholic restrictions on translating and reading the Bible. The obvious danger of allowing the unlearned to read texts that were difficult even for the most learned of men was doubled when ignorant readers were forced to read corrupted translations:

> Thomas Arundel Archbishop of Canterbury in a Council held at Oxford, strictly ordained, that no heretical translation set forth by Wiclif, and his accomplices, nor any other vulgar Edition should be suffered, till it were approved by the Ordinary of the Diocese: alleging S. Jerome's judgement of the difficulty and danger in translating holy Scriptures out of one tongue into another. And therefore it must needs be much more dangerous, when ignorant people read also corrupted translations.

Whilst Protestant reformers had undermined the authority of the Roman Catholic Church by arguing that it was full of distracting, corrupt traditions that had no biblical foundations, Roman Catholics undermined Protestant authority by asserting that the textual foundation of their religion was corrupt. The Hebrew and Greek texts from which Protestant reformers were translating, they argued, were less pure than the Vulgate because the pure texts that Jerome had used had since been lost, leaving only corrupt, late revisions: the texts on which Protestants had founded their own translations. The Vulgate had only recently been declared the authentic text of the Church, in a Council of Trent decree of 8 April 1546, but Allen and Martin argued forcefully for its authority.[11] They asked the reader to consider:

> S. Jerome's learning, piety, diligence, and sincerity, together with the commodities he had of best copies, in all languages then extant, and of other learned men, with whom he conferred: and if we so compare the same with the best means that hath been since, surely no man of indifferent Judgement, will match any other Edition with S. Jerome's: but easily acknowledge with the whole Church God's particular providence in this great Doctor, as well for expounding, as most especially for the true text and Edition of Holy Scriptures.

William Rainolds endorsed Allen and Martin in *A Refutation of M.W. Reprehension* (1583) and applied what he believed to be Gregory Martin's own discoveries of corruptions in the Hebrew texts to the ongoing fight for textual authority. Rainolds employed the example of Psalm 21:

> [W]here the prophet says in the person of Christ, *They have pierced my hands and feet*, which by the Jews being maliciously altered by mutation of one or other letter in to, *As a lion my hands and feet*, without wit, reason, or common sense, whereby is evacuated the best and clearest prophecy in the whole body of scripture touching the manner and fashion of Christ's crucifying, who besides M.W. would so blindly have dissembled it, and yet still sing us the old song of the pure fountains?[12]

In his *An Answere to a certeine booke … entituled, A Refutation of Sundrie Reprehensions, Cavils, &c.*, Whitaker pointed out that the suggestion that this corruption had been made deliberately by the Jews had long since been "repelled thoroughly, orderly, and learnedly," not least of all by Genebrard, their own professor of Hebrew at Paris. He explained that the corruption had occurred

> [B]y reason the two letters were so alike: and proves by testimony of learned Jews, that the best and truest copies had Caaru, they digged, not Caari as a lion, and that when Caari is written, it must be read Caaru. Who ever denied but some fault by this means might come into the Bibles, such as is in your translation are plentifully found?

The incredulous Whitaker asked: "is this a reason then of moment and importance to prove the Hebrew Bibles so full of corruption and errors, that they must be cast away, and the Latin translation Canonized for authentic scripture, and received in their place?"[13]

All Bible translators and revisers who expected to be taken seriously claimed that their text was faithfully translated, unbiased, and authoritative. Whether one was translating according to a Protestant or a Roman Catholic agenda, it was necessary to appear to be translating according to an emerging, if unwritten, code of translation ethics led by the objective pursuit of the true text.

Revision and erasure

That the translations of the English Bible necessarily increased the vocabulary of the English language; that the Protestant emphasis on reading increased the rate of literacy, and that the increased level of literacy in turn created an increased demand for secular as well as religious works is proverbial. With the licensing of the Matthew and Coverdale Bibles in 1538, the English language assumed a higher status than it had hitherto enjoyed. Increasingly throughout the sixteenth century important works were written in English; the vocabulary expanded even further and the rhetorical skills that had formerly been demonstrated only in Latin were now employed in English works.[14] But there was resistance to the way in which the English vocabulary was developing, and a felt need to protect and preserve its identity as a means of protecting national identity. In his preface to *Toxophilus*, Roger Ascham insisted that borrowing words from other languages would be like mixing wine, ale and beer in the same glass, resulting in a sickening mess, "neither easy to be known, nor yet wholesome for the body."[15] John Cheke, who has been called "The outstanding purist of the early Tudor age," endorsed Ascham's position and even translated the Gospel of Matthew to demonstrate that the text could be translated into native English (Barber, p. 62). He replaced "resurrection" with "gainrising," "parable" with "byword," and "apostle" with "frosent" (Westcott, p. 88). He gently reproached Thomas Hoby for not having translated Castiglione's *The Book of the Courtier* as purely as he might have done: "our own tongue should be written clean and pure, unmixed and unmangled with borrowing of other tongues" (Aaa1.r.). Hoby included Cheke's letter in his 1561 translation and added a preface of his own in which he exhorted English scholars to translate great works of learning for the good of the Commonwealth: "that we alone of the world may not be still counted barbarous in our tongue, as in time out of mind we have been in our manners" (C3.r.).

All of the sixteenth-century Protestant English Bibles were in varying degrees revisions of Tyndale's translations, a fact for which he has recently been dubbed the maker of modern English (Daniell, p. 372). But not all revisers followed Tyndale's translation ethics. George Joye thought the Bible ought first and foremost to convey meaning, so he revised mostly prepositions, suffixes, and tenses to create clear English narrative. But he also identified key words for a fuller translation, and even reintroduced "church" in place of Tyndale's "congregation." Tyndale's "Worshipped him" was revised to "fell down before him" (Matt. 15.25); "you are Peter. And upon this rock I will build my congregation" became "you are Stone. And upon this same stone, I will build my church" (Matt. 16.18); and "there is no resurrection" was revised as "there is no life after this" (Matt. 22.23).

Richard Taverner erased confusing repetition within narrative, rendered obscure words and phrases into English that was more appropriate to the context, and occasionally added words to the text to achieve an improved narrative flow. For instance, at Judges 20.38–39 where Tyndale had translated: "And the appointment of the men of Israel with the layers in wait to run upon Benjamin with the sword, was when they should make the smoke rise up out of the city," Taverner revised it as: "And they of Israel gave the privy watch their watch word that as soon as they had taken the City they should fire it, that by the smoke they should show that the city was won." Tyndale followed the Hebrew text closely here, but against the ethos of Evangelical translation that Tyndale had established, Taverner replaced it with a version based on the Vulgate. This is not one of the more famous episodes of Judges, and would have been difficult for a reader to understand. Tyndale's translation strains a reader and would have entirely defeated an auditor. Whittingham was even more dynamic than Taverner. He organized Tyndale's New Testament paragraphs into verses, he introduced intertextual glosses to make meaning clearer or sharpen the polemical edge of a verse, and refined Tyndale's English style. For instance, at Romans 6.1 he introduced a rhythm into Tyndale's "Shall we continue in sin, that there may be abundance of grace?" with "Shall we continue still in sin, that grace may more abound?" He also frequently translated references to written text into speech acts: "learning" with "speech" (1 Corinthians 1.5), "it is showed" with "it hath been declared" (1 Corinthians 1.11), "wisdom of words" with "wisdom of talk" (1 Corinthians 1.17), and "searcher" with "disputer" (1 Corinthians 1.20).

John Rogers and Edmund Becke pursued Tyndale's ethics, generally preferring to make a difference in the margin and to preserve the text, with some notable exceptions. Becke's changes were mostly syntactic; for instance, at Hosea 1.9, where the Matthew Bible had given "therefore will not I be yours," Becke revised it as "therefore will I not be yours." Again at Daniel 10.12, he revised "Then said he unto me," with "Then he said unto me." Edmund Becke's work was mostly paratextual, rather than textual. Rogers tended to revise nouns. For instance, where Tyndale had translated Hebrew place names Rogers revised them as transliterations of the Hebrew name. At Numbers 11.34–35 Rogers replaced Tyndale's translation "graves of lust"

with the transliteration Kibrath Hathavah, consigning Tyndale's translation
to the margin. Again at Numbers 21.20 Tyndale had translated "toward the
wilderness" and Rogers replaced it with the transliteration "Jesimon." In the
margin he noted, "Greek. wilderness." This policy of returning translation to
transliteration in respect of Hebrew place names signified a re-authentication
of the text and a renegotiation of the relationship between text and paratext
in the translation process.

Evelyn Tribble has argued that Tyndale consistently figured glosses, by
which she means the exegetical tradition through which the Roman Catholic
Church read the Bible, as obsfucatory (Tribble, p. 12). Whilst the inculcation
of a reading habit that privileged exegesis at the expense of the biblical text
was generally configured by Protestants as yet another distraction in the
Roman Catholic Church's agenda of distractions from true worship, in his
role as translator what Tyndale objected to most was gloss within the text. In
the preface to his 1534 New Testament Tyndale's stated aim was to keep his
translation as close as possible to his original and: "in many places, me think
it better to put a declaration in the margin, than to run too far from the text."
Tyndale maintained that the meaning of a difficult sentence could often be
gleaned from a text by reading it within the larger biblical context. However,
he did incorporate explanations of some of his word translations, such as this
lengthy paragraph to an explanation of his translation of "Metanoia" as
"repentance":

> Concerning this word repentance or (as they used) penance, the Hebrew
> has in the old testament generally (Sob) turn or be converted. For which
> the translation that we take for saint Jerome's has most part (convererti)
> to turn or be converted, and some time yet (agere penitenciam) And the
> Greek in the new testament has perpetually (Metanoeo) to turn in the
> heart and mind, and to come to the right knowledge, and to a man's
> right wit again. For which (Metanoeo) S. Jerome's translation has:
> sometime (ago penetenciam) I do repent: some time (peniteo) I repent:
> some time (peniteor) I am repentant: some time (habeo penitenciam) I
> have repentance: some time (penitet me) it repents me. And Erasmus
> uses much this word (resipisco) I come to my self or to my right mind
> again. And the very sense and signification both of the Hebrew and also
> of the Greek word, is, to be converted and to turn to God with all the
> heart, to know his will and to live according to his laws and to be cured
> of our corrupt nature with the oil of his spirit and wine of obedience to
> his doctrine.

From this short excerpt we can gauge the amount of detailed collation work
that Tyndale undertook in attempting to render a true translation. Not only
did he compare versions, he surveyed multiple instances of the word in their
contexts throughout the versions. Having assessed the meaning rendered in

translation, he then reread the biblical passage in the original language and made his decision accordingly.

Reformation Bible prefaces were usually taken up with translation and doctrinal points, reading agendas and patronage rhetoric. But in his 1534 New Testament Tyndale included a second preface: "William Tindale yet once more to the christen reader." Tyndale explained that when he was revising his 1526 New Testament another copy of his work, believed to be revised by George Joye, had come to his attention. George Joye had already printed separate translations of the Psalms, Proverbs, Isaiah, and Jeremiah before he undertook the revision of Tyndale's 1526 New Testament. The revision was printed in 1534, but Joye neglected to put his own name on the title leaf. In this same preface Tyndale responded angrily: "it is not lawful (think me) nor yet expedient for the edifying of the unity of the faith of Christ, that whosoever will, shall by his own authority, take another man's translation and put out and in and change at pleasure, and call it a correction." Though there was, in fact, no copyright law to prevent such practice, as far as Tyndale was concerned, there was an ethics attached to correcting another man's translation that Joye had breached, that of making changes without accepting responsibility for them. In his *Apologye*, Joye argued that to claim it as his own would have been inappropriate, "for it had been but a lie to call it my translation for translating and mending a few certain doubtful and dark places."[16] Joye had substituted in numerous places, though not in all, a fuller English translation of "anastasis" that Tyndale had translated as "resurrection." Tyndale marshaled all the authority he could against Joye's substitutions:

> If that change, to turn resurrection into life after this life, be a diligent correction, then must my translation be faulty in those places, and saint Jerome's, and all the translators that ever I heard of in what tongue so ever it be, from the apostles unto this his diligent correction (as he calls it) which whither it be so or no, I permit it to other men's judgements.

Tyndale accused Joye of breeding heresy. Because of Joye's "unquiet curiosity" about resurrection, Tyndale argued, there was now "no small number" who denied the resurrection of the flesh "affirming that the soul when she is departed, is the spiritual body of the resurrection, and other resurrection shall there none be." Their salvation was at stake because of Joye, and Tyndale could do nothing to remedy it: "it were as good persuade a post, as to pluck that madness out of their brains." Clearly Tyndale's attack on Joye goes beyond his own anger at the man who has attempted to attribute a heretical revision to him, to a larger call for an established ethics of translation that would prevent such practice in the future:

> But though it were the very meaning of the scripture: yet if it were lawful after his example to every man to play bo peep with the translations that

are before him, and to put out the words of the text at his pleasure and to put in every where his meaning: or what he thought the meaning were, that were the next way to establish all heresies and to destroy the ground wherewith we should improve them.

The intimate relationship between translation procedure and paratextual procedure is perhaps nowhere better expressed than in this preface. Establishing an English text that is authoritative is foremost in Tyndale's mind as he argues:

> If the text be left uncorrupted, it will purge her self of all manner false glosses, how subtle so ever they be feigned, as a seething pot casts up her scum. But if the false gloss be made the text, diligently overseen and corrected, wherewith then shall we correct false doctrine and defend Christ's flock from false opinion, and from the wicked heresies of ravening of wolves?

Tyndale had already stated his own procedure of leaving the text dark, where necessary, whilst putting light in the margin in order to preserve as much as possible of the source text's characteristics. He was not prepared to turn the text to gloss from which the true text could never be recovered. This was precisely what he felt George Joye had done. Joye utterly rejected Tyndale's criticism and complained that Tyndale "now at last has spewed forth all his venom and poison at once upon me" (Eviii.v.).

Fundamental to our understanding of this disagreement between Tyndale and Joye is the recognition that Joye and Tyndale had competing translation ethics. Tyndale wanted to establish the authority of the text in the English language, whilst Joye wanted a text first and foremost to make sense and to leave, what he called, frivolous glosses out: "I would the Scripture were so purely and plainly translated that it needed neither note, gloss nor scholia, so that the reader might once swim without a cork" (Cvii.r.).

Joye suggested that Tyndale was angry because someone else had dared to steal his glory, thereby suggesting that Tyndale was not as virtuous as he pretended to be. Tyndale insisted that his aim in translating was first to bring the knowledge of the Bible to the ignorant and then: "to weed out all that is not planted of our heavenly father, and to bring down all that lifts up itself against the knowledge of the salvation that is in the blood of Christ." However, Tyndale ended his preface with a final exhortation not to Christian readers, but to irresponsible translators:

> Wherefore I beseech George Joye, yes and all other too, for to translate the scripture for themselves, whether out of Greek, Latin or Hebrew. Or (if they will needs) as the fox when he has pissed in the gray's hole challenges it for his own, so let them take my translations and labours,

and change and alter, and correct and corrupt at their pleasures, and call it their own translations, and put to their own names, and not to play bo peep after George Joye's manner.

Although Tyndale appeared to have a solid stake in the moral high ground of this argument, he too had been accused of irresponsible translation by the Roman Catholic Thomas More. More protested that Tyndale had "translated presbuteros by this English word elders, a word unknown among English men to signify priests, and among whom this word priest was the proper English word well known, and had served in that signification so many hundred year before Tyndale was born."[17] Tyndale observed that in the Old and New Testament the leaders of the people were called elders and he translated accordingly. Although Tyndale's translation ethics were such that the purity of the text was a priority, he also maintained that he did not mind whether his reader called them elder or priest: "it is to me all one: so that you understand that they be officers and servants of the word of God." In the process of trying to put a Bible in the Church, Tyndale had put "Church" out of the Bible. His translation was understood not as an attempt to achieve accuracy, but as an attempt to undermine the Church through the erasure of traditional ecclesiastical vocabulary. More's point was not that Tyndale should not have translated "ecclesia" as "congregation," but that he should not have translated it as "congregation" all the time. More understood that congregation referred to a mixed gathering, whereas church referred to a gathering of Christians: "But I would in no way that as Tyndale takes me, ecclesia should always be translated by this word church, for that were also wrong. For truth it is that ecclesia signifies in the Greek tongue a congregation, without respect of either good or bad Christian or unchristian" (qi.r.).

Whilst Tyndale's translation erased the vocabulary of the Roman Catholic Church, subsequent revisers focused on paratextual strategies of erasure. English Renaissance Bibles carried a table of the principal matters, which were loosely organized alphabetical lists of key words in the Bible followed by brief explanations and biblical reference points. In the Matthew Bible, Roman Catholic key words were included in the tables, but only so that they could be negated. As the reader happened upon such words as "Mass" or "Purgatory" the explanation was given that these terms were not in the Bible. For "Mass," one could turn to the "Supper of the Lord," as for "Purgatory," it was explained: "this word purgatory is not in the Bible: but the purgation and remission of our sins, is made us by the abundant mercy of God." (Bviii.r.). Richard Taverner's strategy was to remove such words from the table, thereby erasing them entirely from his Bible.

In his preface to his 1535 Bible Miles Coverdale exclaimed: "we have great occasion to give thanks unto God, that he hath opened unto his church the gift of interpretation and of printing." In his attempt to defuse the war over words Coverdale argued that since the translation of the Bible had been neglected for so long, the fact that so many now were learning the Hebrew and Greek languages in order to understand the text better was surely to be praised rather than condemned:

> [W]ho is now then so unreasonable, so spiteful, or envious, as to abhor him that does all his diligence to hit the prick [target], and to shoot nearest it, though he miss and come not nearest the mark? Ought not such one rather to be commended, and to be helped forward, that he may exercise himself the more therein?

No translator claimed to have read everything perfectly, and all translators invited learned readers to draw their attention to any faults, but in finding fault Coverdale insisted that "love be joined with knowledge" so that the work of translating the Bible could be a unifying enterprise for the benefit of the whole Church, rather than a source of conflict and division.

The ethics of preservation

Toward the end of the sixteenth century there were numerous biblical texts and commentaries at the disposal of translators; even so there were some words that were deemed to be impossible to translate. Allen introduced this problem to the reader as "the strictness observed in translating some words, or rather the not translating of some" in their 1609 preface. He explained that some Hebrew words were borrowed straight into the Greek text and are therefore present in the Latin text, citing Augustine's illustrations of "Amen" and "Alleluia." Augustine had explained that they were preserved "for the more sacred authority thereof." For the same reason, he argued, many names of feasts and sacrifices were retained in their sacred tongues of Hebrew, Greek, and, he added, Latin. He explained a failure of translation as a failure of the English language to accommodate the equivalent meaning succinctly:

> Again for necessity, English not having a name, or sufficient term, we either keep the word, as we find it, or only turn it to our English termination, because it would otherwise require many words in English, to signify one word of an other tongue. In which cases, we commonly put the explication in the margin. Briefly our Apology is easy against English Protestants; because they also reserve some words in the original tongues, not translated into English: as Sabbath, Ephod, Pentecost, Proselyte, and some others.

Accepting the impossibility of translating some words into English, why, Allen argued, may not the words that the Church already has for those words be maintained, rather than translated into English words that fail to make meaning any clearer?

And why then may we not say Prepuce, Phase or Pasch, Azimes, Breads of Proposition, Holocaust, and the like? rather than as Protestants translate them: Foreskin, Passover, The feast of sweet breads, Show breads, Burnt offerings: etc. By which terms, whether they be truly translated into English or no, we will pass over.

That he recognized no sacred authority resident in such Protestant translations was finally demonstrated here in the glib pun on Passover/pass over. In terms of making more sense, he argued, these translations were as helpful to the English reader as if they had not been translated. Of course, the Roman Catholic translation was not easier, but existing familiarity with ecclesiastical vocabulary was what he insisted made it more accessible. Allen maintained that the Protestant translators were more interested in serving their own agenda than any English reader, and in deliberately corrupting the text "contrary to the Hebrew, and Greek, which they profess to translate, for the more show, and maintaining of their peculiar opinions against Catholics." Fulke preceded his 1589 *Confutation* with a table that offered translations and explications of all of the words that Allen had claimed could not be translated, typically: "Holocaust, a kind of sacrifice, where all was burnt in the honour of God. Heb.10,6." The untranslated words stood as a sign of the broader reluctance of Roman Catholic translators to make meaning clear for the common reader. Thomas Cartwright described the reluctant translators as men "which having a natural hatred of cheese, or some such food, in such sort as the very sight or touch of it does offend them: yet being famished, are content for the safety of their lives even to eat it."[18] Miles Smith similarly understood the obscurity of the Roman Catholic translation as a sign of Allen and Martin's reluctance to translate: "that since they must needs translate the Bible, yet by the language thereof, it may be kept from being understood." Smith maintained that the King James translators had:

> avoided the scrupulosity of the Puritans, who leave the old Ecclesiastical words, and take them to other, as when they put washing for Baptism, and congregation instead of Church as also on the other side we have shunned the obscurity of the Papists, in their Azimes, Tunike, Rational, Holocausts, Praepuce, Pashe, and a number of such like, whereof their late Translation is full.

None of the translators or revisers we have discussed made the substitution of "washing" for the sacrament of "baptism" in their New Testaments. Nevertheless, in his *Refutation* Rainolds mirrored the sacrilegious substitution by making the sacred word serve the crudest of plain contexts: "when one of your ministers goes to be washed and trimmed at the barbers, he goes to baptism." His marginal annotation read "The abuse of ecclesiastical words the ruin of all religion" (p. 271). Whitaker responded by insisting: "we call it the sacrament of *Baptism*, not of washing, as you charge us: notwithstanding that *baptismus* in the general signification of the word, is nothing else but *washing*, and so is used in the scripture often times, and so have your selves translated it. Mark.7.4" (p. 111). Just as More had earlier argued that Tyndale should have translated "ecclesia" according to context, so too, Whitaker argued, should "baptisma" be translated. In his effort to promote the primacy of the King James Bible translation, Miles Smith asserted that both Puritan and Papist ethics of translation foregrounded artifice, where nature was required, and that the King James translators had desired "that the Scripture may speak like itself, as in the language of Canaan, that it may be understood even of the very vulgar."

As William Slights has noted, the English Church had ever been keen to restrain the "interpretative excesses of the more radical preachers, particularly in the margins of any Bible that was to carry the imprimatur of monarch or bishops."[19] After decades of controversy over the marginal notes in English Bibles, King James forbade the King James Bible translators to employ the margins for anything other than language notes and cross-references. King James had taken exception to several notes in the Geneva Bible which he considered to be "partial, untrue seditious, and savouring too much of dangerous, and traitorous conceits: as for example, Exod.1.19. where the marginall note allows disobedience to Kings, and 2.Chron.15.16. the note taxes Asa for deposing his mother, only, and not killing her."[20] Whilst King James's aversion to annotations meant that the committee had to translate without the advantage of qualifying commentary in the margins, they did attempt to shape the reading of the biblical texts with running heads, chapter summaries, and cross-references. For instance, the Geneva Bible had introduced Genesis 3 with a running head "The Woman Seduced," but the King James Bible gave instead a universal running head "The fall of man." The short chapter summaries simply picked out key elements in the text with the appropriate verse numbers immediately before the chapter, but they could also, therefore, powerfully direct the interpretation of the text. The Geneva chapter summary at Genesis 3 gave: "1 The woman seduced by the serpent. 6 Entices her husband to sin. 14 They three are punished. 15 Christ is promised. 19 Man is dust. 22 Man is cast out of paradise." The King James chapter summary gave: "The serpent deceives Eve. 6 Man's shameful fall. 9 God arraigns them. 14 The serpent is cursed. 15 The promised Seed. 16 The punishment of Mankind. 21 Their first clothing. 22 The casting out of Paradise." In the Geneva Bible summary, there is a chain reaction of Eve's seduction and her seduction of Adam. Once incorporated in a state of sin God punishes all three offenders collectively. The promise of the seed is juxtaposed with man's unworthiness and his exile from paradise. The King James Bible summary placed emphasis on the deceptive serpent who caused mankind to fall and was subsequently cursed. The promise to mankind precedes the announcement of punishment and Adam and Eve are then clothed before being exiled. From this summary the reader would anticipate a narrative in which God provides the solution to man's immediate and long-term needs. Although the King James Bible translators were forbidden to use marginal annotations, Miles Smith argued against those who "peradventure would have no variety of senses to be set in the margin, lest the authority of the Scriptures for deciding of controversies by that show of uncertaintie, should somewhat be shaken." He explained that the translators had in fact scattered some words and meanings throughout the Bible, though none pertaining to doctrine since what was required for salvation was plain enough, but "in matters of less moment, that fearfulness would better beseem us than confidence." Smith made it clear that the King James translators had not made a new translation, nor had they sought to make a good one from a bad one, but rather "to make a good one better, or out of many good ones, one principal good one, not justly to be excepted against." As such it attempted to resolve the ethical conflicts that had attended English Bibles up to that moment and to establish itself as the embodied achievement of a century of biblical scholarship.

If Tyndale's translations were subsequently understood as the foundation for Renaissance English Bibles, then the King James Bible was subsequently understood as the crowning achievement. Initially printed as a large lectern Bible, it was quickly printed in a more manageable quarto format for private reading, and even with Geneva Bible notes to increase its popularity. Nineteenth-century histories of the English Bible were created by drawing a line between the work of Tyndale and the Bibles that discernibly contributed, bibliographically or textually, to the making of the King James Bible. The politics of influence ensured that many other Bibles were consigned to the margins in subsequent histories of the English Bible and their role in the development of the English language and English reading practices erased.

It has been well noted, more recently by Richard Griffiths, that the main thrust behind the translation of the Bible was "the emancipation of the people, who would now be able to read it for themselves, and not rely on the teachings of others."[21] Whilst this was certainly the stated aim of the first generation of European and English reformers, throughout the sixteenth century every attempt was made to control the readership through a broad range of paratextual strategies, and restrictive State interventions. The paratext was dangerously ambiguous, and recognized as such from the moment English biblical texts were first printed, for in attempting to constrain the reader paratext signified both the limitations and the endless possibilities of interpretative departures from the text. Allied with the rhetoric of wishing to liberate the reader and reform the Commonwealth was the desire of a generation of Reformation humanists to liberate the text from corruptions and from what it perceived to be the corrupt and corrupting authority that had concealed it for so long. What emerged was an ethics of biblical translation that participated in the formation of an ethics of reading for personal, social, church and state reformation, and, of course, rebellion.

Notes

I wish to express my gratitude to the following: The National Science Council of Taiwan who sponsored this research; Marshall Grossman and David Norton who patiently read drafts of this essay.

1 Otto Dellit, *Uber lateinsiche Elemente im Mittelenglischen* Marburgh (Germany, 1905), cited in Albert C. Baugh and Thomas Cable, eds, *A History of the English Language*, 5th ed. (London: Routledge, 2002), p. 38.
2 See Charles Barber, *Early Modern English* (Edinburgh: Edinburgh University Press, 1997).
3 Henry Sweet, *King Alfred's West Saxon Version of Gregory's Pastoral Care* (London: Oxford University Press, 1871), p. 4.
4 John Foxe, *Acts and Monuments [...]. The Variorum Edition* [online] (hriOnline, Sheffield, 2004). Available from: www.hrionline.shef.ac.uk/foxe (K.iiii.v.) [Accessed: 15.11.2005]. Subsequent citations will be given parenthetically.
5 John Milton, *Of reformation touching church-discipline in England and the causes that hitherto have hindred it* (London: Thomas Underhill, 1641), Wing M2134, pp. 6–7.
6 David Daniell, *Tyndale: A Biography* (London: Yale University Press, 1996).
7 Michael Camille, "Glossing the Flesh: Scopophilia and the Margins of the Medieval Book," in D.C. Greetham, ed., *The Margins of the Text* (Ann Arbor, MI: University of Michigan, 1997), pp. 245–68.
8 B.F. Westcott, *A General View of the History of the English Bible*, 3rd ed., rev., W.A. Wright (New York: Macmillan, 1905), p. 105.
9 Evelyn B. Tribble, *Margins and Marginality: The Printed Page in Early Modern England* (London: University Press of Virginia, 1993), p. 48.
10 Vivienne Westbrook, "Resistant Typologies in Renaissance Women's Writing," in Janet Levarie Smarr, Francis K.H. So and I-chun Wang, eds, *Identity and Politics: Early Modern Culture* (Kaohsiung: NSYS, 2005), pp. 35–64.
11 W. Schwarz, *Principles and Problems of Biblical Translation: Some Reformation Controversies and their Background* (Cambridge: Cambridge University Press, 1955), p. 10.
12 William Rainolds, *A refutation of sundry reprehensions, vacils, and false sleightes, by which M. Whitaker laboureth to deface the late English translation and Catholike annotations of the new Testament* (Paris: Richard Verstegan, 1583, STC 20632), p. 355.
13 William Whitaker, *An answere to a certeine booke, written by M. William Rainolds student of divinitie in the English Colledge at Rhemes* (London: Eliot's Court, 1585, STC 25364b), p. 140.
14 R.F. Jones, *The Triumph of the English Language* (Stanford, CA: Stanford University Press, 1953).
15 *Toxophilus the schole of shootinge contayned in tvvo bookes. To all gentlemen and yomen of Englande, pleasaunte for theyr pastyme to rede, and profitable for theyr use to folow, both in war and peace. ...* (London, 1545, STC (2nd ed.) / 837), a ir.
16 George Joye, *The new Testament as it was written, and caused to be written, by them which herde yt Whom also oure Saveoure Christ Jesus commaunded that they shulde preach it unto al creatures* (Antwerp, 1534, STC 2825), Fvi.r.

17   Thomas More, *The confutation of Tyndales answere made by syr Thomas More* (London: Wyllyam Rastell, 1532, STC 18079), ti.v.

18   Thomas Cartwright, *A confutation of the Rhemists translation, glosses and annotations on the New Testament so farre as they containe manifest impieties, heresies, idolatries [...] and other evills* (Leiden: W. Brewster, 1618, STC 4709), B2.r.

19   William Slights, *Managing Readers: Printed Marginalia in English Renaissance Books* (Ann Arbor, MI: University of Michigan Press, 2001), p. 123.

20   William Barlow, *The summe and substance of the conference [...] at Hampton Court. January 14. 1603* (London: John Windet and T. Creede, 1604, STC 1456.5), p. 47.

21   Richard Griffiths, ed., *The Bible in the Renaissance: Essays on Biblical Commentary and Translation in the Fifteenth and the Sixteenth Centuries* (Aldershot: Ashgate, 2001), p. 4.

Bibles cited

Becke, Edmund, ed., *The Byble that is to say all the holy Scripture*, London, John Daye and William Seres, 1549, STC 2077.

Coverdale, Miles, ed., *Biblia the Bible, that is, the holy Scripture of the Olde and New Testament*, Cologne, Cervicornus and J. Soter, 1535, STC 2063.

——, *The Byble in Englyshe that is to saye the content of al the holy scrypture, both of ye olde, and newe testament, with a prologe therinto, made by the reverende father in God, Thomas archbyshhop of Cantorbury*, London, Rychard Grafton, 1540, STC 2071.

Forshall, Rev. Josiah and Sir Frederic Madden, eds, *The Holy Bible ... with the Apocryphal Books, in the earliest English versions made from the Latin Vulgate by John Wycliffe and his followers*, London, Partridge and Oakley, 1850.

Joye, George, *The new Testament as it was written, and caused to be written, by them which herde yt Whom also oure Saveoure Christ Jesus commaunded that they shulde preach it unto al creatures*, Antwerp, Wyddowe of Christoffel [Ruremond], 1534, STC 2825.

Martin, Gregory, Tr., *The holie Bible faithfully translated into English, out of the authentical Latin*, Doway, Laurence Kellam, 1609/10, STC 2207.

Martin, Gregory and William Allen, Tr., *The New Testament of Jesus Christ, translated faithfully into English, out of the authentical Latin*, Rhemes, John Fogny, 1582, STC 2884.

Parker, Matthew, Ed., *The holie Bible*, London, Richard Jugge, 1568, STC 2099.2.

Rogers, John [Thomas Matthew], ed., *The Byble which is all the holy Scripture: in whych are contayned the Olde and Newe Testament*, Antwerp, Crom [for Grafton and Whitchurch], 1537, STC 2066.

Smith, Miles, ed., *The Holy Bible conteyning the Old Testament, [...] compared and revised, by His Majesties speciall comandment*, London, Robert Barker, STC 2217.

Taverner, Richard, ed., *The most sacred Bible, whiche is the Holy Scripture conteyning the Old and New Testament*, London, John Byddell [for Thomas Barthlet], 1539, STC 2067.

Tyndale, William, Tr., *The Newe Testament dylygently corrected and compared with the Greke*, Antwerp, marten Emperowr, 1534, STC 2826.

Whittingham, William, ed., *The Bible and Holy Scriptures conteyned in the Olde and Newe Testament. Treanslated according to the Ebrue and Greke*, Geneva, Rouland Hall, 1560, STC 2093.

7 Eating Montaigne

Paul Yachnin

Books are deeply loved and greatly feared in *The Tempest*. Prospero praises his enemy's counselor Gonzalo for having given him volumes from his own library. (Gonzalo extended this kindness while piling the Duke and his daughter into an unseaworthy little boat and setting them adrift at sea.[1]) As the play unfolds, the volumes come to seem almost worth the prizing. For one thing, Prospero loves them; if we take him at his word, his affection for them has remained undiminished, even after all that he has suffered. In his account of his banishment, he uses the present tense only about his books: "so of his gentleness, / Knowing I lov'd my books, he furnish'd me / From mine own library with volumes that / I prize about my dukedom" (1.2.165–68).[2] When he promises to renounce his magic, he uses the singular word "book" ("I'll drown my book" [5.1.57]), so perhaps he means to take the rest of them back to Milan. Indeed he might be wise to do so since books are also instruments of power in the world of the play. Caliban warns his fellow conspirators that no act of violence can succeed against Prospero unless his books are first taken from him. Leslie Fiedler, perhaps sharing a certain fantasy of literary power with Prospero, calls the books "those symbols of a literate technology with which the ruling classes of Europe controlled the subliterates of two worlds."[3]

Since they are objects of great emotional investment, the source of Prospero's supernatural powers, and among the primary agents of the dramatic action (they distracted Prospero from his duties as Duke of Milan, which led to his ouster), it is striking that the play-text does not call for the onstage appearance of a single volume. This is particularly remarkable since books are not hard to find in the early modern drama. *Hamlet* has at least two, Marlowe's *Doctor Faustus* features a score of large, manuscript volumes, and books turn up even in action-packed plays such as *Titus Andronicus*, where Lavinia puts a copy of Ovid's *Metamorphoses* to use against the men who raped and mutilated her. Why, then, are there no books in *The Tempest?* I suggest that there are no books in this most bookish of plays because Shakespeare has eaten them. Prominent among the texts on the menu was John Florio's translation of Montaigne, *The essayes or morall, politike and millitarie discourses of*

Lo[rd] Michaell de Montaigne, published in a folio volume in 1603. In what follows, I argue that to understand Shakespeare's eating of Montaigne is to begin to grasp something important about the ethics of reading in the early modern market in literary goods. On this account, ethical reading, as both Montaigne and Shakespeare practice it, is related to a quasi-Levinasian calling toward a recognition of the other within the literary text, but a complex calling because such recognition cannot be prised apart from the instrumentalizing practices of buying and selling and because remembering the personhood of the text is always associated with dismembering the text.[4]

Since the literary field in our own time seems marked by the tension between the impersonal, instrumental procedures of the marketplace and the emotionally weighty, personal closeness of author and reader, it should not be surprising to find a contradictory element also in two of the originators of the field. Montaigne's two-octavo-volume work, put on sale in Bordeaux in 1580, in one duodecimo-volume in Paris in 1585, and in London in Florio's translation in 1603, announced that it was solely dedicated to the private benefit of the author's friends and family – "to the particular commodity of my kinfolks and friends: to the end, that losing me (which they are likely to do ere long), they may therein find some lineaments of my conditions and humors, and that by that means reserve more whole, and more lively foster the knowledge and acquaintance they have had of me" (xxxiii).[5] The very fact that Montaigne's words have been translated into English by an intermediary producer unknown to the author – so that his words are literally not his own – suggests something about the alienation of utterance consequent upon the entry of writing into the marketplace. Publishing format, not usually determined by the author, also affects the overall impression that a work makes upon readers; the shift from the French octavo or duodecimo to the English folio suggests that the London publisher wanted to lure potential buyers by emphasizing the elite provenance of the book.[6]

The prefatory matter of the similarly up-market Shakespeare First Folio (1623) featured the playwright's portrait, an accompanying poem that characterized the plays as the essential expression of his mind, and also Ben Jonson's moving tribute, "To the memory of my beloved, the author." All this seems intended to suggest that the volume was packed full with the author's personality and that conscientious readers could expect to come to know what Jonson calls "the race / Of Shakespeare's mind and manners." But the Folio's prelims also included an exhortation to customers' purses: "the fate of books depends upon your capacities, and not of your heads alone, but of your purses. Well, it is now public, and you will stand for your privileges we know: to read and censure. Do so, but buy it first. ... whatever you do, buy."[7] These instances of the yoking of salability with the promise of readerly intimacy are of a piece with the obsessive attention that early modern writers paid to the question of the value of literary writing in the marketplace. As they presented it, the basic issue had to do with the violation of the private sphere of family, friendship, and authentic utterance by the public categories of commerce, "interest," and strategic self-presentation, not to mention (for writers of high rank) the taint of public commerce upon dignity of gentle birth. It is important to recognize the degree to which – in spite of their many statements to the contrary – early modern writers were able to achieve expressive authenticity and intimacy with their readers precisely because their writing was produced and disseminated in a marketplace.[8] One of the reasons that Montaigne and Shakespeare have been able to fulfill the aspiration toward an epistolary intimacy between writer and reader has to do with how the pressure of mortality registered in their texts (Shakespeare is dead, Prospero and Montaigne anticipate their deaths) seeks out reader-converts and does so in particular from among an anonymous, public readership – a group that, by virtue of its anonymity and far-flung membership, is capable of unlimited growth and deathless longevity.

Montaigne's essay "Of the Cannibals" both reflects upon the literary field and takes a formative position within it. In particular, it gives expression to the ideal of literary incorporation – the responsibility laid upon readers of taking in and making part of themselves the words of another, the generative closeness with the personality of the text that is so productive of the authorial presence characteristic of the high art of modernity – and it also gives expression to the crisis in that ideal that emerged in the face of the trade in culture. The essay itself is in part an unacknowledged pastiche of texts by other writers, especially the "cosmographers," whose work Montaigne affects to disdain.[9] The learned essayist is thus cutting and pasting other texts in order to fashion something new. In contrast, Shakespeare the practical man of the commercial theater is, as I shall argue, deeply involved in a humanist incorporation of Montaigne, even though his play represents reading in terms of ownership and instrumentality rather than as a form of communion. The two texts are products of a formative entanglement of the practices of the school and the market. Taken together, the essay and the play suggest that the rise of a literary marketplace was a necessary precondition for the fulfillment of the humanist, incorporative ideal of reading. Appropriating, owning, and making a profit from the words of another are thus strange but close kin to eating those words and becoming one with the other. I propose that one important figure of this entanglement of practices is the cannibal.

***

A number of Montaigne's essays, particularly "Of Pedantism" and "Of the Institution and Education of Children," develop the language of literary incorporation. Here is Montaigne on the subject of superficial learning and teaching:

> It is a sign of crudity and indigestion for a man to yield up his meat, even as he has swallowed the same; the stomach hath not wrought his full

operation unless it have changed form and altered fashion of that which was given him to boil and concoct.

> ("Education of Children," p. 65)

The practices of bad teachers, he says in a similar observation, are like the nursing habits of certain natural creatures:

> Even as birds flutter and skip from field to field to peck up corn, or any grain, and without tasting the same, carry it in their bills, therewith to feed their little ones; so do our pedants glean and pick learning from books, and never lodge it further than their lips, only to degorge it and cast it to the wind.

> ("Pedantism," p. 56)

To be fair to Montaigne, he acknowledges the degree to which his own writing resembles this kind of pecking and degorging:

> Is not that which I do in the greatest part of this composition all one and the self-same thing? I am ever here and there, picking and culling from this and that book the sentences that please me, not to keep them (for I have no store-house to reserve them in), but to transport them into this ... thereby to make a glorious show, therewith to entertain others and with [their] help to frame some quaint stories or pretty tales. ...

> (Ibid., p. 57)

In contrast, good teaching and learning depend upon the effective digestion of intellectual food: "What avails it us to have our bellies full of meat if it be not digested? If it be not transchanged in us, except it nourish, augment, and strengthen us?" (ibid.). It will be no surprise that the idea of literary incorporation is hardly original to Montaigne; appropriately enough, an unattributed paraphrase from the philosopher Seneca makes the point pithily: "It is not enough to join learning and knowledge to the mind, it should be incorporated into it" (ibid., p. 59).

Of course, the usefulness of literature was a long-standing commonplace. But where the ideal that coupled literary sweetness and usefulness focused on the betterment of the individual reader or student, the rise of a literary marketplace shifted the meaning of use toward an economic register – the interest-bearing "use" of existing literary resources in the production of new and profitable cultural goods. This threat to the traditional ideals of imitation and literary usefulness could tune someone like Jonson (a diehard humanist and also a commercial writer) to the top of his pitch, causing him to be the first writer in England to use the word "plagiary" (to refer to one who plagiarizes) and driving him to condemn others, even Montaigne, for what he himself was more likely to be guilty of:

All the Essayists, even their Master *Montaigne* ... in all they write, confess still what books they have read last; and therein their own folly, so much, that they bring it to the *Stake* raw, and undigested: not that the place did need it neither; but that they thought themselves furnished, and would vent it.

(8:586)

Unlike Jonson (who, it can be noted, uses conjoined imagery of commerce and ingestion very close to that of the *Essayes*), Montaigne did not have to write for his living. As we have heard, his book differs from the Shakespeare First Folio in that it exhorts potential readers *not* to buy the book, which, Montaigne says, is altogether too personal and trivial to be worth their time. Where the First Folio marries its sales pitch with the promise of intimacy, here the personal, intimate nature of the writing is represented as an obstacle to literary consumption:

> Reader, lo! Here a well-meaning book. It doth at the first entrance forewarn thee that in the contriving the same I have proposed unto myself no other than a familiar and private end. I have no respect or consideration at all, either to thy service or to my glory. ... I have vowed the same to the particular commodity of my kinfolks and friends: to the end, that losing me (which they are likely to do ere long), they may therein find some lineaments of my conditions and humors, and that by that means reserve more whole, and more lively foster the knowledge and acquaintance they have had of me. Had my intention been to forestall and purchase the world's opinion and favor, I would surely have adorned myself more quaintly or kept a more grave and solemn march. I desire therein to be delineated in mine own genuine, simple, and ordinary fashion, without contention, art, or study; for it is myself I portray. My imperfections shall therein be read to the life, and my natural form discerned so far forth as public reverence has permitted me. For if my fortune had been to have lived among those nations which yet are said to live under the sweet liberty of Nature's first and uncorrupted laws, I assure thee, I would most willingly have portrayed myself fully and naked. Thus, gentle reader, myself am the groundwork of my book. It is then no reason thou shouldst employ thy time about so frivolous and vain a subject. (p. xxxiii)

On the face of his account, his intended readership is small and well known to him, only his kinfolks and friends, and indeed he tells the person ("Reader, lo!") who is browsing among the new publications in the stationer's shop not to waste his valuable time (or money) on such a "frivolous and vain" book. The irony is not complex, but it is telling. The private world of intimacy with others and oneself is pulled into the teeming, anonymous public domain by dint of the book-trade, both by means of the technology of printing and by the practices of book-selling, which include wide distribution in the original language (and also translation into other tongues, which permits even wider distribution). The private life of the individual writer also enters the public world since the promise of intimacy becomes a selling feature of the publication and since it is the case necessarily that Montaigne wanted his book printed and sold (even if he says that he did not). Perhaps he means every word or perhaps he is doing exactly what the First Folio is doing (enhancing sales appeal with a promise of emotional closeness), but performing more playfully than did Heminges, Condell, and Jonson. In either case, the passage suggests that his book is not untouched by market pressures. "In my region of Gascony," he remarked, "they think it is a joke to see me in print. The farther from my lair the knowledge of me spreads, the more I am valued. I buy printers in Guienne, elsewhere they buy me" (Montaigne, *Works*, III: 2, 614). His reading of others and his writing for others are involved in production, sales, and profit (the author's financial independence does not radically change this fact) as much as his reading and writing are directed toward "no other than a familiar and private end."

Against the background of Montaigne's involvement in the trade in books, his accounts of reading as communion, conversation, or incorporation emerge in part as forms of interested and strategic self-representation. If we want to put the problem in categorical terms, we can say that from the point of view of the market, Plutarch, Seneca, Cicero, and others are objectified and instrumentalized by Montaigne in the processes of translation, quotation, anthologizing, and derivative creation. Is there, in the bustle of all these profitable transactions, any opportunity for the thoughtful digestion and incorporation of the works of antiquity? If this question seems outlandish or anachronistic, we can remember the terms of Jonson's attack or we can consider Montaigne's own account of an ancient Roman case of intellectual property-holding and trading (the example itself is taken from Seneca):

> This fashion puts me in mind of that rich Roman, who to his exceeding great charge had been very industrious to find out the most sufficient men in all sciences, which he continually kept about him, that if at any time occasion should be moved amongst his friends to speak of any matter pertaining to scholarship, they might supply his place and be ready to assist him – some with discourse, some with a verse of Homer, othersome with a sentence, each one according to his skill and profession – who persuaded himself that all such learning was his own because it was contained in his servants' minds. As they do whose sufficiency is placed in their sumptuous libraries.
>
> ("Pedantism," p. 57)

In *The Essays*, Montaigne contends with this implicitly corrosive view of his intellectual work in a number of ways. He emphasizes that his area of expertise begins and ends with himself: "Authors communicate themselves unto the world by some special and strange mark; I the first, by my general disposition; as Michael de Montaigne, not as a grammarian, or a poet, or a lawyer" ("Of Repenting," p. 409). He mocks those, like "that rich Roman," who trade in learning. He suggests that the scholarly goods his own authors bring to his "sumptuous library" serve to deceive – and thereby to humble and educate – his readers: "I will have them to give Plutarch a bob upon mine own lips, and vex themselves in wronging Seneca in me" ("Of Books," p. 204). Even though he confesses to his own intellectual shortcomings and to the poverty of his soil, he implies the depth of his engagement with the original-ity of others by using images of transplantation (ibid.) and incorporation. His taste in books, he says, is plain and simple: "I need no allurement nor sauce; my stomach is good enough to digest raw meat. And whereas with these preparatives and flourishes or preambles, they think to sharpen my taste or stir my stomach, they cloy and make it wallowish" (ibid., p. 207). Eating one's books raw leads of course to "Of the Cannibals," an essay which, among other interests, is concerned with the problems that surround the incorporation (in both senses of the word) of literature.

***

In the West, cannibalism has always epitomized the triumph of appetite over order. From the monstrous Polyphemus in Homer to the tragic, famished Ugolino in *The Inferno* who eats the corpses of his own children to "the barbarous Scythian / Or he that makes his generation messes / To gorge his appetite" (*King Lear*, 1.1.116–18), cannibals have represented the natural / unnatural appetite that is inhibited by no social or symbolic barrier. In the wake of Columbus's news of the existence of a New World, the European obsession with the Amerindian cannibals emerged in part as a sheer fascination with altogether alien and frighteningly violent peoples, but it had also to do with the economic, social, and symbolic violence of European society itself, which found in the Caribs and the Tupinamba a primitive but potentially critical reflection of itself.[10] The widespread reports of New World cannibalism aroused the specter of native-born anthropophagy, which indeed haunts the symbolic order of Christianity, especially the sacrament of the Eucharist. Protestant controversialists grew used to characterizing devout Catholics as no better, and perhaps worse, than the savages of Brazil. To Jean de Léry, French Catholics were "God-eaters" and idolaters (p. 41).[11] Indeed, the repressed physical counterpart of the Eucharist could return with a vengeance, as it did in 1572, in the thick of the French Wars of Religion, when a human heart, torn from the chest of a Protestant known as "Coeur de Roy," was grilled, chopped into pieces, auctioned by the piece, and eaten with much enjoyment by his Catholic neighbors (Lestringant, p. 80).

Money-lenders and capitalists were also cannibals – consumers of other people's property and labor whose appetite for wealth was unchecked by any sense of membership in the human community. Shylock, with his appetite for Antonio's flesh, is the most notorious example, but the stages of Shakespeare's London featured a population of human cormorants, foxes, ravens, and flesh-flies, as if the hell-mouth of the medieval drama had fractured into hundreds of gaping mouths, all of them compelled by the conjoinment of power, will, and appetite, which Ulysses characterizes as the principal enemy of order – the "universal wolf ... [that] Must make perforce an universal prey" (*Troilus and Cressida*, 1.3.121–23). Finally, as Montaigne has told us, readers *should* be eaters of their own kind because they must incorporate knowledge into their souls (not just carry it on their lips); of course, his advice is vexed because literary incorporation, including his own eating of books, is potentially of a piece with the inhuman consumption and use of others' bodies, labor, and material and intellectual property as it was practiced variously by New World (and French) cannibals, European usurers and capitalists, and cultural producers in the book trade.

When Montaigne came to write about the cannibals of Brazil, he was entering a long-standing debate about the comparative merits of Europeans and Amerindians, and his cultural relativism and open-mindedness marked an advance on the extreme position-taking exemplified by the opposing views of Bartolomé de Las Casas (who saw the Amerindians as innocent children in need of salvation) or Juan Ginés de Sepulveda (who saw them as natural slaves).[12] David Quint has argued that the interpretive tradition has misunderstood Montaigne's view of the cannibals.[13] According to his reading of the essay, they are not noble but cruel; "a culture that cannot pardon," their conduct epitomizes the mercilessness and pointlessness of warrior values. Quint is surely right to emphasize the violence and cruelty of the cannibals, but not even the most brilliant ironic reading can dispose of Montaigne's heartfelt admiration for the Tupinamba. Beyond that, violence and even a degree of cruelty are not half-hidden features of the cannibals. On the contrary, they are made prominent and paramount because Montaigne is imagining, not a nation without violence (there can be no such place in a fallen world), but rather a nation where violence can be assimilated to an ethos of community. The Tupinamba kill and eat their enemies, but they kill and eat only the ones they admire; they treat their captives well ("with all the commodities they can devise" [p. 95]), and once they kill them, which they do with dispatch (p. 96), they make their enemies' flesh a part of their own bodies.

"Of the Cannibals" is also implicitly concerned with the problem of reading and writing in a European literary marketplace, and its defense of the cannibals bears on the threatened ideal of incorporative reading. This dimension of the essay helps explain why Montaigne is the inventor of the cannibal as social critic (as opposed to a mere monster of appetite). In spite of his initial comments about the differences between European artifice and Amerindian naturalness (p. 94), he describes Brazilian anthropophagy as fully cultural and symbolic ("It is not, as some imagine, to nourish themselves with it, as anciently the Scythians wont to do, but to represent an extreme and inexpiable revenge" [p. 96]). On the whole, the cannibals are virtuous, courageous, and generous; they are gifted with a taste for beautiful poetry and with a keen eye for European social disorder and injustice. The three members of the Tupinamba tribe that he met in Rouen in 1562 commented on the unequal distribution of wealth in French society (and note how physical violence becomes here an instrument of social justice):

> Second, they have a manner of phrase whereby they call men but a moiety one of another. They had perceived there were men among us full gorged with all sorts of commodities and others which, hunger-starved and bare with need and poverty, begged at their gates; and [they] found it strange that these moieties so needy could endure such an injustice, and that they took not the other by the throat or set fire on their houses. (p. 98)

Amerindian cannibalism emerges as a critique of the European hypocrisy that affects horror at the customs of the Tupinamba but is blind to greater inhumanity at home:

> I think there is more barbarism in eating men alive than to feed upon them being dead, to mangle by tortures and torments a body full of lively sense, to roast him in pieces, to make dogs and swine to gnaw and tear him in mammocks (as we have not only read but seen very lately, yea and in our own memory, not among ancient enemies, but our neighbors and fellow citizens; and, which is worse, under pretence of piety and religion) than to roast and eat him after he is dead. (p. 96)

Invoking the virtues of "barbarians" as a form of social critique goes back at least as far as Tacitus; the particular form it takes here makes the cannibals the ancestors of a highbrow, anthropophagous social commentator such as Hannibal "the Cannibal" Lector (whose name is an uncanny epitome of Montaigne's defense of incorporative reading). More important in the present argument is the fact that Montaigne represents the eating of one's own kind, not only as a symbolic form of revenge, but also as an (admittedly fierce) form of long-term community building. Cannibalism mixes together the flesh of enemies with enemies and ancestors with descendants: the eaters take into themselves the very substance of their forebears along with the flesh of their prisoners of war. Montaigne quotes one of the victims:

> I have a song made by a prisoner, wherein is this clause: Let them boldly

come together and flock in multitudes to feed on him, for with him they shall feed upon their fathers and grandfathers that heretofore have served his body for food and nourishment. "These muscles," saith he, "this flesh, and these veins are your own; fond men as you are, know you not the substance of your forefathers' limbs is yet tied unto ours? Taste them well, for in them shall you find the relish of your own flesh." (p. 97)

On this account, cannibalism provides the corporeal foundation for the quasi-Christian idea of community (all men are moieties of one another) that lies behind the Tupinambas' disapproval of the "civilized" system of property that makes some moieties fat and others emaciated with hunger. Indeed, the man-eaters are complete strangers to the social violence of the European economic order that impoverishes the majority of people and also threatens the ideal of disinterested reading and writing. I am suggesting that Montaigne's account of New World cannibalism speaks to the problem of literary incorporation by building on the ideal of reading as eating in order to provide an anthropophagous model of cultural production over the long term where the consumption and recycling of the books of the past are acts of communitarian violence rather than self-interested forms of accumulation and exploitation. Writers like Montaigne, we might say, do indeed practice a kind of violence by consuming and using the books of the past, but their writerly cannibalism also participates, within the writer-eat-writer milieu of the book trade, in the creation of a transhistorical literary community. Important in this regard is how the Preface requires readers who wish to become intimate with the writer to violate the private territory of his book, which was, after all, "vowed ... to the particular commodity of my kinfolks and friends." Our purchase and reading of Montaigne's book therefore trespasses on the writer's privacy; but, where we turn his words into ours (as Florio and Shakespeare did), our trespass is also a continuation of the communitarian violence embodied in the writer's own work.

***

In *Love's Labor's Lost*, Sir Nathaniel mocks the unfortunate Dull, and he does so in terms with which we are already familiar. He addresses his remarks to his fellow pedant, the schoolmaster Holofernes:

Sir, he hath never fed of the dainties that are bred in a book;
He hath not eat paper, as it were; he hath not drunk ink; his intellect is
not replenished; he is only an animal, only sensible in the duller parts.
(4.2.23–27)

Shakespeare's ridicule of the ideal of incorporative reading in the persons of the two "book-men" (4.2.34) Nathaniel and Holofernes seems connected to the pragmatic, commercialized practices of reading and writing that were mandated by his work as a professional playwright. We know a great deal about Montaigne's reading, including his favorite authors and genres, how much time he liked to spend with this or that writer, which authors he read as a boy and which as an adult ("Of Books," pp. 204–11). What kind of reader was Shakespeare? While Shakespeare might also have read widely for pleasure and instruction, pursuing his own fancy and changing interests in a non-instrumental fashion, it is difficult not to get the impression that his reading was instrumental to his practices as a maker of dramatic texts. The impression arises because the only books that we know he read are those that demonstrably provided him with raw material in the form of literary genres, dramatic plots, character ideas, thematic elements, and the numerous passages he reproduced nearly verbatim and without acknowledgment, such as Gonzalo's lines about his utopian kingdom (from Montaigne) or Prospero's renunciation speech (from Golding's translation of Ovid).[14] These instances of the undigested, exploitative use of other writers' work make Shakespeare resemble the bad teachers who "glean and pick learning from books ... only to degorge it and cast it to the wind" ("Pedantism," p. 56), or the superficial readers who fail to incorporate what they read, or the cannibals (not Montaigne's) whose violence is unredeemed by the assimilation of the flesh of others into long-term community building.

Shakespeare's "bad" literary cannibalism is consonant with his critique of the love of books in *The Tempest*. His apparent antipathy toward books might have something to do with how his plays were normally promulgated by the collective talents of the King's Servants rather than by way of the printing press. Perhaps this is one reason why books usually appear in Shakespeare as vessels of alienated intellectual labor that are able to precipitate a corresponding alienation in their readers. A more likely explanation, however, is that Shakespeare shared the skepticism that working professionals sometimes feel toward upper-class amateurs or the distrust that practical men often have of book-learning, as when Iago disparages the "bookish" Cassio – "Mere prattle, without practice / Is all his soldiership" (*Othello*, 1.1.26–27).[15] *The Tempest* elaborates this conflict between practical knowledge and book-learning in Caliban's recollection of how he shared with Prospero the knowledge of the island's geography essential to the Duke and his daughter's survival, revealing to him "all the qualities o' th'isle, / The fresh springs, brine pits, barren place and fertile" (1.2.337–38). The play begins in the midst of a dire natural emergency that highlights the limits of statecraft embodied in Gonzalo on the one side and the collaborative resourcefulness and practical working knowledge of the sailors on the other. "You are a councillor," the Boatswain says to Gonzalo, "if you can command these elements to silence ... we will not hand a rope more. ... If you cannot, give thanks you have liv'd so long, and make yourself ready in your cabin for the mischance of the hour, if it so hap. – Cheerly, good hearts! – Out of our way, I say" (1.1.20–27).

Since Prospero's books are volumes of magic and are fit for a ruler, we are evidently to think of them as handwritten, arcane, and rare – not products of the printing house and not involved in the book trade. They make challenging reading, even for an accomplished scholar, and they also call forth a profound emotional attachment from their reader and owner. All this helps align Prospero's reading with Montaigne's, but Shakespeare draws out less appealing features too: the Duke's books are instrumental to his will-to-power rather than contributory to his spiritual well-being, and they are antithetical to the interests of community and even to rudimentary justice. It is important that Prospero comes to know himself and his humanity, not by way of his powerful books, but by dint of fraught interactions with his daughter, his fellow Italians, and his servants Ariel and Caliban. If anything, his books prevent him from acknowledging or caring fully for other people. Prospero must bury his book, not only because it embodies questionable magic-making, which he must renounce, but also because it interferes with his progress toward self-knowing, his compassion for others, and his ability to govern a human community. Books can be powerful, but they are also inhuman: without them, Prospero might be "but a sot" (as Caliban describes himself [3.2.93]); with them, he remains irredeemably cut off from his fellow creatures. Where Montaigne suggests the community-building capacity of books, even when reading and writing are involved in the marketplace, Shakespeare seems impressed by but also suspicious of literature and bookish knowledge, especially when the books belong to the members of the upper ranks. With the exception of Lavinia's Ovid, which serves to reveal the identity of her attackers and to galvanize communal action, Shakespeare tends to represent books as instruments of policy (like Ulysses' book of moral philosophy in *Troilus and Cressida* or Ophelia's prayer-book) or as compendiums of dubious wisdom (like Hamlet's book of "words, words, words" [2.2.192]).

While Shakespeare's skeptical attitude toward books and book-learning chimes with his work as a commercial dramatist, his engagement with Montaigne seems nevertheless to have been both sustained and thoughtful. The evidence for this relationship is necessarily open to question since the places where Shakespeare followed Montaigne's ideal of reading by incorporating him fully are the very places where the essayist's words are "transchanged" into the playwright's; however, the cumulative work of a number of scholars (Gail Paster, tellingly, finds herself imagining Shakespeare reading one of the essays [p. 94]) has begun to substantiate the lines of connection between the two writers by revealing Shakespeare as a literary cannibal, to be sure, but as a cannibal capable of the intellectual and ethical digestion and incorporation of the texts of others.[16]

On this account, Shakespeare is an intellectual as well as a practical man of the theater. His "use" of "Of the Cannibals" in *The Tempest* is strong evidence for the truth of this claim, especially since the essay could not have been particularly useful in the process of composition: it supplies little by way of plot or character or applicable background material; and the issues that are central in the essay were also the subject of a large body of sixteenth-century New World writing, most of it more detailed than Montaigne (and, in any case, the play is not even directly about the Americas). In comparison to his use of Plutarch, Holinshed, or Ovid, Shakespeare's reading of Montaigne seems altogether impractical. His critique of incorporative reading notwithstanding, therefore, he seems to have engaged deeply with the author of *The Essays*, digested him, transmuted his writing into his own dramatic art and, in consequence, was nourished, augmented, and strengthened by eating Montaigne ("Pedantism," p. 57).

As a final example of Shakespeare's incorporation of *The Essays*, let us consider the connection, first noted by Eleanor Prosser, between "Of Cruelty" and *The Tempest*. Shakespeare takes over Montaigne's idea of virtue as a capacity different from goodness and makes it key to Prospero's hard-won forgiveness of the men who betrayed him. This is Montaigne:

> Methinks virtue is another manner of thing and much *more noble than the inclinations unto goodness*, which in us are engendered. Minds well-born and directed by themselves follow one same path, and in their actions represent the same visage that the virtuous do. But virtue importeth and soundeth somewhat, I wot not, greater and more active than by a happy complexion, gently and peaceably, to suffer itself to be led or drawn to follow reason. He that through a natural facility and genuine mildness should neglect or condemn injuries received, should no doubt perform *a rare action* and worthy commendation; but he who being *stung to the quick* with any wrong or offence received, should arm himself with *reason against this furiously blind desire of revenge*, and in the end after a great conflict yield himself master over it, should doubtless do much more. (p. 211, italics added)

In *The Tempest*, Montaigne's passage about virtue is subsumed in this conversation between Prospero and Ariel:

ARIEL
Your charm so strongly works 'em
That if you now beheld them, your affections
Would become tender.

PROSPERO
Dost thou think so, spirit?

ARIEL
Mine would, sir, were I human.

PROSPERO
And mine shall.
Hast thou, which art but air, a touch, a feeling
Of their afflictions, and shall not myself,
One of their kind, that relish all as sharply,
Passion as they, be kindlier mov'd than thou art?
Though with their high wrongs I am strook to th' quick,
Yet, with my nobler reason, 'gainst my fury
Do I take part. The rarer action is
In virtue than in vengeance.

(5.1.17–28)

Clearly, I think, this is a moment of intense readerly engagement on Shakespeare's part (at least the verbal parallels make the case reasonably convincing). There was evidently something appealing to Shakespeare in Montaigne's idea of virtue as something more noble than natural goodness, in virtue as a quality that the person makes actively and by dint of struggle, and in the alignment of virtue and forgiveness. Yet aside from a few phrases, there is nothing here of Montaigne's book. Indeed, Shakespeare has rewritten his own reading as a scene pointedly without any book, where Prospero comes to feel his own humanity in the face of the weirdly suspended fellow-feeling of his spirit servant Ariel.

We do not need, finally, to speculate about Ariel as the transmutation of Montaigne's book (a powerful non-human agency able to hold the mirror up to human nature), or indeed about Montaigne himself as the original of Prospero (even through they are both bookish recluses who have withdrawn from active political careers and who commune more with invisible spirits than with living people) in order to assess the depth of Shakespeare's engagement with Montaigne. Most important here is the contribution Montaigne has made to the way we are inclined to read and to use Shakespeare's play. I am suggesting that Shakespeare's incorporative reading of Montaigne – incorporative in terms of both intellectual digestion and marketplace appropriation – is connected to the sense readers often have that Shakespeare himself is the subject of his play and connected also to the entry of *Shakespeare*'s play into a literary economy (especially since his felt presence has enhanced the play's authority and thereby its usefulness). Montaigne helped induct Shakespeare and afterwards generations of Shakespeare's readers into an experience of reading as a form of incorporation and communion and also helped make the play a valuable source-text. Is there any work in literature more cannibalized than *The Tempest*? There is nothing remotely mysterious about this effect. Shakespeare is present to us (as conversation-partner and as ingestible, transformable material) because his reading of Montaigne deepened his ability to create verisimilitude in characters like Prospero, because magicians like Prospero and poets like Shakespeare are close kin by literary convention, and because we are interested in knowing what the playwright thinks about the essayist, just as we are interested to know what the essayist thinks about Plato, Seneca, Plutarch, and the other writers that he ate.

Notes

1 This important detail of the back-story, which has been surprisingly unregarded by critics, was first noted by Harry Berger, Jr., "Miraculous Harp: A Reading of *The Tempest*," *Shakespeare Studies* 5 (1969): 253–83; see also the discussion of Gonzalo and Renaissance politics in Paul Yachnin, "Shakespeare and the Idea of Obedience: Gonzalo and *The Tempest*," *MOSAIC* 24 (1991): 1–18.

2 All Shakespeare quotes refer to *The Riverside Shakespeare*, textual ed. G. Blakemore Evans *et al.* (Boston, MA: Houghton Mifflin, 1974).

3 Leslie A. Fiedler, *The Stranger in Shakespeare* (New York: Stein and Day, 1972), p. 238.

4 I say "quasi-Levinasian" because Levinas's idea of a fully present face-to-face relationship that demands our responsibility to the other is necessarily suspicious of aesthetic representation. Reading a book is not like confronting the face of the other; therefore a "Levinasian" ethics of reading, which would certainly provide an apt language for how many readers would describe their love of Montaigne or Shakespeare, requires a theoretical argument that could recuperate the authorial presence in the textual representation. For a particularly lucid argument along these lines, see Robert Eaglestone, *Ethical Criticism: Reading After Levinas* (Edinburgh: University of Edinburgh Press, 1997), pp. 98–174.

5 All Montaigne quotations are from *The Essayes of Michael Lord of Montaigne*, trans. John Florio, ed. Henry Morley (London: George Routledge and Sons, 1893). I have silently modernized old-spelling titles and texts.

6 For the early publishing history in France, see Donald M. Frame, *Montaigne's Essais: A Study* (Englewood Cliffs, NJ: Prentice Hall, 1969), pp. 1–3.

7 References are to *Riverside Shakespeare*, pp. 58–59, 66, 65, 63.

8 For a brilliant discussion of the emergence of literary personality in the 1590s in London's burgeoning book-trade, see Douglas Bruster, "The Structural Transformation of Print in Late Elizabethan England," in *Shakespeare and the Question of Culture: Early Modern Literature and the Cultural Turn* (New York: Palgrave Macmillan, 2003), pp. 65–93.

9 Gérard Defaux, "Un cannibale en haut de chausses: Montaigne, la différence et la logique de l'identité," *MLN* 97 (1982): 919–57.

10 For a critical survey of the Renaissance "ethnography" of the Amerindians, see William M. Hamlin, *The Image of America in Montaigne, Spenser, and Shakespeare: Renaissance Ethnography and Literary Reflection* (New York: St Martin's Press, 1995), pp. 1–36. A striking example of Amerindian violence is Peter Martyr's report on the fate of some of the Taino Indians: "The Cannibals take them as small children and castrate them, as we do to capons or pigs which we want to fatten and make tender for our food." Quoted in Frank Lestringant, *Cannibals: The Discovery and Representation of the Cannibal from Columbus to Jules Verne*, trans. Rosemary Morris (Berkeley, CA: University of California Press, 1997), p. 23.

11 *History of a Voyage to the Land of Brazil*, trans. Janet Whatley (Berkeley, CA: University of California Press, 1990), p. 41.

12 For the debate between Las Casas and Sepulveda, see Lewis Hanke, *All Mankind Is One: A Study of the Disputation between Bartolomé de Las Casas and Juan Ginés de Sepulveda* (DeKalb, GA: Northern Illinois University Press, 1974).

13 *Montaigne and the Quality of Mercy: Ethical and Political Themes in the Essais* (Princeton, NJ: Princeton University Press, 1998), pp. 75–101.

14 For Shakespeare's borrowings from Montaigne and Ovid, see *The Tempest*, ed. Stephen Orgel (Oxford: Oxford University Press, 1987), pp. 227–41; see Barbara A. Mowat, "'Knowing I Loved my Books': Reading *The Tempest* Intertextually," in "*The Tempest*" *and its Travels*, ed. Peter Hulme and William H. Sherman (Philadelphia, PA: University of Pennsylvania Press, 2000), pp. 27–36, for an excellent discussion of the play's intertextuality. On Shakespeare's reading, see Robert S. Miola, *Shakespeare's Reading* (New York: Oxford University Press, 2000), esp. pp. 152–69.

15 It is worth noting that Iago is one of Shakespeare's most accomplished sub-dramatists and therefore a disturbing reflection of the playwright himself.

16 See Robert Ellrodt, "Self-Consciousness in Montaigne and Shakespeare," *Shakespeare Survey* 28 (1975): 37–56; Hugh Grady, "Shakespeare's Links to Machiavelli and Montaigne: Constructing Intellectual Modernity in Early Modern Europe," *Comparative Literature* 52 (2000): 119–42; Arthur Kirsch, "Virtue, Vice, and Compassion in Montaigne and *The Tempest*," *Studies in English Literature* 37 (1997): 337–52; Gail Kerns Paster, "Montaigne, Dido, and *The Tempest*: 'How came that widow in?,'" *Shakespeare Quarterly* 35 (1984): 91–94; Eleanor Prosser, "Shakespeare, Montaigne, and the 'Rarer Action,'" *Shakespeare Studies* 1 (1965): 261–64. For a survey of other recent scholarship on Shakespeare and Montaigne, see Kirsch, "Virtue," p. 37.

8 Marvell's "*Scaevola Scoto-Brittannus*" and the ethics of political violence

David Norbrook

Renaissance humanism has much to offer for contemporary understandings of the relations between poetry, ethics, and politics. Humanist pedagogy was intensely concerned with ethical efficacy, offering elaborate frameworks for guiding practical decisions in the public life. In the belief that such decisions were bound up with particular linguistic choices, and that the classical world offered the fullest guidance for such choices, the humanist curriculum encouraged minute attention to language, from basic vocabulary to the minutest details of quantitative prosody. There was a truth in Andrew Marvell's satiric comment that he studied Latin for poetic form before meaning: "this *Scanning* was a liberal Art that we learn'd at Grammar-School; and to *Scan* Verses as he does the Authors Prose, before we did, or were obliged to understand them."[1] I would like to explore the ethical implications of a neglected poem by Marvell, a late but remarkably full representative of the fruits of this pedagogy.

"Scaevola Scoto-Brittannus" has claims to forming the climax of Marvell's poetic career: it was probably his last or at least his penultimate surviving poem, and it engages with issues which preoccupied him throughout his life and which have a continuing resonance today. The poem has been neglected because of a residual critical difficulty in seeing Marvell's works as a whole, in opening his canon to the full formal, ethical and political range of early modern discourse. It is arguable that recent historicist criticism has sometimes underplayed questions of poetic form. This does not mean, however, that the heyday of the New Criticism offered a preferable alternative. Cleanth Brooks and others were drawn to the extreme formal self-consciousness of his lyric poetry but failed to recognize the rhetorical brilliance of his satirical works in verse and prose, encouraging a steady shrinking of critical focus and of the number of texts deemed canonical. Moreover, they did not acknowledge Marvell's quintessentially humanist commitment to writing in Latin verse – a medium which indeed put their formalist credentials to the test. The playfulness and formal self-consciousness inherent in the practice of emulating the register and prosody of poems written a millennium and a half previously offered a kind of excess with which the New Critics, always concerned in the end to vindicate the sacramental unity of form and content, were uneasy.[2] As a neo-Latin satire, "Scaevola Scoto-Brittannus" has been doubly marginal in the Marvell canon, and has been omitted from some standard editions of his poetry. As a very late but formally tight poem, it also resists a standard narrative according to which the young, residually royalist, poet's sensitivity to literary form is gradually crushed by his descending to radical polemic.

That narrative has been steadily complicated by a growing body of historicist research, culminating in the *Prose Works* under the general editorship of Annabel Patterson, Nigel Smith's edition of the poems, and Nicholas von Maltzahn's *Chronology*.[3] Work by Smith, Estelle Haan, and Paul Mathole has offered a persuasive case for Marvell's authorship of "Scaevola Scoto-Brittannus" and begun to set the poem in the context of Marvell's later writings.[4] The omission of the satires from the 1681 *Miscellaneous Poems*, which has created so many problems of attribution, may in itself reflect the volatile political climate on which they commented, since the book's publication capitalized on a brief opening of the press and was then curtailed by a renewed crackdown.[5] In drawing on recent scholarship, I would like to examine aspects of the poem's formal and allusive play which turn out to heighten the forcefulness of its ethical and political intervention; and to explore the sometimes disquieting resonance of humanist tyrannicidal ideals in the current age of terror and counter-terror.

Marvell was addressing a dangerously controversial subject. In 1668 a Covenanter named James Mitchell tried to assassinate the Archbishop of St. Andrews, James Sharp, as he sat in his coach in the High Street in Edinburgh; he missed Sharp but one of his bullets struck a fellow-passenger, Andrew Honeyman, Bishop of Orkney, in the hand in a wound that eventually proved fatal. Mitchell made his escape to the Continent, but when the tumult had died down he returned to Edinburgh. In 1674 Sharp recognized his assailant in the street. Mitchell was arrested and made a confession on a promise that his life would be spared. He refused to repeat the confession, however, and in January 1676 the authorities resorted to torture to try to uncover further information about the rebels' networks. According to one source, "Some moved the cutting off his right hand. Others said, he might learn to practise with his left hand, and to take his revenge; therefore they thought both hands should be cut off. Lord Rothes, who was a pleasant man, said, How shall he wipe his breech then?"[6] Instead of his hands they tortured his leg with a sinister instrument named the boot, which had something of an avant-garde status in Scotland but had been used by the French absolutist monarchy, as in the torture of François Ravaillac, the assassin of Henri IV.[7] Mitchell refused to confess, but the authorities decided to make an example of him and in 1678 he was put on trial. Though Sharp had promised Mitchell that a confession he had been induced to make would not be used against him, he now perjured himself by denying that he had made such a promise and Mitchell was executed. The story was not finished, however: in 1679 a group of Covenanters, provoked rather than deterred by the trial and torture, finished the task Mitchell had attempted, murdering Sharp with the most horrific brutality in front of his daughter.

These incidents pose problematic issues of the ethics of political violence and the counter-violence of torture. As we shall see, Marvell addresses them in a characteristically humanist, universalizing manner, projecting precedents from classical antiquity on to the Scottish present. He does so on terrain that has recently become characteristic of a very different, radically historicist approach. The practice of torture and the spectacular display of power have become defining features in the new historicist portrayal of early modern culture. On the model of Foucault's *Discipline and Punish*, and in turn of Nietzsche's *The Genealogy of Morals*, it has become commonplace to argue that liberal humanist principles of punishment as moral reform, and the modern quest for objective truth, were sublimations of pre-modern principles of marking power on the body. Reactions of moral indignation against state torture were condemned as appealing to a false and anachronistic universality.[8] There is validity in the broad point that modes of corporeal discipline have radically changed, and it can be argued that humanist pedagogy represented an early phase in this shift, transferring the emphasis from royal inscription of the body to the disciplining of the young citizen's body for civic virtue.[9] The chronology of those changes, and the forms of agency involved, however, need careful definition. I write as a late recipient of Scottish humanist pedagogy, having had any inattention to grammar schooling punished by a leather belt administered to my right hand, which one was expected to receive with Scaevolan fortitude; it is not long since corporal punishment was finally abolished in Scotland. As for public punishment of the body, with the new millennium the deficiencies of the stock new historicist model have become graphically apparent. If not long ago we were urged to read Nietzsche and Heidegger to try to banish liberal humanist illusions about corporal punishment, today's neoconservatives, sometimes informed by a very different reading of those masters, have been offering increasingly vigorous justifications. Torture no longer serves as defining mark of difference between our own age and a past Other. It is more productive, I would argue, to explore texts as participating in dialogues which reflect and develop political and material conflicts whose timeframe may extend far beyond the specificities of a single conjuncture. Indeed, the closer the analysis of the conjuncture, the more the longer-term implications will emerge.

Marvell's poem was in fact entering highly polarized terrain. If the authorities resorted to extreme means, they claimed in justification that they faced a threat equally extreme: escalating political violence that threatened civil war. For some of those who had fought for Kirk and King, the unexpected episcopal settlement in Scotland in 1660 meant a split between loyalty to an earthly and a heavenly king. In 1666 there was an armed rising and when the government under the Earl of Lauderdale cracked down on dissenting meetings the Covenanters turned to holding outdoor meetings, field-conventicles, which the authorities regarded as menacing displays of force. The Covenanters raided the Old Testament for bloodcurdling justifications of political violence of a kind more often associated in current political discourse with radical Islam.

The beginning of Marvell's poem distances itself from such discourse, condemning Mitchell's act with ethically laden words like "nefas," "peccat," "culpa," "scelus."[10] There is a striking contrast with a contemporary neo-Latin "Deploratio" for Mitchell which asked if God would never come to avenge the bishops' sins with his right hand:

> nunquam ne aderit Deus vltor, inulti
> Dum pereunt justi, dextrâque inulti furorem
> Comprimet?[11]

Mitchell's act was often seen as in itself providential, with a distinction made between his own agency and a separate level of divine intervention against Honeyman's apostasy: "People could not but observe the Righteousness of Providence in disabling Bishop Honnyman's Hand, which was no way designed by Mr. Mitchel". . . . "God does, as it were, beat the Penn out of his Hand, by a Bullet that lighted on his Arm, or Wrist."[12] Marvell casts such claims in a rather satirical light when he comments that heaven's justice seemed slow to Mitchell: the implication would be that his own right hand should have been more patient.

As the poem proceeds, however, this clear-cut ethical framework becomes compromised – in part by the poem's epigrammatic form. The elegiac couplet which Marvell favored for most of his Latin poetry, with the expansive hexameter tightening into an increasingly regular pentameter, encouraged crisp antitheses.[13] His "Et fas in talem credidit omne Nefas," "believed that against such a many every wrongdoing was right" (l. 4), though ascribed to Mitchell, has the effect of leveling the distinction between the bishop's cruelty and Mitchell's violence. In lines 5–6, the conventional conjunction of "insonti ... praesule," "an innocent bishop," is shockingly deflated by the parenthetical question as to whether any bishop can be innocent. The balanced couplet at lines 7–8 is bracketed with condemnatory terms, "Culpa par ... idem ... scelus," which then highlight the off-balance "dispar ... fortuna," "unequal ... fortune." Again a moral equivalence is implied between Sharp and his attempted assassin, with the difference lying in the greater "fortuna" of the more powerful man; "mitra beat ... scelus," "the mitre blesses the same crime," shockingly turns the emblem of moral and spiritual authority into an apologist for crime. Though the poet declares at line 5 that the bullet sins, "peccat," the verb, in a more pragmatic register to be found in Martial's epigrams, simply states that the bullet failed to meet its target;[14] an interpretation potentially reinforced by "Errorem Dextrae," "the error of his right hand" (l. 14). Marvell would certainly have picked up Milton's pun at *Paradise Lost* 4.239, where "error" in the Latinate sense of "wandering" has a buried ethical sense; here, in a Latin text, the situation is potentially reversed, offering the purely factual comment that the bullet wandered off course. The effect is to temper moral condemnation.

The poem now moves to Mitchell's interrogation, and signals a further turn in ethical perspective in the claim that his virtue expiated, "piavit," his crime. From being balanced against Sharp, he is now raised to a higher ethical plane as a heroic martyr. As Haan has noted, the poem works by a series of role reversals (p. 222), and if in the second line Sharp is presented as a wolf to his flock, at line 10 Mitchell is "Reverendus," claiming an honorific conventionally applied to clergymen. Agency and suffering are inverted; in an untranslatable zeugma (l. 12), Marvell states that Mitchell at once pays the penalty and makes the laws. At one point this claim of control does correspond to the records of the trial: Mitchell voluntarily offered his right leg for the torture as "the best of the two, for I freely bestow it in the cause" – though he was in no position to "order" this ("iubet").[15] As will be seen, Marvell makes this moment of agency the center of the poem's symbolism. The other role-reversals, however, are a series of conceits, pushed to the point of discomforting incongruity: Mitchell is ordering a new shoe, which is compared to a "Cothurnum," an actor's shoe, and trying it for size, he has leisure, he is a master smiling at an incompetent servant, and he is a spectator of his own torture.

In invoking the trope of royal punishment as a spectacle, Marvell makes a characteristic humanist leap from his own epoch to classical Rome, inter-weaving a complex set of allusions to Martial's epigrams. Several times Martial wrote of Gaius Mucius, who in the early years of the Roman republic was sent to assassinate the Etruscan leader Lars Porsena, but slew his secretary by mistake. When he was seized and threatened with torture to reveal his plot, he displayed his readiness to endure any torture by voluntarily thrusting his right hand into the fire, hence becoming known as "Scaevola," "the little left-handed one." The parallels with Mitchell's missing Sharp and hitting Honeyman, and with his choice of the right leg for punishment, were clear. In one of the epigrams, Martial writes that had Scaevola not erred the glory of his right hand would have been less: "maior deceptae fama est et gloria dextrae: / si non errasset, fecerat illa minus" (*Epigrams*, 1.21, ll. 7–8). These words are echoed in Marvell's "errorem dextrae." In another of the Scaevola epigrams, however, the moral meanings are less clear-cut. Marvell's description of Mitchell as viewing "the spectacle of his own torture," "proprii ... ad spectacula" (l. 19), borrows from Martial's description of a Scaevola whose hand reigns in the flame and who is "sui spectator" (*Epigrams*, 8.30, l. 5). This epigram, however, describes the reenactment of the Scaevola story at an imperial game: the gladiator in this situation is keeping his life, at the cost of extreme pain, by acting out the story, with the attendant role reversal of a condemned slave acting out a nobleman. As a somewhat amplified English translation put it:

> In *Brutus* time, what was *Rome*'s highest Praise
> Is as a Pastime shew'd, in *Caesar*'s days:
> The Presentation, the true Story shames,
> His Valiant Hand so bravely grasps the Flames,
> Enjoys its Torment, and derides their Ire,
> Frolicks and Reigns in the astonish'd Fire![16]

Martial tinges a conventional Roman lament at the decline of the virtues of the early republic with the defiant pride in the Empire's aesthetic superiority to be expected of a poet whose first collection had been in praise of imperial spectacles: the representation is better than the original. Here we certainly seem to encounter an aestheticized power in which the spectator is drawn to collude with authority by the force of the spectacle.

Marvell's allusions, however, point to a studied inversion of the mechanisms of aestheticized terror. He adds a further level to Martial's role reversal: if the Empire has reduced republican heroism to spectacle, Mitchell is reversing the process, recovering something of the Livyan republican ethos which Martial's wit had distanced. As Martial comments in another epigram, the slave's courage is in fact less formidable than it seems because in entertaining the Emperor by plunging his hand into the flame, he is able to save himself from the death penalty (*Epigrams*, 10.25, ll. 5–6). Mitchell's courage is worthy of the original Scaevola. Marvell's representation of his suffering has been described as Stoic,[17] but the details of the figurative language, rather than offering the sublime transcendence of Stoic virtue, cast him as a member of the Roman ruling class, giving orders to servants, taking in the spectacle of the games, even shopping for shoes. This language provocatively rejects the stock social sneers with which government officials were attacking the Covenanters: "As for [Mitchell's] original, 'tis so obscure, that the mean Proletarian condition of his Parents affords me no notice of his birth," wrote Lauderdale's chaplain George Hickes.[18] In a symmetrical move, Marvell presents those to whom Mitchell gives orders as degraded lackeys; "Laniu[s]" (l. 24), apparently the personal name of the torturer, could also be a generic name for a butcher, and potentially by extension an executioner. The fact that Mitchell fainted under the torment is presented as a choice ("vult," 26) of a leisurely state starkly contrasted to the degradingly sweaty labor of the torturer. He is no longer "conscius," a word that Marvell used around the same time in the sense of "guilty, complicit":[19] as the direct focus on the scene of torture fades away, we are left with an image of martyred innocence. And we are made part of an emergent and ethically authorized response: we are told that the people commiserate with him (l. 20), but the only people allowed to witness this performance were the legal officers, and describing them as "populo" implies the wider diffusion of Mitchell's story through public opinion in which the poem itself participates. Throughout his career Marvell knew how to target his poems effectively for those with the maximum political influence – his knowing the torturer's name carries a warning of inside knowledge – but by the later 1670s a major widening of the political public sphere was in process.[20] It is possible that Marvell also touches on the sensitive issue of his abused confession by having him not admit, "confessus," his pain (l. 21, Haan, pp. 230–33): interestingly, there seems to have been revision at this point since the Yale manuscript instead reads "testatus."

The poem now abruptly reaches its climactic turn: after "pati," with its emphasis on submission, we are confronted with ominous, bristling alliteration:

> Scaevola si Tuscum potuit terrere tyrannum,
> Fortius hoc specimen Scotia nostra dedit.
> Numina quum temnas, homines ne spernito Sharpi,
> Hic è tercentum Mutius unus erat.
> (lines 29–32, but following Haan's "quum"
> for *MPL*'s "quam")

(If Scaevola was able to terrify the Etruscan tyrant, our Scotland has given in this man a braver example. Sharp, although you spurn the divine powers, do not despise men; this one was Mucius out of three hundred.)

Like Scaevola, and Mitchell, the poem tries to instill terror in tyrants. It returns to the initial theme of heavenly as opposed to earthly justice: having initially criticized Mitchell for taking justice into his own hands instead of waiting for heaven, the poem ends by vigorously asserting the discourse of a secular classical republicanism which has been latent but as yet not fully actualized. Martial was offering witty variations on a narrative central to Livy's story of the foundations of the Roman republic (*Ab Urbe Condita*, II.12). In the larger narrative, the royal Tarquins, having been driven out of Rome, ally themselves with Lars Porsena, warning him that if republicanism is allowed to stand in one city, all kings will be in danger. Porsena lays siege to Rome, and Scaevola makes his assassination attempt. When caught, he asserts that this is not the isolated attempt of a single individual: three hundred young noblemen have sworn an oath to kill him and drawn lots for the honor.[21] Fortune has not favored him, but there will be many further attempts. Marvell's poem presents "our Scotland" as a worthy successor to the ancient Roman republic: setting aside any question of divine intervention, there is a huge stock of human resistance available. The "virtus" for which Mitchell is praised (l. 9) would then shade into a Machiavellian *virtù* in seizing the occasion as forcefully as Scaevola had done. The story of an oath can be adapted rather precisely to a Scottish context, where old traditions of taking "bands" of loyalty were adapted by the Covenanters to mobilize popular resistance to tyrants.

The question of resistance is raised still more starkly at the start of a four-line tailpiece which should probably be regarded as a separate epigram rather than part of the poem, a structure also found in the sequence of the "Deploratio" and "Epitaphium":[22] "Explosa nequiit quem sternere glande Michellus, / Explodet saevum Scotia Pontificem." Here the poem's ethical position pivots on questions of linguistic temporality. Marvell makes a kind of pun possible only within neo-Latin poetry. In classical Latin "explodo" meant "to hiss off the stage" and hence "condemn." In English, the word retains that sense (cf. *Paradise Lost*, 10.546, 11.669), but the word was starting to take on the senses of "to drive forth (air), to emit," "to drive out with violence and sudden noise," with reference to gunpowder; the *OED* lists the first usages in this sense from after the Restoration. In the former sense, the poem calls only for Sharp's banishment, but the latter sense is imported from postclassical usage into the poem's classical register to refer to the assassin's bullet. If it can then be taken to infiltrate into its anaphoric repetition, one might argue that the poem incites violence. Arguably the sense of lurking menace is not entirely dispelled. On the other hand, in the epigrammatic genre parallels are designed to highlight differences, and the second usage is wittier if it is making a significantly different point. The poem's outrage against cruelty would surely carry over to the cruelty of political murder. Moreover, the rhetorical contexts of poem and epigram suggest that they place at least their immediate hopes in negotiation rather than violence.

In a meticulous reconstruction of those contexts, Paul Mathole has shown that the poem's circulation in England would have been a significant blow against Sharp's overlord in London, the Earl of Lauderdale. As chief minister responsible for Scotland, Lauderdale had powerful enemies, many of whom were working in concert with powerful English statesmen such as the Earl of Shaftesbury to oust him and his instrument Sharp. A few years earlier, as a member of the "Cabal" ministry, Lauderdale had favored a policy of conciliation with Scottish dissenters as part of an Erastian settlement which Marvell had praised in his poem "The Loyal Scot." A return to such policies with support at high levels was not impossible, and to that extent the speech-act of Marvell's poem is compatible with a non-violent constitutional settlement. Sharp's actions outraged figures who were far from sympathetic to the Covenanters, and who may not have had any generalized humanitarian objection to torture, but who were angered by the combination of legal irregularity and political ineptitude displayed in the Mitchell case. Strong criticisms of the trial were voiced by the Anglican Gilbert Burnet, who was involved in mobilizing opposition to Sharp and who may therefore have read Marvell's poem – as recurrent hand imagery in his own later narrative perhaps suggests. Mitchell's execution, he wrote, "was probably that which, both in the just judgment of God and the inflamed fury of wicked men, brought him two years after to such a dismal fate." Burnet's account of Sharp's death cannot shake off a critical note: his comment that "This was the dismal end of that unhappy man" and that the Covenanters "murdered him most barbarously" was tempered in the manuscript by the phrase "who certainly needed more time to fit him to pass into an unchangeable state," and he went so far as carefully to delete the "most" before "barbarously."[23]

Burnet and Marvell agreed that the Covenanters showed remarkable forbearance in the face of state violence and provocation. Burnet commented that "when they saw a rebellion was desired, they bore the present oppression more quietly than perhaps they would have done, if it had not been for that." In his last surviving letter, Marvell wrote that "The Patience of the *Scots*, under their Oppressions, is not to be paralleled in any History. They still continue their extraordinary and numerous, but peaceable, Field Conventicles" (*MPL*, vol. 2, p. 357): like Mitchell they gain stature through suffering. The Scaevola story, after all, ends in reconciliation: the Etruscan king so admires Scaevola's courage – and is so daunted by the idea that it is fully representative of the collective valor of the young republic – that he frees him to negotiate a settlement. Some aspects of Marvell's poem are calculated to rally support for such a settlement, by countering fears of the Covenanters as violent antinomian fanatics. Its choice of a highly disciplined and allusive Latin medium in itself distances the poem from the register of rhapsodic Biblical prophecy within which so many of the Covenanters' public speeches were framed. Hickes complained that English readers were being misled by the circulation of doctored texts into underestimating the Covenanters' religious fanaticism; *Ravillac Redivivus* conspicuously omits Mitchell's final speech and other utterances which adopted a milder tone, and a later printing amplified Hickes's warnings.[24] Marvell's poem plays down Biblical rhetoric; and in fact, as recent scholarship has emphasized, Scottish religious radicalism was not as single-mindedly religious as stereotypes from Sharp's propagandists down to Scott's *Old Mortality* have suggested.[25]

While today's political climate may suggest that one can hardly overestimate the importance of religion in public affairs, it remains deceptive to consider the deployment of religious texts in abstraction from the pragmatics of their particular speech-acts, which may be informed by less otherwordly factors. The Covenanters combined a fierce insistence on the independence of their church with a radically democratic belief in giving "a right of resistance to ordinary people, acting without the sanction of their parliament or social superiors."[26] They drew on humanist as well as Biblical sources: one of their main points of reference, the neo-Latin poet George Buchanan, had effectively naturalized certain forms of Roman Stoic and republican political discourse in a Scottish Protestant context, producing a history of Scottish liberties to parallel Livy's. Buchanan's role as readily-chastising tutor to the young James VI had dramatically brought home the potential conflict between monarchist and humanist notions of corporeal discipline. In justifying Mitchell's attempted, and the subsequent successful, assassination of Sharp, Covenanter theorists invoked Buchanan and drew on a huge array of classical and later works of secular political theory. Marvell's poem offers the Covenanters' cause a very different resonance and builds bridges between English and Scottish political discourses, enacting the "Scoto-Brittannus" of his title. His choice of the neo-Latin medium is attuned to the Buchanan tradition, which was continued in at least one Latin verse tribute to Mitchell.

All the same, a Scoto-British movement might be a two-way process, with certain forms of populist radicalism feeding into English opposition circles as the political polarization that was to become the exclusion crisis emerged. The Covenanter leader John Welsh, whom Marvell praised for his passivity, was seen very differently by Hickes, according to whom he had composed a discourse on the theme that "they are blessed that shall take the prelates and dash their brains against the stones."[27] Certainly the Covenanters did arm themselves, even if they claimed that their purpose was defensive. Hickes wrote of a Covenanter who was arrested with a seditious tract in one pocket and a loaded pistol in the other: the doctrine in one pocket and the use in the other.[28] As Sharon Achinstein has argued, in English dissenting discourse the boundaries between symbolic and physical violence were often blurred.[29] And Biblically-based activism could blend easily with the powerful classical cult of tyrannicide which is often disavowed in current discourse on terrorism. The word "assassinate" is redolent of an earlier phase of Orientalist discourse and occludes Roman precedents for politically motivated violence. When repressive actions in the wake of Sharp's assassination provoked an open rebellion in Scotland in 1679, Algernon Sidney hoped that it would precipitate a republican rising in England. A few years later, Shaftesbury would be offering his equivalent of Scaevola's three hundred Romans in the "thousand brisk boys" he claimed to have ready for rebellion; very much in the Buchanan tradition, he proclaimed that tyrants had put themselves outside the laws of society and might therefore be hunted down like wild beasts. If Marvell's poem does not exactly glorify terrorism, it does contribute to a cult of martyrdom, and a renewal of republican imagery, that might have the effect of inflaming active resistance. Hickes himself seems to have thought so. He warned: "I doubt not, but if all the Fathers of our Church, and all the Clergy under them had but one Neck, that there are at least 300. Covenanted *Mitchels* behind, that would strive to cut it off."[30] As Paul Mathole points out, the otherwise unmotivated allusion to the Scaevola story suggests that he had Marvell's poem in mind as one of his targets.

The poem's rhetoric suggests that Marvell was trying to steer a line between Hickes's absolutism and the readiness of some oppositionists to gloss over the cruelty of political murder; but "Scaevola Scoto-Brittannus" shows the difficulty of defining such a space in the intensifying political polarization of the later 1670s. What does seem clear from the poem's links with other Marvellian texts is that its questions run deeply through his writings. Most obviously there are links with "The Loyal Scot," which likewise tried to forge Anglo-Scottish unity through an image of a martyred Scot. In that case, in the spirit of the Cabal's mood of religious toleration, the martyr was a Catholic, Archibald Douglas, whose death is presented in witty religious terms quite parallel to Mitchell's. David Baker has argued that there is a connection between that poem's exploration of new political territories and its strongly homoerotic subtext, a pattern that seems to apply to the Mitchell poem too.[31] The imagery of mutilation does seem to connect with contemporary attacks on Marvell as himself mutilated, as a eunuch. In one epigram he praises a eunuch precisely because his artistic productivity far exceeds the merits of physical propagation, which is described, like Scaevola's errant bullet, as "peccare," sinning.[32] Marvell's imaginative exploration of mutilated or androgynous figures who can nonetheless take bold public action seems in part a response to such attacks.

Such action, however, did not need to be seen in directly violent terms. The symbolism of hands runs through Marvell's writings in different genres, and combines rather than opposes the senses of writing and action, placing the emphasis rather on the ends and contexts of action. There are significant parallels between theological debates in which Marvell actively engaged and more recent debates over the status of the hand in writing, with what is often described as a materialist position stressing the impossibility of an abstract mental intention's fully governing the hand's action. Not long after writing the Scaevola poem, Marvell launched into a controversy with the high Calvinist writer Thomas Danson, and took particular exception to a passage implying that God had moved Adam to sin. Danson, he complains,

> parallels God's moving him to that Act rather than to another, *with a Writing-Master's directing his Scholars hand.* If the Cause be not to be defended upon better terms than so, what Christian but would rather wish he had never known Writing-Master, than to subscribe such an Opinion; and that God should make an innocent Creature in this manner to do a forbidden Act, for which so dreadful a vengeance was to insue upon him and his posterity?
>
> (*PW*, 2, p. 469)

Here Marvell offers a humanist resistance to Calvinist determinism, in a manner parallel to his resistance to providential accounts of Mitchell's hand. His position, however, was a complex one, for he had earlier attacked with equal vehemence Samuel Parker for, he alleged, claiming that *"All Religion must of necessity be resolved into Enthusiasm or Morality. The former is meer Imposture; and therefore all that is true must be reduced to the latter."* (*PW*, 1, p. 93.)

High Calvinists like Danson and his ally John Owen spoke contemptuously of Aristotelian ethics as a discourse inherently subversive of a proper acknowledgement of God's agency in all worldly affairs. Parker, at the opposite extreme, exalted ethics at the expense of Providence. Marvell had always been ready to acknowledge the possibility that divine agency could tinge human action in momentous ways, as in his earlier hopes for Cromwell's hand: "Sure, the mysterious Work, where none withstand, / Would forthwith finish under such a Hand[:]" ("The First Anniversary," ll. 37–38, *Paradise Lost*, I, 112). Marshall Grossman has argued that though Marvell presents moral validation as "subsequent to the act" his poetry is constantly aware of "the problems of eschatological ethics," and his theological writings share these preoccupations.[33] Marvell's representation of Mitchell resists the anti-nomian potential of Providential language – though as has been suggested, the resistance may have had a tactical element.[34]

Within a secular perspective, the imagery of hands also carried diverse meanings. The Latin "manus" could refer to an armed force, and in a Latin epigram on Cromwell Marvell speaks of his leading such "manus" in the people's cause.[35] Like a lot of Roman military vocabulary, however, "manus" could also have rhetorical connotations. In a play on the two senses, Algernon Sidney copied out a personal inscription while on a diplomatic mission to Copenhagen: "MANUS HAEC INIMICA TYRANNIS EINSE PETIT PLACIDAM CUM LIBERTATE QUIETEM" ("This hand, enemy to tyrants, by the sword seeks peace with liberty").[36] Unlike Sidney, Marvell had not fought in battle and when he visited Copenhagen on a diplomatic mission six years later he was serving Charles II and charged with an apology for the regicide. He may have come to feel Sidney's boldness as a reproach, for soon afterwards he embarked on a series of increasingly outspoken oppositional poems. In difficult political times, using the hand in rhetoric could involve elements of risk and courage directly comparable to military engagement. In what was probably the first of a series of interventions against Edmund Waller's flattering portrayal of the second Dutch war, his narrator declares:

> Nay, Painter, if thou dar'st design that fight
> Which Waller only courage had to write;
> If thy bold hand can without shaking draw
> What ev'n the actors trembled when they saw;
> Enough to make thy colours change like theirs,
> And all thy pencils bristle like their hairs.[37]

The fleeting pun on "draw" makes the critical poet's courage greater than that of those who actually saw battle.[38] And in "Last Instructions to a Painter," Marvell contrasts such bold and critical use of language with that of the man he blames as the war's architect. As Clarendon moves from drafting a proclamation against the Dutch republicans to a recall of Parliament his hand wavers:

But when he came the odious Clause to Pen,
That summons up the *Parliament* agen;
His Writing-Master many a time he bann'd,
And wish'd himself the Gout, to seize his hand.
Never old Letcher more repugnance felt,
Consenting, for his Rupture, to be Gelt[.]
      (ll. 469–74; *MPL*, vol. 1, p. 159)

Here there is a striking anticipation of the Scaevola poem: Hyde's desire for his gout to afflict his hand will be inverted by Mitchell's receiving in his leg the punishment due to his hand. In a modulation of the eunuch epigram's contrast between poetry and the sin of propagation, here Hyde becomes a type of Cavalier libertinism, his desire for gelding the climax of a life of debauchery and closely associated with a form of ultra-royalist writing that denies the rights of Parliament.

Marvell thus called for the writer's hand to show the boldness necessary to confront tyranny; but he remained acutely aware of the dangers. He identi-fied his own writings in the public service with a Scaevolan sacrifice: in 1661 he wrote to the Mayor of Hull that "if I wanted my right hand yet I would scribble to you with my left rather then neglect your businesse" (*MPL*, vol. 2, p. 28). His constituency letters, however, are generally cautious in what they commit to paper. In a poem probably written in the same year as "Scaevola Scoto-Brittannus," and hence possibly his very last, he satirizes a graphologist who had tried to infer his character from his handwriting: who, he asks, would entrust his feelings to paper if he believed that the guilty paper might find out things in his life he wished concealed: the ignorant hand, "Ignaram ... Manum," betrays the inner soul.[39] The poem perhaps hints at resistance to those who pried into his personal mutilation. It also evokes the political situation when his writings were being called in by the authorities and a search was out for their author – a topic he plays with just after discussing the Covenanters in his last letter. In 1674 a court satirist had raised the threat of physical punishment when he attacked "Marvell, who yet wears his ears."[40]

In this light, the Scaevola poem's Mitchell can be seen as representing not so much the antithesis of the languorous poet Marvell as a close parallel to the public-spirited writer. Mitchell wittily controls the symbolism of his punishment, inverting the meaning the authorities try to attach to it; he takes a festive pleasure in this inversion; and even the grotesque imagery of the foot has a poetic subtext. The words "commodat usque pedem" (l. 16) fall at the point in the elegiac couplet where the potentially variable metre of the first half-line in the second line of a couplet modulates into the regular dactyl/dactyl/long syllable of the second half-line, ending precisely on the word "pedem," "foot." Poetic form and ethico-political import are tightly connected: Marvell's hands were ready to resist tyranny as best they could; and his feet had a kick in them.

I have tried to focus in this essay on the historical contexts of Marvell's writing, but to keep some contemporary debates in mind. In current methodological disputes over the ethics of writing, the status of the hand engages much attention: how far does its involvement in the process of writing symbolize a material restraint that necessarily renders illusory the apparent agency of the disembodied mind? As has been seen, Marvell himself recognized the case to be made both for constraint and for agency, but he would surely have insisted on his moral responsibility for writings whose circulation could have led to the most materially physical forms of punishment. It remains true that his writings are haunted by ambiguities of agency. A letter that has not survived contained the comment: "Praeterea magis occidere metuo quam occidi; non quod Vitam tanti aestimem, sed ne imparatus moriar" (*MPL*, vol. 2, p. 357). If, as Legouis argues, "occidere" has a long 'i', the maxim means: "Besides, I rather fear to kill than to be killed [and if I fear at all to die a violent death it is] not because I hold life of such a price but to avoid dying unprepared" (*MPL*, vol. 2, p. 396). Marvell's biography reveals frequent incidents of sudden outbursts of physical violence: during a diplomatic mission in 1665 he brandished a pistol at a dilatory servant. Margoliouth, however, believed that the 'i' was short, implying that Marvell feared falling through some unexpected natural cause more than potential death in battle. Both versions offer some parallel with Seneca's frequent moralizations of the Scaevola story, e.g. "Vide quanto acrior sit ad occupanda pericula virtus quam crudelitas ad inroganda," "see how much more eager virtue is to embrace dangers than cruelty is to inflict them" (*Epistulae*, 24.5), "Mucio manus in hostili ara relicta instar occisi Porsinae fuit," "The hand that Mucius left on the enemy's altar was as glorious as if it had killed Porsina" (*De Beneficiis*, 7.15.2). But the dividing line between suffering and agency, patience and violence, remained as thin as an accent mark.

Notes

1   *Mr. Smirke*, in *The Prose Works of Andrew Marvell*, ed. Annabel Patterson, 2 vols (New Haven, CT: Yale University Press, 2003 hereafter *PW*), 2, p. 46.

2   If space permitted, a contrast could be developed with William Empson, whose interest in the linguistic play of Marvell's lyrics was always combined with an alertness to social dimensions which subsequently allowed him to write enthusiastically about the satires. For the relative thinness of the Formalist critical lexicon in comparison with traditional rhetoric, see Gérard Genette, "Rhetoric Restrained," in *Figures of Literary Discourse*, trans. Alan Sheridan (Oxford: Blackwell, 1982), pp. 103–26.

3   Nigel Smith (ed.), *The Poems of Andrew Marvell*, revised edition (London: Pearson Longman, 2007); Nicholas von Maltzahn, *An Andrew Marvell Chronology* (Basingstoke: Palgrave Macmillan, 2005).

4   Estelle Haan, *Andrew Marvell's Latin Poetry: From Text to Context* (Brussels: Éditions

Latomus, 2003); I am grateful to Dr. Paul Mathole for providing me with extracts from his unpublished Ph.D. dissertation, *Marvell and Violence* (University of London, 2004).

5 Nicholas von Maltzahn, "Marvell's Ghost," in Warren Chernaik and Martin Dzelzainis (eds), *Marvell and Liberty* (Basingstoke: Macmillan, 1999), pp. 50–74 (53–56). The running title "Miscellanies" has been taken as indicating an original intention of including some of the post-Restoration polemic in prose and verse: Andrew Marvell, *Miscellaneous Poems* (Menston: Scolar Press, 1969), prefatory note.

6 Gilbert Burnet, *A History of my Own Time*, ed. O. Airy, 2 vols (Oxford: Clarendon Press, 1897–1900), 2, p. 137. For a modern analysis, see Julia Buckroyd, *The Life of James Sharp, Archbishop of St. Andrews, 1618–1679: A Political Biography* (Edinburgh: J. Donald, 1987), pp. 100ff.

7 Discussing the Covenanters' suppression in 1679, Algernon Sidney writes of "the boots my lord of Latherdale hath brought into fashion" (p. 92), "my lord Latherdale's boots," *Letters of Algernon Sydney*, in *Discourses Concerning Government with his Letters* (London, 1763), pp. 92, 94. The instrument is depicted facing the title page of Anon., *A Hind Let Loose*, n. pl., 1687.

8 Michel Foucault, *Discipline and Punish: The Birth of the Prison*, trans. Alan Sheridan (London: Allen Lane, 1977). For documentation and critique, see James Holstun, *Ehud's Dagger: Class Struggle in the English Revolution* (London: Verso, 2000), pp. 48–49, and cf. David Norbrook, 'Life and Death of Renaissance Man', *Raritan*, 8:4 (Spring 1989): 89–110.

9 On humanism, hands, and discipline, see Jonathan Goldberg, *Writing Matter: From the Hands of the English Renaissance* (Stanford, CA: Stanford University Press, 1990), a work closely parallel in approach to *Discipline and Punish*, with hands consistently viewed as the authorities' tools rather than participating in critical agency.

10 *The Poems and Letters of Andrew Marvell*, 2 vols, ed. H.M. Margoliouth, 3rd ed., rev. Pierre Legouis and E.E. Duncan-Jones (Oxford: Clarendon Press, 1971), 1, pp. 213–14. Unless otherwise specified, citations from Marvell's poems and letters are from this edition, hereafter *MPL*. I follow Haan's translations of the Latin, which are also provided in the revised edition of Smith's *The Poems of Andrew Marvell*.

11 [George Hickes], *Ravillac Redivivus* (London, 1678), pp. 54–55; cf. Haan, *Andrew Marvell's Latin Poetry*, p. 237 n. 87.

12 Robert Wodrow, *The History of the Sufferings of the Church of Scotland*, 2 vols. (Edinburgh, 1721), 1, p. 293; Anon., *The Life of Mr. James Sharp* (Edinburgh, 1719), p. 119, cited by Haan, *Andrew Marvell's Latin Poetry*, p. 230.

13 So assured is Marvell's Latin verse that critics have found grounds for querying his authorship of the poem in an irregularity in the scansion: the first syllable of "feriatur" is long but it is placed as the first of two short vowels in a dactyl that breaks a sequence of spondees enacting the torturer's sweaty labor. Margoliouth in his edition wrote: "A false quantity in l. 25 is the only contrary evidence" to Marvell's authorship; but Legouis noted a false quantity in an indubitably authentic poem (*MPL*, 1, p. 419).

14 Cf. "pecccavit anulus," "a ringlet had gone amiss," in the context of female cosmetics, Martial, *Epigrams*, 2.66.1.

15 *State Trials*, VI, 1228, cited by Haan, *Andrew Marvell's Latin Poetry*, p. 236.

16 Anon., *Epigrams of Martial, Englished* (London, 1695), p. 181.

17   Haan, *Andrew Marvell's Latin Poetry*, p. 235.
18   Hickes, *Ravillac Redivivus*, p. 11.
19   "Illustrissimo Viro Domino: Lanceloto Josepho de Maniban Grammatomanti,"
     MPL, 1, pp. 55–56l, l. 3.
20   Such a poem could not of course have been printed except on an underground
     basis. Severe attempts were made to restrict the public sphere in Scotland, with
     Edinburgh's first coffee houses having been closed down in 1677: Clare Jackson,
     Restoration Scotland, 1660–1690: Royalist Politics, Religion and Ideas (Woodbridge:
     The Boydell Press, 2003). The poem must have been composed between January
     1676, the date of Mitchell's torture (as established by Mathole), and Marvell's
     death in August 1678, on the cusp of a major shift toward a widening of the
     audience for polemic in manuscript and print: Harold Love, *English Clandestine
     Satire 1660–1702* (New York: Oxford University Press, 2004), pp. 122–23. In
     addition to being included in the manuscript poems added to a printed copy of
     the 1681 *Miscellaneous Poems* (Bodleian MS Eng.poet.d.49, pp. 264–65), "Scaevola
     Scoto-Brittannus" appears with an attribution to Marvell in a MS collection of
     poems on affairs of state probably compiled by members of the Northamptonshire
     Danvers family, British Library Additional MS 34362, fols. 43r–v, and in a
     miscellany containing entries up to 1681, Beinecke Rare Book and Manuscript
     Library, Yale University, Osborn Collection b.54, pp. 1225–26. See Peter Beal,
     Index of Literary Manuscripts, vol. 2: 1625–1700, 2 vols (London: Mansell, 1993), 2,
     pp. 23, 46; I thank Elizabeth Scott-Baumann for collating the Yale MS, which is
     not recorded in *MPL* or in Smith's edition. The evidence suggests that the poem
     circulated, albeit in small numbers, amongst members of the gentry beyond
     immediate court circles. Love includes the contents of the British Library and
     Yale MSS in an appendix, *English Clandestine Satire*, pp. 303–414.
21   Scaevola in fact appears to be bluffing here (I owe this point to Ray Bossert); but
     as Sharp's assassination was to show, Mitchell did have many emulators.
22   *MPL*, 1, p. 420. These lines do not occur in the Bodleian MS and are set apart
     from the rest of the poem in the British Library MS, though they do appear
     without a break in the Yale MS; cf. Hickes, *Ravillac Redivivus*, pp. 54–55.
23   Burnet, *A History of my Own Time*, 1, p. 502, 2, pp. 136, 142, 236. In 1677 George
     Hickes linked Burnet with the diffusion of anti-Sharp propaganda: *The Manuscripts
     of his Grace the Duke of Portland*, 4 vols (London: Historical Manuscripts Commission,
     1891–97), 2, p. 41.
24   *Jackson, Restoration Scotland*, p. 42; [George Hickes], *Ravillac Redivivus*, second edi-
     tion (London, 1682). For contested versions of Mitchell's final speech, see Robert
     Wodrow, *The History of the Sufferings of the Church of Scotland, from the Restauration to the
     Revolution*, 2 vols (Edinburgh: James Watson, 1721–22), 1, p. 517.
25   For Scott's use of the Mitchell episode, see *Old Mortality*, ed. Peter Davidson and
     Jane Stevenson (Oxford: Oxford University Press, 1993), chapter 36, and on his
     difficulty in resolving his own view of the Covenanters, see the introduction, pp.
     xxi–xxvii, xxxvi–xxxix.
26   Ian B. Cowan, "The Political Ideas of the Scottish Covenanters, 1633–88,"
     History of Political Thought 1 (1980): 167–93, 193; Jackson, *Restoration Scotland*, moves
     beyond romance and religious polemic to offer a pioneering study of the rationale
     of Scottish political thought in this period, but more work remains to be done on
     oppositional discourse and publication.
27   *The Manuscripts of his Grace the Duke of Portland*, 2, p. 46.

28 [George Hickes], *The Spirit of Popery Speaking out of the Mouths of Phanatical-Protestants* (London, 1680), p. 67. The names of Sharp's murderers were printed "in Letters of Blood," p. 63.

29 Sharon Achinstein, *Literature and Dissent in Milton's England* (Cambridge: Cambridge University Press, 2003), pp. 84–114.

30 Hickes, *Ravillac Redivivus*, 1678 edition, p. 52.

31 David J. Baker, *Between Nations: Shakespeare, Spenser, Marvell, and the Question of Britain* (Stanford, CA: Stanford University Press, 1997), pp. 152–68.

32 "Upon an Eunuch: A Poet", *MPL*, 1, p. 57, l. 3; Paul Hammond, "Marvell's Sexuality," *The Seventeenth Century* 11 (1996): 87–123.

33 Marshall Grossman, *The Story of All Things: Writing the Self in English Narrative Poetry* (Durham, NC: Duke University Press, 1998), p. 212.

34 It is also worth noting Marvell's unusual phrase "lame Faith" in his 1674 poem defending *Paradise Lost* against potential critics of its theological heterodoxy: "On Mr. Milton's *Paradise lost*," *MPL*, 1, pp. 137–38, l. 14.

35 "In eandem Reginae *Sueciae* transmissam," *MPL*, 1, p. 108, l. 6.

36 Jonathan Scott, *Algernon Sidney and the English Republic, 1623–1677* (Cambridge: Cambridge University Press, 1988), p. 133.

37 Lines 1–6, *The Poems of Andrew Marvell*, ed. Smith, p. 332.

38 The case for Marvell's authorship of this poem, in part or in whole, looks increasingly strong: see Smith's edition, p. 329.

39 "Illustrissimo Viro Domino: Lanceloto Josepho de Maniban Grammatomanti," l. 8.

40 "A Charge to the Grand Inquest of England," l. 10, in *Poems on Affairs of State: Augustan Satirical Verse, 1660–1714. Volume 1, 1660–1678*, ed. George de F. Lord (New Haven, CT: Yale University Press, 1963), p. 222.

Part IV

Philosophy and Renaissance ethics

9 The ethics of inspiration

Gordon Teskey

Do poets make their poems alone, or are they aided by supernatural powers? Do poets, to use a word that began to be associated with them only in the Renaissance, create their own creations? If poets create their own creations, does poetic creativity encroach on the creativity of the Creator, the Creator with a capital "C"? If poets do not create their own creations but are aided by the muses, can these muses, the daughters of Memory, be appropriated to the Creator, to the Spirit, or must poetic inspiration always stand apart from the unified ideological field of a world that was created in six days by God? *Inspiratio* was the Latin translation of Greek *enthousiasmos*, which means the state of "having a god within," to which I would add "having a god within that wants to come out as an artifact." The word is cited in E.K.'s notes to Spenser's "October" eclogue and stands behind the phrase "goodly fury" in the last complete book of *The Faerie Queene* (6 proem 2). In aspiring to add something to the world that is totally new, is the poet or the artist in some sense another god, *alter deus*, like Michelangelo, who was called *il divino*? Is the laurel crown a halo, glowing with empyreal fire?

Using such terms to replace the Creator God with the creative artist reflects a narcissism that is not absent from our own ideas of the artist, ideas that were mocked by Baudelaire in "Perte d'auréole," but which have remained persistent in the shamanistic delirium of modern art. In Baudelaire's comic sketch, which is one of the *Petits Poèmes en Prose*, the poet loses his halo while crossing the chaotic traffic of the street. The halo, or *auréole*, sticks in the tarry muck of the macadam – "*dans la fange du macadam*" – and the poet is too leery of the traffic to retrieve it. He is content to go about now *incognito* and drunk, like a "simple mortal," resigning his exalted status altogether, and to laugh at inferior poets who will take up his halo and wear it. Baudelaire uses the word *simple* in the classic sense of "unmixed," a unity that is no longer divided into two persons by the presence of a god within, by inspiration. The point of Baudelaire's poem is that to be a mature creative artist it is necessary to become a "simple mortal," going beyond the naïve substitution of the self for the Father Creator into that acceptance of contingency and of human abjectness – acceptances that breed skepticism and humor – exhibited in Baudelaire's poem.

Milton at least partly displaces the same narcissism in the invocation to the seventh book of *Paradise Lost*, which leaves him "standing on earth," and he continues to struggle to do so in *Paradise Regained* and *Samson Agonistes*. When artistic creation is regarded as being analogous to divine Creation, as Sarah Kofman puts it, the artist kills God only to put himself in God's place. Kofman goes on to claim (she is to some extent paraphrasing Freud, in the Leonardo essay) that art can mature only from a religious fixation to a narcissistic fixation, which is why religion and art are not truly incompatible, both being forms of infantile regression, although the narcissism of art is just a little more mature than the infantile dependence of religion.[1] Only through science – or, in Hegel's system, *Wissenschaft* – can the mature state be attained in which the rational and the real coincide. It remains an open question, however, whether inspiration can be brought under the regime of the ethical, which depends on a unified subject.

Ethos means "custom, usage, manners, habit," all of which may be summarized in English as *character*, where what is referred to is a single agent – in drama, a single actor's part. But in Greek, as in English, especially in the discipline of sociology, *ethos* also denotes the underlying spirit determining the beliefs and customs of a society. (The biological science of *ethology* is the study of animal behavior in relation to environment.) In the singular sense, ethics, more precisely, deontological ethics, is prescriptive: deontological ethics are concerned with duty and with binding obligations. (The Greek verb *deo* "to bind, tie, fasten, fetter" is connected with the word for chain links.) In the plural sense, by contrast, *ethics* is not prescriptive but descriptive: it is concerned with the moral in the Latinate sense of *mos*: a custom, usage, or rule in a society. *Ethos* is therefore ambiguous with respect to number, referring either to the single or plural, either to a "self," as in *ethics*, or to a society of selves. In the first case, the ethical speaks of conscious rules of *conduct* binding the self from within. In the second case, the ethological speaks of unconscious rules of *behavior* that are binding on selves from without. In both cases, however, the ethical is close to what we call *fate*: hence the implied equivalence in Heraclitus's statement: character (*ethos*) *is* fate, which is one of the meanings of *daimon*.

In *Paradise Regained* the obedient Son, hungering to do his Father's will, replaces the Father with himself by uniting the Father to himself, thus achieving the state of ethical integrity. This is not a narcissistic state because the integrated self that emerges in the poem is a symbol of the human as well and does not glory in having God within: it is a simple, imaginative fact. Henceforth – so Jesus prophesies – crimes against humanity are crimes against God. Having displaced the Father in *Paradise Regained*, Milton turns in *Samson Agonistes* to the problem of displacing the narcissistic self that is now in the place of the Father. But displacing the narcissistic self entails giving oneself over to contingency, to what is referred to in *Paradise Lost* as necessity and chance, and that means giving oneself over to irony and laughter.

Tragedy is a narcissistic literary form that in its more extreme examples presses against the limits of its narcissism to border on farce, as in *King Lear*, in *Antony and Cleopatra*, and especially in *Timon of Athens*, that tragedy of the unified ethical subject everlastingly entombed "upon the beached marge of the salt flood."[2] There is indeed something marginally farcical and comic about *Samson Agonistes*, giving it its resemblance to *Waiting for Godot*, and there is something of Timon of Athens in Samson, too. Milton's drama remains in the sphere of narcissism, but Milton chose the dramatic form so that his own narcissism, as an inspired poet, could be displaced onto the hero, a hero who is his own destroyer. Milton fantasized about pulling the temple of the Restoration government down on its philistine king and his lords. What he could not do, at least in his art, is laugh at them.

***

The question whether the laurel crown is a halo, glowing with celestial fire, is the quintessentially Renaissance question about the poet and about the artist in general: the question of what it means to bring into being what has never existed before. This question is directed, however, not just at the thing that is made, the poem. It is directed also at the *ethos* or character of the poet. Why should the act of creating entangle the poet with the divine, and in such a way that it places the poet's ethical responsibility in question?

It may be supposed that from the earliest human times any act of making, including the making of tools, carried with it a sense of guilt for disturbing the existing order of the world. But in the Christian tradition the act of making bears in a particularly exposed way on the doctrine of divine Creation and even on the dominion Man has been given over that Creation. In Charles Frazier's novel *Cold Mountain* a particularly wicked character, in a book in which there is no shortage of scoundrels, shows the hero, Inman, his tobacco pouch, made from the scrotum of a bull, and sermonizes on it as follows: "'Bull sack,' he said. 'A Man can't make a better pouch than God did. Such things are a test from God to see if we will make do with what He provides or if we will shun dominion and seek improvement by our own weak devices.'" Even with the character in question it is hard to tell whether or not he is being ironical about the theological correctness of using a bull's scrotum for a tobacco pouch – thus exercising a Biblically-ordained dominion over nature. It is also hard to tell whether he is joking or sincerely thinks that adding to nature, seeking improvement by our own weak devices, is a sin. But there can be no doubt that the question he raises is fundamental in a Christian worldview: should we accept nature as it is or seek to improve it? Clearly, we have no choice but to improve nature, but the reason we must do so is that when we fell nature fell with us and is no longer hospitable to us, as it was when we were in the garden of Eden. Our creativity is evidence of our sinful restlessness. A different view of human work appears in Milton's *Of Education*, where he says that the end of education is "to repair the ruins of our first parents."[3] Milton clearly thought the same thing of poetic creation: far from being mere evidence of our sinfulness, poetic creativity belongs to the effort of "regaining to know God aright," as we did in the garden of Eden. Self-fashioning is really self-restoration. In the ethical system of *Paradise Lost* the moral being of creatures is grounded in the recognition that they *are* creatures, owing their being to a Creator. It is therefore with considerable difficulty that Milton can allow himself to be a creator in his own right. He is the last major poet in the European literary tradition for whom the act of creation is centered in God and he is also the first major poet in the European literary tradition for whom the act of creation begins to find its center in the human. It was only by oscillating rapidly in his unconscious between those two, contradictory positions that Milton was able to create. This process of oscillation between contraries, or of continual deviation from and return to an ethically stable position, is what I call *delirium*. Over the course of the seventeenth century what was formerly a poetics of *hallucination*, in which the poet creates a stable illusion of Fairy Land, or of Arcadia, delivering an experience without truth (but then finding moral truth in it), gives way to a poetics of delirium, in which an unstable series of hallucinatory moments is delivered through the mediation of the poet. Whereas in the poetics of hallucination the poet delivers an experience to us, in the poetics of delirium the poet undergoes an experience on our behalf.[4]

Creating a poem is partly the act of production, of *poiesis*, and partly the action of speaking, a speaking that is necessarily public, however private and merely "overheard" (as Mill said of poetry) the utterance may seem. It would appear to be under the action of speaking in public that the ethical responsibility of poetry falls. For any act of speaking in public, in the open, political space, is an act for which the speaker assumes responsibility. The ethical potential in poetry would appear, therefore, to lie within the realm of interpretation and to be inseparable from it. What the poet *says* lies open to interpretation, even if what the poet *does* does not. For it is not through the craft of making in itself, of *poiesis*, but rather through what this craft supports – speaking with a public voice – that the poet is burdened with the responsibility of speaking an efficacious word. The responsibility is complicated by two things: by the impossibility of the inspired poet's ever being wholly responsible for what he says (one thinks of Mayakovsky) and by the embeddedness of poetic speaking in poetic making, that is, in the fashioning of a work of art. It is the act of artistic creating and its entanglement with the divine that concerns me here, especially with respect to the character, or *ethos* of the poet. What ethical problems come into view when the character of the poet is entangled with something with a will that is other than its own?

***

There appear to have been two forms of such entanglement. The first is a traditional, classical entanglement with the divine, in which the poet is the bringer of a vision accorded by the muse, a vision that leaves the poet relatively unchanged. In this situation it is the vision itself – the hallucination – that is transmitted by the poet to us. We experience the vision as another world, a heterocosm, like Spenser's Faerie, or the myth-world of Renaissance Ovidian verse, from Thomas Lodge's *Scillaes Metamorphosis* to Marlowe's *Hero and Leander* and Shakespeare's *Venus and Adonis*. The second form of entanglement with the divine is a deeper, more alarming, and more atavistic (rather than traditional) involvement, one resembling the practices of shamanism, in which the poet undergoes partial transformation, oscillating between opposite states. No longer does the poet merely transmit a vision given by the muse, a vision that is distinct both from himself and from the muse. The structure of distinct elements in the situation – the muse, the vision, the poet – collapses in upon the poet himself. The poet becomes a medium, or conductor, by which an undefined spiritual power breaks into the world. In this situation, as I have mentioned, the poet does not deliver an experience to us but undergoes an experience on our behalf. Over the course of the later Renaissance in England, from Spenser to Milton, it appears that the situation of poetry shifted from the first of these entanglements to the second, from what I have termed a poetics of hallucination, where the involvement with the muse is lighter, to a poetics of delirium, in which the deeper involvement of the poet with a now relatively undefined spiritual power fixes our attention more on the poet than on what the poet says.

***

I spoke of this difference between hallucination and delirium as a transition taking place over the course of the later Renaissance in England, from Spenser to Milton. But the transition appears to be one of even greater scope, defining an underlying condition for the making of art in modernity. Surely the most striking single fact about the most influential poetry in the modern world is its emphasis on the character of the poet, almost independently of what the poet says or shows. Whether we are considering the English romantics, or French poetry from Hugo to Baudelaire and Rimbaud, or modern poets as different, and yet definitive, as Rilke and Pound, what they all exhibit is an almost mantic deformation by the act of poetic creation. With varying degrees of intensity, this disfiguring resembles shamanistic possession, the transmission of spirit from beyond. The ethics of such a situation for art are still largely unreadable.

***

The greater medieval poets were aware, as serious artists always are, of bringing into being what has never existed before, but they tended to legitimate their creations, often ironically, as retellings of old events reported by some authority, or "auctor," and written down in a book. When Chaucer speaks of writing "som newe thing" he means that the new thing is a subject that exists but has not yet been treated in verse. He does not mean *new* in the sense of making something up that never existed before. Even Petrarch, that laurel-crowned creator of the Renaissance idea of the poet as inspired by the muses, is praised in Chaucer for his "rethorike sweete." "Invention" – which is the term for the first part of rhetoric, *inventio* – does not mean "making it up new"; it means what the Latin word implies: "discovering what already exists." Robert Henryson perfectly expresses the medieval view of poetic originality when at the outset of his remarkable poem *The Testament of Cresseid* he disowns any credit for its invention, asserting that when he opened a volume of Chaucer's *Troilus and Criseyde* he discovered an extra gathering of leaves. That is his new invention, his poem: something he *found*, not something he *made*. Even the *Commedia* and the *Roman de la rose* have this structure, although in them the *auctor* is the author himself. The being of a poetical work lies not in its fashioning as an artifact, which is what the word *poem* implies, but rather in its *reproduction* from an original event and its status as a "book," as in Chaucer's *Bok of the Duchess* and his *liber Troili*.

The difference between the idea of a *bok* and the idea of a *poem* is the difference between what has been merely recorded and perhaps rhetorically elaborated upon and what has been fashioned, or produced, that is, "brought forth" as an artifact, virtually out of nothing. This is not to deprecate the art of the middle ages but only to recognize that our own concept of "art" is an inheritance of the Renaissance, one that we tend to impose on earlier times. It is in some respects a question of emphasis. Renaissance poets were certainly preoccupied with the idea of art as imitation, *mimesis*, and medieval poets were not unaware of their own originality. But it remains true that in the Renaissance a relatively new concept of art emerges, one that binds together originality and the shadow of divine inspiration.

***

Storytelling, or, more broadly, verbal invention, by which I mean the production of fixed, reproducible structures in words, is perhaps the definitive action of human nature. Language itself was in all probability created by stories, rather than the other way around. Language did not develop in all its modal complexity and only then did people decide to tell stories with it. It was the impulse to fashion propositional structures in sound – poems – that drove the development of human language beyond animal signaling onto a plane of articulate complexity transcending the immediate experience of the world, giving us a second world founded on words. Poetry creates the very substance out of which poetry is made.

The thought of this second world founded on words and created by art is everywhere in Renaissance critical theory. One of the purest images of it is Spenser's dance of the Graces, accompanied by "an hundred naked maidens lily white," on Mount Acidale, a vision altogether beyond the immediate experience of the world.[5] The transcendency of the vision Spenser gives us is indicated within it by the simile of Ariadne's crown, which is placed in the heavens as a circle of stars:

> Looke how the Crowne, which *Ariadne* wore
>   Upon her yvory forehead that same day,
>   That *Theseus* her unto his bridale bore,
>   When the bold *Centaures* made that bloudy fray
>   With the fierce *Lapithes*, which did them dismay;
>   Being now placed in the firmament,
>   Through the bright heaven doth her beames display,
>   And is unto the starres an ornament,
>   Which round about her move in order excellent.
>
> Such was the beauty of this goodly band. . . .
>   (*The Faerie Queene* 6.10.13–14)

The vision is called into being by the poet, represented as the piping shepherd, Colin Clout, and is dispelled by the intrusion of the real, in the person of the armed knight, Calidore:

> He durst not enter into th'open greene,
>   For dread of them unwares to be descryde,
>   For breaking of their daunce, if he were seene;
>   But in the covert of the wood did byde,
>   Beholding all, yet of them unespyde.
>   There did he see, that pleased much his sight,
>   That even he him selfe his eyes envyde,
>   An hundred naked maidens lilly white,
> All raunged in a ring, and dauncing in delight. . . .
>
> Much wondered *Calidore* at this straunge sight,
>   Whose like before his eye had never seene,
>   And standing long astonished in spright,
>   And rapt with pleasaunce, wist not what to weene;
>   Whether it were the traine of beauties Queene,
>   Or Nymphes, or Faeries, or enchaunted show,
>   With which his eyes mote have deluded beene.
>   Therefore resolving, what it was, to know,
> Out of the wood he rose, and toward them did go.
>
> But soon as he appeared to their vew,
>   They vanisht all away out of his sight,
>   And cleane were gone, which way he never knew;
>   All save the shepheard, who for fell despight
>   Of that displeasure, broke his bag-pipe quight,

> And made great mone for that unhappy turne.
> But *Calidore*, though no less sory wight,
> For that mishap, yet seeing him to mourne,
> Drew neare, that he the truth of all by him mote learn.
> (*The Faerie Queene* 6.10.11 and 17–18)

No one has troubled to guess where those Graces and hundred naked maidens lily-white go when they disappear from Colin and Calidore's sight, but I think the Ariadne simile informs us: they take their place in the heavens, as stars, and perhaps not just as the crown of the Pleiades but as the entire Milky Way, a great shining band across the night which, if we could see it more clearly, as a poet sees more clearly, would appear to us as innumerable maidens dancing for joy. Spenser's power as an allegorical poet breaks out in these strange moments of visionary intensity, moments when allegory itself – with its need to connect stories to the real – stands condemned for its incapacity to let the hallucination float free on its own.

Yet people seem always to have been nervous about the impulse to create hallucinatory structures in words, structures that become visions like the dance of the maidens. It is a talent which may or may not have come to us from the gods, like Promethean fire, a dangerous thing, arousing the resentment of the divine because of its encroachment on the realm of celestial fire, the empyrean. I am convinced that the fire Prometheus steals is not just literal fire, indispensable to culture – for the word *culture* means "cooking" – but is also what happens around a fire or a hearth: storytelling, the invention of hallucinatory structures in words. Literature is the fire that is stolen from the gods, from the empyrean – a word that means "in fire" – and we have always been nervous about its origin in a place that is remote from our concerns.

People have usually sought, therefore, in one way or another, to attach stories by some remote but secure means to the world, from the simple formula, "a long, long time ago in a place far, far away," to etiological "Just So" stories, such as the origin of a flower or of a confluence of streams, or why the tail of Opossum is bare. The story does not exist to explain the existence of the flower, of the narcissus, or the hyacinth, or the anemone. Instead, it is the flower that is seized on to explain the more mysterious existence of the story, of a youth, beloved of a nymph, who loved only himself, and of youths who were loved by the gods, Apollo and Aphrodite. The theory that art is an imitation of the real, and the craft of representing the real with vivacity and force – in short, *mimesis* – is another means of assuring ourselves that the stories we tell are not free-floating things. The various medieval formulae by which a story is connected to the real through a chain of witnesses going back to an original witness or *auctor*, are likewise means of assuring ourselves that the stories we tell are not free-floating things.

The most complicated and self-consciously literary means of tethering stories to the world is *allegory*, where it is supposed by convention that everything in the unreal story *signifies*, often mysteriously, something else in the real. According to this justification, a "vain, amatorious poem," the phrase with which John Milton derided Sydney's *Arcadia*, is not a *vanity*, something empty, but rather something full, rich with the hidden meanings of the world. Milton uses the word *poem* to mean something that is merely inexistent and, what is worse, simply *untrue*. Each word in his phrase – *vain, amatorious, poem* – transmits a more damaging ethical charge than the last: emptiness, gratuitous erotic excitement, and lying. As Spenser says, " ... ne let him then admire, / But yield his sence to be too blunt and bace, / That n'ote without an hound fine footing trace" (2 proem 4). This condemnation of the impercipient reader who cannot without assistance discern the presence and the meaning of Faerie almost turns back on the poet, who will admit much later that he too requires assistance to his steps through the bewildering "waies" or paths:

> Such secret comfort, and such heavenly pleasures,
>> Ye sacred imps, that on *Parnasso* dwell,
>> And there the keeping have of learnings threasures,
>> Which doe all worldly riches farre excel,
>> Into the mindes of mortall men doe well,
>> And goodly fury into them infuse;
>> Guyde ye my footing, and conduct me well
>> In these strange waies, where never foote did use,
> Ne none can find, but who was taught them by the Muse.
>> (*The Faerie Queene* 6 proem 2)

Where never foote did use: this is Spenser's shadowy claim: to be bringing into being what has never existed before. He does so, however, not on his own, human power but under the tutelage of a higher power, the muse.

***

It is strange that the very creativity that makes us human, placing us, in our own conceit, above or apart from the animals, is mysteriously bound up with something other than the human: the divine. But the concept of the human seems always to have resided in this tension between different states, this feeling of being above one state – the inhuman as well as the animal (for they are not the same thing) – and yet below another state, which is that of the gods. Being human is thus not so much a state, a condition, like being an animal or being a god: it is instead a choice, a decision. Or, rather, it is continual decision, a decision we have continually to remember to make. To be human is to decide not to sink to certain impulses by which we are nevertheless powerfully drawn. It is to decide not to lose oneself in appetite and cunning, like an animal, or in the savagery of inhuman actions. But to be human is also to recognize something higher than the self and to reach for it by fashioning stories.

***

The question of the originality of what the poet makes is thus oddly bound up with that of inspiration, as if originality were impossible to the merely human actor and can occur only when the character of the poet is invaded by another. That invasion of the character of the poet by another raises questions about the ethics of the poet which were first raised – and answered – by Plato. We know how they were answered: with the banishment of the poets from the ideal republic, even as their sacred status was recognized. Nor was Plato wrong to do so, if the ideal republic is based on the principle of the indivisible, ethical subject, which is answerable to everything it does and everything it says. For Plato, the poet is incapable either of being ethical himself or of obeying the instructions of an ethical superior – the philosopher king – just because the poet is inspired; for the inspired poet can never be an ethical subject. Regardless of what the poet says, the very fact of being inspired and thus ethically divided makes the poet, in the exact sense of the word, irresponsible. Lord Burleigh would not have been reassured by Spenser's assurance of being inspired by the muse.

***

Matters will stand differently from the Christian point of view if, and only if, the inspiring god and the higher ethical authority, the Christian God, are one and the same. That was Milton's solution, and not only Milton's. But perhaps only Milton could make it convincing:

> Descend from Heav'n, Urania, by that name
> If rightly thou art called, whose voice divine
> Following above th'Olympian hill I soar,
> Above the flight of Pegaséan wing.
> The meaning not the name I call for thou
> Nor of the Muses nine nor on the top
> Of old Olympus dwell'st but Heav'nly born.
> Before the hills appeared or fountain flowed
> Thou with eternal Wisdom didst converse,
> Wisdom thy sister, and with her didst play
> In presence of th'Almighty Father, pleased
> With thy celestial song.[6]
>
> (*Paradise Lost* 7.1–12)

For Milton, the separateness of the inspiring muse from the Judaic and Christian God is an illusion that he now sweeps aside, revealing his own poem to have been created by the same force that created the world, like a leaf on the tree of Creation. Milton's own talents, after all, and his other advantages of character, have themselves been created by his Creator.

Through the action of the Spirit on him, moreover, the Creator continues to create. This is an extreme position, one to which Milton himself cannot consistently adhere, although neither can he consciously abandon it.

***

The problem of the *ethos* or *character* of the poet in the Renaissance is precisely that this inspiring force, this *enthousiasmos*, is incompatible with the orderly conception of the creative act as performed by the Judaic and Christian God. God creates once, in six days, and his subsequent work is to sustain his creation in being, not to add to it. He is now concerned only with saving Creation, in other words, with redemption, which involves God in history, a history that is playing out on the stage of a world he created long ago. God is called the *Creator* because of what he has done, not because of what he is doing now. Poetic creativity adds to the world and is therefore subversive of the God who is the maker of that world and who has entirely finished with making. This means that inspiration, which is strangely necessary to making the new, cannot be inspiration from God: it must be given by some other spiritual power. If the foundation of Christian ethics is where Milton thought it to be – in the recognition that one is created by God – then poetic creativity places the poet outside Christian ethics. Moreover, inspiration places the poet outside any conceivable ethics based on the unity of the responsible subject. For inspiration divides the poet in two, allowing the poet to speak for himself even as another speaks through him.

***

Although the Renaissance saw the revival of the most technical theories of the rules to be followed in making poems – theories, as Milton expressed it, of "what the laws are of a true epic poem" – the Renaissance was also the period in which the question of enthusiasm in poetry, of divine inspiration, arose with peculiar force; and it was peculiarly, even illogically, connected with the idea of originality. When Sir John Davies said that to create "to God alone pertains," he was responding to a widely-felt anxiety that poets were treading profanely upon holy ground. (Davies himself, profane enough in his day, became an attorney general.) So far as I can tell, our earliest witness for this idea of the poet as creating in a manner disturbingly similar to God is Cristoforo Landino's commentary on the *Commedia* of Dante, at the outset of which he remarks that the word *poet* derives from the same Greek word used in the Septuagint Bible when God creates the world: *poieo*, "to create": "*en arche epoiesen ho theos ton ouranon kai ten gen*," "In the beginning God created the heaven and the earth."

If poets are aided by supernatural powers, or if in some more mysterious and disturbing fashion it is they, the poets, who are aiding supernatural powers, helping those powers break into the world, what is the relation of these powers to official religion? What ethical responsibility can there be in a poet who is letting another force into the world, a power over which the poet has no control, and indeed over which society, the giver of the system of *ethics*, has no control? Will this spiritual power be demonic or divine, or will the very starkness of that choice, which was achieved by the fathers of the church in suppressing the Roman country religions, be lost? In the Renaissance, poets begin to traffic with new and mysterious messengers and spirit helpers – Wordsworth would call them mighty powers roaring with one voice – that threaten Christian ethics not only because belief in such powers appears to be idolatrous but also because inspiration by another pulls away the cornerstone of any possible ethical system: the notion of a unified ethical subject who is responsible for what she or he says. The oldest tactic of the prophets, from the first book of Samuel to seventeenth-century women prophets such as Lady Eleanor Davies (wife of Sir John), is to deny personal responsibility for what is being said: "thus saith the Lord."

These are some of the questions that began to emerge again in the Renaissance, which in this sense at least was not so much a "rebirth" of antiquity as it was a resurgence of an atavistic impulse that a Christian worldview had kept down for a long time. The alarm Ruskin describes being felt when the ancient statues were dug out of the soil in Rome – it was as if an ancient plague pit had been opened – suggests that the Renaissance was not just the deliberate, mathematical recovery of antiquity, giving us linear perspective, architectural proportion, and the first dome built in Europe since the Pantheon. The Renaissance was not so much a rational appropriation of the past for the conscious purposes of the present as it was a "rebirth" in the more alarming sense of releasing spiritual forces that that had lain dormant for a very long time.

We find some of the questions I have posed brilliantly stated in Plato, and of course Renaissance authors found them in Plato too, encapsulated in Greek words – *daimon, enthousiasmos* – that found their Latinate counterparts in our words *genius* and *inspiration*. For Plato the words associated with the poet – being possessed by a daemon, or genius, and being inspired from within by a god – meant that the poet must be ethically irresponsible for what he says. Socrates himself claimed he had a daemon: it accompanied him everywhere but never told him what to say, only when to say it. In older English uses of the word *genius* – as when one says that a person "*has* a genius" – indicate how one's genius is alien to oneself, how a person whom we call a *genius* – and the word was most commonly given to poets – must be a divided self, the possessor of a *daemon*, like Socrates. Likewise, if the poet is inspired, then someone different from the person of the poet is breathing through the poet from within and inspiring the song.

The questions concerning the relation of the supernatural to art are more exposed and raw in the period extending from Spenser to Milton: that narrow rift in time between the dominion of an omniscient Creator and the domination of all areas of human activity by reason. In the Renaissance, the mystery of the artist in alliance with supernatural power suddenly bursts upon our sight. What is then exposed is not the question of the nature of art – what is art? – but rather the question of the nature – or, as I have termed it, the character – of the artist. What the character of the artist may be, what the artist is supposed to be doing when becoming entangled with the divine, is the basis of every other possible question concerning the ethical in art. Before we ask how poetry may be ethical, how it may, as Spenser puts it in the "Letter to Raleigh," "fashion a gentleman or noble person in vertuous and gentle discipline," how it may have the power to "ensample a good governour and virtuous man" or, as Sidney says, to make many Cyruses out of one, to ask, in short, how poetry may or may not accomplish something progressive in the world, we need to ask the more radical question: what kind of *ethos* or "self" is the poet?

Yet in asking that question we find that the poet cannot be reduced to one kind of "self" or another because of this troubling relation of the poet to the divine. For it is a relation that splits the selfhood of the poet in two. The poet speaks, or sings, but someone else, or something else, is giving him the breath of his song. If someone else is present, alongside the poet or within him, how can we speak of the character of the poet? "Let me sing it all the way through," says Homer (I paraphrase), of the catalogue of the commanders of the ships that went to Troy, "for you are goddesses, and you are present, and you know."[7] If so, who is he?

Notes

1 *L'enfance de l'art: une interpretation de l'esthétique freudienne*, 3rd ed. (Paris: Galilée, 1985), p. 212.
2 *The Life of Timon of Athens*, 5.2.101, *The Riverside Shakespeare*, 2nd edn, ed. G. Blakemore Evans and J.J.M. Tobin (Boston: Houghton Mifflin, 1997).
3 *Complete Prose Works of John Milton*, ed. Ernest Sirluck (New Haven, CT: Yale University Press, 1959), 2.366.
4 For a fuller discussion, see Gordon Teskey, *Delirious Milton* (Cambridge, MA: Harvard University Press, 2006).
5 *The Faerie Queene*, ed. Thomas P. Roche, Jr., with the assistance of C. Patrick O'Donnell, Jr. (London: Penguin, 1978).
6 *Paradise Lost*, ed. Gordon Teskey (New York: W.W. Norton, 2005), 7.1–12.
7 *Iliad* 2. 484–93.

10 Shakespeare against morality

Richard Strier

> Moral judgments and condemnations constitute the favorite revenge of the spiritually limited against those less limited.
>
> Should moralizing not be – immoral?
>
> Nietzsche, Beyond Good and Evil, §§ 219 and 228[1]

One of our most important recent moral philosophers, the late Bernard Williams, devoted a good deal of his career to distinguishing between the terms "morality" and "ethics," arguing that the second identifies a much larger domain than the first, and that the first identifies a very limited and peculiar realm indeed. Williams denied that there is a single standard against which all human activities can or should be measured; he denied that the things that we value can be arranged into a coherent system and shown to be compatible with one another; and he specifically faulted "morality" for its commitment to the ubiquity and priority of its own relevance.[2] This might all seem distinctively "modern" or "post-modern," and certainly seems to us distinctively post-Nietzschean. But Bernard Williams drew his inspiration more from Homer than from Nietzsche (though Williams was increasingly interested in Nietzsche), and Nietzsche drew his inspiration from Aristotle and from Homer.[3] Williams's "Nietzschean" perspective, therefore, might not have been unavailable to an early modern person like Shakespeare. The argument of this essay is that Shakespeare shared Bernard Williams's sense of the irrelevance of the moral to much of what we value, and that as Shakespeare's career proceeded, Shakespeare developed more and more fully and explicitly his sense of the limitation of the moral perspective.

1.

A sub-thesis of this essay is going to be that Shakespeare's commitment to the theater, perhaps especially to the popular theater, is part of what allowed him to attain this peculiar perspective on morality. Something like this perspective is, I think, required by the theater. Aristotle, after all, invented the notion of the aesthetic in the context of seeking to account for tragic pleasure (we enjoy seeing things represented that we do not enjoy seeing).[4] But we need not go so far from Shakespeare to locate the conditions of possibility for an attitude of the sort that I have schematically described and will attempt to fill in. We only need to remind ourselves of the first great "hit" of the Elizabethan popular theater as a vehicle for serious poetry: Marlowe's *Tamburlaine* plays (1587–88). In these plays, we are invited to enjoy the magnificence of Marlowe's writing ("high astounding terms") and to view the "picture" of a powerfully compelling figure to whom moral terms seem, at best, trivially relevant. After all the cruelties that we have witnessed Tamburlaine performing, Part One of the play concludes with his happy marriage, and Part Two with his quiet death and successful passing on of his kingdoms to his sons.

But Marlowe was a notorious iconoclast and free-thinker. Can we assume that Shakespeare followed him into the realm beyond (moral) good and evil? A way into this question might be to spend a bit of time on one of Shakespeare's first and most enduring "hits," *The Tragedy* (as it is called in both the Quarto and the Folio texts) *of King Richard III*. This is a play that explicitly manifests an extraordinary degree of metatheatrical awareness. Shakespeare wants his audience to think about their pleasure in watching this play. In the second scene of the play, Lady Anne asks Richard Aristotle's question about tragedy. She wonders whether he delights "to view [his] heinous deeds" (p. 53).[5] Delight is indeed the question. We delight in seeing Richard play the villain – in a number of senses of "play." In this tragedy, the character who is Richard says that he "can counterfeit the deep tragedian" (3.5.5). Even more startlingly, Shakespeare has his title character remind the audience of his native theatrical lineage – that is, of the theatrical pleasure they have received from a stage villain. Richard states that in playing with words, he is acting "like the formal Vice, Iniquity" (3.1.82).

But Shakespeare has already given Richard a special intimacy with the audience by opening the play with Richard's soliloquy.[6] Richard's "villainy" is never in question; he says he is "determinèd to prove a villain" (which relies on a great pun, and sounds, oddly and significantly, as if the endeavor might be difficult). The audience's interest is in watching his will (which, in "determinèd," he punningly presents as fate) work itself out. The energy that might have gone into moral judgment is preempted – "I am subtle, false, and treacherous," says Richard. So what we get to do is to watch his villainy – announced as such – unfold. It is hard not to feel that we are witnessing an exercise in skill and superior intelligence. Clarence speaks powerfully and eloquently to the two murderers Richard has set upon him, but it is (again) hard not to feel some contempt for "simple plain Clarence," as Richard calls him, for being so utterly taken in by Richard. It is hard not to side with the witty and intelligent. It is hard to avoid being seduced by wit and audacity.

The erotic power of eloquent audacity has already been demonstrated in the scene with Lady Anne. As in *Taming of the Shrew*, Shakespeare knows (and has Richard know) that banter, however hostile-seeming, is a form of flirtation ("this keen encounter of our wits," Richard calls it [1.2.119]).[7] When Richard succeeds in appealing to Anne's vanity – "Your beauty was the cause" (1.2.125–84) – the audience can only be as amazed as Richard is at his success. Of course, it is villainous. But so? We are having fun – just as Richard is.

Many of the memorable scenes in the play have this quality of co-opting us into enjoyment. There is no mystery about the moral dimension of these scenes, and no interest in it. The scene with Richard as zealous contemplative "enforced" to take the throne is a major (and hilarious) set-piece – a coup de théâtre staged as a coup de théâtre which is also a coup d'état. Can anyone in the theater keep a straight face when Richard thanks God for his humility (2.1.73 and elsewhere) or when he points to his withered arm as proof that he has been "bewitch'd" (3.4.68–72)? And Shakespeare enjoyed the outrageous wooing scene so much that he repeats it later in the play. He has Richard seduce (or at least apparently seduce) Queen Elizabeth, the widow of Edward IV, into securing her daughter for Richard as his second wife (Anne has already "bid this world good night"). The means of seduction here are distinctively Marlovian. Shakespeare has Richard appeal to the imagination of earthly power – "The high imperial type of this earth's glory"; "th' aspiring flame of golden sovereignty" (4.4.245, 328–29).[8]

The mention of "this earth's glory" and the claim that Richard's arm has been "bewitch'd" raise the issues of Providence and the supernatural in the play. Whether or not the audience is meant to share Richard's mockery of witchcraft beliefs (or his superstition about curses), the awareness of a world beyond this life surely adds a moral dimension to the play. Or does it? Shakespeare gives Richard a favorite joke. He uses it twice in the opening scene and again in the "keen encounter" with Lady Anne (and he, and other wicked characters, keep using it). This joke has an unsettling effect – as it does, to some extent, in *Twelfth Night*, where Shakespeare uses it again. The joke is unsettling because it works by taking a standard moral and religious belief with unusual seriousness. Richard says of "Simple plain Clarence," "I do love thee so / That I will shortly send thy soul to Heaven" (1.1.117–18). This form of the joke recurs almost identically in 1.2. Anne says of Edward VI that "he was gentle, mild, and virtuous"; to which Richard responds, "the better for the King of Heaven that hath him" (1.2.107).[9] The second occurrence of the joke in scene one, however, adds another dimension. "God take King Edward to his mercy," says Richard, "And leave the world for me to bustle in" (1.1.151–52). This sense of enjoyment of the world seems to place known experience over against an abstract belief in someplace beyond. "Heaven" seems some place offstage that doesn't matter, while the word associated with "the world" – "for me *to bustle* in" – seems full of humorous and delighted energy.[10]

But, of course, Richard does get his comeuppance. The representative of God in this world is not the priesthood (which Shakespeare seems to see as part of the political world), but what Milton calls God's "Umpire, Conscience" (*PL* 3:195). Villainy is punished here. Almost all the villains in the play have attacks of conscience: the Second Murderer of Clarence; the two men suborned by Sir James Tyrrell to kill the young princes; and, of course, Richard himself. On the eve of the battle with the invading Richmond, Richard finds himself without what he wonderfully calls "that alacrity of spirit" that (as we have indeed seen) he was wont to have (5.3.74–75). He interprets the experience of being visited by the ghosts of his victims as a troubled dream, an attack of "coward conscience" (5.3.180). He falls into a state close to the despair to which all the supposed ghosts had called him. But he does not, contrary to their instructions, "despair and die." His "alacrity of spirit" returns.

He rouses himself to stir his army powerfully to nativist and aristocratic contempt for the invaders ("A scum of Bretons and base lackey peasants"), and he renounces the idea of an objectively valid internal moral arbiter: "Conscience is but a word that cowards use, / Devis'd at first to keep the strong in awe" (5.3.310–11). This is desperate, of course, and meant to be seen as such. I am not suggesting that Shakespeare accepted this analysis – one which we would call Nietzschean and Shakespeare would trace to Machiavelli and Machiavelli's classical sources.[11] But what is important to see is that this is *Richard*'s final word on the matter. His conscience does not, finally, affect him. He loses his kingdom not, famously, for want of virtue or out of mortification, but for want of a horse. When we last see Richard, he is still "bustling," and his famous last line is wonderfully unplaceable in terms of genre. Is it comedy or pathos – or some mixture that allows us to leave the theater with a smile that is not simply (or primarily) that of moral satisfaction. The line reminds us of the solidity and reality and value of the ordinary physical and social world.

The critique of moralism in *Richard III* is largely implicit; it is implicit primarily in the audience's experience (the discussion of conscience is an exception). Obviously one could leave the play imagining that one had witnessed a moral (or a pro-Tudor) spectacle. In the remainder of this essay, I will try to show that, as Shakespeare's career developed, he sought to make it more and more difficult to be like the melancholy Jaques in *As You Like It*, and "moralize the spectacle" (*AYL* 2.2.44) of his plays.

The role of Falstaff in the *Henry IV* plays is, as I will try to show, a crucial turn in this development – perhaps the crucial turn in it. Falstaff is another descendant of (among others) the Vice of the old Moralities (he threatens Hal at one point with the "dagger of lath" that was apparently the emblem of this figure [2.4.134]).[12] As with Richard, Falstaff's moral status is never in doubt; he is, as we are told, a "vice," an "iniquity," a "vanity" (3.4.447). As with Richard, Falstaff's deviation from the moral norm is as marked as his deviation from the physical norm. Falstaff's moral, like his physical, condition is "gross as a mountain, open, palpable" (2.4.220–21). The interesting question then is why this is not all there is to say about Falstaff. Again, our pleasure betrays us. What Erasmus's Dame Folly (one of Falstaff's other ancestors) says about herself is true of Falstaff as well; like Dame Folly, Falstaff merely has to appear and "the faces of all of [us]" immediately brighten up "with a strange, new expression of joy."[13] Men of all sorts take a pride to gird at both these characters (Part II: 1.2.5). Dr. Johnson, a serious and professional moralist, gave some thought to the problem. He put the question in terms of Falstaff's appeal to Hal. After listing a number of Falstaff's faults, Johnson stops and notes that "the man thus corrupt, thus despicable, makes himself pleasing to the prince that despises him, by the most pleasing of all qualities, perpetual gaiety."[14] Johnson does not explain why "perpetual gaiety" should have this remarkable status, but again, Dame Folly can enlighten us. This "gaiety" is, as she constantly says, the opposite of and antidote for "*taedium vitae*," weariness of life – what the first line of *I Henry IV* calls "care."[15] Johnson attributes this power to Falstaff's "wit." But Johnson cannot allow himself to remain at this level of appreciation. He has to diminish both Falstaff's wit ("not of the splendid or ambitious kind") and Falstaff's wickedness ("he is stained with no … sanguinary crimes"); and Johnson has, finally, to moralize the spectacle:

> The moral to be drawn from this representation is, that no man is more dangerous than he that with a will to corrupt, hath the power to please; and that neither wit nor honesty ought to think themselves safe with such a companion when they see Henry seduced by Falstaff.[16]

But does Shakespeare want us to moralize the spectacle even in this way, even in a way that acknowledges Falstaff's power and charm? After all, we do not see "Henry seduced by Falstaff." As Auden, Empson, and Falstaff himself suggest, the situation seems more the other way around.[17] Shakespeare's Falstaff might be more wicked than Johnson allows – he is, in fact, stained with "sanguinary crimes" in getting his ragamuffins "peppered"(5.2.36–38) – and he might be more totally independent of the moral realm. The gaiety and the wit are certainly part of the answer, but they must also be related to the most striking feature of Falstaff, certainly on stage: his fatness. Falstaff first significantly enters the play not in his own first speech, but in the first speech about him (he is, as he says in the equivalent scene in part two, "not only witty in [him]self, but the cause that wit is in other men" [Part II: 1.2.8–9]. As we would expect, the opening speech about Falstaff gives us many clues. His own first words seem innocuous enough – intimate and loving, but not especially noteworthy: "Now, Hal, what time of day is it, lad?" (1.2.1). Hal's response, however, is noteworthy. He rebukes Falstaff (also familiarly) for asking the question:

What a devil hast thou to do with the time of the day? Unless hours were cups of sack, and minutes capons, and clocks the tongues of bawds, and dials the signs of leaping-houses, and the blessed sun himself a fair hot wench in a flame-colored taffeta, I see no reason why thou shouldst be so superfluous as to demand the time of the day.

So: the time of the day is an abstraction; it has no physical existence and is, therefore, "superfluous" to Falstaff. As Hal tells him later, "there's no room for faith, truth, nor honesty in this bosom of thine; it is all filled up with guts and midriff" (3.3.152–54). But Hal's opening vision does not merely substitute the physical for the abstract; it transforms the abstract into the physical. Hal imagines Falstaff living in a kind of Land of Cockayne, where (as in such visions) cooked chickens (here capons) fly through the air.[18] The transformative aspect of the vision culminates in its final item, in which the symbol of reason, lucidity, kingship, spirituality, and masculine authority is transgendered, transformed, and made much more approachable ("the blessed sun himself a fair hot wench in a flame-colored taffeta"). This is imagination at work – Hal's imagination stimulated and tutored by Falstaff. Such a faculty has the power not to be tied to abstractions, to cares, to duties, and, ultimately, to the reality principle. It offers, as Bacon says poetry does, "satisfaction" to the mind of man where "the nature of things doth deny it."[19]

Falstaff soon himself gives an example of this capacity (thieves as "Diana's foresters"), but the most important case is his response to the trick that Hal and Poins play on him. Dr. Johnson underestimates the significance of Falstaff's "easy escapes and sallies of levity." Poins assures Hal that the sole purpose behind robbing Falstaff of the goods Falstaff has robbed from the travelers is to hear what "incomprehensible lies" Falstaff will tell (1.2.180–81). But the further point, after the lies have been exposed, is the important one. Can Falstaff be "put down" by "a plain tale" (2.4.25)? Can he be forced to face the facts? His first response is to refuse to be bullied by the facts – "Give you a reason on compulsion?" he asks (2.4.231). He uses the technique for dealing with abstractions that Hal borrowed for the opening speech – "If reasons were as plentiful as blackberries, I would give no man a reason on compulsion." But simply resisting "compulsion" by the facts is not enough. The bullying reality principle must be defeated, not simply refused. The facts must be transformed – which is what happens when the low-comic scene in the forest becomes, in Falstaff's account, a high romance tale in which "the lion will not touch the true prince" (2.4.267).

None of this has anything to do with morality – unless, of course, one wants to take the view that Falstaff (like the poets) is simply a liar. The realm that Falstaff inhabits is a realm of freedom, of indifference to time, and, most of all, of play.[20] Hal might be taken to be saying something fundamentally true when he says that "If all the year were playing holidays, / To sport would be as tedious as to work" (1.2.199–200), but it is important to recognize these lines as expressing Hal's perspective.[21] For him, playing is work. But for Falstaff, it is not. "If all the year were playing holidays," Falstaff would happily play away. It is worth spending a moment on one of Falstaff's favorite roles. His special favorite might be that of repentant Puritan; the only competitor would be the role of lusty young man. Both are important for our purposes, but I want to focus on the latter. Falstaff's stance as Juventus is an especially astonishing and important denial of the reality principle. His age competes with his girth as his most notable physical characteristic. He is a "*reverend* vice," a "*gray* iniquity," a "vanity *in years*." In a gerontocracy like the Elizabethan world, age was supposed to bring with it not only the diminution of physical power but, more importantly, the accession of moral gravity.[22] In the second scene of *Henry IV*, Part Two, the Lord Chief Justice is especially outraged at this role of Falstaff's – "Do you set down your name in the scroll of youth, that are written down old with all the characters of age," the Justice asks, before enumerating these "characters." Falstaff responds – no doubt completely accurately – "My Lord, I was born about three of the clock in the afternoon, with a white head, and something a round belly" (II 1.2.186–88). It is as impossible to imagine Falstaff young as it is to imagine him slim or virtuous. Part of his identity is to refuse the gravity, decorum, and proper "wisdom" of age.

This aspect of Falstaff's identity is thrust into the foreground in Hal's rejection of him. When Falstaff addresses the newly-crowned monarch as "My King, my Jove," and says, "I speak to thee, my heart," Hal begins his rejection thus: "I know thee not, old man. Fall to thy prayers. / How ill white hairs become a fool and jester" (Part II: 5.5.46–47). Hal speaks for decorum, for morality, for responsibility here. It is impossible not to know that he is doing the right thing in rejecting Falstaff. Yet it is equally impossible for Shakespeare not to have known that a great deal of his audience would experience this prudence and moralism as a form of cruelty. And recognizing the biblical reference does not help. The exultantly rigorous Jesus whose surrogate in the parable of the shut door says to those who claim to have eaten and drunk in his presence, "I know you not" (Luke 14:27), is difficult to recognize as the sacrificial proponent of mercy and undifferentiating love. Shakespeare, by committing himself to writing a series of plays that would follow Prince Hal on his well-known route from Eastcheap to Agincourt, was pre-committed to the rejection of the comic character that he had created in Part One and had eventually, after the Oldcastle debacle, named "Falstaff."[23] The equipoise of Part One – with Hotspur heroically dead and Falstaff comically resurrected – could not be maintained.[24] Prudence, order, and morality had to prevail, and Shakespeare never forgave himself for that. He never again put himself in a position of seeming to favor (as Falstaff puts it) "Pharoah's lean kine" (Part I: 2.4.467).

2.

The next time in Shakespeare's career that we see an old man told to act his age, we are not in any doubt as to how to feel about this judgment. The entire confrontation between Lear and Goneril in which Goneril first begins her personal assault on Lear's dignity is structured as a confrontation between prudence and folly. Goneril cannot abide Lear's Fool:

> Not only, sir, this your all-licensed fool,
> But other of your insolent retinue
> Do hourly carp and quarrel, breaking forth
> In rank and not-to-be-enduréd riots. Sir,
> I had thought by making this well known unto you
> To have found a safe redress, but now grow fearful,
> By what yourself too late have spoke and done,
> That you protect this course, and put [it] on
> By your allowance; which if you should, the fault
> Would not scape censure nor the redresses sleep,
> Which in the tender of a wholesome weal,
> Might in their working do you that offense
> That else where shame, that then necessity
> Must call discreet proceedings.
>
> (1.4.188–201)[25]

There is no doubt that Goneril is speaking, very grandly and precisely, for decorum and for a proper, morally (or at least socially) sanctioned punitiveness. Goneril "know[s] [Lear] not" in his "foolish" state – "I would you would make use of that good wisdom / Whereof I know you are fraught, and put away / These dispositions that of late transform you / From what you rightly are." Lear takes up the theme of not being known – "Does any here know me?" – and develops it with comic hyperbole: "Why, this is not Lear. / Doth Lear walk thus? Speak thus?" (1.4.213–14). Goneril is not amused. She sees Lear's mock-wonder – "This admiration" – as "much of the same savor" of Lear's other "pranks." Her final extended speech to him in this scene explains to Lear how ill white hairs become a fool and jester – "As you are old and reverend," she tells Lear, "[you] should be wise."[26]

This scene is no anomaly in *King Lear*. Goneril and Regan always speak with the voice of decorum. At the end of scene 1, they tell Cordelia, in perfectly good faith, that she has "obedience scanted" (line 267).[27] In Act II of the play, Kent (in his role as Caius) is another irreverent old man who must be taught to behave. Cornwall is now the voice of "reverence" and decorum, and Cornwall characterizes Caius in terms borrowed from the condemnation of Falstaff – "You stubborn ancient knave, you reverend braggart" (2.2.118). With the true voice of moral authority (as well as political power), Cornwall tells Kent / Caius, "We'll teach you" (2.2.119a). Kent answers, "I am too old to learn" (2.2.119b). This is a wonderful protest against what Bernard Williams calls the presumed ubiquity and priority of the moral perspective. Kent's line implies a model of acceptance rather than of teaching and reformation. It is related, on the one hand, to Kent's earlier assertion of the "privilege" of anger (2.2.64), and, on the other, to Lear's later assertion of the privilege of "need" (2.4.234). At the end of Act II, when Goneril, Regan, and Cornwall are all seconding and congratulating each other on the decision to leave Lear out in the storm, the unmistakable note of punitive moral superiority returns. Goneril explains the exact moral propriety with which they are acting. Lear is getting what he deserves. It would be wrong to interfere with the punitive (and, presumably, reformative) precision of the moral universe – "'Tis his own blame hath put himself from rest, / And needs must taste his folly" (2.4.260–61). When Gloucester points out the actual circumstances to which they are condemning Lear – "Alack, the night comes on, and the bleak winds / Do sorely [rustle]. For many miles about / There's scarce a bush"[28] – Regan assumes the task of moral explication: "O sir, to willful men / The injuries that they themselves procure / Must be their schoolmasters" (271–72). Cornwall agrees that Regan "counsels well" (278). Lear must "learn."

Interestingly, this is the view of many critics. Shakespeare has set up *King Lear* so as to invite moralizing. Lear is an old fool; he makes a disastrous set of mistakes; his men might be as unruly as Goneril says they are.[29] Yet must he "taste his folly"? Does he have to be made to "learn"? Gloucester is a credulous old fool and has had a child out of wedlock. Does this mean – as Edgar asserts and many critics from Robert Heilman to Stanley Cavell have argued – that there is a beautiful logic to Gloucester's blinding?[30] The play certainly provides the materials for these views. But before moralizing about Lear's follies and need for reformation, we should notice the characters in the play with whom this perspective associates us. The problem with moralizing the represented experiences of Lear and Gloucester is not that it is difficult to do so. It could hardly, in fact, be easier. The problem is that it seems irrelevant to do so. Their sufferings are such as to make the whole question of "desert" seem irrelevant – or, as in the case of Goneril and Regan's moral certainty, both niggling and cruel. Perhaps moral judgment, however precise, is not the way to approach even some situations to which, it seems, such judgment should apply. That, I would suggest, is one of the "messages" of *King Lear*.

But even after *Lear*, I would argue, Shakespeare had still not finished atoning for the high-minded ending of *Henry IV*, Part Two. There is another character in the canon who plays the fool and refuses to act with the dignity and solemnity suitable to his age. I am referring, of course, to "the old ruffian" and reprobate, Mark Antony (4.1.4).[31] But, of course, in *Antony and Cleopatra*,

Shakespeare adds another aged reprobate, developing the full implications of "Falstaff as Mom" as well as a full range of other erotics.[32] One would not know from Shakespeare's play, in which Cleopatra describes herself as "wrinkled deep in time" (I.v.30), that she died at the age of 39. *Antony and Cleopatra* can be seen as Shakespeare's final apology for the rejection of Falstaff, his final refutation of the claim of the moral perspective to ubiquitous priority and relevance. My reading of the play might sound oddly "Nietzschean" – to which I am willing to say, so be it. But, before anyone descries anachronism, let us be sure to remember Dame Folly.[33]

In *Antony and Cleopatra*, as in *Richard III* and in *Lear*, the moral perspective is not denied by being downplayed or excluded. As in the earlier plays, this perspective could hardly be more available. Just as *Richard III* begins with Richard describing himself as a villain, and the first Act of *Lear* seems to confirm, over and over again, Goneril's view of Lear, *Antony and Cleopatra* begins with an elaborate speech describing Cleopatra as a strumpet and Antony as "a strumpet's fool." The very first speech of the play is an invitation to "behold and see" Antony and Cleopatra in just this way. As in *Richard III*, if the play is going to offer us anything other than the rather thin pleasure of seeing what we already think we know confirmed over and over again, Shakespeare has to offer us something other than such confirmation. What he does offer us is truly astonishing. If we are seeing a strumpet and a fool in action, their action turns out to be high play. The absurd public game that Lear devises – "Which of you shall we say doth love us most" – is replayed in its proper key: in private, and as a game. Cleopatra walks onto the stage asking, "If it be love indeed, tell me how much" (1.1.14). Antony answers in the only way that is truly responsive; he rejects the gambit – not militantly and curtly as Cordelia does, but eloquently and grandly. He will not play the quantity game, and rejects it in principle: "There's beggary in the love that can be reckoned." But Cleopatra wants to play further. She accepts his point but decides on an arbitrary act of will: "I'll set a bourn how far to be beloved." This, in turn, provokes Antony to move from a grand statement of principle to a cosmic hyperbole: "Then must thou needs find out new heaven, new earth." We are back to the playful imaginative dialogue of the opening interaction between that other pair of lovers in the second scene of *Henry IV, Part One*, but here in the mode of high-style poetry rather than the mode of low comic prose. And we are again in a world of biblical reference, but, again, not in the mode of parody and perversion (thievery as a "vocation") but in the mode of straightforward allusion.

But why would Shakespeare give his "strumpet's fool" a reference – that no biblically literate member of the audience could have missed – to one of the grandest and most resonant apocalyptic promises in the New Testament: "a new heaven, and a new earth" (2 Peter 3:13, Revelation 21:1)? Is Shakespeare somehow suggesting that these morally debased characters have access to some sort of spiritual wisdom, or to some equivalent thereof?

I suppose that it might be possible to read Antony's line ironically, as a case of unconscious and damning blasphemy, but the line seems to accept rather than to parody a visionary perspective. The first "action" in the play, after this extraordinary opening dialogue, consists of the entrance of the messenger from Rome. When Cleopatra twits Antony about his (very minimal) willingness to hear the message from "the scarce-bearded Caesar," Antony rejects the idea with another grand and apocalyptic vision: "let Rome in Tiber melt, and the wide arch / Of the ranged empire fall" (34–35). Antony declares a separate realm of value, one that contrasts in its compactness with the "wide arch": "Here is my space" (35).[34] As in Donne's most affirmative love lyrics, the grandeur of the assertion of private "space" – "the world's contracted thus" ("The Sunne Rising," line 26) – depends upon the rejection of the world at large, of all the (secular) aspirations, ideals, and activities of "the world."[35] Shakespeare has his old reprobate express a *contemptus mundi* that would make any ascetic proud: "Kingdoms are clay! Our dungy earth alike / Feeds beast as man." But just at this point, Shakespeare has Antony not simply reject all public values, but reclaim and redefine one of the most important of them, one of the most "Roman" of them, in a new sense: "The nobleness of life / Is to do thus," says Antony, as he presumably kisses or embraces Cleopatra. The explanation that Antony offers for this conception of "nobleness" is as striking as his appropriation of the term: "The nobleness of life / Is to do thus, when such a mutual pair / And such a twain can do't." The meter is emphatic in its stress on "such" in both lines, and that stress seems to be the point. The way in which Antony and Cleopatra each and jointly occupy their particular identities seems to be the source of the special value that is being asserted here.[36]

This idea – that personality includes and trumps all other values, including moral ones – is explicitly thematized in the play, and constitutes one of its most original and striking motifs. When Cleopatra persists in twitting Antony about the presence of the ambassadors and about his marital status (the messenger who is prevented from speaking is to announce, among other things, Fulvia's death), Antony does not lose patience with Cleopatra, but, oddly, praises her for relentlessly teasing him. He responds to her mock-insistence that he "hear the ambassadors" with an apparent rebuke that turns into praise:

> Fie, wrangling queen,
> Whom everything becomes – to chide, to laugh,
> To weep; whose every passion fully strives
> To make itself, in thee, fair and admired!
> (1.1.49–52)

This does not mean that "everything" turns into Cleopatra – though there is a momentary flicker of this meaning – but that everything suits her, looks well on her (is "becoming" to her). The claim is aesthetic, not metaphysical. But what can it possibly mean? Somehow actions that are normally negative and perhaps disfiguring are flattering to Cleopatra (compare Katherine in *Taming of the Shrew* on "a woman mov'd" as "bereft of beauty" [5.2.144]).[37] The second half of the statement is clearly meant, in some sense, to explain the first. The focus is not action but passion, and the claim is that Cleopatra's being is the locus in which "every passion" seeks to be beautiful. This, however, is still quite opaque. The explanation seems to lie in two phrases in these lines: "fully strives" and "in thee." The idea seems to be that in the completeness of their expression, Cleopatra's passions become beautiful, and that this is what her mode of being leads them, essentially autonomously, to "strive" to do. Passion is the focus. As Enobarbus says in the following scene, "This cannot be cunning in her" (1.2.157). Antony is describing a process or a phenomenon through which – in the very realm in which ethics operates, that of the passions – aesthetics trumps, transcends, and confounds the moral.

This is a truly surprising perspective, and it is not one for which I know of any direct precedent. The closest I can come to providing an intellectual-historical genealogy or context for it is in certain aspects of the neo-Platonic tradition, in the thought, particularly, of Plotinus. Plotinus was the great theorist of diffusiveness as an essential property of the Good, and of multiplicity as benign: "It is not by crushing the divine into a unity but by displaying its exuberance ... that we show knowledge of God"; without such diffusive energy – which, Plotinus repeatedly insists, is a matter of nature and not of deliberation – "the Good would not be Good."[38] Plotinus is also the great theorist of fullness as a positive aesthetic quality, and of the desirability of lesser creatures and of imperfection as part of this fullness: the essentially generative Reason-principle "produces even what we know as evil: it cannot desire all to be good" (p. 147). In explaining this rather startling assertion, Plotinus resorts to an analogy with the arts: "an artist would not make an animal all eyes; and in the same way, the Reason-Principle would not make all divine" (ibid.). And again, Plotinus says that those who complain that the presence of non-beautiful aspects of the universe are a defect, "are like people ignorant of painting who complain that the colours are not beautiful everywhere in the picture" or like those who censure a drama "because the persons are not all heroes." These aspects are "part and parcel" of the total beauty of the aesthetic objects in question (ibid.).

So, do I think that Shakespeare was echoing Plotinus in Antony's praise of Cleopatra? It is not impossible. Ficino was certainly known in England, and Ficino translated and popularized Plotinus.[39] It is often hard to say where Shakespeare "got" his ideas, since his absorptive powers were obviously so remarkable. Maybe he found the neo-Platonism of Plotinus – widely echoed in many Christian and non-Christian texts – "in the air."[40] What is clear is that this motif – of seemingly negative phenomena, especially passions –

"becoming" particular, very special individuals, and being part of what makes them special, is repeated and emphatic in *Antony and Cleopatra*. In the next scene in which we see Antony and Cleopatra together, Antony has resolved that his "pleasure" and his "business" – both terms being put under pressure in the play – require him to return to his "many contriving friends" in Rome (1.2.189; for "business," see I.ii.178–80). Cleopatra, of course, rebukes him for this resolve, reminds him of his erotic hyperboles ("Eternity was in our lips and eyes" [1.3.36]), calls him a liar and a cold-hearted betrayer of women ("I see / In Fulvia's death how mine received shall be" [65–66]), and then uses exactly the same vocabulary which Antony has used for her to describe the effect that she has produced in him. As she continues to mock and rebuke him, she says to one of her women: "Look, prithee, Charmian, / How this Herculean Roman does become / The carriage of his chafe" (1.3.85–86). She suddenly and humorously takes a purely aesthetic view of Antony's anger. She admires his anger, finding that it becomes, in him, fair.

For the culmination of this motif in the play (though not, as we shall see, its final appearance), Shakespeare returns to Cleopatra. After Enobarbus' wonderful and hyperbolic account of Cleopatra's first appearance to Mark Antony, Enobarbus' Roman interlocutor refers to Cleopatra's history (her relationship with Julius Caesar); this leads Enobarbus to recall, somewhat unsequaciously:

> I saw her once
> Hop forty paces through the public street
> And, having lost her breath, she spoke and panted,
> That she did make defect perfection.
> (2.2.239–41)

This is the most striking and abstract formulation yet of the principle that Shakespeare celebrates and repeatedly articulates in this play, the phenomenon of somehow, through personal charisma, making "defect perfection."[41] And if hopping and being breathless seems like too trivial a matter to bear the weight of this remarkable theme, Enobarbus proceeds to a much stronger formulation. Hopping may be undignified, and panting unlady-like, but they are hardly serious defects, and they have no moral dimension whatever. Enobarbus' next formulation is his and Shakespeare's strongest. Enobarbus does not hesitate to make the claim absolute, and to exemplify it with a seemingly impossible case:

> vilest things
> Become themselves in her, that the holy priests
> Bless her when she is riggish.
> (2.2.248–50)

Nothing could be further from traditional morality, and nothing could more clearly exalt the aesthetic over the moral. It may be proof of Shakespeare's awareness of the intellectual background to this perspective that these amazing lines are at the end of the speech that opens with Enobarbus' famous praise of Cleopatra's "infinite variety" (245–46). The praise of "variety" is a hallmark of the Plotinian tradition. The sentence in which Plotinus explains that "the Reason-principle" produces even what we know as evil ends by explaining that the whole cosmos, with all of its creatures, is "the expression of Reason teeming with intellectual variety" (p. 146). Whenever this tradition is invoked, variety is praised. Aquinas insisted that variety "was needful in the creation."[42] To draw closer to Shakespeare's time and place, Richard Hooker explained that "the general end of God's external working is the exercise of his most glorious and abundant virtue." And this abundance "doth shew itself in variety."[43]

That this motif, in Shakespeare at least, is meant to flout or transcend traditional morality is indicated with regard to Antony as well. At the end of Act I, Alexas reports that in Rome Antony is manifesting something like an Aristotelian mean in his emotions – "between the extremes / Of hot and cold, he was nor sad nor merry" (1.5.54–55). Cleopatra approves of this in the situation ("O well divided disposition"), but when she really starts to think about him, praises Antony not for his avoidance but for his manifestation of extremes; she says, to her mental image of him, "Be'st thou sad or merry, / The violence of either thee becomes, / So does it no man else" (63–64). This returns us to "such a mutual pair / And such a twain." This quality of being released from the moral into the aesthetic is unique to these characters.[44]

The motif is so deeply embedded in the play that it surfaces even in contexts that are meant to be morally condemnatory. In responding to Caesar's characterization of Antony as "the abstract of all faults / That all men follow" (1.4.9–10), Lepidus says:

> I must not think there are
> Evils enough to darken all his goodness.
> His faults, in him, seem as the spots of heaven,
> More fiery by night's blackness.
>
> (10–13)

Lepidus means to say that Antony's faults do not completely overwhelm his virtues, and that the faults are made more obvious by the co-presence of the virtues. But within the simile, the faults are glowing and energetic stars that light up the night. Instead of wasting the lamps of night in revel, as Caesar has just said, Antony's faults suddenly become the lamps of night in revel. We even get the characteristic interjected clause of uniqueness, "in him" (compare "To make itself, in thee, fair and admired"). Caesar rebukes

Lepidus for being "too indulgent" to Antony, and mocks the idea that Antony's low pleasures are somehow redeemed by being his. It is as if Caesar has heard the passages on what "becomes" Antony and Cleopatra. About Antony's lustfulness, foolish overgenerosity, and pleasure in standing "the buffet / With knaves that smell of sweat," Caesar sarcastically challenges Lepidus to "say this becomes him – / As his composure must be rare indeed / Whom these things cannot blemish" (20–23). "Rare indeed" seems to be exactly the idea. Even the final use of the word that signals the "defect perfection" motif is complex in this way. Again, the usage is Caesar's. Here it is probably meant to be neutral rather than condemnatory. After Antony's defeat and disgrace at Actium, Caesar sends one of his captains to "Observe how Antony becomes his flaw" (3.12.34). The presumption, of course, is that his defeat has humbled and lowered Antony, but in the next scene, we see Antony, after some false moves, become himself again. It turns out that this flaw too "becomes him."[45]

Even apart from the "becoming" motif, moral condemnation has a way of turning into praise in this play. The opening lines of the play, meaning to condemn Antony's lack of "measure," praise the heroic extremity of his heart "which in the scuffles of great fights hath burst / The buckles on his breast" before complaining that he now "reneges all temper" (1.1.6–8). The description of Antony as "ne'er lust-wearied" functions equally ambiguously (2.1.53); even Maecenas' biblically inflected condemnation of "th' adulterous Antony" presents him as "most large / In his abominations" (3.6.95–96). The most "puritanical" speech in the play, the one most sure in its moralism – like Edgar's analysis of the reason for Gloucester's blindness – is spoken by Antony himself. He calls Cleopatra a "boggler ever," and offers a generalized reflection on how utterly precise is the "justice" of the gods: "when we in our viciousness grow hard ... the wise gods seel our eyes, / In our filth drop our clear judgments, make us / Adore our errors" (3.13.115–19). This is a powerful evocation of the curse of moral blindness, and yet, in the context of this play, it is not clear that it is such a bad thing to "Adore our errors." And the speech is part of the scene after Actium between Antony and Cleopatra before Antony becomes himself again. The turning point in this scene is worth noting. Instead of trying to answer Antony's insults, Cleopatra asks him a completely different sort of question, one that has nothing to do with the moral or even practical register. She asks him, "Not know me yet?" (3.13.162). She does not point to any list of qualities, but urges him to consider and address himself to the full particularity of the person that she is.[46] Instead of saying to her "I know thee not," and turning against his heart, Antony recalls his heart (3.13.177) and thereby regains his identity by recognizing hers, and by committing himself to rather than rejecting what Hal turned King Henry terms "gormandizing" – "one other gaudy night."

The links between Antony and Cleopatra and Falstaff are subterranean, but real. One such link is the odd fact that these characters are perhaps the only ones in Shakespeare for whom a happy post-mortem existence is evoked. Post-mortem existence is mostly imagined as terrifying in Shakespeare, so that oblivion becomes a positive term – "to die, to sleep."[47] The angels that Horatio postulates for Hamlet are in the optative mode. But Falstaff is, we are quite confidently told, "in Arthur's bosom, if ever man went to Arthur's bosom" (*Henry V*, 2.2.9–10). Shakespeare gives Falstaff a strikingly and unironically "christom" death, a highly "reformed" one (he cried out against sack, and against women).[48] This is perhaps Shakespeare's direct apology to him, but Shakespeare saves Falstaff's death from piety and moralism only by Mistress Quickly's urgings (that "a' should not think of God") and by her wonderful malapropism, that puts him in the realm of myth rather than that of orthodox religion, in Arthur's rather than Abraham's bosom. The deaths that Shakespeare gives Antony and Cleopatra do not need to be saved from piety or moralism. They are entirely within a different realm. Both Antony and Cleopatra have the imagination of death as a peaceful sleep, but they, in deep consonance with their characters and with the play as a whole, add an erotic dimension – he as a bridegroom (4.14.101), she as both bride and as mother (5.2.286, 308–9).[49] They are given, moreover, a less metaphysical and more active vision of the afterlife. Antony imagines them as continuing the party: "Where souls do couch on flowers, we'll hand in hand / And with our sprightly port make the ghosts gaze" (4.14.52–53). Cleopatra imagines meeting Antony in the afterlife as she did at Cydnus ("I am again for Cydnus" [5.2.227]); there Antony had been "barber'd ten times o'er" (2.2.234); in the afterlife she will meet and kiss "the curled Antony" (5.2.300). The *contemptus mundi* of the sensualists is rewarded with an erotic and "sprightly" paradise. These "green fields" have nothing to do with the Lord. Shakespeare here gives the idea of rewards in the afterlife an entirely non-moralistic dimension. Greatness trumps wisdom and prudence once again.[50]

Notes

For helpful comments on this essay, I am indebted to audiences at the University of Maryland, College Park, the Shakespeare Association of America (New Orleans, 2004), and to the Renaissance Workshop at the University of Chicago. I am especially indebted to Jeff Collins, Steve Pincus, and Josh Scodel.

1 Friedrich Nietzsche, *Beyond Good and Evil: Prelude to a Philosophy of the Future*, trans. Walter Kaufmann (New York: Vintage, 1966), pp. 147, 158.

2 See Bernard Williams, *Morality: An Introduction to Ethics* (New York: Harper and Row, 1972), esp. the chapters (not numbered) entitled "Moral Standards and the Distinguishing Mark of Man" and "God, Morality, and Prudence," pp. 59–67 and 68–78 respectively; and Williams, *Ethics and the Limits of Philosophy* (Cambridge, MA: Harvard University Press, 1985), esp. chapter 10 ("Morality, the Peculiar Institution").

3 For the depth of Williams' interest in Homer and in Greek tragedy, see his *Shame and Necessity* (Berkeley, CA: University of California Press, 1993); for his increasing

interest in Nietzsche, see his *Truth and Truthfulness* (Princeton, NJ: Princeton University Press, 2002), esp. chapters 1–2. For Nietzsche and Homer, see *Beyond Good and Evil*, p. 151 *et passim*; for Nietzsche and Aristotle, see Kaufman's notes on pp. 138 and 228.

4 See Aristotle, *Poetics*, 1448b5–20, in *Introduction to Aristotle*, ed. Richard McKeon (New York: The Modern Library, 1947), pp. 625–26.

5 All quotations taken from *King Richard III*, ed. Antony Hammond (London: Methuen, 1981). Unless otherwise specified, quotations from and references to Shakespeare's plays will be from the second series of Arden editions.

6 On the hero-villain's "startling intimacy" with the audience, see Harold Bloom, *Shakespeare: The Invention of the Human* (New York: Riverhead, 1998), p. 70.

7 Marlowe noted that "Women are woon [won] when they begin to jarre," in "Hero and Leander," 1: 332 (*Elizabethan Narrative Verse*, ed. Nigel Alexander [Cambridge, MA: Harvard University Press, 1968], p. 64).

8 Compare "The sweet fruition of an earthly crown," in *Tamburlaine*, Part 1: 2.7.29 (Christopher Marlowe, *The Complete Plays*, ed. J. B. Steane [Harmondsworth: Penguin, 1969]).

9 For the occurrence of the joke in *Twelfth Night*, see 1.5.64–69, in which Feste "proves" that Olivia is a fool for mourning her dead brother.

10 Bloom advises, "Think of Falstaff as the author of *Richard III*, and you cannot go too far wrong," *Shakespeare: The Invention of the Human*, p. 66.

11 See Niccolò Machiavelli, *The Discourses*, ed. Bernard Crick, trans. Leslie J. Walker with revisions by Brian Richardson (New York: Penguin, 1974), I: xi. The ultimate classical source might be the speeches of Callicles in Plato's *Gorgias*, esp. 483b–c; see *The Collected Dialogues of Plato*, ed. Edith Hamilton and Huntingtron Cairns, Bollingen 71 (New York: Pantheon, 1961), p. 266.

12 Quotations from *I Henry IV* unless otherwise indicated.

13 Desiderius Erasmus, *The Praise of Folly*, trans. Clarence H. Miller (New Haven, CT: Yale University Press, 1979), p. 9. For this connection, see Walter Kaiser, *Praisers of Folly: Erasmus, Rabelais, Shakespeare* (Cambridge, MA: Harvard University Press, 1963).

14 *Selections from Johnson on Shakespeare*, ed. Bertrand H. Bronson with Jean M. O'Meara (New Haven, CT: Yale University Press, 1986), p. 188.

15 See *Praise of Folly*, ed. cit., pp. 21, 30, 48, 109.

16 *Johnson on Shakespeare*, p. 188.

17 In Part I: 2.2, Falstaff says "thou hast done much harm upon me, Hal, God forgive thee for it" (89–90), and he repeats this claim often. For William Empson, see *Some Versions of Pastoral* (1935; New York: New Directions, 1960), chapter 3 ("They that Have Power"); for W.H. Auden, see "The Prince's Dog," in *The Dyers Hand and Other Essays* (1948; New York: Random House, 1962), pp. 182–208.

18 For a Middle English Land of Cockayne, see *Early Middle English Verse and Prose*, ed. J.A.W. Bennett and G.V. Smithers, 2nd ed. (Oxford: Clarendon, 1968), pp. 138–44. For an Italian version in which it rains ravioli, see Carlo Ginzburg, *The Cheese and the Worms: The Cosmos of a Sixteenth-Century Miller*, trans. John and Anne Tedeschi (Baltimore, MD: Johns Hopkins University Press, 1980), pp. 82–83.

19 Francis Bacon, *The Advancement of Learning*, ed. G.W. Kitchin (London: J.M. Dent, 1973), 2.4.2, p. 82.

20 On "the bliss of freedom gained in humor" as "the essence of Falstaff," see A.C. Bradley's wonderful essay, "The Rejection of Falstaff," *Oxford Lectures on Poetry* (1909; London: Macmillan, 1959), p. 262; see also pp. 269, 273.

21 I believe this is in accord with C.L. Barber, *Shakespeare's Festive Comedy: A Study in Dramatic Form in Relation to Social Custom* (1959; Cleveland, OH: World Publishing Co., 1963), p. 196.

22 See Keith Thomas, "Age and Authority in Early Modern England," *Proceedings of the British Academy*, 62 (1976): 205–48.

23 On Shakespeare having substituted the name "Sir John Falstaff" for the name of the character originally named "Sir John Oldcastle," see, *inter alia*, Jonathan Goldberg, "The Commodity of Names: 'Falstaff' and 'Oldcastle' in *I Henry IV*," *Bucknell Review*, 35 (1992): 76–88, and David Kastan, "'Killed with Hard Opinions': Oldcastle, Falstaff, and the Reformed Text of *I Henry IV*," in *Textual Formations and Reformations*, ed. Laurie E. Maguire and Thomas L. Berger (Newark, NJ: University of Delaware Press, 1998), pp. 211–30.

24 For a recent study that emphasizes (rightly, to my mind) the profound thematic and tonal differences between Part I and Part II of *Henry IV*, see Hugh Grady, *Shakespeare, Machiavelli, and Montaigne: Power and Subjectivity from* Richard II *to* Hamlet (Oxford: Oxford University Press, 2002), esp. pp. 128, 182–83.

25 All quotations from *King Lear* will be from the Quarto text in René Weis, King Lear: *A Parallel Text Edition* (London: Longman, 1993). Departures from this text, as in the interpolation of "it" in line 195 here (which does appear in the Folio text), will be noted.

26 See William Empson, "Fool in *Lear*," in *The Structure of Complex Words* (London: Chatto and Windus, 1964), chapter 6.

27 On the paradoxes of obedience and disobedience in the play, see Richard Strier, *Resistant Structures: Particularity, Radicalism, and Renaissance Texts* (Berkeley, CA: University of California Press, 1995), chapter 7.

28 I have departed from Weis's text here because he departs from the Quarto text without, I believe, sufficient reason for doing so. He substitutes the Folio reading, "ruffle," for Q's "rustle" ("russel"). No other recent editor of the Quarto agrees with Weis in making this substitution. See William Shakespeare, *The Complete Works, Original-Spelling Edition*, gen. eds, Stanley Wells and Gary Taylor (Oxford: Oxford University Press, 1976), p. 1044; *The First Quarto of* King Lear, ed. Jay Halio (Cambridge: Cambridge University Press, 1994), p. 74; *The History of King Lear*, ed. Stanley Wells (Oxford: Oxford University Press, 2000), p. 177.

29 The text(s) leave this matter genuinely open. Peter Brook's 1971 film decisively accepts Goneril's view.

30 See Robert Bechtold Heilman, *This Great Stage: Image and Structure in* King Lear (Baton Rouge, LA: Louisiana State University Press, 1948), chapter 2 ("I Stumbled when I Saw"); Stanley Cavell, "The Avoidance of Love: A Reading of *King Lear*" (1969), rpt. in *Disowning Knowledge in Six Plays of Shakespeare* (Cambridge: Cambridge University Press, 1987), pp. 44–50, esp. p. 49: "Gloucester suffers the same punishment he inflicts."

31 I am using the third series Arden, ed. John Wilders (London, 1995).

32 "Falstaff as Mom" was the title of a talk at MLA given, I believe, by Sherman Hawkins in 1977, and not published. For Falstaff's "femininity," see Auden, "The Prince's Dog," p. 196; and Valerie Traub, "Prince Hal's Falstaff: Positioning Psychoanalysis and the Female Reproductive Body," *Shakespeare Quarterly*, 40 (1989): 456–74.

33 On the place of *The Praise of Folly* in the general intellectual landscape of Renaissance and Reformation Europe, see Richard Strier, "Against the Rule of Reason: Praise of Passion from Petrarch to Luther to Shakespeare to Herbert," in

Reading the Early Modern Passions: Essays in the Cultural History of Emotion, ed. Gail Kern Paster, Katherine Rowe, and Mary Floyd-Wilson (Philadelphia, PA: University of Pennsylvania Press, 2004), pp. 23–42.

34 I am not sure why Harold Bloom finds this speech "unconvincing" (*Shakespeare: The Invention of the Human*, p. 553).

35 The poems in which Donne makes this kind of assertion are probably written after the accession of James, since one of the most important of them, "The Canonization," makes what seems to be a clear reference to a male monarch reigning ("the Kings reall or his stamped face / Contemplate" [lines 7–8]). This means that these poems were probably written in approximately the same period as *Antony and Cleopatra*, in, that is, the early years of James's reign (which began in 1603). Why these strikingly similar statements of the absoluteness and transcendent value of the private should have occurred, just about simultaneously but probably completely independently, at this time is a wonderful historical puzzle which has not, to my knowledge, been answered or even, perhaps, sufficiently meditated upon. For a suggestive attempt at something like an answer, see Jonathan Goldberg, *James I and the Politics of Literature* (Baltimore, MD: Johns Hopkins University Press, 1983), chapter 2 ("State Secrets").

36 Compare Nietzsche on egoism as "belonging to the nature of the noble soul" (*Beyond Good and Evil*, p. 215). See also Reuben Brower on the singularity of heroic identity in *Hero and Saint: Shakespeare and the Graeco-Roman Heroic Tradition* (Oxford: Oxford University Press, 1971), esp. chapter 3 ("Metamorphoses of the Heroic").

37 I am not, of course, suggesting that Shakespeare necessarily agreed with the view that Katherine is expressing here (or even that she necessarily does), but only that it was clearly an available, and, as the evidence shows, a dominant view. See Suzanne W. Hull, *Chaste, Silent and Obedient: English Books for Women, 1475–1640* (San Marino, CA: Huntington Library, 1982); and, *inter alia*, David Underdown, "The Taming of the Scold: The Enforcement of Patriarchal Authority in Early Modern England," in *Order and Disorder in Early Modern England*, ed. Anthony Fletcher and John Stevenson (Cambridge: Cambridge University Press, 1985), pp. 116–36; Susan Dwyer Amussen, "'Being stirred to much unquietness': Violence and Domestic Violence in Early Modern England," *Journal of Women's History*, 6 (1994): 70–89.

38 See Plotinus, *The Enneads*, trans. Stephen MacKenna, abridged by John Dillon (London: Penguin, 1991), pp. 119, 111. On the essential diffusiveness of the Good, see (aside from p. 111), pp. 354, 388, 531–33; for Plotinus' repeated insistence that this process is natural and necessary and not a product of intention or deliberation, see pp. 267, 271, 294–95. Further page references in the text.

39 For a useful overview, see *Platonism and the English Imagination*, ed. Anna Baldwin and Sarah Hutton (Cambridge: Cambridge University Press, 1994), Part 3 ("The Renaissance and the Seventeenth Century"). The Pseudo-Dionysian idea of "dissemblant similitudes," strongly stressed in Georges Didi-Huberman, *Fra Angelico: Dissemblance and Figuration*, trans. Jane Marie Todd (Chicago: University of Chicago Press, 1995), pp. 6, 50–56, 123, is perhaps a related conception.

40 On how little Shakespeare required to absorb "all he needed" of various traditions, see T.S. Eliot, "Shakespeare and the Stoicism of Seneca," *Selected Essays* (1932; New York: Harcourt, Brace 1950), p. 119, and see also, "Tradition and the Individual Talent": "Shakespeare acquired more essential history from Plutarch than most men could from the whole British Museum," *Selected Essays*, p. 6.

41 Janet Adelman's chapter on *Timon of Athens* and *Antony and Cleopatra* is entitled "Making Defect Perfection," but she does not particularly focus on this phrase; *Suffocating Mothers: Fantasies of Maternal Origin in Shakespeare's Plays*, Hamlet *to* The Tempest (New York: Routledge, 1992), chapter 7.

42 Quoted in A.O. Lovejoy, *The Great Chain of Being: A Study of the History of an Idea* (1936; New York: Continuity, 1960), p. 76; Lovejoy's book is the great study of the influence of such ideas in the Western tradition. For the quoted passage, see *Summa Contra Gentiles, Book II: Creation*, trans. James F. Anderson (Notre Dame: Notre Dame University Press, 1956), chapter 45 ("The True First Cause of the Distinction of Things"), p. 137.

43 Richard Hooker, *Of the Laws of Ecclesiastical Polity (Books I–IV)*, intro. Christopher Morris (1907; New York: Dutton, 1965), p. 152. I take it that "virtue" here includes both goodness and power, or is meant to indicate an absolute coincidence of the two.

44 Nietzsche sees the problem with the moral perspective as precisely its lack of discrimination; moral laws are unreasonable *because* they are universal, because "they address themselves to all", and "generalize where one must not generalize" (*Beyond Good and Evil*, § 198, p. 109). Without the special cases that matter, Cleopatra notes that "the odds is gone" (4.15.68). Compare Williams, *Morality: An Introduction to Ethics*, pp. 74–77, and William Blake, "One Law for the Lion & Ox is Oppression," Plate 24 of *The Marriage of Heaven and Hell*, in *The Complete Poetry and Prose of William Blake*, ed. David Erdman, rev. edn (Berkeley: University of California Press, 1982), p. 44.

45 It must be said that in Caesar's awed description of Cleopatra's corpse, he too finally subscribes to the "defect perfection" motif in speaking of her "strong toil of grace" (5.2.346) – a phrase in which the negative and the positive exist simultaneously, or rather, are fused, and in which the aesthetic becomes paradoxically spiritual.

46 See Edward A. Snow, "Loves of Comfort and Despair: A Reading of Shakespeare's Sonnet 138," *ELH*, 47 (1980): 462–83, esp. p. 471.

47 For horrifying visions of post-mortem existence, see *Measure for Measure*, 3.1.120–27; *Hamlet*, 1.5.10–22.

48 For a wonderful note on the theological meaning of Falstaff's heart being "fracted and corroborate" (*Henry V*, 2.2.124), see p. 37 of J.H. Walter's edition.

49 On the force and significance of Cleopatra's "Husband, I come" (V.ii.286), in both its claims, see Cavell, *Disowning Knowledge*, pp. 31–33.

50 On "greatness," see Nietzsche, *Beyond Good and Evil*, § 212, p. 139, and the whole of the culminating section of the book, Part 9 ("What is Noble"). On "the recognition of greatness" as "a feat more difficult" for us than for the Elizabethans, see Brower, *Hero and Saint*, pp. 1–2.

11 The skeptical ethics of John Donne

The case of *Ignatius his Conclave*

Anita Gilman Sherman

Is skeptical ethics an oxymoron? If skepticism is defined as a principled refusal to pass judgment, then it may be wise to concede its incompatibility with ethics, the study of the grounds for choice. But if skepticism designates a program of inquiry based on a set of rhetorical techniques that will unsettle preconceived notions, then a skeptical ethics is not a contradiction in terms, but a plan for action.[1] To understand the skeptical ethics of *Ignatius his Conclave*, I argue that it both adopts and disowns a skeptical aesthetic – adopting rhetorical forms associated with skepticism while disowning the aestheticizing tendencies of its skeptical characters. In the process, *Ignatius* asks how a gathering of skeptical personalities goes about decision-making.

***

Donne's skepticism has less to do with the neo-stoicism of the Taciteans and their quietistic regard for self-preservation in a world of courtly duplicity than with a compulsion to take intellectual risks.[2] For much of his life, Donne struggled with an almost pathological propensity to doubt that at times threatened to paralyze him, but in the process he developed an ethics of interrogation that he was able to turn to account in his literary endeavors, stamping them with his remarkable aesthetic signature. While *Ignatius his Conclave* has disappointed readers in search of elegant seduction or ingenious metaphor, it is a satisfying work because in it Donne negotiates the difficult conjunction of ethics and aesthetics as these emerge from skepticism. Written in 1610 and published in January 1611, as many as 15 years after "Satire 3," *Ignatius* at once enacts and condemns a skeptical aesthetic even as it tries to salvage a skeptical ethic from its blistering intellectual rampage.[3]

Donne's "Satire 3," penned in the 1590s, has become the *locus classicus* for a heroic understanding of a skeptical ethic. "To stand inquiring right" involves "hard deeds ... hard knowledge too" as the seeker circles round and round the "cragged, and steep" hill of Truth, striving to win "what the hill's suddenness resists." As early as 1633, in a eulogy appended to a posthumous edition of Donne's poetry, Lucius Cary, second Viscount Falkland, credits the third satire with having set the bar for a skeptical heroism demanding both valor and labor. Cary recognizes that Donne's insistent spiritual questioning requires an almost athletic moral courage.[4] Yet, notwithstanding Donne's strenuous inquiries into all manner of subjects, from suicide to sex to Biblical hermeneutics, Donne's skepticism is often seen as a youthful phenomenon that faded in importance once he took orders, devolving into ethical and political vapidity.[5] While I do not address that biographical narrative here, I do want to show the vibrant, if crabbed, skeptical ethic operating in his seldom read and often misunderstood anti-Jesuit screed.

Usually, *Ignatius* is described as a favor-currying intervention in King James's polemic over the Oath of Allegiance. This view is amply warranted given the prominence in Donne's preface of the phrase "humane infirmity," no doubt lifted from the widely reprinted letter of Cardinal Bellarmine to Archpriest George Blackwell, urging him to desist from that "humane infirmity" that might entice him to take the Oath of Allegiance and so escape martyrdom. With wry humor Donne echoes Bellarmine's coinage, only he turns it against itself, undoing its call for seriousness by admitting up front that "This Booke must teach what humane infirmity is" (5). That Donne may have harbored misgivings about the way its flippancy would be received is suggested by the fact that it was first published anonymously in Latin on the Continent, at Hanau, "farre from the father," as the English preface later put it.[6] Donne's choice of Latin also shows that his implied reader was presumed to belong to that sophisticated confraternity, the international republic of letters.[7] But while *Conclave Ignati* may well have been written to capitalize on the furor aroused in Europe by the King's *Premonition* and his *Triplici Nodo, Triplex Cuneus. Or an Apologie for the Oath of Allegiance*, it is far more than a cagey piece of political ephemera; in it, Donne wrestles with his personal demons.

***

As the preface explains, *Ignatius* is an exercise in "Lightnesse & Petulancy" after the serious, scholarly efforts of *Pseudo-Martyr* a year before. The preface opens with a slap at the "Protectors of the Popes Consistory and of the Colledge of Sorbon," its ostensible dedicatees, who, our narrator claims, will benefit from the account of his journey to Hell while in an "*Extasie*" (5). This narrator appears to be a reliable observer. It is through his privileged eyes that we are granted a view of hell. Never mind that he distances himself straightaway from the special spectacles he is wearing, telling us that they have vouchsafed past visions of fraudulence:

> And by the benefit of certaine spectacles, I know not of what making, but, I thinke, of the same, by which *Gregory* the great, and *Beda* did discerne so distinctly the soules of their friends, when they were discharged from their bodies, and sometimes the soules of such men as they knew not by sight, and of some that were never in the world, and

yet they could distinguish them flying into Heaven, or conversing with living men ... (7)[8]

Although with this line he undercuts his own authority, he nevertheless insists on providing us with a narrative frame and an intrusive authorial voice designed to give us the illusion of stability and ethical centering. The fiction is that "in the twinkling of an eye" he has been raptured to hell (note the perverted echo of 2 Thessalonians) where, not unlike Andrea and Revenge in Kyd's *The Spanish Tragedy*, he gets to pose as a spectator and eavesdropper of infernal doings. Indeed, the narrator in passing refers to himself metaphorically as a member of a theater audience liable to get bored and walk out. "Truly I thought this Oration of Ignatius very long," he says; "yet I was loathe to leave the stage, till I saw the play ended" (63). Evidently, he imagines himself as one of the gallants sitting on stage close to the drama. This spatial relation is significant because he is not looking down (*kataskopos*) from a place outside the arena of activity, as often happens when the theatrical metaphor is used. Instead the narrator is placed within the arena, albeit on the edges, and he is looking across, eye to eye with the devils and the dead.

Yet, it is not merely the unreliability of the narrator's spectacles or his uncomfortable proximity to the action that should give us pause. Hell, by definition, provides a false and twisted perspective. Speakers in an infernal setting can no more be trusted than the Cretan wit who announces that everything he says is a lie. In keeping with Donne's fondness for paradox, in this work he appropriates rhetorical forms that in most circumstances signify the countering of skepticism, but that in this exceptional circumstance – a snapshot of a day in the life of Lucifer – revert upon themselves, the infernal context ironizing and undermining their usual valence. Because we have been forewarned that nothing we see vicariously through Gregory and Bede's spectacles can be trusted and because we are not looking down on hell itself, but are loitering on its stageboards, our position as readers is thoroughly unstable. We must doubt everything and trust nothing. Indeed, we are trapped in what might almost be called a parody of the skeptic's dilemma. Despite our fond hope that the narrator will serve as a sturdy Virgilian guide through the infernal labyrinth, we find ourselves left to our own interpretive resources, trying to make sense of the double-talk as best we can.

In his hallucinatory adventure, the narrator lands in hell on a day occurring only "once in an Age" when petitioners sue to enter a "more honourable roome, reserved for especiall Innovators" – i.e. the conclave room – where they plead "their owne Causes" before Lucifer himself. In making their case for admission into the inner sanctum of hell, the petitioners review their self-styled achievements. Each delivers an oration. Each subscribes to the "great man theory of history," representing his own transgressive exploration as sweeping away the cobwebs of time-hallowed custom. The enduring appeal of the work – and its humor – lies in the fact that the petitioners include

Copernicus, Columbus, Machiavelli, Paracelsus, Aretino and Filippo Neri, the counter-Reformation saint. The peculiar cast of characters – a hit list akin in its quirkiness to Donne's *Courtier's Library* – reveals Donne's anxiety over the ethics of an aestheticized life. His figures are reviled more for their noisy fixation with fashioning an artistic narrative about themselves than for their innovations. This becomes apparent when Donne allows a note of apology to intrude into the characterization of those whose work he grudgingly respects. Ignatius, for example, in addressing Copernicus, concedes that "those opinions of yours may very well be true" (17). Indeed, the presence of Copernicus, Columbus and Aretino in the demonic chamber betrays Donne's internal divisions. He seems unable to summon up much venom about their accomplishments. Donne's critique of their almost Nietzschean aestheticism, however, marries well with the conventions of Menippean satire.

According to Northrup Frye, Menippean satire is characterized by many traits, among them "the ridicule of the *philosophus gloriosus*" and "violent dislocations in the customary logic of narrative" which may strike naïve readers as careless.[9] "The Menippean satirist," Frye adds in words apposite to Donne, "shows his exuberance in intellectual ways, by piling up an enormous mass of erudition about his theme or in overwhelming his pedantic targets with an avalanche of their own jargon."[10] Eugene Korkowski refines Frye's definition, situating Donne's *Ignatius* within what he calls "an almost neo-classical revival of the genre" in the early seventeenth century in which theological *gloriosi* are the primary satirical butts.[11] More recently, W. Scott Blanchard situates Menippean satire within a skeptical tradition that privileges paradox, the violation of generic boundaries and the Bakhtinian grotesque.[12] Insofar as skepticism can be expressed through genre and rhetorical techniques, it is clear that games with Menippean satire can keep readers off balance and provoke inquiry as much as the choice of an unreliable narrator and infernal setting.

While Donne may have been inspired by contemporary satires of puffed up theologians, he was no doubt also working with the skeptical models offered by Lucian and Erasmus. Donne loosely adapts Lucian's dialogues among the dead, setting up a sequence of bombastic, self-congratulatory monologues that backfire against the deluded speakers, exposing their arrogance and hypocrisy instead of their merit. He also borrows from Lucian's games with the moon. In Lucian's *A True Story*, for example, the inhabitants of the moon have eyes that "are removable, and whenever they wish they take them out and put them away until they want to see: then they put them in and look. Many, on losing their own, borrow other people's to see with."[13] As Maria Katharina Carrig explains, "Lucian used the device [of the moon voyage] to mock the whole idea of the absolute perspective."[14] Lucian also makes fun of inflexible viewpoints in *Philosophies for Sale*, in which Zeus and Hermes put ten philosophers on the auction block, the last of whom is a skeptic who refuses to accept that he has been sold (for spare change). "I am suspending judgment on that point and thinking it over," he says.[15] Skeptical doubt has a long tradition of inspiring mirth even when while making inroads into dogmatisms.

The *Colloquies* of Erasmus and his *Praise of Folly* also influenced Donne, even as they themselves bear a Lucianic stamp. (Erasmus's translations of Lucian along with Sir Thomas More's were the best known in the first half of the sixteenth century.)[16] Carrig has shown that when Christian humanists borrowed the techniques of Lucianic dialogue, they steered a perilous course between the multivocality of skepticism and the univocality of satire. Carrig observes that in its classical (Aristotelian-Horatian) formulation "satiric comedy attempts to base its authority on the assurance of a privileged perspective, an ethical centering or stability that skepticism denies";[17] hence, to combat the doubts induced by skepticism, the satirist must locate a vantage point from which she can speak with certainty and pass moral judgment. In Erasmus, for example, the lunar setting is not destabilizing, operating instead as a fixed vantage point from which to look down on the human theater. Rather than mocking the whole idea of an absolute perspective, the moon can provide an omniscient, godlike view of terrestrial pettiness – a place from which a "true" perspective is possible. In *The Praise of Folly*, the allusion to the moon voyage marks a turning point away from Lucianism and from the shifting arguments and unstable rhetoric that has kept the reader at sea, unable to find a firm foothold.[18] Once on the moon, Folly's invective becomes more openly didactic. "If you were to look down from the moon," Folly says, "as Menippus used to do, you would think that you were seeing a swarm of flies or gnats, quarreling among themselves, fighting, robbing, sporting."[19] Here Erasmus has borrowed from Lucian only to leave him behind. As Carrig says, "*The Praise of Folly* attempts to transform Lucianic perspectivism into a form of Christian dialectic, using rhetorical play to forge a compromise between skepticism and Christian humanism."[20]

It may appear as if Donne is attempting an analogous compromise in *Ignatius*. Like the *Colloquys* of Erasmus, *Ignatius* also has an ethical objective that involves exposing credulity, on the one hand, and cynicism, on the other. For example, Ignatius, Machiavelli and Paracelsus share a talent for manipulating people for the sake of securing power, while Filippo Neri is targeted for his faith in miracles and visions. Yet *Ignatius* does not limit itself to ridiculing received notions, as it would if it were wholly Lucianic in spirit. Nor does it seem written in the spirit of compromise characteristic of the Christian dialectic of Erasmus. Like the Pope in Erasmus's *Julius Exclusus*, the characters in *Ignatius* are blissfully unaware that the more they vaunt themselves on their high exploits, the more they provide their putative audience with ammunition against them. Even in this situation of dramatic irony, *Ignatius* complicates the Erasmian set-up because there is no stable position from which to judge the speakers.[21] While in the Erasmian colloquy, St. Peter clearly perceives the highlights of the Pope's life as monstrous, in Donne's satire the petitioners' immediate audience (Lucifer and Ignatius) shares their sensibility; all parties agree that "innovation" should be rewarded in hell.

In short, although *Ignatius* participates in a humanist tradition of Menippean satire, several features put it in a class of its own, not least Donne's deployment of rhetorical devices symptomatic of skepticism. The framework of the *Conclave*'s gallery of rogues is a dream experienced by an unreliable narrator; not only is the framing device an illusion, but the narrator exacerbates our uncertainty.[22] The demonization of all the high achievers – not just philosophers and theologians, but explorers, physicians and pornographers – makes them by definition contestatory figures.[23] Even removed from their infernal setting, however, their self-glorifying spiels would produce a hybrid countergenre – a cross between a mock encomium and a mock eulogy. The moon voyage trope also undergoes transformation in Donne's hands.[24] So far from mocking ideas of perspective in Lucianic style, the moon in *Ignatius* serves as a hypothetical launching pad for epistles aimed at inflating the Jesuits' reputation on earth. While it may seem that Donne is doing nothing more than giving a Menippean spin to hackneyed advice like "watch out for Jesuits," Donne's riff on the moon divulges the arrogance and greed underwriting missionary zeal. Instead of opening his mind to alternate worlds, the prospect of life on the moon exposes the barrenness of Ignatius's imagination.

Lucifer, faced with the contentious rivalry of Ignatius and Machiavelli, each vying to be his chief henchman, seizes on the idea of banishing the Jesuits to the moon so as to get rid of Ignatius. Lucifer tempts Ignatius with the offer of presiding over a "lunatique" Hell, "over which," he tells him,

> you Ignatius shall have dominion, and establish your kingdome & dwelling there. And with the same ease as you passe from the earth to the Moone, you may passe frome the Moone to the other starrs, which are also thought to be worlds, & so you may beget & propagate many Hells, & enlarge your Empire, & come nearer unto that high secte, which I left at first. (81)

Ignatius pretends to consider the offer, shrewdly evaluating its many possible benefits, among them that "a woman governes there; of which Sex they have ever made their profite, which have attempted any *Innovation* in religion" (83). The chief benefit, however, turns out to be that "when wee are established there, this will adde much to our dignity, that in our letters which wee send downe to the earth ... we may write of what miracles wee list: which we offered to doe out of the *Indies*, and with good successe" (87). Ignatius sees the moon as an extension of the New World, a colony to be exploited and a fount for tall tales and miracle-mongering. But in the end he does not decamp. For all his politic humoring of the proposal, Ignatius has no desire to abandon his prized position close to Lucifer's throne. That a different point of view might be available up there never even occurs to him. Yet, as Copernicus's opening salvo makes clear, Donne is acutely aware of that different perspective. "Shall these gates be open to such as have innovated in small matters?" Copernicus asks, "and shall they be shut against me, who have turned the whole frame of the world, and am thereby almost a new Creator?" (15). Donne's fascination with upturned and overturned frames infuses new life into the moon-voyage trope. Neither a site from which one sees better or more truly (like Folly) nor a site from which one mocks the possibility of perfect vision (like Lucian), the moon in *Ignatius* serves as host to a Satanic fantasy: relief from a Jesuit dystopia.

If games with framing, point-of-view and genre comprise the principal strategies of the skeptical aesthetic enacted in *Ignatius*, it is also important to reckon with the role that memory plays in the work. Donne's games with memory not only increase the instability of our perspective, but they bring out the problems and contradictions of a skeptical aesthetic, especially with regard to the ethics of counter-exemplarity. Donne's *Übermenschen* are both champions of skeptical inquiry and competitive narcissists, each one self-legislating and self-grounding like Nietzschean aestheticizers. They give long speeches about their lives, remembering their exploits and boasting. While their convoluted rants have an obnoxious quality, as heroical innovators these figures nevertheless exert appeal. Their counter-exemplarity, made evident in bouts of amnesia and obsessive reminiscence, at once amuses and repels us.

As part of his skeptical strategy, Donne aligns his readers with Lucifer by constructing both as untutored and forgetful, in constant need of nagging reminders. Lucifer's mind seems to be a blank – or, if you will, a tablet of soft wax available for the violations of stamping or incision. He is often clueless as to the identity of his petitioners. "Quis tu?" he asks Copernicus (13). "Et tu, quisnam es?" he asks Paracelsus (19). The petitioners unload their résumés onto him, strutting and swaggering for his benefit. But Lucifer seems beleaguered, harassed and inclined to escape the onerous duty of listening to these self-congratulatory memorial narratives. The irony is that Lucifer is a stand-in for us. Donne positions us so that we in effect are like Lucifer, forced (inasmuch as we continue reading) to listen to the tedious, pompous suitors that besiege him. Our minds, like Lucifer's, are also figured as blank slates unable to deflect the importune ramblings of innovators high on memory. The audience – be it Lucifer, James or random readers – is represented as desiring the freedom not to listen. In other words, while Lucifer may not desire amnesia or forgetfulness, he does want the freedom to refuse knowledge and memory. Evaluating the relative merits of each speaker's life story is a burden he would prefer to cast off. Their memories (presented as encomia/eulogies) oppress Lucifer who, could he shut his ears to them, would lead a lighter-hearted and more carefree existence as the grand panjandrum of hell.

Nevertheless, the customs, traditions and ceremonies of hell require that "once in an Age" he listen to memorial narratives of innovation (13).

By contrast to Lucifer's distraction and forgetfulness, Ignatius has an amazing memory stored with all the learning necessary to counter the pretensions of his rivals. His rhetorical thrusts have a distinctly humanistic tone, appealing to authors and exemplars from Antiquity in order to attack his opponents. Indeed, for every one of his rivals' self-glorifying speeches touching on memorial places, Ignatius comes up with a parallel and substantially longer vituperation, touching on an alternate set of classical *topoi*. This display of Ignatian erudition is awkward enough that the narrator feels obliged to account and apologize for it:

> And though when hee died he was utterly ignorant in all great learning, and knew not so much as *Ptolemeys*, or *Copernicus* name, but might have been perswaded, that the words *Almagest*, *Zenith*, *and Nadir*, were Saints names, and fit to bee put into the *Litanie*, and *Ora pro nobis* joyned to them; yet after hee had spent some time in hell, he had learnt somewhat of his *Jesuites*, which daily came thither. And whilst he staied at the threshold of *Hell*; that is, from the time when he delivered himselfe over to the Popes will, hee tooke a little taste of learning. (15)

Although Ignatius had a reputation for being a rustic autodidact, more a warrior than a man of words, Donne repairs this fault, glossing over the inconveniences of history so as to accommodate his narrative. He does this openly and facetiously so as to expose once more the liberties routinely taken by those who purport to remember the past.[25]

Ignatius ultimately becomes so threatening to Lucifer that Lucifer tries to find another demonic innovator who will be his match. At first, he believes he has found such a counterweight in Machiavelli. As the narrator explains, "since *Ignatius* could not bee denied the place, whose ambitions and turbulencies *Lucifer* understood very wel, he thought *Machiavel* a fit and necessarie instrument to oppose against him; that so the skales being kept even by their factions, hee might governe in peace, and two poisons mingled might doe no harme" (31). But despite Lucifer's hope to balance the Ignatian faction with the Machiavellian faction, Ignatius overpowers Machiavelli, causing him to vanish. Then Lucifer casts about for another candidate and spots Filippo Neri at a distance, deep in a crowd, "who acknowledging in his owne particular no especiall merit towardes his kingdome, forebore to presse neere the gate" (71). For once, in a last ditch effort to repel Ignatius, Lucifer's memory kicks into gear. He begins to recite Neri's accomplishments, remembering his many dastardly innovations.

Filippo Neri, however, has nothing to say for himself. He neither responds to Lucifer's encouragement nor to the attacks of Ignatius. The narrator describes his behavior as verging on the catatonic: "To all this *Nerius* sayde nothing, as though it had beene spoken of some body else. Without doubt, either he never knew, or had forgot that he had done those things which they write of him" (75). Perhaps Donne's dislike of Neri has as much to do with the pious visions and improbable stories purveyed in the *Vita beati patris Philippi Nerii* by Antonio Gallonio (1602) as with a general antipathy towards divines who prize non-rational experience (*Erlebnis*).[26] Insofar as Donne may have longed for an experiential sense of the holy, he may have despised it all the more in those who, he felt, came by it cheaply or fraudulently. Thus, Neri's vacuity elicits his contempt. Since Neri can neither confirm nor dispute Lucifer's account of his career, Lucifer carries on, borne on the waves of his own eloquence, spinning a wild narrative featuring the "free, open, and hard fashion against *Princes*" (75) allegedly championed by Neri. Since the Jesuits were routinely accused of promoting regicide, Lucifer finds it expedient to invest Neri with dastardly Jesuitical attributes. To secure his power and ensure his own autonomy, Lucifer shapes a narrative about Neri and his followers that will compete with and squelch the narrative that Ignatius tells about his all-conquering Jesuits. Whereas before Lucifer seemed indecisive and inarticulate, if not senile like Neri, he now realizes that if he is to have any breathing space at all, he must activate his memory and come up with a narrative that effectively silences Ignatius as an author. He fails, of course. The satire ends with Ignatius secure in his power over Lucifer.

In *Ignatius*, where the scene comes to be dominated by sharp-elbowed individuals shouting one another down, boasting about innovation is inextricably tied to personal memory. The assurances of collective memory seem to have receded far into the background. Indeed, *Ignatius*, with its free-for-all of competing narratives, enacts the crisis of collective memory in post-Reformation Europe. As an institution, the Catholic Church had been a powerful locus of collective memory – its rituals, spaces and stories together created an understanding of the past that amounted to doctrine and dogma. With the advent of "cultural innovations" like the Reformation, the collective memory of the church became a site of struggle, each camp claiming greater antiquity and purity for its rituals than the other. Protestants of every stripe insisted that their innovations represented a return to the traditions of the primitive church. They accused Catholics of having introduced superstitious practices, while the Anglicans blamed the Puritans for affecting singularity. Not unlike the characters Donne unleashes in *Ignatius*, the Reformation set loose a pack of polemical writers, each mustering all the rhetorical and scholarly resources at their disposal to demolish their opponents. Each aimed to put a spin on the controversy in question. The virulence of their pamphleteering shows that social narratives were still malleable. From the King to the anonymous pamphleteer afraid of having his ears chopped off for publishing seditious material – all believed that the narratives of collective memory were up for grabs and needed to be controlled. The vitality of debate testified to a tacit recognition that individual players with loud voices had a sporting chance against those with strong arms.

Historians and critics have long pointed out that, despite the upheavals that decisively transformed society in this period, the rhetoric of the time was conservative, resolutely pitted against change. Robert Weimann, for example, observes that "there simply was not available, in the contemporary framework of formulated thought, any room for dramatically usable concepts and symbols of social change, let alone revolution"; therefore, "in science, astronomy and philosophy, the inescapable breach with the past was not conceived in terms of radical change or innovation."[27] Similarly, Lawrence Stone explains, "all change had to be interpreted as the maintenance of tradition."[28] J.P. Sommerville, however, has recently modified this view, arguing "That Englishmen expressed hostility to innovation is true but unimportant ... The crucial point is that Englishmen were far from united on what constituted innovation."[29] Judging by *Ignatius*, Donne himself was torn on the subject. Although he was an experimenter at heart, tampering with traditional literary forms and embracing change in his verse so successfully that his voice continues to enchant readers with its idiosyncratic sounds, in his statements he often disavows novelty, castigating it.

Ignatius stands at the epicenter of this tension. As the narrator explains early on,

> Now to this place, not onely such endeavor to come, as have innovated in matters, directly concerning the soule, but they also which have done so, either in the Arts, or in conversation, or in any thing which exerciseth the faculties of the soule, and may so provoke to quarrelsome and brawling controversies: for so the truth be lost, it is no matter how. (13)

In *Ignatius*, quarrelsome and brawling controversies are the order of the day. The innovators break the taboo forbidding them to crow about the changes they have wrought and unabashedly revel in their overthrowing of tradition. Their outrageousness consists precisely in their refusing to pay lip service to the pieties of social memory. All the characters (except Neri) are Machiavellian inasmuch as they revel in personal glory and shun the passivity that Machiavelli associated with Christianity and blamed for corrupt government. Donne's Machiavelli himself refers to "the language of the Tower of *Babel*, too long concealed," which Ignatius, Lucifer and the Pope, like an unholy Trinity, "have raised to life againe" (27). So it seems plain that Donne has his knives out for the braggadocio of the man-on-the-make and his babble of memories. In my view, the posturing over innovation in *Ignatius* dramatizes a rupture between personal and religious collective memory that invites skepticism.

Yet, for all its protestations, *Ignatius* seems fascinated by change. In effect, it challenges us with implicit, although unstated, questions. How shall we handle cultural change? Shall we utter blanket condemnations as the tract ostensibly recommends? Shall we take it on a case-by-base basis, one innovation at a time? Scurrilous as *Ignatius* may seem at times, I suggest that it provides a narrative about a European republic of letters that occupies an intellectually more fertile ground (if not a morally higher ground) than the sectarian, provincial wrangling that was the norm. It attempts to make sense of what is happening on several intellectual fronts, setting the issue of cultural innovation in a broad, European framework encompassing the arts and sciences. The strategy of using satire to criticize the history and character of religious polemic has a long and illustrious pedigree dating back, not only to Lucian and Erasmus, but also to Donne's great-uncle, Sir Thomas More. Like More, whose "whole life and thought were a protest against the parochial and the national,"[30] Donne also registers a protest against the parochial and the national in *Ignatius*. Yet unlike his great-uncle, he speaks from a Protestant position, intervening in a conversation about continuity and change, tradition and innovation.[31]

Donne's scholarly sensibility was offended by the inaccuracies and distortions routinely perpetrated in the religious polemic of his time. All through his career, Donne makes jibes at the expense of pedants and controversialists, pointing out their errors and flights of fancy. *Ignatius* is no exception. In it, Donne fashions a burlesque of controversy, complete with scrupulously documented marginalia, and beats other polemicists at their own game, mimicking their belligerent poses and digressive argumentation. The whole mock-historical apparatus is a joke at the expense of zealots who construct their tendentious arguments by appealing to ancient and venerable sources. By representing the pettiness of intellectual infighting, *Ignatius* in effect invokes a cosmopolitan worldview of cultural change.

In a sense, *Ignatius* conjures up the ghost of healthy political debate by anatomizing its corpse. B.J. Smith has associated noise with the animated political arguments characteristic of republics:

> ... public life always has been associated with vociferous speech. Republics generally have been noisy places, home to oration and dialogue, catcall and epithet. Wherever public life has emerged, the din of *res publica* has always been heard: clamoring voices, sometimes reduced to jabbering, rarely in unison (although sometimes in harmony), the howl and prophecy of disorder to the inexperienced ear. So much has this been the case that some have suggested that public liberty might be measured by decibel alone. In short, the republic has been characterized by the presence of voices.[32]

If the noisy voices of *Ignatius* are meant to remind us of republics, then Donne is probably anti-republican. Nevertheless, implicit in the unruly clamor of *Ignatius* is a vision of productive conversation. Like the negative of a photograph, constructive talk is the reverse image of *Ignatius*. An ethical take on debate emerges from the skepticism of the satire – hence, my view of its skeptical ethic.

While *Ignatius* distances itself from the aestheticizing postures of its skeptical characters even as it uses rhetorical forms associated with a skeptical aesthetic, its skeptical ethic responds to the paucity of functional debate. It is always difficult, as J.R. Mulryne says, "to reconcile interpretation of broad cultural developments with the micro-politics, not always fully recoverable, of a particular occasion."[33] But since I believe that what drives *Ignatius* is distress over noise and dysfunctional debate, together with an implicit longing for more harmonious dialogue, it stands to reason that Donne's conflicted feelings about conciliarism play a role in the work. *Ignatius* expresses the frustration Donne shared with King James over his inability to organize a general ecumenical council, once the controversy over the Oath of Allegiance had irreparably damaged this prospect. The energy animating *Ignatius* has other sources as well – his feelings about dissent in general, including parliamentary dissent, and most obviously, his rage against the Jesuits. John Carey has described Donne's bitterness toward the Jesuits as the residue of his "apostasy," explaining that Donne considered the Roman Church "an adversary with which he hoped he might finally be reconciled."[34] Carey understands Donne's fascination with councils in therapeutic terms, saying that "by healing the rift in the Church, he could heal himself."[35] While the therapeutic effects of a united Christendom should not be minimized, Donne's preoccupation with the verbal process entailed by councils has political and ethical implications involving the public sphere that need to be taken seriously.

In keeping with his vision of himself as a statesman and peacemaker, James began agitating for a general council early in his reign. As W.B. Patterson comments, "the striking feature of James's proposal ... is that he appealed to the pope to convene a council," evidently recognizing that religious disputes could not be resolved without the Pope's leadership.[36] But the discovery of the Gunpowder Plot exacerbated tensions between Catholics and Protestants in England, while the controversy over the Oath spoiled relations between James and the papacy. Nevertheless, the Oath "seems actually to have been an attempt by James and his advisers to conciliate modern Roman Catholics in England" by allowing them to declare their loyalty to the King and to distance themselves from the Jesuits.[37] In the *Premonition*, published in 1609 in Latin, French and Dutch as well as English so as to reach a wide European audience, James reiterated his case for the Oath of Allegiance and once again called for an ecumenical council from which only Jesuits and Presbyterians would be excluded.[38]

The *Premonition* aroused consternation across Europe and prompted a flood of responses on diverse topics. But, as Patterson points out, "one of the conspicuous features of the controversy was the attention given to the history, nature, and purpose of general councils."[39] While the interest in councils was by no means new, Richard Hooker, for example, having devoted a part of his *Lawes* to their purpose, now theologians and intellectuals as diverse as Francisco Suarez, Isaac Casaubon and Hugo Grotius were impelled to address issues of conciliarism and religious reconciliation. Casaubon, for example, believed that the Roman Church would have to purge some of the innovations it had made in the ancient faith, while the Reformed churches needed to reinstate much of what was valuable in the traditional liturgy.[40] In 1609, when the English ambassador to France, Sir George Carew, wrote of a "third party" that sought to steer a middle course between the extremes of Protestantism and Catholicism, he was referring to Jacques-Auguste de Thou and his friends, among them Isaac Casaubon, the Huguenot Jean Hotman de Villiers and several Roman Catholics. While Donne's biographer has no proof that Donne met with Casaubon or Grotius, he speculates that it is highly likely, given the many friends and acquaintances they shared;[41] it is virtually certain that he knew George Carew and would have visited him in France, having overlapped with him in Egerton's service.[42] In other words, independently of the King's influence, Donne would have been familiar with the ideas of de Thou's irenic "third party" and its interest in conciliarism.

Notwithstanding the guarded attitude toward councils apparent in the twenty-first of The Thirty-nine Articles, Britain had long been in the vanguard of conciliarist thought, thanks in part to the Parisian theologian John Major or Mair (d. 1550), who came from Scotland with its robust tradition of conciliarist ecclesiology.[43] While Henry VIII's interest in councils revived opportunely in the course of his divorce, the historian Francis Oakley argues that those who expressed similar interests at the time should not "be dismissed as royal propagandists deftly responding to the shifting imperatives of their royal master's policy."[44] Even Sir Thomas More, Oakley observes, "out of office, out of royal favor, and finally imprisoned, came to focus more intently than heretofore on the teaching function of the general council and on its role as ultimate legislative authority in the government of the church."[45] Donne would also likely have known about what Patterson designates as "the fullest exposition of English conciliar theory," the fifth book of Richard Field's *Of the Church* (1610). Field emphasized the importance of freedom of speech, although he added that those attending an ecumenical council would be expected to seek "the common good, that private respects, purposes and designes bee not set forward under pretence of religion."[46]

Donne's irenic agenda is most visible in the *Sermons*.[47] In them Donne deplores the way zeal trumps charity in religious disputes,[48] saying,

> And truly it is a lamentable thing, when ceremoniall things in matter of discipline, or problematicall things in matter of doctrine, come so farre, as to separate us from one another, in giving ill names to one another. *Zeal* is directed upon God, and charity upon our brethren; but God will

not be seen, but by that spectacle; nor accept any thing for an act of zeal to himself, that violates charity towards our brethren, by the way. (II.111)

In the interests of peace, he opposes "the sharp and virulent contentions arisen, and fomented in matters of Religion." He asks his auditory to desist from recondite questions and, in a phrase oddly reminiscent of Descartes's "clear and distinct ideas," to rest content "in those places, which are cleare and evident" (II.308). Certainty can be found so long as the mind is trained to focus on that which will elicit consensus. True doctrines are taught in the church, he says, "but for doctrines which were but to vent the passion of vehement men, or to serve the turns of great men for a time … for these interlineary doctrines, and marginal, which were no part of the first text, here's no testimony that God sees that they are good" (II.242). In *Ignatius*, doctrines that vent the passion of vehement men take center stage. But in the sermons they are relegated to the wings, cited only to be dismissed.

The *Sermons*, of course, are full of references to councils old and new. The Council of Trent, for example, comes in for much criticism, on the one hand for taking hard-line positions, and on the other, for indecisiveness and waffling.[49] But there is no need to jump ahead to the *Sermons* or to Donne's participation in the Synod of Dort to make a case for his engagement with conciliarism. Already in *Pseudo-Martyr*, written just prior to *Ignatius*, Donne takes on the most distinguished contemporary historian of councils, Severinus Binius, a German Counter-Reformation scholar, whose five-volume work Donne seems to have known well. Donne may also have known that Paolo Sarpi was working on a history of the Council of Trent.[50] If, in addition, one remembers that as a trained lawyer, former MP, and omnivorous reader, Donne would be *au courant* about discussions regarding contract, consent and the limits of free speech,[51] one can see that Donne's concerns in *Ignatius* occur in the context of a debate over political and religious reconciliation that preoccupied the international republic of letters.

If the failures of conciliarism were on Donne's mind in 1611, then the final incident of *Ignatius* has more bite than is at first apparent. The last we learn of Ignatius is that he covets "the principall place, next to Lucifers owne throne" (95), which happens to be occupied by Pope Boniface. Outraged to find him there, "*Ignatius* flyes upwards, and rushes upon *Boniface*, and throwes him out of his Seate" (97). This may be a sidelong thrust at the deposing power of councils, an issue that troubled discussion of conciliar theory. It is difficult to extrapolate from so brief an incident any distinctions about conciliar preroga-tives to depose monarchs indirectly and popes directly. Suffice it to say that the Council of Constance provided an important precedent for dismissing popes.[52] The impetuous removal of Boniface by Ignatius may thus be more than a barb at the ambition of Jesuits. As a sour joke about the deposing power, it may represent a muffled allusion to a prominent feature of conciliarism.

***

Although Donne's interest in conciliarism is apparent as early as *Biathanatos* and amply set forth in *Pseudo-Martyr*, it continues into the *Sermons*, which postdate *Ignatius* by six to seven years – years during which Donne struggled to understand the genealogy of his religious beliefs and to deepen the extent of his religious commitments. In a sense, *Ignatius* is his last hurrah, his last flamboyant expression of doubt and discontent. In it, his imagination delights in exploring,

> a secret place, where there were not many, beside *Lucifer* himselfe; to which, onely they had title, which had so attempted any innovation in this life, that they gave an affront to all antiquitie, and induced doubt, and anxieties, and scruples, and after, a libertie of believing what they would; at length established opinions, directly contrary to all established before. (9)

Ignatius confronts us with the innovations of doubters, the noise of personal memory and an onslaught of trivial ceremony. At the same time, it acknowledges the truth and value of some of the innovations, grants eloquence and erudition to its arch-malefactors and aligns the politicking in the inner chambers of Hell with the maneuvers of a dysfunctional public sphere.

In short, the skeptical ethics of *Ignatius* are geared to communal concerns. While "Satire 3" investigates the dilemmas confronting the individual who seeks "true religion" – when "To adore, or scorn an image, or protest, / May all be bad" – *Ignatius* stages the nightmare of individuality run amok, each ego proclaiming his own all-sufficient truth. While critics may disagree about the extent to which "Satire 3" imagines the possibility of a just earthly power,[53] I argue that the infernal cacophony of *Ignatius* asks us to envision what a corporate form of strenuous inquiry might look like. Hence, my claim that the skeptical form of the tract, while disavowing the aestheticizing tendencies of its skeptical counter-exemplars, nevertheless summons into view a skeptical ethic involving a community of disputants. No longer at issue is the individual's Stoic integrity vis-à-vis tyrannical government – his ability to "stand / Sentinel" in the face of various political and ecclesiastical pressures. By 1611, Donne has moved on, as it were, having already explored in the third satire the diffidence of Phrygius and the promiscuity of Gracchus. He is no longer seeking a mean between the extremes represented by these figures; in the intervening years Donne has become interested in the group dynamics of decision-making. Not only has he attended parliamentary sessions and read obsessively about the Tridentine council, but he has also become personally acquainted with the vicissitudes of those who jockey for power. *Ignatius* testifies to his conviction that the process whereby groups choose is corrupt, with the weak as much as the strong accountable for specific failures. Yet, his satirical indictment of meetings as conclaves shows that at the back of his mind Donne is pondering an important question: what would heroic skeptical inquiry look like if conducted by a gathering of reasonable, dispassionate men?

Notes

I would like to thank Theodore Leinwand and David Norbrook for their invaluable help with this essay.

1 If my definition of skepticism recalls the Socratic method, it is no coincidence. After Plato's death, the Academy limped along until Arcesilaus (295–42 BCE) and later Carneades (219–129 BCE) arrived and invigorated it; the philosophy taught at their "new" Academy forms the basis of the "Academic skepticism" described in Cicero's *Academica* and *De Natura Deorum* and debated by Augustine in his *Contra Academicos*. See R.J. Hankinson, *The Sceptics* (London: Routledge, 1995) and Luciano Floridi, *Sextus Empiricus: The Transmission and Recovery of Pyrrhonism* (Oxford: Oxford University Press, 2002).

2 Andrew Shifflet has recently taken issue with this description of neo-Stoicism prevalent in the work of Quentin Skinner, Richard Tuck and Markku Peltonen, all of whom conflate it with skepticism. Shifflet argues for "the republican, liber-tarian, and oppositional possibilities of the Stoic tradition" and against "pessi-mistic and absolutist interpretations." He understands Taciteanism as endorsing, not withdrawal, but "a rhetorical mediation of anger" for political ends. See his *Stoicism, Politics, and Literature in the Age of Milton* (Cambridge: Cambridge University Press, 1998), pp. 3, 10.

3 All citations are from *Ignatius his Conclave*, ed. T.S. Healey, S.J. (Oxford: The Clarendon Press, 1969).

4 See Reid Barbour, *Literature and Religious Culture in Seventeenth-Century England* (Cambridge: Cambridge University Press, 2002), pp. 69–74.

5 See Herschel Baker, *The Wars of Truth* (London: Staples Press, 1952); Louis I. Bredvold, "The Religious Thought of Donne in Relation to Medieval and Later Traditions," in *Studies in Shakespeare, Milton and Donne*, ed. English Department of the University of Michigan (New York: Haskell House, 1964), pp. 191–232; John Carey, *John Donne: Mind, Life and Art* (New York: Oxford University Press, 1981); Arthur Marotti, *John Donne, Coterie Poet* (Madison, WI: University of Wisconsin Press, 1986); Richard Strier, *Resistant Structures: Particularity, Radicalism, and Renaissance Texts* (Berkeley, CA: University of California Press, 1995).

6 See Willem Heijting and Paul R. Sellin, "John Donne's *Conclave Ignati*: The Continental Quarto and its Printing," *Huntington Library Quarterly* 62.3–4 (2001): 401–21.

7 I have borrowed the phrase "republic of letters" from David Norbrook, who applies it to Donne in the context of More's *Utopia*, the circulation of which "helped to outline a space for an international republic of letters, an ideal community to which entry was freely offered to those with ability and whose values were critical of tradition, struggling to replace the arbitrary exercise of power by rational political debate." See "The Monarchy of Wit and the Republic of Letters: Donne's Politics," in *Soliciting Interpretation: Literary Theory and Seventeenth-Century English Poetry*, ed. Elizabeth D. Harvey and Katharine Eisaman Maus

(Chicago, IL: University of Chicago Press, 1990), pp. 3–36, 7–8. Perhaps *Ignatius* can be seen in part as a mordant response to the *Utopia*.

8 In his edition of Ignatius, Healey notes that Thomas Morton, Dean of Winchester, on pp. 217–19 of his *Apologia Catholica, Pars II* (1606) singles out Gregory and Bede as "the worst offenders" with regard to fraudulent visions and private revelations (p. 103). As for the trope of the special spectacles that confer X-ray vision, Traiano Boccalini uses it to describe how Tacitus enables ordinary people to read the secrets of princes' hearts (*Raguagli da Parnassus* Bk.2, ch. 71, cited in Peter Burke, "Tacitism, Skepticism, and Reason of State," in *The Cambridge History of Political Thought 1450–1700*, ed. J.H. Burns and Mark Goldie (Cambridge: Cambridge University Press, 1990), p. 490). While to my knowledge no evidence links Donne and Boccalini, it may be useful to think of the narrator of *Ignatius*, if not of John Donne, as a neo-Tacitean.

9 Northrup Frye, *Anatomy of Criticism: Four Essays* (Princeton, NJ: Princeton University Press, 1957), pp. 309–10.

10 Ibid., p. 311.

11 Eugene Korkowski, "Donne's *Ignatius* and Menippean Satire," *Studies in Philology* 72.4 (1975): 419–38.

12 W. Scott Blanchard, *Scholars' Bedlam: Menippean Satire in the Renaissance* (Lewisburg, PA: Bucknell University Press, 1995).

13 Lucian, *Works*, trans. A.M. Harmon (London: William Heinemann, 1913), 1.279.

14 Maria Katharina Carrig, "Skepticism and the Rhetoric of Renaissance Comedy" (Diss. Yale University, 1995), p. 115.

15 Lucian, op. cit., 2.511.

16 See Craig R. Thompson, *The Translations of Lucian by Erasmus and St. Thomas More* (Ithaca, NY: Cornell Studies in English, 1940), p. 28.

17 Carrig, op. cit., p. 4.

18 Ibid., p. 115.

19 Desiderius Erasmus, *The Essential Erasmus*, ed. John P. Dolan (New York: New American Library, 1964), p. 138.

20 Carrig, op. cit., p. 117.

21 But see P.M. Oliver, *Donne's Religious Writing: A Discourse of Feigned Devotion* (London: Longman, 1997), pp. 183–84. Oliver contrasts "Satire 3" with *Ignatius*:

> The sharing of assumptions – in the present instance about such topics as the Jesuits and equivocation – is essential for the proper functioning of satire, and this is one of the reasons why *Ignatius his Conclave* is successful as satire while Satire III is not. The ebb and flow of the poem generates too much uncertainty, while the prose work's more fixed viewpoint allows readers to laugh in the knowledge that their laughter will not rebound on them. They will not suddenly find themselves undermined by any moment of textual sympathy with Loyola … the narrative voice and the voice of Loyola … remain recognisably stable.

22 One of the satire's most distinguished early readers, Johann Kepler, seems to have been quite thrown by its use of the framing device. See his *Somnium*, ed. and trans. Edward Rosen (Madison, WI: University of Wisconsin Press, 1967), pp. 38–39. Astonished to find himself named in the opening lines of *Ignatius*, Kepler willfully disregards Donne's own sidenote that he is citing Kepler's *De Stella in Cygno* (1606) and instead surmises that the author has come across his *Somnium* in

manuscript. In note 8 appended to his *Somnium* (1622), he writes:

> I suppose that a copy of this little work fell into the hands of the author of the
> bold satire entitled *Ignatius his Conclave*, for he stings me by name at the very
> outset. Later on he brings poor Copernicus to Pluto's court, which is entered,
> unless I am mistaken, through the chasms of Hekla.

Hekla is an Icelandic version (so Kepler explains in the following note) of Mount
Etna where Empedocles died according to the account of Diogenes Laertius.
Given that Donne nowhere mentions Hekla, volcanoes or Pluto, it is worth asking
why Kepler misreads Donne. In my view, Kepler links *Ignatius* with his *Somnium*
owing to the conceit of the transported dreamer as a framing device. In an access
of *amour propre*, he falls prey to the mistake that Donne has lifted the device from
him; it is, after all, in the middle of Donne's narrator's "*Extasie*" and survey of
"the swimming Ilands, the Planets" that Kepler gets named. Unlike Kepler's
dreamer, however, who, having been transported in an ecstasy to the moon, is
able to make important astronomical calculations from his new and different
vantage point, Donne's dreamer is thrust into a murky perceptual universe where
he can provide no new empirical foothold on reality. Kepler tells us that he feels
stung. His sense of injury allows him to make common cause with "poor
Copernicus," whose unjust sufferings at the hands of blinkered readers occupies
the bulk of the previous note 7. Kepler feels mistreated, in my view, not just
because he is singled out, but because his dream trope has been borrowed,
subverted and traduced. For him, the salient feature of *Ignatius* is the bizarre use
of the framing device.

23 Balachandra Rajan, for example, associates a contestatory stance with skepticism.
See *The Form of the Unfinished: English Poetics from Spenser to Pound* (Princeton, NJ:
Princeton University Press, 1985), p. 20.

24 Donne's rhetorical games with the moon depend on a number of previous
models, besides Lucian. As Korkowski puts it, there was a "rash of moon-satires
in the early seventeenth century" (op. cit., p. 436). Korkowski lists the following
as the most likely inspirations for Donne's *Ignatius*: *Pasquillus Ecstaticus* by Caelius
Secundus Curio; the third edition of the *Satyre Menippée* to which was added
Nouvelles des Regions de la Lune (Paris, 1594); and *Munsterus Hypobolimaeus, sive Hercules
tuam Fidem* by Daniel Heinsius (1608). He also notes that in 1612, the Dutch
classicist, Petrus Cunaeus, published a Menippean satire called the *Sardi Venales*
that "takes place just under the region of the moon" (ibid., p. 429).

25 Early on, Donne finds precedents for the propensity to invent speeches for
historical figures when he alludes to his special "spectacles" as an "instrument":
"I think truly, *Robert Aquinas* when he tooke *Christ's* long Oration, as he hung upon
the Crosse, did use some such instrument as this, but applied to the eare: And so I
thinke did he, which dedicated to *Adrian* 6, that Sermon which *Christ* made in
prayse of his father *Joseph*: for else how did they heare that, which none but they
ever heard?" (9.1–6).

26 See Donne on Neri in *Biathanatos* 119–20, *Pseudo-Martyr* 59, and *Sermons* 1.186–87
where Neri is referred to as a "Puritan Papist."

27 Robert Weimann, "Society and the Uses of Authority in Shakespeare," in
Shakespeare, Man of the Theater, ed. Kenneth Muir, Jay L. Halio, and D.J. Palmer
(Newark, NJ: University of Delaware Press, 1983), p. 186.

28 Lawrence Stone, *The Crisis of the Aristocracy 1558–1641*, abridged ed. (Oxford:
Oxford University Press, 1967), p. 16.

29 J.P. Sommerville, *Royalists and Patriots: Politics and Ideology in England 1603–1640* (London: Longman, 1999), p. 103.

30 Myron P. Gilmore, *The World of Humanism, 1453–1517* (New York: Harper, 1962), p. 215.

31 Stephen Toulmin discusses *Ignatius* in *Cosmopolis: The Hidden Agenda of Modernity* (New York: Free Press, 1990). Toulmin argues that Renaissance philosophy responded to religious violence, first, by adopting a skeptical stance and, second, by repudiating skepticism in a renewed search for certainty. In Toulmin's words,

> If uncertainty, ambiguity, and the acceptance of pluralism led, in practice, only to an intensification of the religious way, the time had come to discover some *rational method* for demonstrating the essential correctness or incorrectness of philosophical, scientific, or theological doctrines. ... If Europeans were to avoid falling into a skeptical morass, they had, it seemed, to find *something* to be "certain" about (p. 55).

Toulmin's bifurcated narrative of early modernity, ranging on one side the "sweet reasonableness" (p. 79) of Erasmus and Montaigne with their "modest, skeptical lights" (p. 71) and on the other, the penchant for increasingly dogmatic axioms of rationalists like Descartes, fixes on the assassination of Henri IV in 1610 as the turning point. This was the moment (and even more so after 1618 with the onset of the Thirty Years' War) after which "everyone now talked at the top of his voice, and the humanists' quiet discussions of finitude, and the need for toleration, no longer won a hearing" (p. 79). Toulmin singles out *Ignatius his Conclave* as a response to the assassination of the French king. Following Hiram Haydn's account of Donne as a representative of the "counter-Renaissance," he concludes that Donne is "a highly conservative figure" (p. 63) whose "attitude to intellectual innovation ... finds bilious expression in *Ignatius*" (p. 64). That "poem" [*sic*] and "The First Anniversary" together show that Donne laments the downfall of "Cosmopolis," that unified worldview where the Order of Nature and the Order of Society match. As Toulmin puts it, "With the antennae of an author who picks up the 'feel' of his time, Donne voices regret that the world is out of hand in not one, but a dozen ways" (p. 66). While Toulmin's overall view of philosophical developments in the seventeenth century is helpful, his take on *Ignatius* overlooks its Menippean ironies and discursive negotiations.

32 Bruce James Smith, *Politics and Remembrance: Republican Theories in Machiavelli, Burke and Tocqueville* (Princeton, NJ: Princeton University Press, 1985), p. 18.

33 J.R. Mulryne, Introduction, *Theatre and Government under the Early Stuarts*, ed. J.R. Mulryne and Margaret Shewring (Cambridge: Cambridge University Press, 1993), p. 13.

34 Carey, op. cit., p. 35.

35 Ibid., p. 36.

36 W.B. Patterson, *King James VI and I and the Reunion of Christendom* (Cambridge: Cambridge University Press, 1997), p. 69.

37 Ibid., p. 78.

38 Sommerville, op. cit., pp. 206–7.

39 Patterson, op. cit., p. 110.

40 Ibid., p. 128.

41 R.C. Bald, *John Donne: A Life* (Oxford: Oxford University Press, 1970), pp. 283–84.

42 Ibid., p. 150.

43 See Francis Oakley, *The Conciliarist Tradition: Constitutionalism in the Catholic Church 1300–1870* (Oxford: Oxford University Press, 2003), p. 143.

44 Ibid., p. 134.

45 Ibid., p. 135.

46 Richard Field, *Fifth Booke of the Church* (London, 1610), pp. 377–78; cited in Patterson, op. cit., p. 119.

47 All citations are from John Donne, *The Sermons*, ed. George R. Potter and Evelyn M. Simpson, 10 vols (Berkeley, CA: University of California Press, 1953–59).

48 But see Norbrook, op. cit., p. 23, who says that in 1626–27, Donne "preferred evangelical 'zeal' to the 'decency' that was so much a feature of High Church rhetoric."

49 For a typically trenchant attack, see *Sermons* VI.15.314–27. In examining Donne's attitudes to the Council of Trent, Jeffrey Johnson uses the word "innovation" to explain Donne's objections to that gathering's pronouncements: "Donne reacts to a variety of the council's rulings that, from Donne's perspective, were innovations that redefined orthodoxy." This ties in well with my sense that conciliarism haunts the pages of *Ignatius* with its parade of belligerent innovators. See Jeffrey Johnson, "John Donne and Paolo Sarpi: Rendering the Council of Trent," in *John Donne and the Protestant Reformation: New Perspectives*, ed. Mary Arshagouni Papazian (Detroit, MI: Wayne State University Press, 2003), p. 94.

50 See William J. Bouwsma, *Venice and the Defense of Republican Liberty* (Berkeley, CA: University of California Press, 1968), p. 571.

51 Donne sat for Brackley in the Parliament of 1601 and was later to sit for Taunton in the "addled" Parliament of 1614.

52 See Oakley, op. cit., pp. 32–51.

53 See, e.g., Richard Strier, op. cit., and Joshua Scodel, *Excess and the Mean in Early Modern English Literature* (Princeton, NJ: Princeton University Press, 2002).

12 Winning the initiative

Angus J. S. Fletcher

The present essay belongs to a mixed genre, since it mingles matters of traditional ethics, political history and literature, while in turn this mixture is intended to provide a place especially for the cardinal question for modern science, a discipline determining the shape of the modern world, namely the problem of describing motion. This ultimate scientific concern is so broad in its application that virtually no sphere of human life or thought escapes its influence. Furthermore, our modern world depends historically for its exacting pragmatic experimentalism, leading to a materialist ethics, upon revolutionary changes in the science of motion that effectively began in the late sixteenth and early seventeenth centuries.[1] Much has recently been made of a material use of mechanical devices like clocks, pumps, thermometers and telescopes in these developments, but all such devices depend upon their deep relation to movement, which remains conceptually fundamental. Nor does this founding statement apply merely to Hobbesian thought; it has general force in all the major modern philosophic systems. If these claims are just, there is no way to avoid mixing science and ethics, or literature and ethics, as soon as we cast a philosophical eye upon the omnipresence of movement in human life, including the twists and turns of thought itself.

The politic body

In the West, during virtually all stages and periods of ethical debate, there has been no doubt that ethics involves behavior. Behavior means action, hesitation or inaction, and hence it follows that ethics, while it seems to require reflection upon "values," finally comes down to the study of human behavior as a way of acting. Aristotle classically takes generative form to be a universal logos or principle of change, and then argues in the *Nichomachean Ethics* that "human good turns out to be activity of the soul in accordance with virtue" [1097b–1098a].[2] In this ancient Greek context of *eudaimonia* to be happy implies performing this "activity" of the soul, and the discussion of ethics frequently turns upon subtle readings of the term "active" as applied to soul or mind. (Activity in this radical kinetic sense always means alteration of an object's place or state, whether in and by itself, as when animals grow, occupying more or less space through organic development, or when inanimate things change speed or location.) For Aristotle the ideal testing ground of such action will be the polis, with its swirling social *inter*-actions, and if we carry his thought down toward its ground, we always find that ethics finally requires the study and the understanding of motion as an attribute of social existence.

That extremely general societal claim provides the premise and persistent concern of the present essay, which may be stated as follows: In order for a human to act, he or she must *begin* to act, that is, must somehow initiate a course of action or movement. This start-up will apply to all modes of action, including those where to act is to begin to think and intend with a certain purpose. Students of the origins or *archai* of social customs tell us that source and beginning are not the same, and much obscurity surrounds their difference. Yet we may begin our discussion by noting certain initiatory moments. We reach at once beyond movements of mere physical bodies, and it will be helpful to enlarge our perspective by considering action in a social context, where the agent is a body politic. Leaving aside all subtleties regarding belief, for English-speaking peoples English history provides an archetypal case of articulated political motion.

In a celebrated – indeed classic – article on the powers of the House of Commons Wallace Notestein showed, many years ago, that it was only when the Commons divided and then acted as an ensemble of committees that it was able to win legislative power over the Crown.[3] In the period leading up to the English Civil War the Commons managed, through committee, to move various agendas to the forefront; finally, by the end of the seventeenth century, the lower house became a virtually independent governing body, empowered to make, change and enforce statute law in England. In politics this capacity to act is an equivalent of the individual's power to proceed as an ethical being, by making decisions and plans and then acting upon such initiatives. Now while this analogy is broadly obvious on the political scale of government, it is not so obvious what altogether comprises the problem of "committee" for an individual. Even so, the idea that larger scales could be reduced to individual actions and ethics was not new, and during the early seventeenth century this analogy underwent radical, even catastrophic change. In politics England underwent a civil war before the main issues began to be clear. Meanwhile in scientific matters an immense shift occurs, whereby the Copernican revolution and its legacy influenced all intellectual life. My belief is that science and social awareness initiate by means of articulating subcommittees of the mind. They allow unexpected changes of value to emerge, including necessarily those required for ethical reflection. Modes of self-reflection also change, as with extended dramatic soliloquies in the theater. Articulation is as old as the Greeks, but there appears now to be a different openness to deliberately ambiguous expressions, where articulation becomes increasingly tonal.

If so, it follows that in order to grasp the determining character of the seismic shocks to both politics and intellectual choices, we need to understand their underlying issue, which is to consider how ideas of motion, of movement itself, provide a disturbingly relativistic viewpoint.

In the early seventeenth century motion was redefined, as a basic scientific concern, by Galileo, who gradually developed new concepts and experimental demonstrations (through geometric analysis), in part by thinking about the meaning of the cosmic reorientation devised by Copernicus.[4] This was primarily a reorientation of concern, away from a medieval theory of immanent qualities (as in the theory of impetus), to the modern quantitative theory of inertia, which Galileo discovered. If one were to isolate one cardinal attribute of the new theory, it would be the statement that, in the absence of any interfering or impinging outside force, any object will either stay at rest forever or will continue moving forward in a straight line, forever. *The controlling archetypal shape of all motion in the universe is no longer the circle, as most ancient and medieval philosophers thought, but the rectilinear straight line.*[5] Even Galileo had difficulty in giving up the prestige of circular motions, as distinct from his scientific correspondent, Johannes Kepler, who showed that planetary orbits had to be elliptical. This new idea focuses upon what is called "local motion,"[6] which has the following properties:

a   The new science or "philosophy" singles out movement of some thing from one place to another, as when a rock falls through the air to the ground, a projectile moves from the cannon's mouth, or a ship slides through the water.

b   As a model the local viewpoint keeps the study of motion mainly on the surface of the earth, and only gradually does its implication become clear for extraterrestrial, cosmic spaces as well.

c   Despite all differences from Aristotelian views of movement, this new concept of movement still remains a model of motion for human action – we are terrestrial movers – if we can see the link between local motion in physics and human action in ethics.

d   We may say that even if not often obviously, the Galilean influence would tend to localize thoughts about action as a kind of movement, and this localization confers upon the analogy a distinctly earthbound, experimental and realistic aspect, as occurs in the greatest contemporary play centering upon the problem of motion, namely *Hamlet*.

One wonders, of course, what link exists between the inherently remote world of physics and the immediate scene of ethics, where mind is brought to bear on patterns of human behavior. In the Renaissance period this question was not as stark and forbidding as it is today, for at that time philosophers and poets alike crossed back and forth between their sciences and their imagined constructs by means of endless analogical comparisons – systems were felt to have power if their internal relations of parts bore strong similarities to other loosely parallel networks of relations. Analogy was the central cosmic figure, as it had been for centuries. A great Epicurean vision, Lucretius's *On the Nature of Things*, acquires major intellectual and poetic influence, for its theory of atomism uses the *clinamen* or swerve of the atoms – its cosmogonic initiating moment – as linked by Lucretius to universal forces of desire, sublime energizing powers. In this context the intricate obscurities surrounding what it is to move, to have the quality of motion, had not yet given way to a fully modern quantitative account. Science and art, science and religion, science and politics were all understood as having figurative relations among each other. They become cognitive cousins; one transitional phase of this kinship is to be seen in the persistence of interpreting nature as if it were a sacred text, a piece of the Bible. Most divisions of thought were believed to share in natural magic, as they mirrored each other by analogy. Such was the character of the late Renaissance world picture. When Galileo says that mathematics is the language of science, he is drawing a magic circle that contains both artificial and natural languages.[7]

If we find parallels between the New Science and the Old Philosophy, this promotes translation and navigation between two realms. We may draw analogies between physics and ethics. Aristotle and his followers had classic-ally established the belief that life in general was virtually coterminous with motion and change. The classic text of the *De motu animalia* codified early observations of the most obvious fact in question, namely that animals are seen to be self-moving creatures, whose power to move was a matter of central philosophical concern for Aristotelian science. Given that humans are clearly a kind of animal, albeit animals endowed with manifestly "higher" powers and purposes, it became natural enough in this Aristotelian tradition to ask why they possess such gifts. The question of purposes and ends colored all the interests of science, so that *Why* assumed dominant sway over Aristotelian science at large. This broad picture needs recalling, if we are to ask what happened when the interests of early modern science shifted to questions of *How*.

The familiar simplification – admittedly a cliché – of the shift from Why to How is not entirely without merit here. If medieval scientists felt obliged to ask why things and animals moved, Galilean science began to ask rather how they moved. A medieval scientist like the fourteenth-century Paris master, Jean Buridan,[8] was beginning to limn the new science, but only with Galileo does the commitment to mathematics assume a central ontological as well as epistemological place. Galileo sought better geometric demonstrations and descriptions of the shapes and amounts of movement occurring in any particular case, and for him this search implied a universal principle. The privilege now accorded to rethinking the ancient concern, "Why does motion exist?" pressed heavily on a further higher-order question: How best, how exactly in the most objective fashion, shall we construct our descriptions of movement? Scholastic philosophers had long been preternaturally exacting in their formal and logical concerns for argument, but now the scientist had to construct arguments that also took the palpable actual world into consideration, while holding to the demands of mathematics. Despite all metaphysical implications of the New Science, and resistance from the Church shows how stressful these might be, the answers in physics now were increasingly composed in the form of how-accounts. This is true even with Galileo's major treatises written in dialogue form, where we today may be inclined to neglect the clear scientific exposition, beguiled by the spell of Galileo's rhetorical brilliance. If a stone fell straight down or a projectile moved along a parabolic curve, these phenomena had to be described accurately as objective phenomena, measurable in geometric or numbered quantities. Only after the How of motion had been addressed, could there be found an intelligible Why of motion.

Staging ethics in the drama

Meanwhile this shift applied subtly to human behavior, which, as action, is always a kind of motion or state of rest. Suppose then that we make a more than casual reading of Hamlet's eloquent phrasing, when he describes mankind. Suppose we lean on his lexicon in the following rather alchemical apostrophe, where he rejects the Why in favor of the How, albeit in the usual sense of "how much":

> What a piece of work is a man, how noble in reason, how infinite in faculties, in form and moving how express and admirable, in action how like an angel, in apprehension how like a god: the beauty of the world, the paragon of animals – and yet to me, what is this quintessence of dust?
>
> (2.2.303–8)

In order to communicate Hamlet's inexplicable loss of delight in the world and its beauty, this speech grounds its thought in a new awareness, which is the idea that all our activity, whether on stage or in actual life, is a movement interesting to us chiefly in its mysterious presence rather than for its mysterious Why. Its Why, as we have said, depends upon its How and this dependency becomes the new central interest of philosophy, from which indeed we have not recovered. The Sunday morning world, in Wallace Stevens's vision, serves "an old dependency of day and night," and we may ask, is this a material contingency discovered by science, does the dependency share partially in an older Christian tradition, or are the two worldviews pitched forever in ironic conflict? Such was the Renaissance question also.

Given the analogical framing so common to Renaissance thought, it is convenient to give the drama a cardinal philosophic role as the imaginative theater of acting and taking actions, with all their performing presence and deliberate display. Drama does what other genres only talk about or narrate or perhaps emotively express; but drama enacts, and in that sense gives the noblest presentation of the central philosophic issue for the Renaissance, namely the newly defined and fully reinterpreted Aristotelian question of action and its life-giving or life-denying nature. "For they are actions that a man might play," says Hamlet, as it were deploying an unprecedented economy of social motility, the human version of natural motions in the physical universe. (Much later, in our own time, bodies in nature interact according to the emerging principles of modern physics, and the same equivalence, *pari passu*, aligns a quantized natural philosophy and a fragmented human society.) On this analogy ethics is increasingly reducible to a kind of social physics. The great plays of the Renaissance analyze the sources and designs of all movement in human life and experience; Shakespeare and Galileo are born in the same year. Such historical accidents, even if we include another even more materialist author, Christopher Marlowe, also born in 1564, are perhaps not much more than the convenient markers of a new worldview opening its doors upon a new world of thought. Yet these inventors were typical of their age.

What really counts is the expanding manifold of beliefs and new procedures, all of which seek to make the workings of man, as a "work," part of a controlled *outering* of the objective environment of physical process. Man's inner life is turned outward, as upon a stage. In a sonnet Edmund Spenser had once spoken of a "continual cruel civil war within myself,"[9] and now this war could be seen as a relevant field of transport back and forth between microcosmic and macrocosmic scales of action. Taking opposite sides and finding their mechanisms became a new possibility, as we discover in major analytic dramas of internecine conflict such as *Troilus and Cressida*. As we have said, Professor Notestein showed in his British Academy lecture how the Commons acquired its initiating powers. Prior to the later sixteenth century their role was silently to approve royal prerogative, by *passively* assenting to agendas and orders of the Privy Council. Thereafter, at first slowly and then with gathering speed, the Commons above all found a *voice* through the forming of secondary bodies, those critical Subcommittees of the House, so that eventually a whole new mechanism of governance – politically modeling the governance of the self – broke out into rapid legislative movement on all fronts. What Notestein calls "the rapid evolution in the ways of doing business, the change from a comparatively simple to a highly complex machine"[10] marks the sort of change and motility that we have come to identify in all areas of human activity, as a consequence of social and individual emergence into the modern era.

Returning now to the Aristotelian ground plan, we see more clearly how

Western philosophy in all periods has sought to understand human life in terms of motions on many levels. The ethical question may be reduced to one rather broad issue: where does ethical movement with its principles of action come from, if motion indeed is the sign of human participation in the life process? In his radically important article on the idea of "Self-motion," Professor David J. Furley sets forth the continuing question as to how we shall draw lines, ethically, between the inner life of man (as an animal) and the outer environment of the natural world.[11] Furley discusses the intricate Aristotelian reflections on the role of desire in prompting animal action, whereby the *orekton*, the object of desire, would in some sense appear to cause the animal to move, as for example in its acting to satisfy a hunger. But then, one asks, is not the movement of the self-motion somehow being determined "from the outside?" This raises the issue of decision and especially of intentional thought (*dianoia*), whereby desire becomes a "middle term, which causes motion by being moved" (*De motu animalia*, 703b23–24). As Furley notes,[12] regarding the *De anima* 2.5, Aristotle is troubled by "the difficulty of finding the right language to describe the relation between the soul and the objects of perception," and in turn with the problem of distinguishing between animals that move themselves and inanimate natural bodies which do not have this power to move themselves.

This problem, Furley writes,

> comes into particularly sharp focus in the *Ethics*. In the *Physics* and the biological works, including the *De anima*, Aristotle was concerned with fitting the movements of animals into certain general patterns of explanation. In the *Ethics* he has to find the distinguishing characteristics of a subset of animal movements – namely, human actions for him to decide whether a man is really a self-mover, and in what sense, and when. The notion that the object of desire is what moves a man to action becomes a challenge to the whole concept of moral responsibility.[13]

These questions, we may say, are the essential problems that drive plays like *Troilus and Cressida* and *Hamlet*. They point precisely to the fact that whatever questions of guilt or innocence, good and bad choice, decent and indecent behavior, proper and improper conduct arise in such plays, these points of decision will depend finally upon a higher question: What indeed prompts humans to act in the first place? Hence arises the famed theme of delay in *Hamlet* or the theme of the prompting intermediary (the Pandarus theme) in the *Troilus*. Drama enacts desire and its blockage, actions allowed and actions started, stopped, continued, diverted, and finally interrogated. Ethics, *for the early modern period*, becomes in this light the study of the conditions of winning the initiative.

Gazing toward relative motion

Like the drama then, the New Science asks questions about the first steps taken toward any movement. Ethical reflection is soon led to question something like the relativity in human affairs, as it appears more intelligibly in the celestial universe. Ethical considerations necessarily share in the Galilean revolution of ideas about the correct way to understand starting and stopping motion in the physical world, because at heart all ethical questions involve human behavior, and that in turn is always a modality of action, of acting on the stage of life. Galileo is fully, cautiously aware of theological implications of his research.[14] Numerous shifts occur therein, the most basic being Galileo's persistent search for objective natural fact, towards which he takes several fundamental approaches, guided by his faith in geometrical treatment of instrumental observations. A mathematician by training, he seeks with unerring practicality to perfect observational devices of his time, as with the telescopic discovery of four tiny satellites of Jupiter or the hitherto confusing phases of Venus. (Galileo's mistakes, for example regarding the tides, are not to the purpose here; they involve errors in specific physical assumptions, rather than reversions to medieval Aristotelian science.) Among the issues serving the present set of suggestions might be noted the fact that despite certain deep-seated reservations, he grounded his theory of inertia on the idea that unimpeded movement in straight lines is the founding lawful principle of all natural change and process. Unimpeded rectilinear motion provided Galileo with a new model of "perfection" – we might even call it "imperfection" – supplanting the older circularities, and in turn this preference implied a freedom from the enclosures of what had been seen as a "closed" Ptolemaic world. The larger determining cultural effect will be apparent at once, involving ethics directly and indirectly insofar as ethics ties human action to ultimate reality.

The circle implies stasis; the line implies movement that gets somewhere. The circle implies perfection; the line implies an unknown distance yet to cross before anything like perfection is reached. The circle implies permanence; the line implies progress. The circle permits no promise of deviance; the line allows for digression. In short, no schematic mythology could have shown more stark or profound ethical influences upon judgments of ethical issues than the cosmology arising in the period in question from, let us say, 1564 to 1664. Then, with Newton formulating general laws of motion starting from his perfected law of inertia, along with gravitational theory, modern science inspired a rationalized mechanistic model of universal order. In due course the revolution set in motion by Copernicus, Kepler and above all Galileo was also about to inspire one of the greatest and most deeply relativistic epic visions, namely *Paradise Lost*. This poem has often been thought the high point of the metaphysics of light; equally, and I think more important, it represents the modern world of relative motions. These had long been associated with speculations about possible plural worlds, where celestial bodies would be so numerous as to imply extreme cosmic variability. But with Galileo's telescopic discovery of the moons of Jupiter in 1610 there was no longer any way that cosmology could allow a vision of fixed, ideal, absolute centrality, as of the previous earth-centered model, to carry conviction. All sufficiently massive planetary or astral centers could in turn become sub-centers, dependent upon yet other centers; the ideal, orthodox circles of ancient and medieval astronomy were not tenable. In the Copernican universe, Galileo had hypothetically shown, all motions were relative to each other, and each reference point (each inertial frame) could be taken as "central," depending upon the point of view the astronomer found most convenient. If the four newly discovered satellites orbiting the planet Jupiter implied a new vision of the Medici court (a satellite is literally a courtier, a hanger-on), then there could no longer be any centrally privileged super-center, for Earth too had its satellite, our Moon, and there was every reason to find the system of satellite dependency proliferating forever, to produce in fact a virtually infinite universe. The Papal court, on this plan of motion, could no longer claim absolute centrality; all separate bodies had their own separate inertial frames of reference, providing what came to be known as "Galilean relativity."

In brief, since there now existed a new founding model for any and all major conceptions of the cosmic dance, motion itself – what Spenser had memorably presented as cosmic "change" in his *Mutabilitie Cantos* – at once acquired its own paradoxical mode of centrality, that of the moving center, the opposite of an unmoving central Earth or the even grander deific Aristotelian "unmoved mover." The larger cosmic structures would remain stable as long as all bodies were allowed to continue moving, as if the universe were an immense structure of perpetual motions. Whereas motion other than circular had earlier been the mark of dangerous instability, it now in Newton's world became the emblem of stability. Instead of aspiring to the endless circle and its enclosure, the new picture saw the orbits of planets as continually aspiring to unimpeded rectilinear movement, ever outward, ever expanding. Gravity maintained the ellipses, but the aspiration remained hidden within them. This is the scientific ground for Shakespeare's and Montaigne's vision of human life, where all things change even as we seek to hold them fixed. Indeed they seem to change in direct proportion to our attempt for desperate fixity, as if we suffered obsessive drives to regain the ideal unchanging center.

Nothing could be more powerful for the transformation of modern ethical debate into its many skeptical and relativistic shapes, and we live to this day under the influence of the cosmological transformation, in which the basic theory of how movement works still controls our meditations. In this spirit we have become practical.

A last brief word, then, on what was lost: The Aristotelian universe had been filled with animation, matter embodying self-moving personal souls, and now all that seemed true was the abstracted lawfulness of the geometric descriptions of lines, trajectories, relativities and empty absolute Newtonian space. *Paradise Lost* analyzed thoughts of free will and necessity and especially the *initiating* moments of merely human action, when Adam and Eve discover the consequences of their dangerous curiosity. Thus Milton makes Galileo the half-hidden intellectual hero of his poem, an epic designed, as Doctor Johnson saw so clearly, to render the new knowledge in imaginative, humanized form:

> The heat of Milton's mind may be said to sublimate his learning, to throw off into his work the spirit of science, unmingled with its grosser part. ... He sent his faculties out upon discovery, into worlds where only imagination can travel, and delighted to form new modes of existence, and furnish sentiment and action to superior beings.[15]

Such intellectual voyaging recalls the Elizabethan period, as it always implicitly and more than once explicitly praises Galileo's cosmic voyaging by means of the telescope. The poem succeeds so powerfully no doubt because it comes into being *before* Newtonian orthodoxies of cosmic knowledge take over completely. *Paradise Lost* is still written on the cusp, while the late vision of *Paradise Regained* ends the period when plays like *Hamlet* or Marlowe's *Faustus* could be made.

Anti-poetic, rationalistic, anti-figurative forces would soon become apparent in literary and philosophic history; the field of literature in Europe was soon to be dominated by the realistic novel and by journalism. While a fully rationalized mechanistic worldview promises immense control over nature, the wayward souls of humans – the concern of ethics – seem to have been a modern loser in some sense. The soul, to employ anachronistic language, would more than ever be vulnerable to the dreams of reason. Of all the adjectives commonly applied to the Newtonian world picture, none is more frequent than the word "cold." This would seem to tell us that no advance comes without a loss, and the more we note our awesome control over nature, through technology, the more we note the shadows falling over this dread consequence. Our ethics are still entangled, no doubt threatened, by the expanding vision and the contracting global fact first set forth by the New Science with all its inevitable extensions.

Western ethics were thus cast into a troubled, yet promising Faustian worldview, as baroque skepticism pitched philosophy (natural and moral) into a changed modern condition. Necessarily this had to be what we might call "ethics after the New Philosophy" – as John Donne wrote, "And new Philosophy calls all in doubt" – the plague of uncertainty shows the iron hand of modern science enforcing doubt about ethical assumptions. On that basis, as Bernard Williams puts it in a survey of ethical reflection, the New

Science might be seen to have introduced a "proposition about the universe [its fundamental relativity of motion] which, if true, seems to threaten the possibility of moral thought or some vital part of it."[16] Much has been written about this Pyrronism of the early modern world, except that insufficient attention has been given to what might, fundamentally, be called its positive potential, whereby it intersects with ethical imaginings. Sextus Empiricus, so important to Montaigne, outlined the skeptical philosophy under the prime heading *modes* of thought, those modes leading to suspension of dogmatic judgment. Sextus perceived the central issue here, namely that doubt had to proceed modally and this, as he said, assumed that every mode was in fact a trope, and this would include every mode of what is called a belief. Modernity begins to earn the logical weight of its name, as a way of seeing the world *modally*, in terms of values and beliefs as uncertain, merely possible structures of thought.[17] For example, the grandest figurative equivalence of the seventeenth century, the prestigious rise of the Sublime, was in fact a poetic "displacement" of the Supreme Being.

The suggestion is clear: in some sense the New Science forced ethics to notice the extent to which ethical values and beliefs were more like poetic figures than ontological propositions. This may seem strange to the present account, owing to its focus on Galileo, but my point is that increasingly the poetry of the modern period has for us a deeply scientific cast, and science often seems our best poetry. The onset of modernity implies such an acceptance of figuration, and in that sense, the intellectual initiatives of the New Philosophy – its powers of committee-like articulation – opened up simultaneously new powers of action and new dangers in taking premature or unwarranted action. (How readily today in the United States we see dangers in the unchecked misuse of committee!) I have allowed free rein to the game of late Renaissance analogizing, seeing Commons' committee-driven initiative as a macrocosmic parallel to decisions taken microcosmically in the mind. That free rein is itself a troped idea. It remains an irony of intellectual history that a hardening physical science of motion should generate a new vision of ethical ambiguities, but that I believe to have been the case, as if following an Emersonian law of compensation. At the very least it appears that the New Science separates ethics from the authority of prescriptive religion and custom, impelling ethical reflection to accommodate the rationalized science of the Newtonian world, much as we find later, fully assimilated, in Alexander Pope's *Essay on Man*.

If the broad cultural transition into this deist worldview saw the rise of a new cosmology based on the primacy of motion, what follows is that the historian has no choice but to redefine the role of fixity as a source of framing authority. If motion in every discernible aspect provides a disturbing source of ethical questioning, then the very idea of a conceptual scheme, as Donald Davidson put it, comes under scrutiny. As so often before, a critical issue emerges: how can a system based on cosmically primary physical motion ever acquire framing fixity? The idea of frame itself must either dissolve in deconstructive Derridean fashion or else be redefined according to the virtually gyroscopic vision I have proposed, motion and mobility themselves becoming an independent object of modern ethical study. This, of course, is what skeptics like Montaigne had understood in rough and ready terms.

Since antiquity there had been many confrontations between philosophy and the mutable aspect of worldly phenomena. Plato's "idea of the good," the Stoic's withdrawal into a controlled *apatheia*, a Kantian logic of categorical imperatives, even a Humean associative belief in benevolence or later the Nietzschean cult of "noble" human powers – all these are instances of philosophy meeting ideas of phenomenal change. When mystery enters the ethical picture, we get theories of personal illumination, as with a Meister Eckhart, or the mixed resources displayed in American Transcendentalism.

With all such systems aimed at grounding ethical thought, there seems to exist a way, if only metaphorically, to link the discourse to common human needs. It is significant, therefore, that when modern science bases its chief study upon the analysis of motion, it shifts the inward humanized aspect of the ethical to an outward naturalistic aspect. By pointing outward, as it were, motion-study disturbs the inner frame, because motion in all its complex human experience is precisely most present in what we call *the actual environment*, where life occurs and for which the term "life" names a meaningful concept for creatures existing beyond and outside the merely human. In fact movement or, as we say, actions taken in our uncertain world, lead to periodic crises and anomalies which are caused especially by our clinging to improperly fixated axioms of Whitehead's "misplaced concreteness." By contrast, with any significant human action and choice there are always too many factors to be considered, making rigid adherence to fixed frameworks a most unlikely route toward success. Our human world, as genuinely gifted political leaders know, differs from the practice of logic and mathematics or the strictly controlled technological manipulation of physical processes. Deliberate human choosing is rarely an elegant affair. There is always something experimental about it.

The issue then is to accept that with the coming of modern scientific artifice the disciplines of ethical control and choice need somehow to link up with human uncertainties. One slightly comforting thought remains: Galilean science *in Galileo's hands* had itself deliberately opposed the "perfection" of Platonic vision and Aristotelian essentialism; it had countered a medieval inheritance that tended to find authority in the absolute. It sought a method rather resembling poetics. By admitting that action disturbs frame, Galileo had argued that the controlling orders of nature are not inherently opposed to our human acceptance of destabilizing counter-forces. The symbolic distance between Galileo and poets like late Shakespeare or the Spenser of the *Mutability Cantos* is by no means as great as their mere professional differences might suggest. They are all asking how initiating an action or making a move can occur, without losing grip on some stable idea of good and evil. In this context a poet like Milton is even more powerfully alive to the philosophic issues. We are left, I believe, wondering if the imperatives of dream and imagination are not necessary components of all modern ethical inquiry, since the dream is the scene of all movements occurring in our less than conscious minds.

What finally then is "the committee?" Clearly it implies a kind of philosophical tropology, that aspect of our actions that requires turning from the path of mere authority. It would seem that the committee is a partial agency – in the mind and in society – that manages to resist the global dominance of "monarchic" power claiming the rights of undisputed consistency. In a post-Newtonian situation we ourselves cannot but remember that ethics is also entangled with poetry, and as with all poetry it requires that we learn how to read the rhythms and the ambiguities. If there is a metaphoric link between mind and politics, we shall have to learn the interpretation of that link. If empowered mind is a system of mental committees, that neurophysiological parallel also needs skilled reading. Imagination continues to imply an ethical dream, and while, ironically, we know that art is never successfully composed by committee, science customarily involves just such group effort, as if employing a self-organizing, self-perpetuating Committee of the House.

We must therefore ask, should we not defend the committee of the self, the committee of the singular mind? Today, as earlier in the Renaissance, ethics simultaneously asks how the individual person "takes arms against a sea of troubles" and also how society manages to achieve a comity of constraints, to prevent individual action from excess. Like Hamlet, we must interrogate the dream, in order to discover what is right and what is possible. In all such modern situations we are asking about the ways we humans engage with ethical turnings, as a matter of the ways in which, as the Bible says, we "live, and move, and have our being."

Notes

1 This essay grew out of research for a book from Harvard University Press (Cambridge, MA), due to appear in January 2007, entitled *Time, Space and Motion in the Age of Shakespeare*.

2 I quote from a longer passage quoted in turn by Jonathan Lear, *Aristotle: The Desire to Understand* (Cambridge: Cambridge University Press, 1988), p. 162. In the context of motion theory, see Martha Nussbaum, *De Motu Animalium* (Princeton, NJ: Princeton University Press, 1978). Nussbaum has written extensively on relations between literature and philosophy.

3 "The Winning of the Initiative by the House of Commons" (1924), in *Studies in History: British Academy Lectures*, ed. by Lucy S. Sutherland (Oxford: Oxford University Press, 1966), pp. 145–203.

4 See Thomas Kuhn, *The Copernican Revolution: Planetary Astronomy in the Development of Western Thought* (Cambridge, MA: Harvard University Press, 1956), chapter 6, "The Assimilation of Copernican Astronomy."

5 On the complex matter of rectilinear motion, see Dudley Shapere, *Galileo: A Philosophical Study* (Chicago, IL: University of Chicago Press, 1974), pp. 87–125.

6 On local motion and its implications, see E.A. Burtt, *The Metaphysical Foundations of Modern Science*. Doubleday Anchor reprint of the 1932 revised edition; this volume is now reprinted by Dover Books. See chapter 3 on Galileo, and especially on "The Science of Local Motion," pp. 72–78. Burtt's book, despite the obviously personal animadversions of Russell, remains in my view the most suggestive of all studies of the interaction of science and metaphysics in the seventeenth century. The reader may wish to consult Gerald Holton on Burtt: *Thematic Origins of Scientific Thought: Kepler to Einstein* (Cambridge, MA: Harvard University Press, 1980), pp. 456–60.

7 The passage occurs in *The Assayer*. See Stillman Drake, ed., *Discoveries and Opinions of Galileo* (New York: Doubleday Anchor Books, 1957), pp. 237–38.

8 On Buridan, see A.C. Crombie, *Medieval and Early Modern Science* (New York: Doubleday Anchor Books, 1959), pp. 2.67 ff.

9 *Amoretti*, No. 44. For a concentrated Renaissance use of the various senses of motion, see Shakespeare's Sonnet 94 ("They that have power to hurt, and will do none ... "), where images of movement illuminate problems of wealth, power and dignity, with all their paradoxical mutability. The topos is old; the treatment by Shakespeare is new and memorable, as Empson showed in *Some Versions of Pastoral*. The reader may wish to consult my recent article on Spenser's final vision of universal motility: "Complexity and the Spenserian Myth of Mutability," in *Literary Imagination*, 6:1 (Winter 2004): 1–22. This article makes use of Complexity Theory as developed by John Holland, Murray Gell-Mann and other complexity theorists.

10 Notestein, op. cit., *Studies in History*, 190.

11 This essay appears in Amélie Rorty, ed., *Essays on Aristotle's Ethics* (Berkeley, CA: University of California Press, 1980), pp. 55–68 and appears also in M.L. Hill and J.G. Lennox, eds, *Self-Motion: From Aristotle to Newton* (Princeton, NJ: Princeton University Press, 1994), pp. 3–14.

12 Furley, "Self-Motion," in Rorty, ed., op. cit., p. 61.

13 Ibid., p. 62. In this context self-motion becomes the ethicist's "autonomy."

14 See especially the Galileo "Letter to the Grand Duchess Christina," in Drake, ed., *Discoveries and Opinions of Galileo*. See above, note 7. The horrifying history of Bruno's fate indicates fully how fearful might be the scene of dogmatic debate over authority and belief.

15 I quote from my copy of the first American edition of Johnson's *Works*, the "Life of Milton," in *Works of Samuel Johnson, LL.D* (New York: Alexander V. Blake, 1843), 2.42b.

16 "Ethics," in A.C. Grayling, ed., *Philosophy 1: A Guide Through the Subject* (Oxford: Oxford University Press, 2003), p. 575. This issue arises in the course of Williams's commentary on free will, a theme central to all of Milton's poetry, early and late, always advanced by Milton in connection with the New Science, mainly cosmology, but also early modern biology. On the latter, as regards vitalism and political philosophy, see John Rogers, *The Matter of Revolution: Science, Poetry, and Politics in the Age of Milton* (Ithaca, NY: Cornell University Press, 1998). Rogers focuses his discussion of late seventeenth-century British politics on the influence of William Harvey's discovery of the circulation of the blood. Rogers's very interesting materialist study, while not treating conceptual philosophic issues, shows how vitalism made certain ideas of movement, e.g., the blood circulating,

symbolically available to poets and politicians, even as it promoted a "poetic" escape from all the more fundamental problems of motion. As distinct from this vitalist account, I stress fundamental conceptual issues of thinking itself, such as scientists and philosophers – not the politicians – worried over and argued about. These more basic questions belong mainly to physics and astronomy, of course, and their secondary literature, available to us in the present, is extremely large. The reader may usefully consult the text and extensive bibliography in Peter Dear, *Discipline and Experience: The Mathematical Way in the Scientific Revolution* (Chicago, IL: University of Chicago Press, 1995); also, on experiment and Cartesian mechanism, Dear, *Revolutionizing the Sciences: European Knowledge and its Ambitions, 1500–1700* (Princeton, NJ: Princeton University Press, 2001), with its documentation and scientific "Dramatis Personae."

17 The suggestion that skeptical interest in modal figuration leads directly to modal logic would be incorrect, since C.I. Lewis did not invent modal logic, to deal with conditionals, until the early twentieth century. However, there is a family resemblance: when poets and ethical thinkers pursue the contingent aspect of choice, decision and action, they are thinking modally. Strict entailments become virtually impossible and are replaced by relations of possibility versus necessity, so that ethical situations are understood as a) actually true, but might be otherwise, b) might possibly be true, or c) must be true, although this claim is itself subject to worries over contingency. My concern here is broadly to indicate that, with the early modern period, *occult forces* were liberated from their medieval immanent status and became interesting only insofar as their operations could be discerned as law-bound names for recurrent phenomena, e.g., as in Newton's account of gravity, the "laws of motion." Gravity remained occult – a mysterious action at a distance – but its operation was knowable under a law. This advance resulted, I believe, from a finer Galilean appreciation of the *modalities of our perception of motion* in the universe and then by extension in human affairs. Our perceptions come under fresh questioning during the seventeenth century, as with Hobbes and his concern with ever-shifting theatrical personae.

Part V

Assessments

13 Ethics or politics?

An exchange passing through the *Areopagitica*

Sharon Achinstein and Marshall Grossman

Headnote

This exchange between Sharon Achinstein and the editor began several years ago – viva-voce – when Sharon and I were "down the hall" colleagues at the University of Maryland, and I was at the beginning of what she thought an ill-advised project on the ethics of reading. Sharon's concern that the turn to ethics would indicate a turn away from politics needs to be addressed, and as the present volume is intended to stimulate a broader conversation on the modes of and implications of an ethical engagement with Renaissance literature, I proposed including our exchange of views on the subject in the volume. When Sharon decamped for Oxford, the exchange continued cyber-spatially, punctuated by occasional "in real life" encounters at conferences mutually attended. Unlike essays, conversations are interminable by nature. A portion of this one, however, is here edited and fixed in print.

***

MG: We might begin with definitions. I started this project with a simplistic argument that ethics was about determining what the good is and politics about achieving it. Thus ethics would be about desire (what should I want?) and politics about power and strategy (how do I get what I want?). Is the turn to ethics necessarily a turn away from politics?

SA: Is the turn to ethics a turn away from politics? As a "political critic," I cannot of course accept the distinction between ethics and politics. Because the conditions in which we are able to *do* ethics, as you say, to "determine what the good is," are indeed political conditions. These conditions include not only our access to information, scholarship, and other people; our awareness of multiplicities in culture, society and status; our freedom from basic wants such as illness, hunger and violence; and our identity structures in which respect is enabled or denied (e.g. as "irrational women," or even under slavery, torture, or threat, can we "determine what the good is"?). But it seems to me that you are asking not about a "dialectical" ethics, but whether there can there be a transcendental ethics, that is, where politics or ethics can be morally good and not simply ideological? That is, can we escape dialectic?

MG: I'm not all that sure ethical and moral notions of the good are compatible. Reading the essays in this volume that deal with questions of political violence and reading the *New York Times* have conspired to show me how difficult this question is. Richard Strier's essay in this volume (Chapter 10), representing morality as a prescriptive and institutional mandate at odds with the personal responsibility assumed by ethics, suggests that ethics is precisely a dialectical alternative to ideological morality. I am not quite ready to give up on the idea that ethics is prior to politics and so, all politics has either a recognized or unrecognized ethics on which it is grounded. But I would not want to argue it as though power is not in itself an object of desire and "the good" is, not only there to be discovered, but universal. When we juxtapose the idea that ethics is prior to politics with the dynamic reality of contradiction, the recognition that one person's benefit is often another's cost, a couple of questions emerge: 1. Does the turn to an ethical ground for political actions necessarily produce an appeal to the absolute? Can there be a dialectical ethics that stands against, or at least apart from, the morality supported by the various "ideological state apparatuses?"[1] 2. Conversely, can politics produce an ethics that is anything other than an ideology? If not, what, if any, are the proper restraints on political violence – other than greater violence?

SA: The historian in me knows there have been many answers to this question, Kant's being one of the most notable; but more recently, and in wake of the post 9/11 situation, even anti-foundationalists have found themselves in knots about it. Slavoj Žižek, for example, following on a romantic tradition of sublime violence, advances:

> The notion of the radical political Act as the way out of this democratic deadlock … an Act [that can] retroactively [change] the very co-ordinates into which it intervenes … an Act proper cannot be contained within the limits of democracy (conceived as a positive system of legitimizing power through free elections). The Act occurs in an emergency when one has to take the risk and act without any legitimization, engaging oneself into a kind of Pascalean wager that the Act itself will create the conditions of its retroactive "democratic" legitimization.[2]

This admission of an actuating violence has a long history of romantic engagement, with the appeal to the extraordinary, or the sublime, or the Holy Spirit, or the revolution: but I would rather put in my lot with the flawed Enlightenment and think that human rights, justice and the rest are indeed implicated in histories of oppression and opportunism, but that as ideals they can indeed ground movements for change in the political and in the material. I like my ethics transcendental; so that leaves me endlessly attached to the ongoing – and fallible – process of Enlightenment.

Perhaps it is indeed closer to what Derrida came to at the end of his life, with his concept of "a democracy to come": not to be the future *implementation* of democracy, but the presence of hope, futurity, and openness that enables justice to be distinguished from the law. As Derrida wrote in 2004, "the locution 'democracy to come' should above all not mean, namely, a regulative Idea in the Kantian sense, but also what it *remained*, and could not but remain (*demeurer*), namely, the inheritance of a promise."[3] Derrida elaborates,

> The expression 'democracy to come' … calls for an urgent and interminable political critique. A weapon aimed at the enemies of democracy, it protests against all naiveté and every political abuse, every rhetoric that would present as a present or existing democracy, as a de facto democracy, what remains inadequate to the democratic demand, whether nearby or far away, at home or somewhere else in the world.
>
> ("Rogue States," 331)

In this essay, with reflections on "rogue" states and the binary opposition between rational and irrational political orders that the post-9/11 discourse has let fly, Derrida uses deconstruction not only to query the terms of polemical division, but the systems of thought that underlie the "clash of civilizations" approach. I feel Derrida was coming to sound more and more like a Habermasian socialist; indeed a very recent collection of essays shows him to be in the same orbit as Habermas drawing attention to the merging, or at least the convergence, of these two thinkers recently over issues such as Europe, terrorism, and foreigners' rights.[4]

That kind of justice – yet-to-come – is what can overcome the untranslatable: what Derrida has called a "messianicity without messianism." In his essay "Faith and Knowledge," Derrida movingly wrote of the advent of justice as an "opening to the future." There justice would be distinguished from right, for it alone

> allows the hope, beyond all "messianisms" of a universalizable culture of singularities, a culture in which the abstract possibility of the impossible translation could nevertheless be announced. This justice inscribes itself in advance in the promise, in the act of faith or in the appeal to faith that inhabits every act of language and every address to the other.[5]

MG: Leaving aside whether, or for how long, Derrida and Habermas walk together, we seem to find ourselves at some kind of chiasmic crossing here – with you looking to the specter of the transcendental haunting dialectics and me looking for the specter of the dialectical in an otherwise immanent ethics.

The phrase "messianicity without messianism" suggests that Derrida was thinking about Walter Benjamin. I wonder whether Vicky Kahn's discussion of Benjamin's reworking – in the *Origins of the German Tragic Drama* – of Carl Schmitt's theory of the exception moves in the direction of an ethics that does not displace the political.[6] The situation of the baroque as Benjamin described it resonates with Benjamin's political situation and, unfortunately, with ours too. Is an ethics derivable from his study of seventeenth-century German melodrama that remains valid in twentieth-century Germany and twenty-first-century America? If so is that ethics inscribed within or grounded by a political similarity among the three?

Consider the case of iconoclasm: is seventeenth-century Christian iconoclasm fundamentally different from contemporary Islamic iconoclasm? Were the roundheads wrong to smash up churches? Had they destroyed Kings College Chapel, would the act resemble the Taliban's destruction of those ancient images of Buddha? Burning the Danish embassy and smashing saints and crosses both appeal for ground to the same Hebraic proscription of graven images. But as a political act, seventeenth-century iconoclasm looks to me much more promising than contemporary Islamic iconoclasm. When we go down the path of a politically defined or contested ethic, do we wind up justifying fundamentalist Mullahs as reacting against neocolonialism – as some on the left do? I find this unpalatable. What in politics allows us to say something is wrong? Alternatively, how might we formulate an ethics that efficiently distinguished the iconoclasm of the seventeenth-century Puritans or the twentieth-century Taliban from, say, German legal proscriptions of the Swastika?

Is there a place for the enlightenment in this? Like you I'm partial to the enlightenment, but precisely because it presents or promotes a notion of "reason" as absolute and even as I embrace that notion of reason, I am persuaded by Adorno and Horkheimer's very reasonable demonstration that the same shadow of the absolute that enlightens the enlightenment inevitably darkens it as well.[7]

SA: I don't think I have much to say about iconoclasm in the abstract: the many histories of iconoclasm tell me that there is not "one" iconoclasm that can be blamed and another forgiven: each must be understood, I think, in relation to the particular social, economic, and political conditions in which it occurs: if I were a sixteenth-century adherent of the Old Faith, I would have found the Reformers' iconoclasm obscene, but as I view it from today, I can now understand that iconoclasm as enabling a particular formation of early modernity; I can see it as a "rational" mode of political action and as a kind of speech. Surely iconoclasm speaks a violence that is the demise of politics and law: that is, where politics and law have failed to adjudicate conflict. But there are perhaps conflicts that politics and law fail to recognize: cannot violence against women be understood in the same light?[28] In these conflicts which politics and law fail to recognize, ethics is needed; but ethics understood as within the material, the real, the here and now: a call to justice, but a call that cannot be made outside lived experience.

With this thought in mind, I turn to *Areopagitica*, and its building on the momentum of iconoclasm, and ask how it becomes engaged with its political, legal, and ethical projects. I do think that the civil war context has been inadequately addressed in *Areopagitica*: it is, after all, a text written in time of war. What must it have meant to stand up for freedom of speech in the autumn of 1644 when Parliament was tendering to the King in Oxford its Propositions to be considered at the Treaty of Uxbridge and at the same time, waging yet another campaign of the civil war? There was in November 1644 a sense of the long war behind, and the long war ahead to come: the twenty-seven propositions were in fact totally unrealistic, and Charles' typically shrewd and terse reply practically throws them out of court.[9] I think of *Areopagitica* as a wartime tract, for its rousing evocations of the "vast city of Refuge," a city "beseig'd and blockt about," a city where warring and seeking after truth are identical: "the shop of warre hath not there more anvils and hammers waking, to fashion out the plates and instruments of armed Justice in defence of belieaguer'd Truth."[10] It's a wartime tract, also for its metaphors, and particularly for its figuring books as assailants. The "Dragons Teeth" metaphor too – springing up "armed men" (YP.2.592).

MG: As a wartime tract, the *Areopagitica* makes overt the fissuring of the revolutionary front, does it not? The tract works on at least three different and ascending levels of generality. On a personal level, Milton responds not only to the legal suppression of *The Doctrine and Discipline of Divorce* but to a vicious smear campaign conducted against him by Presbyterians in the Westminster Assembly and their allies in Parliament – who branded him a libertine.[11] On a political level both the divorce tracts and the *Areopagitica* work to undermine the Presbyterian legislative attempts to claim divine grounds for civil law after the reformation's reduction of the sacraments from visible rites governing and structuring communal living to a few, largely memorial and personal transactions. This is especially clear in the divorce tracts, which attack the one "civil" institution that could advert to the scriptural endorsement of Jesus Christ. On this level the politics of the divorce tracts become portable, in the sense that they operate not only in the immediate historical situation of 1644–45, but in other situations in which forces are similarly opposed.

One needs only to follow the present debates on same-sex marriage and civil unions to see the vitality of Milton's arguments against legislating sacraments. While George Bush invokes the state's obligation to protect the sanctity of marriage between a man and a woman, for Milton sanctity is simply not a legal category. "What God has joined" is sanctified. But neither the state nor the individuals the state "marries" are in a position to know what matches have been so joined.[12] Following Milton's logic, the state has only to do with civil unions – the material, contractual obligations couples have to each other and the children they might produce – but nothing to do with any sacramental joining, which falls entirely outside its worldly ordinance.

On the most general level, however, the *Areopagitica* operates ethically as well as politically, because it internalizes the determination of right and wrong, rendering it as a conflict to be resolved – again, and again – by individual judgment:

> Good and evill we know in the field of this World grow up together almost inseparably; and the knowledge of good is so involv'd and inter-woven with the knowledge of evill, and in so many cunning resemblances hardly to be discern'd, that those confused seeds which were impose'd on *Pysche* as an incessant labour to cull out, and sort asunder, were not more intermixt. It was from out the rinde of one apple tasted, that the knowledge of good and evill as two twins cleaving together leapt forth into the World. And perhaps this is that doom which *Adam* fell into of knowing good and evill, that is to say of knowing good by evill. As therefore the state of man now is; what wisdome can there be to choose, what continence to forbeare without the knowledge of evill?
>
> (YP 2.514)

It seems to me that this passage vitiates any appeal to a prescriptive morality in the fallen world. The *Areopagitica* posits civil society as the result rather than the cause of a collective process through which just judgments are – eventually – recognized by a community of truth seekers. In this respect Habermas is a Miltonian and the public sphere he associates with the eighteenth-century is already imagined in the middle of the seventeenth. If one thinks about the presentation of the fall in *Paradise Lost*, one sees Milton implicitly extend this ethic of personal confrontation and choice even to the prelapsarian garden. There the prescriptive morality of the single prohibition, enforced by a present and accessible creator, derives its nobility from extension in time. It is not just that Adam and Eve must not eat the forbidden fruit, but that they must choose not to eat it each and every minute – again, and again – to eternity. Anticipating this in the *Areopagitica*, Milton paradoxically represents the fall itself not simply as *felix culpa*, but as something approaching a moral necessity:

> If every action which is good, or evill in man at ripe years, were to be under pittance, and prescription, and compulsion, what were virtue but a name, what praise could be then due to well-doing, what grammercy to be sober, just or continent? many there be that complain of divin Providence for suffering *Adam* to transgresse, foolish tongues! when God

gave him reason, he gave him freedom to choose, for reason is but choosing; he had been else a meer artificiall *Adam*, such an *Adam* as he is in the motions.

(YP 2.527)

The universal to which Milton appeals is not dicta or revelation but reason. The ethic of the *Areopagitica* demands a commitment to one's reason over one's passions on the one hand, and the prescriptive determinations of moral or political institutions on the other. Whether such a commitment is possible or not, and particularly whether "reason" is itself anything other than politically determined, remains, however, an elusive question.

Because the *Areopagitica* is a wartime text, taking sides in a context in which books really do "spring up armed men," the more concrete question of political violence cannot be avoided. As much as Milton's resistance to licensing is principled and reasonable, his conviction that *unlicensed* printing will help "truth" prevail is also a conviction that "truth" is not going to displace the Presbyterian establishment unless it first prevails in the army. Having already lived through a civil war and given the political alignments of 1644, he knows that lives are at stake. He knows with some urgency that if the Presbyterians succeed in engineering the return of Charles I, people to whom he feels close will die. Within a few years, he will write that to prevent such an outcome, Charles I had to die. Milton will argue that Charles's death was both just and necessary. He will also accept the political violence of Pride's purge, the murderous suppression of the army levelers and Cromwell's dissolution of the rump.

The *Areopagitica* is a political document, engaged in a context that includes war. But operating in this context, the *Areopagitica* calls for a separation of divine and civil law that is as applicable now as it was then, because its application remains reasonable, which is to say, because my reason mandates that I choose to affirm it. It looks also to an ethic that gives a concomitant privilege to an individual's reasoned judgment and demands that an individual accept responsibility for the consequences of the judgments he or she makes. This ethic extrapolates from its political context a procedure that purports to apply universally. This is where Adorno and Horkheimer would, I believe, locate the violence that inheres in the negative moment of "the dialectic of reason." The "natural" law of reason remains outlaw, in the sense that it trumps the legislated laws of civil society. But reason also kills – outside the law. Milton accepts that in a fallen world, in which reason confronts unreason, reason sometimes mandates violence. Milton, however, still lives in a world in which reason is right reason; personal judgment is still mediated by the absolute good that is its origin and the continued advisory presence of the holy spirit. In our present world, unmoored from and justly suspicious of any such appeal to the absolute, however, the privilege Milton grants to reason is itself politicized. I wonder if, in our political context, a Miltonic reliance on reason would not turn out to be the sovereignty of the individual, in the sense of an ethic that equated reasoned choice to declaring the exception? (I'm not sure whether to think of this as a modernist baroque or a baroque modernism.) Is there at that point a functional distinction between Schmitt's sovereignty and Hobbes' submission?

SA: Which is why the turn to Schmitt is at once intriguing and disturbing. With this conservative critique of liberalism emerging out of the experience of failed Weimar democracy, Schmitt gives us an essentially Hobbesian account of power (and yes, one can see why in our post 9/11 moment, that could seem relevant); but I am wary of this flirtation – it's one which threatens as I see it to negate the political and even the concept of the state by refusing to accept any normative claims. Milton's "armed men" vocabulary seems to draw upon the necessity of a "law preserving violence" that, as Benjamin, with an indebtedness to Schmitt's theory of sovereignty, points out, is always "a threatening violence."[13] But when Habermas criticizes Benjamin's violence essay (and the figure of Schmitt lurking there), he warns that these authors championed "the violent destruction of the normative as such," a "politics of pure means."[14] Schmitt's approach to tyranny – the tyrant as one who suspends positive law but thereby effects sovereignty – is radically different from Milton's description, not solely because Milton believes in God, but because for Milton, the normative critique is still very much possible, the structures of reform are *working*. He engaged within known political (and aesthetic) structures *always*.

Does Milton reflect on violence in ways that lead him to present a new case for liberty? Verses pinned to his door in 1642 "when the City expected an assault" make light of the conventions of epic heroism at the same time as calling upon their power, with the hope that poetry can be a "counterforce to force."[15] But in the military-minded *Areopagitica*, there seems to be a move to distinguish kinds of violence and to conflate others. War in *Areopagitica* is present in the term "warfaring," but the editorial correction there may signal an uncertainty (2.515).[16] Milton describes his ideal soldier: "He that can apprehend and consider vice with all her baits and seeming pleasures, and yet abstain, and yet distinguish, and yet prefer that which is truly better, he is the true warfaring Christian." But this is not an incitement to do violence, to attack: it is rather a defensive posture that deploys its better knowledge and discretion for the purpose not even of self-defense, but of withdrawal: the Stoical norm is in place. (One wonders how it would have been possible to "abstain" in this sense when faced with Prince Rupert's troops bearing down on Brentwood in summer 1642, when it looked to all Londoners as if the King's army would strike the city with like brutality, what one pamphlet called "the inhuman and barbarous actions of the Cavaliers," as that town, just ten miles from Westminster, had suffered.)[17] Milton's speaker of *Sonnet VIII*, "When the assault was intended to the City," calls his doors "defenceless," hardly to be considered "warfaring" – the protection sought seems rather that of a noncombatant, one whose allegiance is to Art not War. There is something peculiarly withdrawn from the fierce hatreds of Milton's divorce tracts and the earlier anti-episcopal, iconoclastic writings when we get to his *Areopagitica*. Towards the end of the tract, Milton takes up his martial imagery in earnest, with the "free and open encounter" between Truth and Falsehood taking place whilst the doors of the Temple of Janus are open, a time of war; and yet their encounter, their "grappling" (561), is still within the field of sport. The "warfaring" Christian is not really heading out into battle, but into an athletic contest.

In the end, I think *Areopagitica*'s warfaring posture not only stays away from the actualities of conflict, but also refuses the Hobbesian genealogy of society out of warfare; he rejects the Hobbesian wartime origins of the normative (*Leviathan*, xii, 8).[18] Milton's warring violences are at best moderated through classical sport or romance convention, and this is a reluctance to consider violence as the starting point for an account of liberty. And all too soon in *Areopagitica* the imagery turns to "mining knowledge" (562): this metaphoric instability to me suggests a refusal to be truly "warfaring." The tract refrains from cheap propagandizing protest against the monstrous behavior of the Cavaliers, the infamies of Prince Rupert or the inflated barbarity of the Irish enemy; there is a measured posture that must have something to do with accommodation and inclusiveness. But in *Areopagitica*, there is a lived experience of collective action: even in disagreement, in times of war, the city-dwellers *and their enemies alike* are pursuing common aims: the pursuit of Truth.

MG: Would you agree, then, that the ethic of the *Areopagitica*, as distinct from Milton's ethic, is neither for nor against any specified political violence? It seems to me that what you have described is an ethic of restraint mediated by the submission of passion to reason that tends to restrict violence to defensive action. Milton anticipates the enlightenment insofar as he implies that if judgment is deferred until reason discerns truth, violence becomes unnecessary because truth commands the agreement of the reasonable. By invoking his belief in the absolute truth of God, Milton defers this moment of collectively perceived truth "till her masters second comming." It is interesting, however, that Milton steps back from this pacific deferral (which perhaps seems perpetual to us, but which many of Milton's contemporaries expected to be finite and brief) to the present tasks of collection and construction embodied in "the sad friends of Truth" who "went up and down" to gather her up "limb by limb still as they could find them" (YP 2.549) and the builders of the temple "some cutting, some squaring the marble, others hewing the cedars." Like the placement of *Samson Agonistes* after *Paradise Regained* in the 1671 volume, these figures return the reader from the vision of unity in the truth to daily and enduring engagement with the work of this world. "There must be many schisms and many dissections made in the quarry and in the timber, ere the house of God can be built. And when every stone is laid together, it cannot be united into a continuity, it can but be contiguous in this world" (YP 2.555). The implied ethos is subtle because the formal fullness and sufficiency of truth must be anticipated without presuming to know its full content. Judgment must be made – to motivate correct action in the present, but judgment must also be withheld to the anticipated end of time. Is this "messianicity without messianism"? To be sure Milton says the messiah has come and will return to make Truth whole. But, in the meantime, it remains necessary that her "sad friends" gather up the scattered limbs, judging them according to the justice to come. In the meantime, their task entails confronting and resisting those who would obstruct it.

We should recall that the *Areopagitica* – in its immediate historical context – was an act of civil disobedience: published without a license and bearing Milton's name on the title page (though not that of the printer). The printing of the pamphlet enacted the distance between civil law and individual ethos invoked within it. *The Doctrine and Discipline of Divorce* had been called in and its author denounced as a libertine in sermons delivered before Parliament, so Milton had to know that putting his name on the title page of the *Areopagitica* put him at legal (and in those violent and unstable times, possibly extralegal) risk. Because Milton knows that books sometimes spring up armed men, I would not assume that this act of non-violent resistance implies any rejection of violence. It is rather what Milton's judgment demands of Milton in the moment.

SA: Yes, disobedience: but nowhere is disobedience presented as violence. We need a more careful distinction between "violence" and "power" than what is offered in any Schmitt-inspired analysis. Even the daring angel Abdiel, in his great act of resistance in *Paradise Lost*, has only the authority of his words until *later* he's vindicated by the deity. Abdiel's signal presence at the beginning of the war in heaven – he strikes the first blow – in *Paradise Lost* is justified by God's having commended his actions and given him super-supernatural powers. Milton's *Samson Agonistes*, an exploration of the inexplicability of divine action, makes violence wholly instrumental. The ethical teaching of that drama is not about violence, but about responsibility and faith. The "politics" I see with both Abdiel and Samson is in recognizing that power is what abides, and in power, it is possible to distinguish earthly incomplete knowledge as means from ends: power here I take in the Arendtian sense of the condition enabling people to think and act in terms of means and ends in the first place.[19] I would say that the God who transcends in Milton does not prevent politics, but is the designated point of origin for being within politics, even before the fall, as Satan shows – but I'd like to think that Milton's deity is only one possible point of origin; one that in his time, in his day, prompted the assessment of actions.

MG: When discussing the *Areopagitica*, you described Milton as "one whose allegiance is to Art not War"; I think that observation is right and important. Ethos is story. Confrontation and resistance are integral to Milton's discovery of himself as a "friend of truth" and a "warfaring Christian," and insofar as Milton is a teller of stories, I think his commitment is to mimesis. When he writes, especially when he writes poetry, his first and last obligation is to "decorum ... which is the grand master peece to observe" ("Of Education," YP 2.405) – and which comes down to the created illusion that represented action issues from represented character. What makes Milton, in my view, an ethical writer is that when imitated character and action contradict dogma, prescription, or accepted theology, he complicates his thought rather than compromising his characters. I'm thinking, for instance, of the many ways in which, in *Paradise Lost,* Eve exceeds the prescribed and customary assumptions about female inferiority or subordination – even when those assumed positions are explicitly stated, as when Raphael chastises Adam for adoring Eve and Adam offers cogent and determined resistance.[20]

Perhaps now I can amend the simple definition I started with. Ethics might be about the desire to desire the good: that is, the practice of life, which one judges is most likely to bring one's best self into being. Politics is the context in which ethos becomes manifest both to itself and others. In other words politics is the language in which the ethos is written and read. In good dialectical style each is the ground of the emergence of the other. But the dialectical subject that emerges, emerges from, and is recognized by, a kind of aesthetic cognition. This is why Milton's ideal curriculum places poetry both before and after logic – "subsequent, or indeed precedent, as being lesse suttle and fine, but more simple, sensuous and passionate" ("Of Education," YP 2.403).

Perhaps I can illustrate the preference for the "simple, sensuous and passionate" persistence of story over the QED of logic by returning briefly to the evocation of a "messianicity without messianism" in Derrida's later work. In *The Gift of Death* (1992) Derrida discusses at length Kierkegaard's reading of the story of Abraham and Isaac, in which Abraham comes to exemplify the "knight of faith," by remaining silent about the command to sacrifice his son:

> [F]or Abraham, Kierkegaard declares, *the ethical is a temptation.* He must therefore resist it. He keeps quiet in order to avoid the moral temptation which, under the pretext of calling him to responsibility, to self-justification, would make him lose his ultimate responsibility along with his singularity, make him lose his unjustifiable, secret, and absolute responsibility before God.[21]

I, however, am disturbed by Abraham's silence. Because we, the readers, know what Abraham doesn't – that the same God whose demand compels

Abraham to "declare the exception" will, in the moment, cancel Abraham's agency and prevent the act – I'm tempted to read the episode as a bit of biblical baroque. The death of Isaac would have been tragic. But the story as told veers toward *Trauerspiel*.

I have in mind a counter-Abrahamic reading that recuperates ethics. In this reading, Abraham is the wrong example, an example, perhaps to be admired, but to be questioned and rejected rather than emulated. In Torah, God on several occasions reacts positively to being questioned. Abraham is able to argue with him about Sodom, albeit unsuccessfully. Moses persuades him not to slay the Israelites for their apostasy at Sinai by arguing that to do so would make Pharaoh look good. So why assume that Abraham's unquestioning acquiescence in the sacrifice of Isaac should be emulated? The counter example is Jacob, who tends not to accept the hand he has been dealt. He resorts to chicanery to get the birth-right, he connives in the matter of the spotted lambs, he is devious and cautious about his reunion with Esau in Edom and, most important, when he wrestles all night with the "man" who appears at Peniel, he refuses to let go until he gets the blessing and the name Israel, and is also crippled. This moment of holding on, being renamed and hobbled, I read as the moment when Jacob becomes the ethos of Israel. He places himself against God and holds to his own narrative. God both rewards and punishes him for it (Genesis 32). If Abraham had been like Jacob, he might have told God to stop being ridiculous, that he had circumcised himself on the basis of God's promise to bring a nation from his loins and that a deal is a deal. But even before this there is a telling incident when Abraham again keeps silent: when Sarah insists that he drive out Hagar and Ishmael. This foreshadowing sacrifice of his *first* son – not to God but to the envious fears of his wife – is of course what created all that trouble during *Samson Agonistes* and has Israel building walls to this day. Jacob replaces the apocalyptic decision with the model of endless and open-ended discussion, supple engagement and prevailing struggle. Why not an ethics of reading that is like Jacob not like Abraham? The God of meaning is protean and the reader to be blessed never lets go.

SA: May I bring us down to earth? I remind us, very humbly, that the transcendent powers mediating our meaning – the meaning you and I have been creating – are not simply the 'context' of our communication, but the very conditions of their possibility: the internet; my university email account; my ethernet connection: all supported by the institutions of higher education that the good people of the United States and the United Kingdom still deem to maintain through public funds (and which demand an ongoing struggle to secure amidst governmental interference or repressive surveillance); to say nothing of the commercial backers enabling this exercise, that is, the publishing house; the booksellers; and the readership this volume may attract or bring into being. I don't think this is an, "of course, all that goes without saying; all that is *prior* to what matters": we are living in a time when it is especially evident to me that our ethics of reading is a fragility that requires a politics to maintain its protection.

Notes

1 Louis Althusser, "Ideology and the Ideological State Apparatuses: Notes toward an Investigation," in *Lenin and Philosophy and Other Essays* (New York: Monthly Review Press, 1971), pp. 127–86.

2 Slavoj Žižek, *Welcome to the Desert of the Real!: Five Essays on 11 September and Related Dates* (London: Verso, 2002), pp. 152–53.

3 Jacques Derrida, "Last of the Rogue States: The 'Democracy to Come,' Opening in Two Turns," *South Atlantic Quarterly* 103 (2004): 327.

4 See Martin Beck Matuštík, "Between Hope and Terror: Habermas and Derrida Plead for the Im / Possible," in Lasse Thomassen, ed., *The Derrida–Habermas Reader* (Edinburgh: Edinburgh University Press, 2006), p. 279; and see, Jürgen Habermas and Jacques Derrida, "February 15, or What Binds Europeans Together: A Plea for a Common Foreign Policy, Beginning in the Core of Europe," trans. Max Pensky, originally in *Frankfurter Allgemeine Zeitung*, 31 May 2003; reprinted in Thomassen, op. cit., pp. 270–78.

5 Derrida, "Faith and Knowledge. The Two Sources of Religion at the Limits of Reason Alone," pp. 42–101 (p. 56), in *Acts of Religion*, ed. and with an intro. by Gil Anidjar (London: Routledge, 2002).

6 See Victoria Kahn, "Aesthetics as Critique: Tragedy and *Trauerspiel* in *Samson Agonistes*," Chapter 5, in this volume.

7 [Max Horkheimer and] Theodor W. Adorno, *Dialectics of Enlightenment*, trans. E.B. Ashton (New York: Continuum, 1987): "The Critique of every self-absolutizing particular is a critique of the shadow which absoluteness casts upon the critique; it is a critique of the fact that critique itself, contrary to its own tendency, must remain within the medium of the concept" (p. 406).

8 Catharine A. MacKinnon, "Women's September 11th: Rethinking the International Law of Conflict," in *Are Women Human? And Other International Dialogues* (Cambridge, MA: Harvard University Press, 2006), pp. 259–78: "That day [September 11, 2001] being a man was no protection, hence the world's response. The losses of September 11th were real to power in a way women's losses never have been" (p. 274).

9 See Charles's reply in Samuel Rawson Gardiner, ed., *Constitutional Documents of the Puritan Revolution* (Oxford: Clarendon, 1906; reprinted 1979), pp. 286–87.

10 *The Complete Prose of John Milton*, 8 vols, ed. Don M. Wolfe *et al.* (New Haven: Yale University Press, 1953–82), 2.553–56.

11 For an account of the campaign to label Milton a libertine and his reactions to it, see Thomas H. Luxon, *Single Imperfection: Milton, Marriage and Friendship* (Pittsburgh, PA: Duquesne University Press, 2005), pp. 58–71.

12 See, for example, *Tetrachordon*, re: Matt 19.6:

> [*Let no man put asunder.*] That is to say, what God hath joyn'd; for if it be, as how oft we see it may be, not of Gods joyning, and his law tells us he joyens not unmatchable things, but hates to joyne them, as an abominable confusion, then the divine law of *Moses* puts them asunder, his owne divine will in the institution puts them asunder, as oft as the reasons be not extant, for which

God ordain'd their joyning. Man only puts asunder when his inordinate desires, his passion, his violence, his injury makes the breach: not when the utter want of that which lawfully was the end of his joyning, when wrongs and extremities, and unsupportable greevances compel him to disjoyne. … In a word, if it be unlawful for man to put asunder that which God hath joyn'd, let man take heede it be not detestable to joyne that by compulsion which God hath put asunder." (YP 2.651)

13 Walter Benjamin, "Critique of Violence," in *Walter Benjamin: Selected Writings*, ed. Marcus Bullock and Michael W. Jennings (Cambridge, MA: Harvard University Press, 1996), 1.242.

14 Jürgen Habermas, "The Horrors of Autonomy: Carl Schmitt in English," in *The New Conservatism: Cultural Criticism and the Historians' Debate* (Cambridge: MIT Press, 1989), pp. 128–39.

15 Janel Mueller, "On Genesis in Genre: Milton's Politicizing of the Sonnet in 'Captain or Colonel,'" in Barbara Kiefer Lewalski, ed., *Renaissance Genres: Essays on Theory, History, and Interpretation* (Cambridge, MA: Harvard University Press, 1986), pp. 213–40 (p. 238).

16 Ernest Sirluck's note discusses the alteration of "wayfaring" to "warfaring" in the 1644 texts: "The printed text has *wayfaring*. All four presentation copies and 'F' [Bodleian Wood B.29] have the *y* crossed out and *r* written above it. … It can scarcely be doubted … that the change has Milton's authority" (YP, 2.515, n. 102).

17 [Anon.], *The Valiant Resolution* (London, 1642).

18 Thomas Hobbes, *Leviathan*, ed. Edwin Curley (Indianapolis, IN: Hackett, 1994), p. 76.

19 Hannah Arendt, *On Violence* (New York: Harcourt Brace, 1970), p. 51.

20 This view of Milton's presentation of Eve is elaborated and supported in Marshall Grossman, "The Rhetoric of Feminine Priority in *Paradise Lost*," *English Literary Renaissance* 33 (2003): 424–43.

21 *The Gift of Death*, trans. David Wills (Chicago, IL: University of Chicago Press, 1992), p. 61. Derrida here refers to Søren Kierkegaard, *Fear and Trembling* (Problema III).

14 Afterwords

Reading *Reading Renaissance Ethics* "with modesty enough"

Theodore B. Leinwand

Why do many progressive, early twenty-first-century men and women describe themselves as being unable simply to look at images of President George W. Bush, because, well because of his oft-noted smirk? What do they – what do I – read in this expression? Smugness? Indecency? Pride? A taunt? A salvo? There is often, as well, a squint, which we suspect signifies haziness or discombobulation. This squint makes it even more difficult to decipher the smirk, with which it seems to be at odds. He cannot really be smirking about his confusion, we tell ourselves. It is inconceivable that he takes pleasure in the wages of ignorance. Is this, then, a tactical demeanor? Does it signify a well wrought *hexis*: a passive/aggressive squint smirk, at once disarming and dismissive? "You think I'm an idiot. I've thought that myself. But I'm not. And by the way, I'm still the boss." If we cannot bear to look, it must be because the squint and the smirk are the composite sign of half a dozen years of our defeat. This post-modern male Medusa, this anamorph of Alfred E. Newman, the grinning *MAD* magazine mascot ("What, me worry?"), and John Wayne, cocksure and impenetrable, has not quite slain us (only thousands of others), but he has paralyzed many of us. Like Ferdinand, we find that our "nerves are in their infancy again / And have no vigor in them" (*The Tempest*, 1.2.485–86).[1]

What is it that we long for but do not see? Something ethical, I think. Not something pious – we certainly get enough of that – rather something that speaks to the effort of ethics (Paul Yachnin [Chapter 7] reminds us that Montaigne deems "virtue … another quality of thing and much more noble than inclinations unto goodness"; Richard Strier [Chapter 10] remarks on the paltriness of moralizing). Since I have already referred to Bush's *hexis*, then still keeping with Aristotle, I think we are looking for signs of *energeia*. We want an index of achieved, not merely assumed or proclaimed, moral stature. As Yachnin puts it, "virtue [is] a quality that the person makes actively and by dint of struggle." This must be what Bush's smirk, in all of its now maddening, now dispiriting, complacency, short circuits or side steps. And yet, there is something else for which this smirk is responsible, something to which it categorically attests: where there is a smirk there is settled immodesty.

What we long for, what would betoken careful consideration or effort, and so evidence of ethics, is a facial hint of modesty (the fully bodily *hexis* extends to Bush's swagger, to his outpacing his Secret Service detail on his bicycle, and to other immodest, largely cinematic gestures). But the school of Bush (under headmaster Cheney) appears to correlate modesty with the likes of the oft-noted, never forthcoming apology that this president and his administration programmatically resist. The Rovian conviction must be that genuine modesty and apology smack of "consider[ing] too curiously" (5.1.194), as Horatio puts it ("Consider it not so deeply" [2.2.33] is Lady Macbeth's version), hence of over-intellectualization and/or feminization (Lady Macbeth, again: "Are you a man?" [3.4.59]). That modesty might, as Hamlet hopes, govern "imagination" (5.1.192), is to George Bush *uni*maginable (is damning evidence of Hamletism). Would that Maynard Mack had taught undergraduate Bush that imagination deployed with what Hamlet calls "modesty enough" (5.1.197) may be the very hallmark of ethics.

Speaking of former Governor Bush and of modesty, it is notable that for "modesty," the *OED*'s first citations derive from Sir Thoms Elyot's *The Boke named the Governour* (1531). For Elyot, the word had a largely Ciceronian inflection, pertaining to "discretion" and "moderation." This latter sense follows from Aristotle, for and in whose ethics all virtues correspond with mean, therefore appropriate, states. But "states" is at once too static and too passive to capture the action implicit in an ethical stance, so I recur to *hexis* – not, that is, to the moral disposition one has but to the moral disposition one attains ("each and every minute – again, and again" is the way Marshall Grossman puts it in his exchange with Sharon Achinstein [Chapter 13]). On one hand, there is a morality that one asserts that one has or embodies – what, following Angus Fletcher (Chapter 12), we may correlate with "immanent qualities" – and I am tempted to refer to this as an ethics of smugness. On the other hand, there is a morality that one en*acts* – what Fletcher describes as following upon "inertia" – hence an ethics that begins when action begins, an ethics of motion or action. The latter is what the play *Hamlet* worries, from "the actions that a man might play" (1.2.84) to the "act / That blurs the grace and blush of modesty" (3.4.40–41; again, modesty) right down to the gravedigger's "an act hath three branches – it is to act, to do, to perform" (5.1.11–12). Hamlet himself methodically works his way toward an ethics of action in the graveyard. Of course, he does not work the way gravediggers work, rather the way intellectuals work (the way contributors to *Reading Renaissance Ethics* work): as interpreters. His "Here's fine revolution, an we had the trick to see't" (5.1.84–85) situates him right on the early modern cusp that Fletcher describes, making his way, philosophically no less than philologically, from "revolution" as recurrence or circle to "revolution" as overthrow or vector. "With modesty enough," Hamlet employs his imagination to trace what Fletcher calls the "relative motion" that leads to and from Alexander's dust. That intellectual work – Shakespeare's abbreviated

Baconian essay – completed (or interrupted by the funeral procession), Hamlet is ready to act, to pass from the inertial "readiness is all" (5.2.200) to the violent "Drink off this potion. . . . Follow my mother" (5.2.309–10).

Taking my cue from Hamlet and from the essays in this volume, I deem ethics the word for how we conduct ourselves – what we choose to do – in our ignorance (in an essay on the "question of ethics," Lowell Gallagher cites Alain Badiou's question: "How will I link the things I know, in a consistent fashion, via the effects of being seized by the not-known?" ["*mettre la perseverance de ce qui est su au service d'une durée propre à l'insu*"]).[2] Readers and writers alike, we interpret so as to mitigate our uncertainty. "Deliberate human choosing," writes Fletcher, "is rarely an elegant affair. There is always something experimental [essayistic, poetic] about it." We conduct our experiments with modestly (sans smirk, squint, or swagger) because we have reason to doubt both much success and most certainties. Given the preponderance of what Grossman (Chapter 4) calls "indecidable" text, we are well advised to make modest choices, to subscribe to what Grossman characterizes as an "ethics of restraint." For in the end, our choices are us; they publish who we are (in still more undecidable texts). Hamlet also models our alternatives. Literally and figuratively in the dark (circa midnight, "upon the platform" [1.2.213], watching), he comes face to face with an undecidable. His first instinct is to "sweep" (1.5.31) to his revenge, immodestly, almost megalomaniacally imagining that he was born to set everything right. For a while, "accidental judgments" and "casual slaughters" (5.2.365) contend with what Macbeth calls "the pauser, reason" (2.3.109), leaving us uncertain whether "rashness" (5.2.7) or "readiness" (5.2.200) will prevail. Also for a while, for an academic, a critic like Hamlet, wit trumps humility; but once the wit of the gravediggers one-ups Hamlet's own, he is finally ready to puzzle things out – "with modesty enough" – and then to act. Gordon Teskey (Chapter 9) glosses this transformation for me: "displacing the narcissistic self entails giving oneself over to contingency." Also to "necessity and chance" (as Hamlet concedes, "Or I could make a prologue to my brains / They had begun the play" [5.2.30–31]) and, Teskey again, to "irony and laughter" (Hamlet: "Is thy union here?" [5.2.309]). Thinking back to Hamlet's putative delay, it again is helpful to recall Grossman, who writes that "deferral . . . does not mean not interpreting, but rather taking responsibility for one's interpretation." Reading and interpreting *Hamlet*, too long by half, we are perhaps prone to forgive Hamlet for himself suggesting that analysis is interminable. Thinking ahead to what "shall live behind" Folio Hamlet (what Q2 Hamlet "shall . . . leave behind" him [5.2.328]), we have the "story" (5.2.332) that Horatio must live to tell, the story to which Hamlet, *ante mortem*, risks submitting himself. Here, Hamlet acknowledges the very nearness of ethics to aesthetics (in this instance, narrative) that Harry Berger (Chapter 3), Victoria Kahn (Chapter 5), Strier, and Achinstein and Grossman mull over.

Having mentioned Hamlet's wit, I suppose that it is only fair to acknowledge its appeal to intellectuals who read volumes like *Reading Renaissance Ethics*. Does it correspond with the President's smirk? Witty Hamlet presumes to know what's what ("I'll take the ghost's word for a thousand pound" [3.2.281–82]). But incrementally, modesty overtakes presumption ("Why, even in that was heaven ordinant" (5.2.48) vs. the earlier, "O cursed spite / That ever *I* was born to set it right" [2.5.191–92]). And then, finally, even the interpretive reticence implied by "the readiness is all" gives way to "the rest is silence" (5.2.341). If death is tragedy's dramatic catastrophe, then silence is its ethical catastrophe (strophe, in *King Lear*). For a few acts, between certainty and silence, *Hamlet* opens up space for the readiness modestly to interpret. I continue to emphasize modesty because the truism that we have no choice but to carry on the work of interpretation seems less a cause for rejoicing than evidence for "human abjection" (Teskey). Viv Westbrook (Chapter 6) cites Miles Coverdale's delight that God "hath opened vnto his church the gyfte of interpretacyon," but Coverdale was hardly oblivious to the hornets' nest of heresy that Biblical translation/ interpretation threatened. Even the pretense that interpretation could be relegated to the margins is belied by Tyndale's martyrdom. Likewise, as David Lee Miller (Chapter 2) concludes, that justice is always a question of reading only adds to our, as opposed to, say, the gods', ethical burdens and to our doubts. If I have momentarily shifted from Hamlet's momentous ego ("This is I, / Hamlet the Dane" [5.1.246–47]) to "we" and "our," it is because, like Anita Sherman's (Chapter 11) Donne, we too must take account of what a tragedy like *Hamlet* may not equip us to cope with: "communal concerns" (see *Ignatius*), as opposed to individuals' crises (see "Satire 3") . The negative example of immodesty set for us in Donne's raucous conclave of *gloriosi* – evident not just in their pervasive, smirking dogmatism and vehe- mence, but their profound confusion at an historical moment (theirs, ours) when collective memory has failed – tacitly endorses a more tentative, more modest communal "program of inquiry" (not assertion), of "productive conversation" (not extra-legal fiat), perhaps too a "republic of letters" (not politics). Finally, if I plump for (take refuge in?) modesty, it is because there does not appear to be much room in Shakespeare for what Kahn calls radical critique.

Is this a difference between Shakespeare and Milton that escaped Coleridge? Few have failed to notice their distinct egos – supposedly self- effacing versus supposedly self-evident. And yet, contra Keats, I have the sense that the Shakespearean ego is always in evidence, taking considerable pride it its relentless analytical competence.[3] It may be that such competence constitutes a Shakespearean ethos, founded in evaluation not revelation (or, *pace* Teskey's dubiously ethical poet, in inspiration; *pace* Strier, in aesthetics). Via Milton and Benjamin, Kahn opposes complacency to critique, acting to action. Shakespeare and Bush complicate this. The latter, because senti- mentality and posturing first herald and then ratify his actions. Vacuous, affect-rich talk of evil, of tyranny, and of the homeland sponsors aggression (Achinstein and Grossman). Shakespeare, because like Kahn's Samson (who comes to see himself as a character in a Trauerspiel), his (or at least Empson's) Hamlet recognizes that he is playing a part in a revenge tragedy. Indeed, like Kahn's Samson, whose encounters with Manoa, Dalila, and Harapha teach him what he must reject, Hamlet sees in the lyric that is Ophelia, the melodrama that is Laertes, and the essay that is Horatio, the unpersuasive alternatives to his tragic action. The ethical demands of Shakespearean tragic protagonism consistently leave the endearing and the naive sponsors of comic resolutions (the Kents and the Poloniuses) behind. Even in a fiction, but especially in his tragedy, Hamlet must, finally, act. Act even though interpretation (regarding Claudius, Alexander, and Yorick, not to mention his father) has mostly failed him; even though evidence is in short supply; and even though his own deep plots have palled ("*They* had begun the play"). As Grossman writes in his exchange with Achinstein: "The implied [Miltonic] ethic is subtle because the formal fullness and sufficiency of truth must be anticipated without presuming to know its full content." It is possible that in the realm of Shakespeare, characters may find themselves "released," as Strier puts it, "from the moral into the aesthetic"; it may even be that some characters effect this release for themselves. But I do not think that it is ever the case that Shakespeare releases a character from the *ethical* into the aesthetic, or pretends that it is an easy thing either to confound ethics or to subsume it within aesthetics.

For Shakespeare, then, as for us, it is easier to fathom morality than ethics, easier to encourage radical critique than to carry it out. Not that this means that we ought to settle for what Kahn dismisses as "aesthetic contemplation" (or, for that matter, to dismiss the aesthetics that, according to Strier, trump the moral). It is just that doing one's imaginative best modestly to trace the course of Alexander's dust, then acting a part in another's play that, curiously, enables one to take decisive action, bespeaks ethical activity at once ironical and every bit as estimable as Samson's admittedly opaque "rousing motions." "Calm of mind" and "fiery virtue rous'd" are not the only alternatives so much as they are extremes. And while Strier applauds the "extremes" that "become" the likes of Antony and Cleopatra, such extremes are mostly viable as foils for morality, not as guides to ethics. So it is probably temperament as much as politics which explains why I am more favorably disposed toward interpretive modesty than toward either these "extremes" or what Kahn calls the "hermeneutical sublime." Teskey points to the ethical conundrum posed by delirium and by *enthousiasmos*, but I suspect that temperament may also explain my predisposition toward Shakespearean imagination rather than Miltonic passion as the spur to action.

If I read Harry Berger aright, then the ethical terrain that brings acting into such close proximity to action is no less discernible in Hals's Dutch Republic than in Shakespeare's Elsinore and Milton's Gaza. Cast by father and genre as revenge hero, Hamlet (ever the connoisseur of acting styles) would have to be far less self-conscious than we and he know he is not to catch himself in the act, so to speak, of posing. For Coleridge, there is always, "*a tergo*," at the back of Hamlet's mind, a "knowledge, the *unthought-of* consciousness, the *Sensation*, of human auditors."[4] The tissue of formulaic self-recrimination in "O, what a rogue and peasant slave am I ... " (2.2.488ff) and "How all occasions do inform against me ... " (4.4.32ff) attests to a Hamlet who can never forget that he is role playing, who even flaunts his role call, and yet who longs to assimilate his role to himself, not himself to his role. Would that that self were accessible, to him or to us. To have "that within which passes show" (1.2.85), it bears remembering, is to be undecidable to oneself, not just to others and to us. But neither the excuse of command performance ("Revenge his foul and most unnatural murder" [1.5.25]) nor epistemological opacity (and certainly not playing, not his "antic disposition" [1.5.175]) offers Hamlet ethical relief. If anything, to have no choice but to play a part attests to how powerfully history bears down on us. We may take deep pleasure in watching Falstaff and Cleopatra at play, acting as if they inhabit a "realm of freedom" (Strier); but she, at least, never forgets that Rome, hence history, is at the gate. Moreover, we are always, I think, on the lookout not just for playing, but for playing *well*. While playing may "exalt the aesthetic over the moral" (Strier), or for that matter unmoor all certainties, even gesture toward aporia, "well" – the character or quality of our play – retains for Shakespeare and for Hamlet overlapping aesthetic and ethical (not simply moral) force.

This nearness of aesthetics to ethics may help to explain a curious turn late in Berger's essay. For all that he steadfastly recurs to what he calls the "reflexive scenario" – the bracing, deracinated and formal evidence that Hals's sitters pose only as if posing and only in order to pose – Berger and the sitters on whose behalf he speaks can neither resist reviewing their (and Hals's) performance, nor offering a critique quintessentially ethical in its tenor. The painter is commended for his "*stark refusal* to transcend the swerve toward disaggregation" that will vitiate the "corporate occasion." The sitters, in turn, are commended for playing their parts so well: as Berger puts it, the regents and regentesses "persevere," indeed they do so "bravely." "They will not let the painter or themselves down." Hals's profoundly self-conscious sitters, no less than the equally self-aware Hamlet, achieve ethical stature by playing their parts (sitting as patrons, acting out revenge) just as well as they can. Accomplished as they are, they "acknowledge their investment in what they are actually and self-interestedly doing." Still, they must concede that occasion informs (against) them. The sitters know very well what they owe Hals's brushwork, and as Berger shrewdly notes, the "visual epideixis" in which they take part must entail at least a modicum of "performance anxiety" (performing for Hals, for contemporaries, and for us). Hamlet is no less well informed that someone or other has "*cue*[d him] for passion" (2.2.499), also that his performance depends, as he "himself" says, on "memory hold[ing] a seat" in Shakespeare's "[G]lobe" (1.5.96–97). Keeping in mind *Reading Renaissance Ethics*'s dramatis personae, then, Hamlet, Samson, the regents and the regentesses – even the Bible but probably not Britomart – sometimes appear to attain a kind of life of their own, distinct from the voices or brushes or pens that give rise to them. However, their indebtedness to, and competition with, their creators frustrate the assignment of ethical responsibility (this is the flip side of the burden Teskey says we face when we set out to judge an inspired poet). If, finally, we were to triangulate these relations by adding readers/viewers, that is, interpreters like ourselves, to characters/text and to creators/translators, we would significantly complicate the distribution of what Berger has called complicity and responsibility.[5]

If nothing else, it is Marvell's readership, his advocacy directed toward a volatile public that David Norbrook (Chapter 8) calibrates so finely. Keeping in mind Norbrook's (also Kahn's) terms, when should authorial "constraint" leave off, when does it cease to do good, and when should "boldness" or "agency" take over? Where do writers and readers draw what Norbrook calls "the dividing line between . . . patience and violence"? (Is there even a dividing line if, with Yachnin, we imagine both a "writer's own work" and reading itself as "acts of communitarian violence"?) Hamlet knows enough to acknowledge that "the hand of little employment hath the daintier sense" (5.1.64–65); but Norbrook makes the case that in "difficult political times" (like Hamlet's, like Marvell's, and like our own), "using the hand in rhetoric" can involve "risk and courage." First Hamlet sits himself down to devise "a new commission, wr[i]te it fair" (5.2.32) and so send Rosencrantz and Guildenstern, with "many . . . as's of great charge," to "sudden death" (5.2.43–46). Next, he overcomes his daintier sense and employs his hands to commit regicide, perhaps tyrannicide, at long last redressing "th' oppressor's wrongs" (3.1.71). If Marvell's "writings are haunted by the ambiguities of agency," surely *Hamlet* and Hamlet are similarly haunted. Their common indecidability recommends modesty, but it is easy for us to see how this might also argue for the "rashness" that Hamlet praises, for an indigestion (as Yachnin via Montaigne with a dash of Hamlet's wit might say) or "indiscretion [that] sometime serves us well" (5.2.8). If my students are any guide, then readers today typically "root" for Hamlet to "just do it," to kill Claudius (based on ghostly evidence, the majority of people polled in the United States advocated "taking out" Saddam Hussein). We are less sure of ourselves when it comes to enduring the "cursèd spite" of having "to set . . . right" what is "out of joint" (1.5.191–92). For Shakespeare as for Marvell (though evidently not for George W. Bush), neither Christian nor pagan (R/republican) activism, neither quietism nor Stoicism, is quite or sufficiently comforting, authorizing. Said another way: with Horatio on one side, Rosencrantz and Guildenstern on another, Fortinbras on a third side and Laertes on a fourth, one cannot help but feel that Hamlet has to find the "trick to see't" (5.1.84–85) on his own. We too.

Notes

1 All Shakespeare citations are from the *William Shakespeare: The Complete Works*, Stephen Orgel and A.R. Braunmuller, eds (New York: Penguin Books, 2002).
2 Lowell Gallagher, "Faustus's Blood and the (Messianic) Question of Ethics," *ELH* 73 (2006): 4 and 24n12. See Alain Badiou, *Ethics: An Essay on the Understanding of Evil*, trans. Peter Hallward (London: Verso, 2001), p. 50; *L'éthique: Essai sur la conscience du Mal* (Paris: Hatier, 1993), p. 43.
3 See my "Shakespeare Against Doctrine," online in *Literature Compass* 3 (2006): 513–28.
4 Samuel Taylor Coleridge, *The Collected Works of Samuel Taylor Coleridge: Marginalia*, eds H.J. Jackson and George Whalley, vol. 12, part 4 (Princeton, NJ: Princeton University Press, 1998), p. 485.
5 Harry Berger, Jr., *Making Trifles of Terrors: Redistributing Complicities in Shakespeare* (Stanford, CA: Stanford University Press, 1997).

Index

Note: page numbers in *italics* refer to illustrations.